Neuroaesthetics

Tudor Balinisteanu · Kerry Priest
Editors

Neuroaesthetics

A Methods-Based Introduction

palgrave
macmillan

Editors
Tudor Balinisteanu
Neuroaesthetics Lab
University of Suceava
Suceava, Romania

Kerry Priest
Exeter, UK

ISBN 978-3-031-42325-3 ISBN 978-3-031-42323-9 (eBook)
https://doi.org/10.1007/978-3-031-42323-9

The research leading to the publication of this textbook has received funding from Norway Grants 2014-2021, under Project contract no. 18/2020, project code RO-NO-2019-0091

This Palgrave Macmillan imprint is published by the registered company Springer Nature Switzerland AG
The registered company address is: Gewerbestrasse 11, 6330 Cham, Switzerland

Paper in this product is recyclable.

Contents

Editors and Contributors

About the Editors

Tudor Balinisteanu established the first Neuroaesthetics Lab in Romania (https://neuroaestheticslab.usv.ro/), the Neuroaesthetics Lab at the University of Suceava and is currently researching empathy through leading participation in international projects including PoeticA, focusing on the biological universals of the aesthetic experience of poetry, Origins of Dance, focusing on the origins of rhythm in mutual entrainment, and VIVAET, that aims to create empathic visual identities for medical AIs.

Kerry Priest (www.kerrypriest.com) is an interdisciplinary artist and visiting specialist in music at the University of Plymouth. She has previously taught at Von Humboldt University and the University of Eichstaett-Ingolstadt. Her poetry has been published widely and she has written libretti for the Royal Opera House and stage work for the Minack Theatre.

Contributors

Alexandru I. Berceanu is a mixed realities director, researcher, and teacher at UNATC Department of Animation and Interactivity. His practice in art and research has as core the potential of art and games as emotional and social development environments. He established the interdisciplinary research centre CINETic at UNATC where he is conducting research at the intersection of theatre and neuroscience, concentrating on mechanisms and effects of theatrical representation at neurocognitive and biochemical levels.

Anja Borowicz Richardson is a Honorary Postdoctoral Researcher, Entanglement Research Group, Royal College of Art. She is a multimodal artist exploring performed materiality and neurodiverse perspectives through sculpture, sound, and synthetic media. Showcased in: RCA2022, UrbanLab, Sauna Reading Group, The Listening Academy, Aesthetica Art Prize magazine, Fermynwoods Podcast, and 2018 Bangkok Biennial. Kenneth Armitage Young Sculptor Prize recipient.

Pamela Breda is Senior Postdoc, Angewandte University, Vienna. She is an artist, filmmaker, and researcher exploring the intersection between visual imagery, technology, and narratives. She was appointed a fellow in residence at several international art institutions, including Pratt Institute (New York, USA), Cité Internationale Des Arts (Paris, F), Max Planck Institute For Empirical Aesthetics (Frankfurt, DE). Her films have been screened internationally and presented at festivals and art venues.

Claus-Christian Carbon studied Psychology, followed by Philosophy, received his Ph.D. from FU Berlin and 'Habilitation' from U Vienna, and now holds a full professorship leading the Department of General Psychology and Methodology (U Bamberg), the Faculty of Human Sciences as Dean and the EPAEG, a research group specialized in cognitive ergonomics, psychological aesthetics, and design issues.

Mamadou Dramé is full professor in language sciences and didactics of modern French grammar at the Faculty of Science and Technology of Education and Training (FASTEF) of Cheikh Anta Diop University in Dakar (UCAD). He has published several works relating in particular to urban cultures. He teaches linguistics, sociolinguistics, phonetics and communication. Currently, he is the Vice Dean of FASTEF and Publication Director of the journal Liens Nouvelle série, Revue Francophone Internationale.

Johan Magnus Elvemo is an assistant professor, filmmaker, and visual artist. Elvemo has been teaching practical/theoretical film and media courses at the Norwegian University of Science and Technology (NTNU) in Trondheim, for more than 30 years. He has his education from the University of Trondheim, Norway, and Ohio University, USA. His main areas of theoretical research are film and rhythm, and film and audio-visual perception. Elvemo has worked on different types of film and video projects throughout his career: Feature films/documentary films/art films/art and science projects, and as well as information films. He has extensive and varied experience in the industry, working as a director, scriptwriter, photographer, editor, and producer. In the last 8 years, Elvemo has mostly been working on art and art and science projects. These projects have all been a part of an ongoing artistic research into the relationship between music/sound and the moving image. Several of his projects have been shown with live music on stage (symphony orchestras/string orchestra/chamber music groups). Projects that he has been involved in have been presented in Norway, USA, Cuba, Switzerland, and Croatia.

Per Olav Folgerø is a biologist and a researcher in Neuroaesthetics with a special interest in the neurology of perception related to Aesthetics. He has built up a research environment for Neuroaesthetics at the University of Bergen and is a main contributor to the Humanities Research Laboratory. His research investigates the perception of beauty, and the evolution of cognition and perception.

Oana Geman is a senior researcher member at the first Neuroaesthetics Lab, University of Suceava, Romania (https://neuroaestheticslab.usv.ro/). She is a Medical Bioengineer with a Ph.D. in Electronics and Telecommunication and a post-doctoral researcher in Computer Science (2012). She is currently an associate professor at the University of Suceava, Romania and obtained Habilitation in 2018. Within the past five years, she published 10 books, has published over 200 articles, and papers in Q1 and Q2 Journals, with FI over 50, and her various works have been cited over 2060 times, and H-index is 26. She is a reviewer of many top journals and IEEE Senior Member.

Lasse Hodne is Professor in Art History at the Norwegian University of Science and Technology (NTNU). He has written two books and several articles on Italian Medieval and Renaissance art. In addition, he has written several articles on Johann Joachim Winckelmann's art theory, as well as on classical aesthetics, and art theory. Within the field of neuroaesthetics, he has particularly focused on the relationship between facial perception and portrait painting, as well as the central role of symmetry in art and architecture.

Morteza Izadifar is a researcher at the Institute of Human Aesthetics, Coburg University of Applied Sciences & Art and Bamberg University, Bavaria, Germany. His research interests include Neuroaesthetics; Consciousness & Time; Time Perception; Time & Imagery/Imagination; Neurobiological Bases of Self; and Neural Correlates of Music Perception and Composition.

Christer Johansson holds a Ph.D. from Lund University. He also studied at UCSD at the Cognitive Science department and held a two-year postdoc at Rijksuniversiteit Groningen (supported by the Wenner-Gren Foundation, and the Dutch Science Council (NWO)) on the neurological basis of language (PI Dr. Laurie Stowe). He has a second two-year postdoc in Tsukuba, Japan (supported by AIST/STA) on machine learning of language (PI Koiti Hasida). He is employed at the University of Bergen since 2001 and is a full professor since 2005. His early career involved research in Computational Linguistics and Machine Learning. More recently he has built up the Humanities Research Laboratory at UiB. His interdisciplinary research investigates how vision and language interact, utilizing methods in Computational Linguistics, Experimental Psycholinguistics, and Neuroaesthetics.

Emanuela Motrescu is an assistant researcher and member at Neuroaesthetics Lab, University of Suceava (https://neuroaestheticslab.usv.ro/). She is currently pursuing a Ph.D. in Cinematography and Media Studies at Babeș-Bolyai University, in addition to a master's degree in Visual Arts, at the University of Arts and Design, Cluj-Napoca and Documentary Filmmaking, Babeș-Bolyai University. With a focus on experimental research, her interests encompass neuroaesthetics, the exploration of time and timing in film, attention mechanisms, and the aesthetic experience in visual arts and cinematography.

Adrian Nita is a researcher at the "Constantin Radulescu-Motru" Institute of Philosophy and Psychology and Ph.D. supervisor at the "Stefan cel Mare" University in Suceava. He has researches in the field of metaphysics and modern philosophy, especially Leibniz and Kant. He is the president of the Leibniz Society of Romania and coordinator of the Leibniz edition in Romanian (projected in 20 volumes).

Oana Teodora Papuc is an Assistant Lecturer (Ph.D.), currently working for the Department of Foreign Languages for Specific Purposes, Faculty of Letters, Babeş-Bolyai University, Cluj-Napoca. Latest publications include the edited volume *An Introduction to Internet Linguistics* (2021), and the scholarly article 'Exploring Liminal Aesthetics: The "Glitchy And Decayed" Worlds of Vaporwave, Semiotic Assemblages, and Internet Linguistics' (2022), STUDIA UBB PHILOLOGIA, (LXVII), 4.

Karsten Specht is a cognitive neuroscientist. He worked as a neuroscientist at the University Hospital Aachen, the Research Centre Jülich, and the Otto-von-Guericke University Magdeburg, Germany. From the Otto-von-Guericke University Magdeburg, he received his Ph.D. in Cognitive Neuroscience in 2003, and, in 2012, his Habilitation in General and Biological Psychology. Since 2004, he also works at the University of Bergen, Norway, where he got a professorship at the Department of Biological and Medical Psychology in 2012. In 2017, he became the head of the Bergen fMRI group, and he also holds a guest professorship at the Arctic University of Norway in Tromsø, Norway. His main research areas are on the neuroimaging studies of the brain with a focus on auditory perception of speech and music, rehabilitation from speech and language disorders, brain connectivity and plasticity, clinical multimodal neuroimaging, and the development and implementation of new neuroimaging methods. Over the years, he published more than 100 peer-reviewed articles and received several major research grants. Since 2021, he is also the deputy dean of the Faculty of Psychology, at the University of Bergen, Norway.

Marius A. Teodorescu is a theatre director, working in both independent and state theatres. He is currently an assistant professor at the Theatre and Film Department at Babeş-Bolyai University. His main research areas are theatre management, theatre directing, and theatre history.

List of Figures

Unit 1 Lesson: Behavioural Experiments—Research Designs, Statistical Power, Sample Size *Case Study: Empathy and Closeness in Partnered Dance*

Unit 2 Lesson: Portraits as Faces

Unit 3 Overview: Neuroaesthetics Approaches to the Visual Arts—Creation

Unit 3 Lesson: Using Reaction Time and Mixed Models

Unit 3 Lab: Gender and Prototypes

Unit 4 Overview: Symmetry Research in Neuroaesthetics

List of Tables

Unit 3 Lesson: Using Reaction Time and Mixed Models

Unit 3 Lab: Gender and Prototypes

Unit 4 Lesson: Why Is *en face* Associated with Holiness?

Unit 6 Lesson: Coordination Techniques of Instructive-Educational Activities in the Field of Neuroaesthetics Using Problem-Based Learning (PBL)

Foreword: Aesthetics and Neuroaesthetics

Tudor Balinisteanu, Adrian Nita, Mamadou Dramé, and Emanuela Motrescu

Since ancient, if not primordial, times, humans wondered about art: why do we have art? How did we come to have art? What is the value of having art? Why do we experience pleasure in relation to art, and why does some art engender more pleasure than other art, and that only, apparently, for some people and not for all of us? Answering such questions is beyond the scope of a single book. Nor is it appropriate for a course manual to do more than set out the questions, provide informative contexts as well as equip readers and students with a basic set of skills to enable them to at least begin a journey of discovery. Hence, the present textbook aims to offer exactly that. We will begin a marvellous questing journey and walk the sometimes beaten, sometimes arduous, path, together, for a

---

The material on Plato, the Sophists, Nelson Goodman, and Theodor Fechner was written by Tudor Balinisteanu. The material on Nicolas Boileau, Gottfried Wilhelm Leibniz, Alexander Gottlieb Baumgarten, and the Romantics was written by Adrian Nita. The material on Kant was written by Tudor Balinisteanu and Adrian Nita. The definitions of aesthetic experience and neuroaesthetics in bold and the summaries in boxes were elaborated by Tudor Balinisteanu. The exercises/ questions were elaborated by Tudor Balinisteanu, Mamadou Dramé, and Emanuela Motrescu.

T. Balinisteanu (✉) · E. Motrescu
Neuroaesthetics Lab, University of Suceava, Suceava, Romania
e-mail: tudor@texmar.ro

A. Nita
Institute of Philosophy and Psychology, Bucharest, Romania
e-mail: Adrian.nita@usm.ro

M. Dramé
Faculté des Sciences et Technologies de l'Education et de la Formation, Boulevard Habib Bourguiba, Dakar, Senegal
e-mail: mamadou1.drame@ucad.edu.sn

T. Balinisteanu and K. Priest (eds.), *Neuroaesthetics*,
https://doi.org/10.1007/978-3-031-42323-9_21

little while (at least for an academic semester). Hopefully, the journey will prove to be sufficiently interesting for you, the reader, to continue walking the path. Likely, you will never be alone on this sinuous journey. You will meet other scholar-travellers, from many different disciplines, who will walk with you for a longer or shorter period of time. Together, you will find magical oases of thought, Grail-like questions to ask and answer, stormy weather, and calm seas. It will be a wondrous journey.

But let us begin with the first steps. The very first step is to provisionally answer the question: 'What is neuroaesthetics?' An immediate, but not very useful, answer is that neuroaesthetics is the neuroscientific study of aesthetics. Let us postpone for a little while the more informative and useful answer, but only in order to better understand it. For, before we proceed to that answer, a historical overview of philosophical and empirical approaches to the study of aesthetics is in order.

Classical philosophical thought on aesthetics linked aesthetics with beauty. In that regard, it seems, all roads lead to Plato (c. 428–c. 348 BC). In his entry on Plato's aesthetics in the *Stanford Encyclopedia of Philosophy*, Nickolas Pappas points out at the outset that a major thread in Plato's philosophy of aesthetics posits a dilemma for modern readers: while Plato aligned beauty with the greatest good, he aligned art with the greatest danger. How can beauty be good, but art be dangerous? For Plato, beauty meant a perfection of form. However, he argued that perfect forms could only be found in an object's archetype and that all archetypes are located in a transcendental space of perfection. Hence, for each class of objects that exists in our mundane, natural world (say, amphoras) there exists a perfect single form (an archetypal amphora without physical existence) in the transcendental space of ideas, a space that sits beyond the physical world, that is, on a metaphysical plane. Therefore, while beauty belongs on a metaphysical plane of perfection beyond this world, art (or, more appropriately, *technê*, or craft) belongs in our natural, physical world. We may aspire to create the perfect form physically, but we will never be able to do so because the perfect form is without materiality. Hence, to the extent that art, imitating perfect forms, distances us from those forms, it is dangerous. However, if art objects can offer glimpses into perfect forms, then art serves a good purpose. Art can offer glimpses into perfect forms when it has beauty. The more beauty an object has, the more one is attracted to the object and compelled to extrapolate the possibilities of perfection. Attraction can mean love. If beautiful objects (and people!) set forth love, they set forth the beholder on a quest for uncovering the transcendental, otherworldly perfection of ideal forms. Beauty is more a measure of perfection than an intrinsic property of the object, and its correlate is the intensity of love. An object that manifests an ideal form, however imperfectly, may set out beauty according to how it sets forth the love required to propel one towards perfection. Beauty, it seems, is neither a property of ideal, immaterial forms, nor an intrinsic property of material objects that embody those forms imperfectly, but rather a quality of the experience of intuiting perfection. That is not an empirical approach to beauty, but rather one that invites introspection!

If Plato can be regarded as our almost archetypal idealist, around the same time, philosophers identified as Sophists can be regarded as developing philosophical thought that sits directly opposite to that of Plato (although a continuum between these extreme positions existed, as it always does). Much ink has been spilled on discussing Plato in the context of the *sophistēs*, directly proportional to the importance of the issues at stake, as one may surmise. As the root of the word *sophistēs* indicates, derived as it is from *sophia*, meaning 'wisdom', and *sophos*, meaning 'wise', sophist practice cultivated the embodiment of wisdom. 'Embodiment' here must be primarily understood in rather pragmatic terms, in the sense that it refers to the art of speaking and persuasion, and not to a content or corpus that constitutes wisdom. The sophists were purposeful when it came to wisdom, and were even accused of being materialistic by Plato, who disliked them for that reason. In Plato's dialogue, *Gorgias*, the Sophists' sophistry is compared to *kommōtikē*, 'cosmetics' or 'self-adornment', being negatively distinguished from truth and reality as promoting seeming and appearance (but alternative interpretations of Plato's use of the terms have been developed, for example, by Reames) (Reames, 2016). If beauty is a praxis of persuasion, seen by Plato as a cultivation of appearance, one may surmise that the Sophists were both utilitarian ('make things to appear beautiful, whether they are or not') and subjective ('beauty exists if one believes it exists'). And, in addition, they liked to be paid for making things look good and beautiful or teaching others the ways in which this might be achieved through mere use of speech (for a detailed presentation of Sophist practice and method see Wolfsdorf, 2015). Moreover, from the prominent Sophist, Protagoras (c. 490 BC–c. 420 BC), we have inherited the saying that 'Man is the measure of all things', a phrase where 'man' is usually capitalised when it shouldn't be. Protagoras may have not referred to an abstract 'Man', or humanity in the masculine, but rather to each man's individual experiences that inform the ways in which each individual measures, or weighs, what is one thing or other (Mansfeld, 1981). Beauty, then, in spite of the Sophists' pragmatism, is subjective—it is in the eye of the beholder. While pragmatic in its emphasis on factual experience, this approach to beauty, like Plato's, is not empirical. But the experience of beauty, alas (or fortunately?), keeps us closer to the mundane, as opposed to distancing us from it. It is not a measure of the intensity of longing for perfection (as with Plato), but a measure of individual experience, what modern psychologists might call a self-reported score on a self-created scale.

Plato and the Sophists have bequeathed to us frames of thought on which we, mere mortal moderns, like to build all too clear-cut dichotomies, such as the mundane vs. the sacred, realities vs. ideals, or disembodied vs. embodied. But closer inspection of modern philosophical thought, meaning those philosophies that emerged after the scientific revolution of the seventeenth century and the first industrial revolution that began in England in the 1750s, may help us set things right, so to speak.

The seventeenth century, the beginning of European modernity, marks an increasing alignment of art and science. As the century of classicism and later the Enlightenment, the importance of harmony, clarity, and brevity of the work of art is now emphasised along with expression and taste (Ferry, 1990). A true manifesto of classicism, *Poetic Art* (1674) by Nicolas Boileau (1636–1711) marks the departure from ancient and medieval aesthetics, although it continues to keep at the centre previous frameworks that held together aesthetic object, beauty, and imitation. However, according to Boileau, an object is beautiful if it imitates nature on the basis of harmony and utility, and on the basis of general laws. The work of art needs an appropriate language, but above all it needs clarity and brevity, as we see masterfully exemplified in the work of the great French classics Pierre Corneille (1606–1684), Jean-Baptiste Poquelin (Molière) (1622–1673), Jean De La Fontaine (1621–1695), Jean Racine (1639–1699), where no word seems to be unnecessarily used. We see how beauty is sought in art in its original sense of production (from the Greek *to poein*): the artist is a perfect craftsman who creates an object that in turn imitates another object. It is not by chance that classical aesthetics has a huge passion for all things antique. The emphasis on measure, proportion, harmony, and balance is taken forward from Aristotle, Horace, Quintilian, or Vitruvius.

In this context, let us consider the work of Gottfried Wilhelm Leibniz (1646–1716), a man of his time yet often proposing ideas that seem to belong in our own time. If individuality, theory of small perception, and common sense, are some of the elements later used by Alexander Gottlieb Baumgarten (1714–1762), Immanuel Kant (1724–1804), and modern aesthetics more generally, Leibniz emphasises the idea of this world as not only the best but also the most beautiful of all possible worlds (Leibniz, 1985). The quantity of beauty and the ingredients of beauty can be measured with the right instruments, but only God can calculate the amount of beauty and the ingredients of beauty in every possible world. Therefore, based on the law of the optimum, God brought into existence that world, which is the most beautiful, i.e. our world (Leibniz, 1985). However, the important thing for our effort to define neuroaesthetics is the idea that beauty is quantifiable, an idea that brings us one step closer to aesthetics as a science.

As an autonomous discipline, but also as a science, modern aesthetics might be said to begin with Baumgarten, who moves further and further away from Aristotle. According to the Stagirite, there is no science of individual things; knowledge (episteme) is the science of the universal; particular facts are studied by history (see Aristotle, *Poetics*, 1988). In *Aesthetics* (1750), along the lines of the Enlightenment and in line with mid-eighteenth-century advances in science, Baumgarten seeks a place for what Aristotle removed from the purview of aesthetics, namely, particular facts. As a science of individual things researched through the senses, aesthetics is the science of sensible things, but also the theory of liberal arts, the doctrine of inferior knowledge, the art of beautiful thinking, and also the art of the analogue of reason (Baumgarten, 1986). Imposing the autonomy of art and beauty, Baumgarten is modern through his emphasis on science, on reason, even if it is not reason in the Kantian sense. Although he continued to speak of imitation in art, Baumgarten goes a step further towards the aesthetics of expression, restoring the dignity of the imagination, showing that the artist imitates the maximum variety free from contradictions; hence, the role of perfection as an intrinsic value (Baumgarten, 1986).

Fast forward to Immanuel Kant. In the first part of his *Critique of the Power of Judgment* (1790), dedicated to the aesthetic perception and judgement of beauty, Kant distinguishes four moments or, should we say, dimensions, of the perception of beauty that are not necessarily successive: a feeling of disinterested pleasure (first moment), universally 'communicable' or shareable, but not conceptually determinable (second moment), as if it had a purpose but without calling for a definition of its purpose (the third moment), and compelling in others the same emotional response (the fourth moment). One might group these four moments of aesthetic judgement around feeling (first and third moments), and universality (second and fourth moments). However, in spite of its universality, one cannot measure the feeling of beauty because it does not have a determinate purpose. Since it does not have a determinate purpose, we cannot determine conceptually what is beautiful in an object. Beauty is experienced when imagination remains unconstrained by understanding, or, in other words, when the imagination is not mobilised by understanding, or, in yet other words, when the imagination and understanding are free to play. Nevertheless, this state of unconstrained imagination, or ungovernable imagination, or play, can be experienced by any human being, and is therefore universal. Because of that, one is entitled to ask others to agree with one's judgement that something is beautiful. One might say that Kant's envisioning of beauty is more like the Sophists' beauty than Plato's beauty, because it is communicable and persuasive, although the experience of beauty certainly does not serve utilitarian or pragmatic purposes. But one could equally say that Kant's envisioning of beauty is more like Plato's because beauty is an intensity, although, clearly, it is not a purposeful intensity (it does not bring us closer to understanding the perfection of metaphysical, or, say, a priori, forms).

According to Kant, Baumgarten's attempt to base aesthetics on rational principles is unsuccessful, given that the judgement of beauty is not really based on empirical rules (Kant, 2000b). Although in *Critique of Pure Reason* (CPR) and *Critique of Practical Reason* (CPrR) he makes an absolute distinction between sensibility, intellect, and reason, in *Critique of Faculty of Judgement* (CFJ) (1790), therefore only three years after the second edition of CPR (1787), Kant accepts that judgement can take the form of taste, or aesthetic judgement. If in CPR, *Transcendental Aesthetics* is the science of the a priori principles of sensibility (Kant, 2000b), in CFJ he unites the domains he had separated in the first two *Critiques*: feeling (pleasure or displeasure), located between knowledge and desire, is linked to judgement (of taste), having a priori principles and being applicable to art (Kant, 2000a).

Putting aesthetics on new foundations in relation to classicism and the previous attempts to scientifically establish aesthetics in modernity can be seen as an effort to understand the judgement of taste: the judgement of taste is subjective, that is, it belongs to a human individual, but it has the approval of all as if it were objective; the judgement of taste is synthetic, in the sense that it adds to the representation of a thing the feeling of pleasure, and it is a priori, in the sense that it is not obtained from experience, being disinterested (Kant, 2000a) as pleasure can be experienced by everyone, equally. On these grounds, Kant can argue that the judgement of taste is necessary and universal. The departure from the aesthetics of imitation is also observed in the chapter dedicated to the ideal of aesthetic judgement: if in CRP, Kant refers to God (Kant, 2000b), in the aesthetic field the ideal is man with his main modes of expression, the word, taste, and sound (Kant, 2000a). Based on the type of expression, Kant distinguishes the arts of the word (eloquence, poetry), the plastic arts (plastic, painting, gardening), and the arts of free play (the art of colours, music) (Kant, 2000a).

On the Leibniz-Baumgarten line, Kant places common sense as the organ of aesthetic feeling (Kant, 2000a), occupying a place between theoretical reason and practical reason. Without being a proper sense, like sight or hearing, the common sense is rather related to the imagination. Kant thus consents to a removal of the imagination from the area of negative connotations to which earlier aesthetics confined it. From here to the theory of genius is but a small step: if taste is needed to judge an aesthetic object, genius is needed to produce a beautiful object. As a propaedeutic of romanticism, the Kantian theory of genius is based on the idea that genius does not follow rules but provides a model from which rules can be drawn.

We notice now that the purposelessness of the experience of beauty is a recurring theme in the jostle of philosophies we have examined so far. Hence, what we might take forward from Kant in our neuroscientific exploration of aesthetic experience is the emphasis on the feeling of pleasure. Synthesising the philosophical positions presented so far, we might argue that **aesthetic experience is the experience of pleasure of various intensities, commensurate with our individual past experiences of the world, yet universally accessible to all.** But how individual are our individual experiences of the world? Before answering this question, let us take a break for a little imagination exercise.

A LITTLE IMAGINATION EXERCISE: Find one of your favourite photos (it can represent a person, landscape, whatever). First find your relaxed mood, then contemplate the photo for three minutes. At the end, fill in this box:
Intensity on a scale from 0 to 10, where 0 = no intensity of pleasure (this is impossible, actually, but the figure offers and anchor), 10 = My feeling of pleasure was so intense that I had to stop looking/ fell off my chair/ had tears in my eyes, etc.: ☐
Then answer the following questions:

1. **When in the past did I experience such intensity?**

2. **What were my personal circumstances at the time?**

Then ask a friend to follow the same steps, using THE SAME picture. Ask your friend to fill in the same box and questions (provided here again for convenience):
Friend:
Intensity on a scale from 0 to 10, where 0 = no intensity of pleasure, 10 = extreme intensity of pleasure: ☐

1. When in the past did I experience such intensity?

2. What were my personal circumstances at the time?

Compare the numbers, then the text. If our conclusion stated above this box is valid, the numbers should differ, but not by much. The text, of course, will be personal to each of you, but you could still compare the themes, and find them sufficiently different to validate our conclusion. And remember for future classes:

1. When you compared the numbers, you engaged in QUANTITATIVE RESEARCH. You performed a very simple comparison. Comparisons are a very big part of the core of statistical analyses!

2. When you compared the texts and sought common themes, you engaged in QUALITATIVE RESEARCH. You were interested in the depth, reached introspectively, that always lives beneath the numbers.

Romantic aesthetics acknowledged the central place played by emotion and feeling to the detriment of reason in all human experience: if classicism aimed to discipline feeling, and the Enlightenment aimed to replace it with reason, Romanticism places sentimentality in the foreground, dealing a (final) fatal blow to old forms of religion and law (Faure, 1987). However, Romanticism maintains the relationship with science in an eminently philosophical form, as it follows from the romanticism-idealism relationship (in particular, classical German idealism) of Johann Gottlieb Fichte (1762–1814), Friedrich Wilhelm Schelling (1775–1864), and Georg Wilhelm Friedrich Hegel (1770–1831). Schelling, especially, is the one who makes the lectures on the philosophy of art (1802–1803) a strictly scientific approach: aesthetics is (or should be) the science of art within the limits of philosophy. For him, scientific thinking is that way of thinking which, starting from an absolute presupposition, creates a totalizing impression of the world as a whole: the philosophical system is the expression of absolute science. Thus, the scientific philosophy of art, i.e. aesthetics, presents in the plane of the ideal the real that is in art (Schelling, 1985). To build the necessary determinations (that he calls'potencies') of art, Schelling begins with the construction of the universe in the pose of art: the philosophy of art is the science of the universe in the form of art or in the potency of art. For example, lyric poetry is the transformation of the infinite into the finite; epic poetry is the representation of the finite in the infinite; dramatic poetry is the synthesis of the universal and the particular (Schelling, 1985).

Do you have among your friend's answers a piece of qualitative introspection that is so individual that it might be considered Romantic? Does it offer more depth than 'non-Romantic' text? Or simply more drama?

At this point we might wonder whether our provisional definition of aesthetic experience still stands. If the Romantics present an 'extreme case' of truly alienated and idiosyncratically enlightened individuals, like you were as a teenager, the definition still stands. But let us not break the champagne just yet! While we may feel justified in linking art and (disinterested) pleasure, philosophers aligned with constructionism feel justified in regarding art as a means of creating reality itself, pleasurable or not!

In his seminal book, *Languages of Art* (1968), and in subsequent work developing from it, Nelson Goodman proposed that the interface between us and the material world is a space of symbols. One might imagine this interface as a transparent screen, on which we paint what we see behind the screen. What we paint, our representations of the 'real world' behind the screen, is not a copy of that world. Rather, depending on the technique we adopt, the skill we possess, and the degree of creative imagination we employ, our painting will look more or less abstract. That is because we abstracted from the real world some of its features and reassembled them on the transparent screen. The image on the screen might be said to be composed of symbols. We can say that because it is generally accepted that symbols are abstract and by that virtue, well, symbolise features of the 'real world' (or, as a scientist might say, clusters of matter of various kinds arranged or disposed in a fairly systematic manner).

Now, imagine that the transparent screen on which we painted a piece of the 'real world' (that piece which sits behind it) is actually the surface of a sphere and that we are inside that sphere at its centre. Imagine then that we paint the entire surface of this sphere made of a transparent screen. At the end of the process, we will no longer see the 'real world' behind the screen, but a world that we painted, a world composed of symbols. Now imagine that we have always lived, since birth, inside such a sphere, that the sphere is actually a magic bubble that moves with us when we move, and that we have always been at its centre, even when we moved. Imagine that by a magic feat, our brain continuously painted what our eyes saw behind the screen so that the scenes on the sphere surface always changed, as fast as we moved, with no less than the speed of thought. This could mean, as Nelson Goodman argued, that we have always only knew the reality that we ourselves constructed using symbols. In other words, while our eyes touched the 'real world' (and now it becomes clearer why I used inverted commas), that is, our eyes perceived the 'real world', the actual real world which we have always inhabited is the one our brain has been dynamically painting around us since the moment of our birth.

Supposing that this might indeed be the case, imagine that our sphere intersects with another person's sphere so that our brain paints on the interior surface of our sphere what our eyes see on the interior surface of the other sphere. Suppose then that there exist as many spheres as people on earth, and think about how they might intersect on a bus or train. Remember that we don't see anywhere inside a person's sphere their thoughts or emotions! What we see are symbols that their brain defined using those thoughts and emotions! Surely some of the paintings inside other spheres might be similar to those within our sphere at certain times, but not always because the brain paints over the inner surface of our sphere very fast, and it will paint another image when we leave the bus over the one it had painted while we were inside the bus. But while we were inside the bus, we would have contemplated the same seascape running past the window, and within different spheres, it would have been painted various shades of green or blue or in between. Now try something harder: imagine that when you say a word, an image is summoned, and that only images painted by our brain inside our little spherical universe can be summoned. Imagine that all spheres (so to speak) decided to use a certain word to summon a certain colour, irrespective of what the eyes see and the brain paints. Let's say that some used the word 'green', and others 'blue', and some hesitated about which to use. Words, then, are themselves symbols. It looks like it gets very complicated inside the spheres. While people are complex, the spheres on the bus would generally agree among themselves about the general shape of the landscape, and about a generally similar colour of the sea, which all spheres somewhat arbitrarily decided to call 'green' or 'blue', but not, as in Goodman's example, 'grue', which would have been equally justified for symbolising a shade between green and blue.

Finally, imagine that the bus is in fact the whole planet Earth and that the passengers are its human population. The world we live in, according to Nelson Goodman, is one we constructed using symbols, and we did that because we wanted to know this world, but couldn't really touch it in a way that would confirm for us that only this or that world is absolutely true. Indeed, even when we touch a stone, we cannot know the stone's (material, not mystical) truth. We know that something of a certain shape is there and that it has certain texture and temperature. But all these words were decided by consensus among the spheres (sorry, I really like using 'sphere' to denote 'person'). They symbolise a truth that is there only when the spheres congregate, and when they do not, we don't know what happens to the stone. Nelson Goodman thus helps us to understand that the language of science may be as remote from the phenomena it aims to define objectively as any other subjective language (e.g. the many languages of art).

Does this help us rewrite our provisional definition of aesthetic pleasure? Our last version was this: **aesthetic experience is the experience of pleasure of various intensities, commensurate with our individual past experiences of the world.** On the face of it, Goodman's philosophy does not challenge such a definition. However, it adds the critical element of what might be called 'a time line of consensus', and thus forces us to rethink the part that concerns 'our individual past experiences of the world.' When we reflect on these experiences, do we use a language that, as Kant would have it, allows us to persuade others to agree that something is beautiful? If we were to quantify or measure how much individuals agree that something is beautiful, would we obtain a measure of how beautiful something (e.g. an object) is? Would that agreement take place because of some universal factors that channel our judgement of what is beautiful? **What do YOU think?** (Do take ten minutes to ponder!).

►Having spent time reflecting on the questions set forth in the above paragraph, let's see then if you agree with this redefinition of aesthetic experience: **aesthetic experience is the experience of pleasure of various intensities, pleasure caused by universal biological mechanisms specific to human animals, but triggered by non-biological cultural factors, and commensurate with those of our past experiences of the world that can be reported in a language historically validated by consensus.**

Read the definition again and find those words that suggest dimensions we could measure. Add those words and phrases to the list below:

Intensities of pleasure (how would you measure THAT?)
Degree of consensus
Universality (can we measure that?)
.... (for you to fill in)
.... (for you to fill in)

Note the appearance of a new factor in the definition above: the cultural factor. Think about whether cultural factors relate to the phrase 'a language historically validated by consensus'. Think about the language of consensus in which we report our memories, those memories that ground or anchor cultural factors that trigger pleasure. Have you been offered a rose by your beloved? Do you think about your beloved when you see any rose of that particular colour? Have you come across a poem, painting, or song that represents red roses and love and you have experienced pleasure because of the memory of the rose offered to you by someone dear? If the poem, song, or painting is a cultural factor that triggers pleasure, can it do so outside Europe and North America? Can you measure whether the stimulus (sorry!) will have the same effect in other cultures?

'Enough questions!' you perchance now exclaim. Indeed, it would be difficult to answer all of these questions in a textbook, never mind a mere introductory chapter. Suffice it to say that some answers exist, and will be pointed out in various sections of this manual. Let us conclude for now that we can measure scientifically some dimensions of the experience of beauty, and briefly introduce the work of the German physicist and philosopher, Gustav Theodor Fechner (1801–1887) (for a more detailed discussion of his work and its implications, see Skov et al., 2009).

Fechner is credited as the founder of empirical aesthetics, for which 'neuroaesthetics', as some might say, is another term. Fechner's monumental work provided an integrative vision for the study of aesthetic experience by proposing two converging approaches: 'aesthetics from above' and 'aesthetics from below' (Fechner, 1860, 1876, 1878). 'Aesthetics from above' (*Aesthetik von Oben*) refers to the study of the general concepts and ideas about the experience of aesthetic pleasure, much like the kind of philosophical work selectively presented so far in this Introduction. 'Aesthetics from below' (*Aesthetik von Unten*) refers to the study of the simplest empirical facts, leading progressively to the discovery of regularities in, or patterns of, aesthetic response, that can be formulated as general rules and principles, thereby meeting and joining with those general concepts developed by the philosophers. The general principles discovered through scientific enquiry substantiate, so to speak, the philosophical concepts and ideas. Fechner's own description of these **complementary** approaches is worth quoting in full (in translation from his 'Das Associationsprincip in der Aesthetik' from 1866) (Fechner, 1866):

> From the pure heights of these general ideas [of the philosophers], one then descends to the level of simple empirical singularities, of specific beauty bound by time and space, evaluating every individual phenomenon with respect to the general. The Aesthetics from Below sets out from singular experiences of what pleases and displeases. From there, it builds up all concepts and laws that have their place in aesthetics, attempting to develop them with regard to the laws of what is and what ought to be—and to these laws pleasure must always be subordinated. By generalizing more and more, we will arrive at a system of the most general concepts and laws. Whereas the Aesthetics from Above focuses on concepts and ideas, with all explanations being merely based on subordinations to categories of concepts or ideas; the Aesthetics from Below focuses on empirical laws, and all explanations are mainly based on subordinations to such. (Ortlieb et al., 2020, brackets added)

In his empirical explorations of aesthetic pleasure, Fechner developed the theory that aesthetic experience depends on a direct factor (pleasure is determined by the material features of an object, that are objective, measurable dimensions of that object) and an associative factor (different people respond differently to those objective dimensions, because they are biased by their subjective, personal, past experiences). An important legacy of Fechner's work is his effort to integrate the objective with the subjective, or, we might say, the sciences with the humanities.

If so far we have attempted to answer the question 'What is aesthetic experience?' through accounts that might be said to fit Fechner's aesthetics from above approach, let us move on to a brief account of aesthetic experience that might fit the aesthetics from below approach. This will allow us to formulate, by way of conclusion, a tentative answer to the question, 'What is neuroaesthetics?'. Brief this account may be for now, but questions relating to the aesthetics from below approach will be further discussed and refined in subsequent chapters.

► **Stop and think**: Is our provisional definition of aesthetic experience consistent with Theodor Fechner's work? Are Fechner's ideas about a **direct factor** and an **associative factor** taken in in our definition: **Aesthetic experience is the experience of pleasure of various intensities, pleasure caused by universal biological mechanisms specific to human animals, but triggered by non-biological cultural factors, and commensurate with those of our past experiences of the world that can be reported in a language historically validated by consensus.**
Reach out for a green marker and a blue marker and use the green marker to underline the words in the above definition that suggest the direct factor. Then use the blue marker to underline which words suggest the associative factor.

Let's consider the words you have highlighted in green and blue (or did you also use 'grue'?) above. You were asked to group them according to whether they reflect Fechner's concepts of direct and associative factors, but let's attempt a regrouping of these words within the categories of science (green) and philosophy (blue). While you may ponder on why philosophy is blue, and science is green, you will likely also find that some words and phrases, such as 'various intensities' are rather 'grue'! They can be placed in the science category because intensities are measurable, but, as we have seen with Plato, they could also be placed in the philosophy category because the experience of the intensity of pleasure signals the nearness, in our intuition, of transcendental, perfect forms. They can be thus placed because science research methods have their origins in philosophy and logic.

For example, look at the phrase, 'pleasure of various intensities'. Think about how this pleasure is quantifiable by measuring Heart Rate Variability (HRV), and then think about how the same phrase evokes the presence of (forever veiled) transcendental forms (or, if you are a Romantic, the phrase may evoke the idea that intensity of pleasure is the key that opens the gate between our pitiful mundane realm of measurable HRV, and the pure realm of perfection). Do you sense a tension between the two kinds of thinking, or, on the contrary, a seamlessness?

> I know you are curious about which is the correct answer, but I must say that I look up to you, who are now a student, to give us the right answer in a few years (or decades).

We will come back to the definition of neuroaesthetics in the final summative section of this textbook. In what follows, we will take you through six units, each comprising an Overview (for you to read at home before class), a Lesson or interactive lecture, and a practical Lab where you will do simple experiments based on the lesson topics. Unit 5, which introduces the fMRI technique is an exception in that it does not contain a lab, but yet another lecture instead of a lab. This is because access to an fMRI device is still rare for beginners in neuroaesthetics. We aim to offer you merely an introduction to the discipline, in a first effort to create a textbook for this new field of study, that can surely be further improved in new or future editions. We have taken a somewhat daring approach by including topics such as dance arts and human-AI interaction, as well as a Unit on Problem-Based Learning, whereas most 'traditional' neuroaesthetics research focuses on the visual arts. We have thus hoped to signal a growing interest in areas that have benefitted from less attention by comparison to the visual arts within the discipline of neuroaesthetics. While there are many studies on dance arts within the field, they are fewer than the number of studies on visual arts, and there are very few, if any, on human-AI interactions. As regards the latter, we are still tentatively exploring possible links between neuroaesthetics and AI research, yet our inclusion of a second Lecture dedicated to human-AI interfaces signals our strong conviction that AI will play an increasingly important role in the field, even if many will regard it as not quite amenable to the kind of research being currently regarded as falling within the remit of neuroaesthetics. For example, when we react to symmetry in an image, does it matter if our neural response is triggered by an image created by a human, or by an image created by an AI? If not, where is the border between art, as defined by centuries of humanities research and critiques, and reality? If AIs will become capable of eliciting emotional responses from us, as Pamela Breda's 'Blurred Lives' suggests, how can we understand their awareness of beauty? If we fall in love with an AI avatar, can it love us back because it sees beauty in us? In any case, we are confident that by the end of the module, you will have at least tasted some of the pleasures of investigating aesthetic pleasure.

References

Aristotle. (1988). *Poetics* (S. H. Butcher, Trans.). Hill and Wang.

Baumgarten, A. G. (1986). *Aesthetica*. Olms (Original work published 1750).

Boileau, N. (1952). *Oeuvres*. Garnier (Original work published 1674).

Faure, E. (1987). *Histoire de l'art. L'art moderne 2*. Denoel.

Fechner, G. T. (1860). *Elemente der Psychophysik*. Breitkopf und Hartel.

Fechner, G. T. (1866). Das Associationsprincip in der Aesthetik. *Zeitschrift Für Bildende Kunst, 1*(1), 179–191.

Fechner, G. T. (1876). *Vorschule der Ästhetik*. Breitkopf und Hartel.

Fechner, G. T. (1878). Wie es der experimentalen Aesthetik seither ergangen ist. *Im Neuen Reich, 8*(2), 41–51, 81–96.

Ferry, L. (1990). *Homo Aestheticus: L'invention du goût a l'âge démocratique*. Grasset.

Goodman, N. (1968). *Languages of Art: An approach to a theory of symbols*. The Bobbs-Merrill Company.

Kant, I. (2000a). *Critique of the power of judgment* (P. Guyer & E. Matthews, Trans.). Cambridge University Press (Original work published 1790).

Kant, I. (2000b). *Critique of pure reason* (P. Guyer & A. Wood, Trans.). Cambridge University Press (Original work published in 1781–1787).

Leibniz, G. W. (1985). *Theodicy. Essays on the goodness of God, the freedom of man and the origin of evil* (A. Farrer, Trans.). Open Court (Original work published in 1710).

Mansfeld, J. (1981). Protagoras on epistemological obstacles and persons. In G. B. Kerferd (Ed.), *The sophists and their legacy* (pp. 38–53). Steiner.

Ortlieb, S. A., Kügel, W. A., & Carbon, C.-C. (2020). Fechner (1866): The aesthetic association principle—A commented translation. *I-Perception, 11*(3). https://doi.org/10.1177/2041669520920309

Pappas, N. (2009). Plato's aesthetics. In E. N. Zalta (Ed.), *The Stanford encyclopedia of philosophy* (Fall 2020 Edition). https://plato.stanford.edu/archives/fall2020/entries/plato-aesthetics/

Reames, R. (2016). Seeming and being in the 'Cosmetics' of Sophistry: The infamous analogy of Plato's *Gorgias*. *Philosophy & Rhetoric, 49*(1), 74–97. https://doi.org/10.5325/philrhet.49.1.0074

Schelling, F. W. (1985). *Philosophy of art* (D. W. Stott, Trans.). University of Minnesota Press (Original work published 1803).

Skov, M., Vartanian, O., Martindale, C., & Berleant, A. (Eds.). (2009). *Neuroaesthetics*. Routledge.

Wolfsdorf, D. (2015). Sophistic method and practice. In W. M. Bloomer (Ed.), *A companion to ancient education* (pp. 61–76). Wiley. https://doi.org/10.1002/9781119023913.ch3

Introduction: Representative Foci in Neuroaesthetics—Subjectivist, Objectivist, and Interactionist Perspectives

Per Olav Folgerø

Welcome to Neuroaesthetics! This exciting, new, interdisciplinary field brings together subjects as seemingly far apart as neurobiology and art history and puts them in dialogue with one another. This Introduction is intended to briefly provide insights into some recent scientific works and methods in neuroaesthetics and to whet your appetite for the lectures and lab work that will follow.

The disciplinary field of 'Neuroaesthetics' was mapped in 1999 by the neuroscientist Semir Zeki, who is a professor at the Wellcome Centre for Human Neuroimaging, in the Department of Imaging Neuroscience at University College London. Hence, it is a relatively new discipline and one which lies at the intersection between cognitive psychology, neurobiology, and art. Neuroaesthetics uses models derived mostly from cognitive psychology and modern brain scanning techniques in order to study how the brain responds to aesthetic stimuli. Zeki's main interest is in primates' visual brain systems. From 1994 onwards, his studies also included the neural basis for the aesthetic appreciation of art, and in 2001, he founded the Institute of Neuroaesthetics, the first of its kind in the world, at University College London.

There is also another great neuroscientist who should be regarded as a founder of our discipline, namely Vilayanur S. Ramachandran, who is a professor in neurobiology at the Center for Brain and Cognition, University of California, San Diego. Together with William Hirstein, he formulated what he calls the 'eight laws of aesthetics'. We will not go through each of these laws but focus instead on only one in more detail, the one that provides a suitable starting point for discussing the intersections of objective and subjective studies of art.

P. O. Folgerø (✉)
Bergen, Norway
e-mail: Per.Folgero@uib.no

T. Balinisteanu and K. Priest (eds.), *Neuroaesthetics*,
https://doi.org/10.1007/978-3-031-42323-9_1

According to Ramachandran and Hirstein (1999), art will always tend to be a sort of exaggeration of reality. As arguments in favour of their thesis, they draw on artefacts as diverse as the 28,000 year-old so-called Venus of Willendorf, Indian female temple sculptures from the ninth century C.E. showing an exaggeration of female beauty, and modern caricatures, such as one of the American ex-president Nixon, which, as pointed out by Ramachandran, is more Nixon-like than the photo of the ex-President. Ramachandran labels this exaggeration of form in art as *the peak shift effect*. Interestingly, he finds the same mechanism at work in the animal world. There is, for instance, an interesting experiment on seagulls feeding their chicks. The beak of the seagull, which is yellow, has a red stripe on it, on which the chickens peck when they beg for food. If a yellow stick with a red patch on it is placed into the nest, the chicks will peck also at this stimulus. Now, if another stick with, say, three red stripes is placed into the nest, the chicken will peck even more vigorously. The stick with three red stripes appears to be a 'Picasso in the world of chicks', says Ramachandran: being trained to respond to one particular stimulus will lead to a preference for an exaggerated or *peak shifted*-version of the same stimulus. This is, of course, interesting also in an evolutionary perspective on art.

Ramachandran's point is that art will always tend to exaggerate reality. This leads to a most fundamental question in aesthetics: What is beauty? The question debated for at least 2500 years has been given a wide variety of answers. One can broadly distinguish three main positions:

- The *objectivist view*, which dates to Plato, maintains that beauty is a property of an object that produces a pleasurable experience in any suitable perceiver.
- The *subjectivist view* dates to the Greek philosophers known as the Sophists. They maintained that beauty is in the eye of the beholder, which means that taste cannot be debated.
- The *interactionist view* maintains that beauty is grounded in the processing experiences of the perceiver that emerge from the interaction of stimulus properties and the perceivers' cognitive and affective processes. Hence, this position appears as a golden middle between the objectivist and subjectivist positions.

The Objectivist View

Objectivist criteria for beauty include balance, contrast and clarity, symmetry, and proportions. Among the first instances of intended symmetry in hominid evolution are the countless hand axes produced within the Acheulean stone industry, appearing about 1.7 million years before the present (BP) and continuously produced until almost 200,000 years BP in a wide range of geographical locations. They differ from the previous Oldovan axes, first documented in Olduvai Gorge, Tanzania, by their conspicuous mirror symmetry along the mid-axis of the teardrop form.

As the symmetry of late Acheulean tools goes far beyond functional requirements, it has been assumed that an increased cognitive sophistication of hominines must have taken place during this period (Hodgson, 2009). An 'awareness toward symmetry itself tended to now come to the fore' (Hodgson, 2011, p. 39). Throughout the history of art, we find that symmetry is one of the leading principles. A surprising example is portrait painting: in 3/4 profile portraits, the symmetry line, in the majority of cases, passes through one of the eyes. This holds even for Picasso's cubist paintings. Talking about portraits, it is also remarkable that almost all fifteenth c. portraits are in profile, for example, the self-portrait of Albrecht Dürer, while all depictions of Christ, as the Holy Face, are *en face*. In portraits of The Holy Face, the gaze is frontally directed towards the beholder; hence, the face has an almost perfect symmetry. This strongly indicates that *en face* and symmetry were the only acceptable ways to represent Christ in this period of art history.

The question can be raised, as indeed we do in a research project on 'Symmetry in Art and Science', in which I cooperate: Is a symmetric face associated with divinity, and is it so because of qualities that lie in the symmetric form itself? Hence, does our biologically determined preference for symmetry imply that holiness must be represented *en face*, i.e. in the most symmetric manner? Or is it just a convention that determines that Christ shall be represented *en face*? Our research is based on a survey questionnaire where subjects look at faces with different orientations and with different gaze directions. Faces here presented are from the busts of generals who took part in the manoeuvres of Garibaldi (photographs by Lasse Hodne, Figs. 1, 2, 3 and 4). Each photo illustrates an experimental condition.

Subjects are asked to read a list of adjectival allegations in a questionnaire, five positive and five negative, and rate them from 0 to 10 according to how much they agree with them (Fig. 5). Examples of adjectival statements used are given in Fig. 6.

So far, our results seem to indicate that:

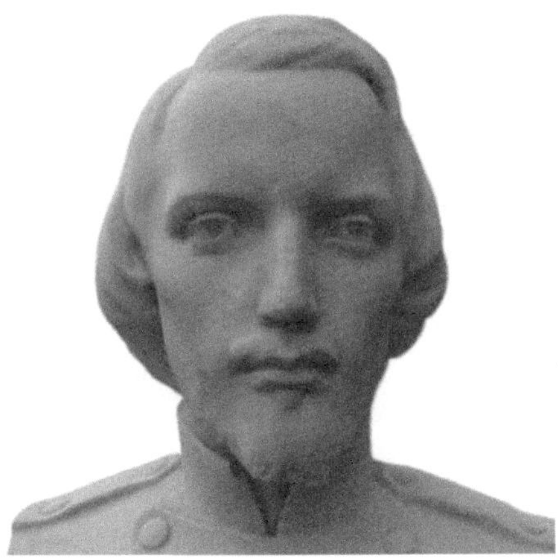

Fig. 1 One of Garibaldi's generals *en face* with gaze directed at the viewer (*Source* Lasse Hodne, 2023)

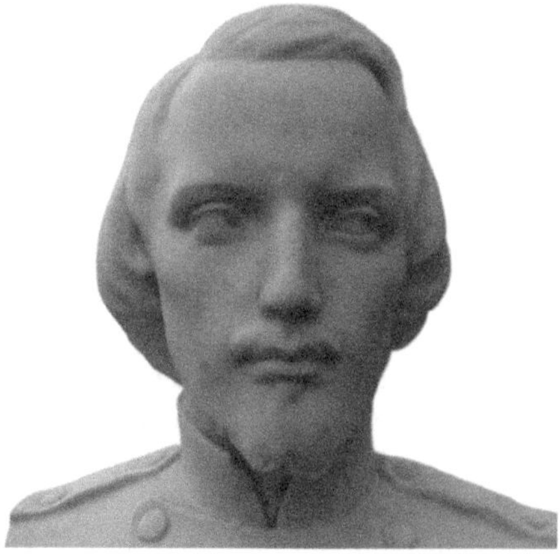

Fig. 2 One of Garibaldi's generals *en face* with gaze to one side (*Source* Lasse Hodne, 2023)

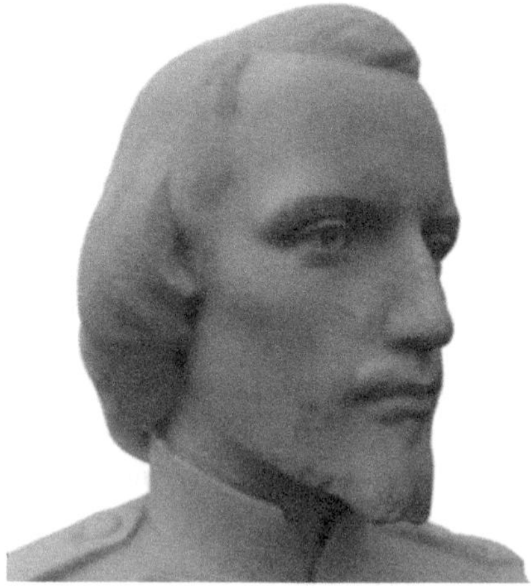

Fig. 3 One of Garibaldi's generals 3/4 profile looking in same direction as head orientation (*Source* Lasse Hodne, 2023)

1. The *en face* gazing at you is more authoritarian, but also more credible, more caring, more trustworthy, more harmonic, and more including (Fig. 6).
2. The profile looking at you is more intimidating and monitoring, not so when looking away (Fig. 7).

Our results, in fact, indicate that the frontal Holy Face is more than a convention. That is, it seems reasonable to suggest that there exist deeper biological and evolutionary reasons for such a convention and preference for facial symmetry.

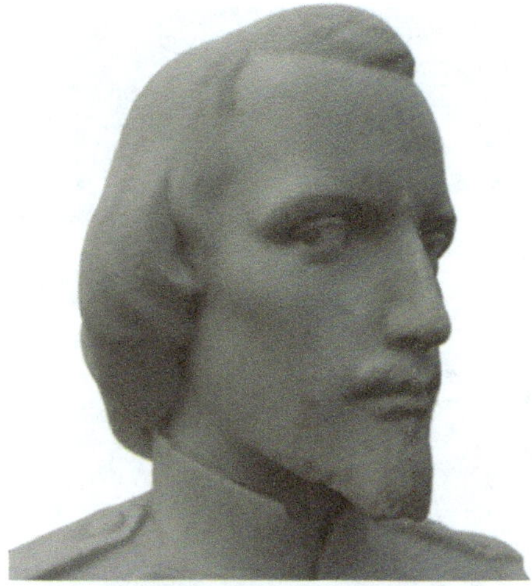

Fig. 4 One of Garibaldi's generals 3/4 profile gazing at you (*Source* © Lasse Hodne)

The following adjectival statements were used:

The person is harmonious	The person is authoritarian
The person is trustworthy	The person is evasive
The person is caring	The person is intimidating
The person is inclusive	The person is monitoring
The person is respectable	The person is dominant

Fig. 5 Adjectival statements rated by participants who looked at Figs. 1, 2, 3, and 4 (*Source* Lasse Hodne, 2023)

Following the objectivist view, we can ask: what about the golden ratio?

Modern research, such as Di Dio et al.'s fMRI study (2007), has significantly improved our knowledge on whether golden beauty has a real and objective impact on the beholder. But let us start with a brief review of the first studies related to this topic in the late nineteenth century, those of the German physiologist Gustav

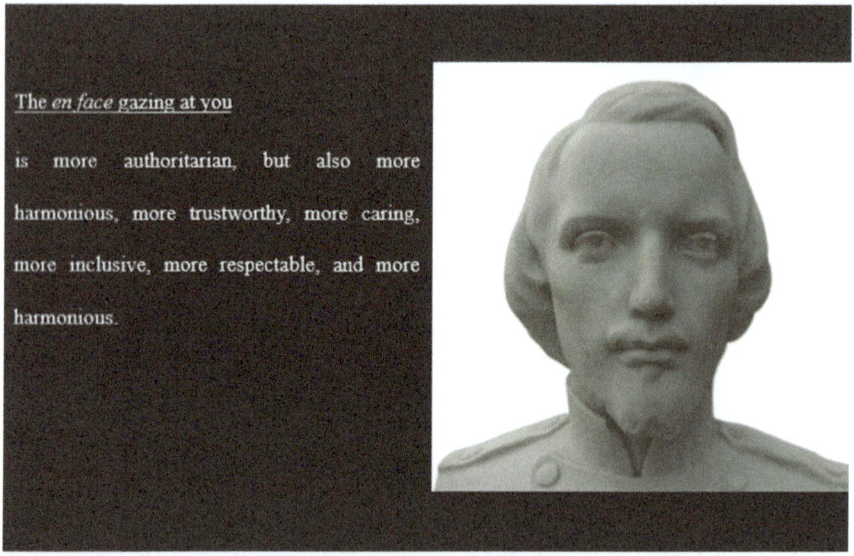

Fig. 6 Faces gazing at you (*Source* Lasse Hodne, 2023)

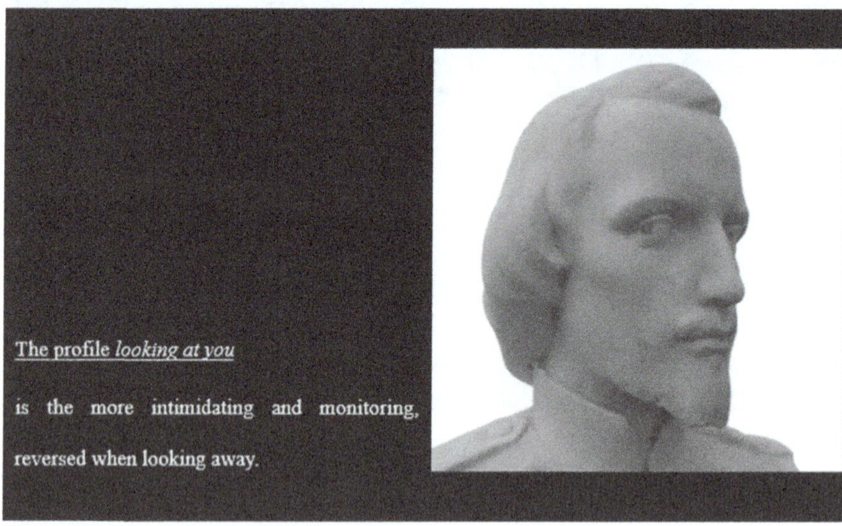

Fig. 7 Faces looking away from you (*Source* Lasse Hodne, 2023)

Theodor Fechner, published in the year 1876. Fechner demonstrated that subjects rated geometrical figures with golden proportions as more beautiful than other figures. The golden rectangle form has been given the highest rating: 35% of the subjects, which were Fechner's students, rated the rectangle with golden proportions as the most beautiful. The ratio between the width and the length of the rectangle was 0.618, which is the golden ratio.

However, it has been strongly questioned whether a biological and inherited mechanism alone can explain these features, or whether they are the result of the frequent appearance in our culture of forms with golden proportions, ranging from huge aesthetic monuments, to those of art and architecture, to the golden rectangle form of the credit cards of modern daily life.

In a brain scanning study on responses to Classical and Renaissance sculptures Di Dio et al. (2007) demonstrated that subjects rated sculptures following the Greek canon of beauty higher than those that were digitally manipulated. Those manipulated generally scored with a negative rating (Fig. 6). Moreover, the canonical sculptures increased activation in distinct areas of the cerebral cortex. As the abstract of Di Dio et al. indicates, the question is whether there are objective criteria for beauty, and whether the golden mean is such a criterion.

The studies were carried out using a *functional magnetic resonance imagining* (fMRI) scanner. The most striking finding is the activation of the *right insula* in those cases when the subjects in the scanner viewed sculptures following Polycleitus' mathematical canon. This is important because the insula is a central structure in the emotional neural network of the brain, also called the limbic system. Observation of canonical sculptures will thus activate the emotional pathways, and these mechanisms seem to be biologically determined. Di Dio et al.'s results suggest that golden beauty may be an objective and biological parameter that elicits activity in particular regions of the brain. Therefore, their results can be taken to illustrate what is meant by the *objectivist* view. However, this is not to say that this Italian group of researchers are pure objectivists when it comes to the question of beauty. It simply means that they have demonstrated how the golden mean affects beholders, and that the golden mean seems to be universally and biologically determined.

The Subjectivist View

As we have already seen, the *subjectivist view* maintains that beauty is in the eye of the beholder, which means that taste cannot be debated. In 2011, Semir Zeki's group in London documented that music and visual artworks, considered to be beautiful by subjects in a test group, where what is beautiful for one person may be ugly for another, nevertheless will activate the same area in the brain, the medial orbitofrontal cortex (mOFC). This has led the researchers to formulate a brain-based theory of beauty: 'Almost anything can be considered to be art, but only creations whose experience has, as a correlate, activity in mOFC would fall into the classification of beautiful art' (http://www.youtube.com/watch?v=NlzanA w0RP4). According to this definition of aesthetics, then, beauty is in the beholder's eye, which here actually means *the brain* of the beholder, within the structure of mOFC, localized frontally, towards the midline, right above the eyes, and the orbits. Ishizu and Zeki (2011) found an overlap between the activation of mOFC as a response to beautiful musical and visual stimuli: subjective beauty activates mOFC. Moreover, this *universal* response to beauty is a physiological *objective* truth. The OFC is part of our neurological reward network, and it is 'perhaps primarily a higher order cortex for smell and taste' (Brown & Dissanayake, 2009). This part of the brain is phylogenetically old, hence significant also for lower animals.

The Interactionist View

In addition to the objectivist and subjectivist views of beauty, we have the so-called *interactionist* view, according to which beauty is grounded in the *processing experiences of the perceiver* that emerge from the *interaction of stimulus properties and perceivers' cognitive and affective processes*, in accordance with models deriving from gestalt psychology.

> ▶ The interactionist view: beauty is grounded in the processing experiences of the perceiver that emerge from the interaction of stimulus properties and perceivers' *cognitive and affective processes.*

Research has documented that the feeling of pleasure in response to a stimulus is greater if the stimulus is easily processed, a process called *fluent processing. Processing fluency* is defined as the subjective experience of ease with which an incoming stimulus can be processed.

> ▶ *Processing* fluency is defined as the subjective experience of ease with which an incoming stimulus can be processed.

What increases the processing speed?

1. The processing fluency increases if the stimulus is symmetrical and if it has a high degree of contrast and clarity.
2. Likewise, processing fluency increases when we recognize the stimulus, i.e. if we have seen it before. We call it the mere exposure effect.
3. The processing fluency will also be increased if the stimulus has been so frequently seen that it can be considered to be prototypical (cf. the seminal article by Reber et al., 2004).

An article by Piotr Winkielman et al. (2006) stresses precisely that prototypes are attractive because they are *easy on the mind*; they are easily processed by our nervous system. Let us, for the sake of simplicity, take an example from everyday life: our preference for a familiar car model, the Volkswagen Beetle with its classical round forms. In a comparison between one of the newest models and an older one; the two forms demonstrate well what is meant by prototypicality. So, one of the reasons why Volkswagen, Fiat, or other successful car industries present their retro models is because we all prefer the prototypical, we want a car that resembles our beloved prototype.

We will now leave this discussion about objectivist, subjectivist, and interactionist positions, to face another question, which has been hotly debated in modern art history: Is art foremost a stimulus for our cognitive processes, a position dominating in the art theory of the twentieth century? For instance, the modernist art theoretician Clement Greenberg stressed the cognitive and analytical content of the pure picture plain. We hereby ask whether art has also a strong emotional impact? This question is among the subjects of the paper, 'Motion, emotion and empathy in esthetic experience', written by the art historian David Freedberg and the neuroscientist Vittorio Gallese.

► Vittorio Gallese and David Freedberg address this issue and challenge the primacy of cognition in responses to art. They propose that a crucial element of aesthetic response consists of the activation of embodied mechanisms encompassing the simulation of actions, emotions and corporeal sensation, and that these mechanisms are universal.

An amazing discovery in neuroscience is the existence of the so-called *mirror neurons*. These nerve cells link *sensory* and motoric parts of the brain in a very particular manner, and they are found in monkeys as well as in humans. They respond to the visual input by activation. When a Macaque monkey looks at a man executing a grasping movement:

a. In the brain of the monkey the mirror neurons are activated. The same neurons will also be activated ahead of a grasping movement done by the (grasping) monkey itself (https://www.youtube.com/watch?v=yacL60710hg).
b. The activation of the mirror neurons during pure observation of a movement will, however, not result in a real movement of the limb. What they do is react '*as if*' in movement.
c. A most significant implication of the discovery of mirroring mechanisms is that the simulation of action by the mirror neurons, the embodied activation, leads to our understanding of a movement executed by others.

The mirror neurons can even interpret the final intention behind a movement, even when the concluding stages of the movement are hidden from vision. Significantly, this motoric understanding also leads to an activation of our emotional nerve networks, leading to empathetic responses to what we see, whether it is an action taking place here and now, in a photo, or in a work of art. Vittorio Gallese and David Freedberg propose that a crucial element of aesthetic response consists of the activation of *embodied* mechanisms within the brain that simulate actions, leading to corporeal sensations as well as emotions and that these mechanisms are universal.

Embodied simulation in aesthetic experience will explain our empathy for pain. As one of their examples, Freedberg and Gallese point to Goya's etching from *Los Desastres de la Guerra* (Disasters of War: Biblioteque Nationale, Paris, France). The viewing of images of punctured or damaged body parts activates part of the same neural network of the brain that is normally activated by our own *sensation* of pain. This accounts for the feeling of physical sensation and corresponding shock upon observation of pressure or damage to the skin and limbs of others. But they will also be activated when a ballerina watches the movements of another ballerina. The mirror mechanisms are mostly localized in the *prefrontal cortex* and in the *inferior parietal cortex*.

Can we mirror the movements of others also when we simply see traces of these movements, as, for instance, in the paintings of Jackson Pollock that reflect the painter's dancing movements as he simulated Indian dance during the very act of painting? Or, to put it in another way: *Does one feel the movement of brush-strokes when looking at the completed work?* Vittorio Gallese proposes 'that even the artist's gestures in producing the artwork induce the empathetic engagement of the observer, by activating simulation of the motor program that corresponds to the gesture implied by the trace.' Gallese stresses that '*despite the absence of published experiments on this issue, the mirror-neuron research offers sufficient empirical evidence to suggest that this is indeed the case*' (Freedberg & Gallese, 2007, p. 202).

What about the pierced canvases of Lucio Fontana? According to the mirror neuron data collected from other experiments, and in line with Freedberg and Gallese's (2007) arguments, it seems reasonable to suppose that neurons in the mirror system will activate, as if they were part of the motor act of cutting the canvas, although the beholder stands still, merely looking at the artwork, not moving as little as a finger. In fact, this is now proved experimentally.

Moreover, how does our brain react to the finger of Thomas piercing the breast of Christ in Caravaggio's famous painting? The discovery of the mirror mechanisms in the brain tells us that we react physically, the mirror neurons mirror the movements, those of Thomas, as well as the imagined *sensory* reaction of Christ; moreover, the mirror mechanisms are not isolated. In the dynamics of the brain, the activation of the mirror neurons will also lead to the activation of emotional centres. Hence, observed motion will lead to emotion, and empathy (Freedberg & Gallese, 2007).

In this introductory lecture, we have focused on different ways to define what beauty is, and discussed the objectivist view, the subjectivist view, and the in-between standpoint—the so-called interactionist view. Whether we prefer one of these views above the others, or adopt an intermediate position, we will ultimately have to deal with the fact that the sense of beauty involves our neurons, neuron networks, rewarding mechanisms, mirroring mechanisms, etc. Moreover, each region communicates with other regions by means of neural connections, for instance, those complex interactions linking the cognitive, affective, and emotional neural mechanisms of the brain. Let us close by welcoming you to this new and fascinating discipline, neuroaesthetics, in the hope that you will find the journey ahead as exciting as we do!

References

Brown, S., & Dissanayake, E. (2009). The arts are more than aesthetics: Neuroaesthetics as narrow aesthetics. In M. Skov & O. Vartanian (Eds.), *Neuroaesthetics* (pp. 43–57). Baywood Publishing Company Inc.

Di Dio, C., Macaluso, E., & Rizzolatti, G. (2007). The golden beauty: Brain response to classical and renaissance sculptures. *PLoS ONE, 2*(11), e1201. https://doi.org/10.1371/journal.pone.0001201

Fechner, G. T. (1876). *Vorschule der aesthetik*. Breitkopf & Härtel.

Freedberg, D., & Gallese, V. (2007). Motion, emotion and empathy in esthetic experience. *Opinion. Trends in Cognitive Sciences, 11*(5), 197–203. https://doi.org/10.1016/j.tics.2007.02.003

Hodgson, D. (2009). Evolution of the visual cortex and the emergence of symmetry in the Acheulean techno-complex. *ScienceDirect, 93–97*. https://doi.org/10.1016/j.crpv.2008.10.009

Hodgson, D. (2011). The first appearance of symmetry in the human lineage: Where perception meets art. *Symmetry, 3*, 37–53. https://doi.org/10.3390/sym3010037

Ishizu, T., & Zeki, S. (2011). Toward a brain-based theory of beauty. *PLoS ONE, 6*(7), e21852. https://doi.org/10.1371/journal.pone.0021852

Ramachandran, V. S., & Hirstein, W. (1999). The science of art: A neurological theory of aesthetic experience. *Journal of Consciousness Studies, 6*(6–7), 15–51.

Reber, R., Schwarz, N., & Winkielman, P. (2004). Processing fluency and aesthetic pleasure: Is beauty in the perceiver's processing experience? *Personality and Social Psychology Review, 8*, 364–382.

Winkielman, P., Halberstadt, J., Fazendeiro, T., & Catty, S. (2006). Prototypes are attractive because they are easy on the mind. *Psychological Science, 17*, 799–806. https://doi.org/10.1111/j.1467-9280.2006.01785.x

Zeki, S. (1999). *Inner vision*. Oxford University Press.

Unit 1 Overview: A Critical Assessment of Neuroaesthetics as Experimental Science—Chances, Challenges, Required Commitments

Claus-Christian Carbon

Preamble: A Late But Sustainable Development of Neuroaesthetics

Neuroaesthetics aims to explore the neural underpinningscited in the text but of aesthetic experience. Due to the reliance on advanced neuroscientific technologies such as non-invasive electroencephalography (EEG) or invasive transcranial magnetic stimulation (TMS) or functional magnetic resonance imaging (fMRI), it was developed as a new branch of aesthetic research only a couple of decades ago. The more systematic research on neuroaesthetics was started around 1999 with a special issue of the *Journal of Consciousness Studies* where prominent figures of this field published seminal works, including Vilayanur S. Ramachandran (where the field is called "Science of Art", see Ramachandran & Hirstein, 1999) and Semir Zeki (who called the field "Art and Brain", see Zeki, 1999a). Already in the same year, 1999, Zeki finally coined the term "Neuroaesthetics" (Zeki, 1999b). Noteworthily, these early sources explicitly and foremostly referred to art and artworks when discussing aesthetics. Typically everyday aspects like kitsch and aesthetically pleasing everyday and ordinary design objects are less addressed or mentioned at all (see Ortlieb & Carbon, 2019). Nowadays, neuroaesthetics is an emerging field of different sorts of scientific endeavours covering nearly all phenomena of aesthetics of a great variety of modalities and phenomena—in 2023, just 24 years after establishing this research field already 230+ scientific papers in Web of Science are listed that explicitly use "neuroaesthetics" in the title or abstract.

C.-C. Carbon (✉)
University of Bamberg, Bamberg, Germany
e-mail: ccc@uni-bamberg.de

T. Balinisteanu and K. Priest (eds.), *Neuroaesthetics*,
https://doi.org/10.1007/978-3-031-42323-9_2

In the following, we will discuss several chances for neuroaesthetics research. However, we will also call some challenges into the mind and demand specific commitment not to fall into some traps of misinterpreting neuroaesthetics data and to contextualize such data into a meaningful interdisciplinary aesthetic framework.

Chances: What We Can Learn from Neuroaesthetics

Neuroaesthetics adds innovative methods and sophisticated measures to address research questions of empirical aesthetics. It can provide insights into the neural basis of aesthetic experiences and contribute to our understanding of how the brain works to phenomena relevant to this kind of experience. We can learn about universal and default mechanisms (Vessel et al., 2012) involved when processing aesthetically relevant items such as artworks. Moreover, we can identify specific brain regions and neural circuits (Kawabata & Zeki, 2004) involved in such processes. Taken such pieces of evidence together can have far-reaching implications for understanding the neural mechanisms underlying the complex interplay between sensory inputs, affective-cognitive processing of the input, and the triggered or executed behaviour. Due to this complex interplay, interdisciplinary co-working seems to be inevitable; among the most important fields are perceptual sciences, emotional research, and behavioural studies. As such, neuroaesthetics is a potential driver and initiator of the cross-disciplinary dialogue very much needed in today's science community, where we try to develop new theories of complexly interacting areas in order to understand and cope with these complexities. We should, however, be very cautious about thinking (or even believing) that by observing the neuronal basis of ongoing processes when perceiving an artwork, we have found any key to understanding the phenomenon of art as such (see Hyman, 2010) and the specifics of aesthetic experience (Carbon, 2019a; Kubovy, 2020).

Challenges: Where We Struggle with the Complexities and Specifics of Aesthetics

Despite its inspiring ways to gain knowledge on brain functionality, neuroaesthetics also faces critical challenges in understanding aesthetics. A serious problem: aesthetics inherently contains so many facets and triggers such a variety of different processes that it is unrealistic to understand the entire complexity by focusedly analysing neuronal activities across the brain. But besides this, the really essential problem is that aesthetics and the appeal of aesthetics, the experiencing of aesthetics including feelings and triggered experiences by the activation of the associative network, is a phenomenological issue, and neuroaesthetics cannot address this critical part of aesthetics adequately. We will discuss all these points in the following in more detail to sensitize the reader to these challenges.

The first challenge is that aesthetics is a multifaceted phenomenon encompassing various forms, styles, and media in terms of the aesthetic object, but there are an infinite number of processes involved and triggered by perceiving and experiencing such an object. The sheer complexity and interdependence of affective and cognitive processes overtax the capability to understand aesthetic experiences. The only chance to gain useful knowledge is to reduce complexity to smaller pieces. This is the typical, and clever, answer of experimental research to overly complex problems. By focusing on a few parameters and changing them systematically, you reclaim scientific land, but you also lose an essential asset and so the key to the treasure island of aesthetics: The emerging Gestalt created by the entire network activity over time will fade out, vanish, and will be ultimately lost. The typical Fechnerian approach to psychophysical research by splitting up the problem into distinct aesthetic qualities and subproblems will self-evidently lead to the so-called *Gestalt Nightmare* (Makin, 2017). To explain complex aesthetic experiences in terms of isolated neural processes is misleading if we are interested in the complexity and true experience of art. Such a reductionist also ignores the default type of perceptual processing: The emerging percept with which we operate, non-consciously or consciously of quality, is not the sum of its sub-processes, but it is a rather constructive process adding Gestalt and meaning by filling gaps in a fundamental (Carbon, 2014) as well as the creative level (Carbon et al., 2022). As our filling-in mechanisms and the creation of the percept are based not only on universal mechanism but the beholder's personal learning history, one of the primary challenges in neuroaesthetics is the inherent subjectivity of aesthetic experiences. Subjectivity is a matter of idiosyncratic associations built up by individual lifetime experiences, framed by a cultural associative space in which we live. This makes it difficult to generalize findings across different persons (cf. Honekopp, 2006), diverse cultures (Darda & Cross, 2022; Yang, et al., 2019), or more general-speaking populations (Nadal, 2013). The issue gets even more complex when we include the dynamics of aesthetic processing that come into play by several factors. Dynamics emerge by the beholder elaborating on the aesthetic object (Belke et al., 2015). Suppose a person is well committed to a deeper dive into an artwork, for instance, so not just looking at it for seconds or milliseconds like in a typical experimental setting, but assigning typical time slots of about 30–60 s for each artwork like in art museums (Carbon, 2017; Smith & Smith, 2001) or even much longer due to a lifetime engagement. In that case, humans typically go through different stages of elaboration (see Carbon & Leder, 2005). These stages are not systematically gone through step by step as some models in empirical aesthetics make believe, but are marked by sudden moments of Aesthetic Aha! (Muth & Carbon, 2013), not evidently followed by insights that lead to dissolving riddles in an artwork, but are typically followed by phases of semantic instability (Muth et al., 2016) which are often demanding but enjoyable. We also face long-term dynamics due to familiarity, elaboration, and context factors such as social factors (Bourdieu, 1984) and Zeitgeist (Carbon, 2010). Thus, in certain contexts, we will process aesthetic items very differently depending on our "social class" (Bourdieu, 1984), the situational demands or the way things are needed, produced and presented in a

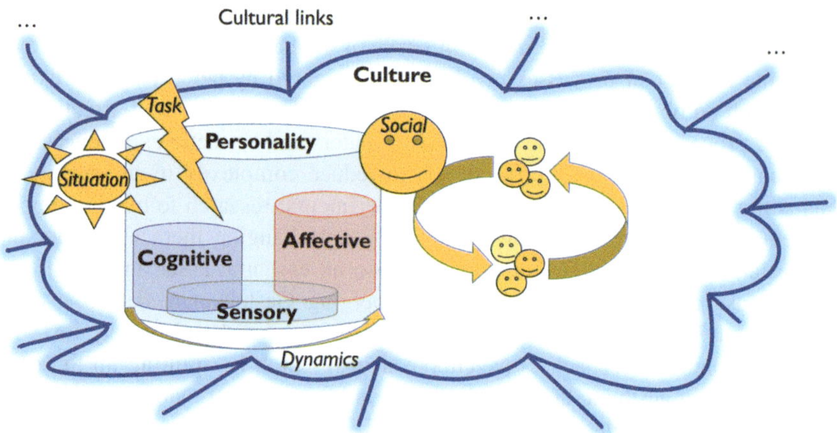

Fig. 1 Model of the interplay of aesthetic processes and relevant factors and facets that modulate and moderate aesthetic experience (MoMo-Model of Aesthetic Experience). Our personality is a significant factor in how we process an aesthetically relevant entity in terms of sensory, cognitive, and affective sub-processes which show dynamic qualities. However, personality is in turn embedded and dependent on the cultural context which has recursive links to other cultures. The current situation, task-dependent requirements, and social interchange will further moderate our aesthetic experience (*Source* © Claus-Christian Carbon, 2023)

time- and cultural-dependent context. For a model of the complex interplay of all these factors and facets, please look up the MoMo-Model of Aesthetic Experience in Fig. 1.

This means that we probably begin to elaborate on an artwork because we are attracted by more superficial attributes or a guiding system that asks us to attend to the artwork. We will assess the quality of the artwork, but also the potential to appeal to us and give us the chance to gain insights (Muth et al., 2015). Then we will often embark on a journey that is characterized by a non-linear perception process with changing perspectives (Carbon, 2020), discussing with others, and further informing us with contextual information about the artwork (McManus & Furnham, 2006); from time to time, we will even stop the process at a certain time to return and elaborate further (Carbon, 2017).

It is essential to realize that these genuine aesthetic processing complexities cannot be ecologically validly (for a critical reflection on this concept, see Holleman et al., 2020) researched by simple lab-oriented experimental approaches (Kubovy, 2020). We will also lack an understanding of the bodily components triggered by aesthetic processing (Nummenmaa & Hari, 2023). We might fall into the trap that experimentally rigorous approaches will always lead to highly complex and large datasets to address certain research questions. Undoubtedly, experimental research in a lab will primarily produce reliable data, often also highly objective data, but it misses the point that people perceive and behave differently in social contexts where typically deeper aesthetic experiences are made. Factors such as the physical setting, the presence of others, and the viewer's prior knowledge and expectations (Muth et al., 2017) can all modulate our perception and appreciation of art (Pelowski et al., 2017). The often-found reductionism in neuroaesthetic research to ignore those factors may also overlook the potential interactions between different levels of analysis when experiencing art (Shapiro, 2011). As long as we do not know the context-specific and context-generic principles of cognition and behaviour, it is wise to simulate at least some typical ingredients used to trigger such experiences, which is done in the so-called path#2-approach (Carbon, 2019a). In contrast, mostly a path#3-approach is employed where participants are exposed to decontextualized and normed artistic stimuli. As testing participants with neuroaesthetic methods in a real-world context (path#1-approach), e.g. a museum, is often extremely challenging as mobile versions of the needed equipment are hardly available or not reliable enough, it is an excellent strategy to balance out experimental control and ecological validity as illustrated in Fig. 2. Such a balanced strategy will definitely not capture the full range of art processing experienced in a museum, but it will capture essential facets of this experience at least.

The most important challenge we will face with the neuroaesthetic approach is to understand that many aesthetic experience, but especially experiences of art, triggers strong, extraordinary responses. These are not only cognitively rooted but often show very expressive affective (Fingerhut & Prinz, 2018) and enactive (Fingerhut, 2018) components. When perceiving the depicted face in Fig. 3, we instantly feel empathy, and we experience a mixture of emotional responses like pain, anxiety, and grief. We will probably have associations with Jesus Christ and

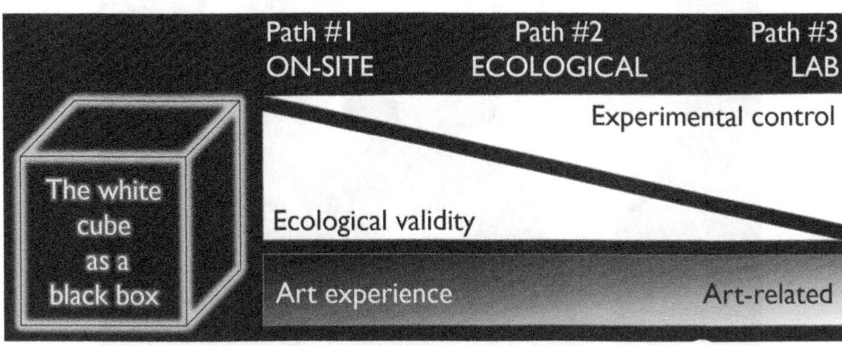

Fig. 2 Different ways of gaining insights into the processing of art. Whereas path#1-approaches are conducted on-site (for instance, in an art museum or gallery) and where participants are, e.g. museum visitors, and so perceive and behave naturally, and so we gain high levels of ecological validity, we have a minimum of experimental control (e.g. randomization of trials and randomized assignment to conditions is hardly achievable), a path#3-approach conducted in the lab offers all commodities of experimental control but lacks true art experience and so can only classified as measuring art-related processes. Path#2 is often the golden path to understanding sub-processes involved in the art experience, as conditions emulate typical context factors but still allow experimental control to a large extent. See more details in Carbon (2019a) (*Source* © Claus-Christian Carbon, 2023)

his story of woe; it deeply touches us, it might even frighten us, and will increase our arousal level. Maybe we will find some stylistic and contentwise parallels to Edvard Munch's scream picture series he painted at the fin-de-siecle (when we are trained in this part of Western art history), but it could also be that we remember a crying person when having attended a recent traffic accident. Anyhow, as said before, these responses might be idiosyncratic or culturally dependent (Hodgson, 2004), but they are real, strong, and personal. We cannot discuss or relativize them: The respective beholders will experience them as they are. With neuroscientific measures, we might identify neural correlates of these responses, but we will never be able to describe the emerging qualia validly. One reason for this is that we never will know all "levels of experience" (Merleau-Ponty, 1964, p. XVI), but also because we can never adequately describe and experience another's perception and experience when processing an artwork.

New technology will develop more sophisticated devices to capture parts of these experiences in the field, for instance, at an art vernissage, within a concert at the philharmonic, or when attending a dance performance at the opera or a sophisticatedly cooked dish at a food festival. Additional observations of the

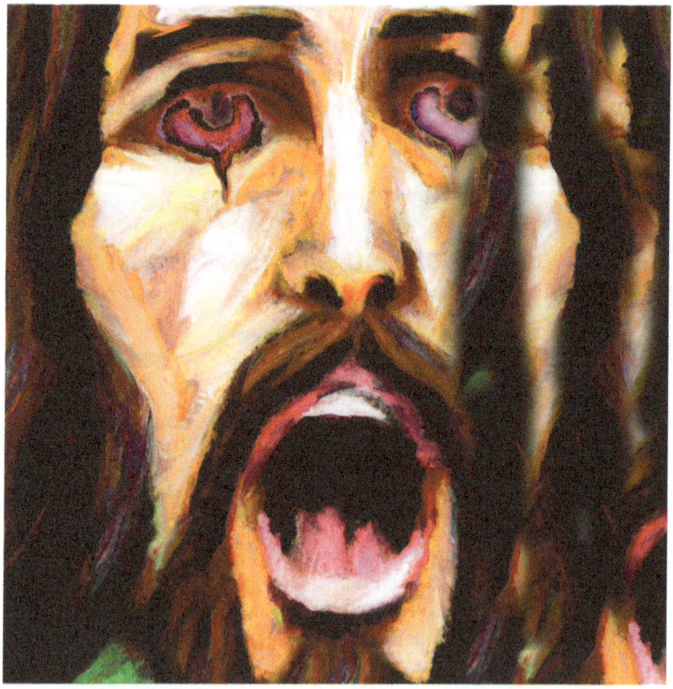

Fig. 3 Illustration of the expressive affective component often triggered by artworks (*Source* © Claus-Christian Carbon, 2023)

behaviour in time, qualitative data about feelings and interpretations, and information about the personality, situation, and further context seem inevitable to create a comprehensive picture of a person experiencing aesthetics.

Commitments: Contextualize Neuroaesthetic Research

After having introduced the reader to the promising opportunities and great chances neuroaesthetics research offers and discussing typical challenges of neuroscientific approaches in aesthetics, we have to sum up which commitments we have to make to use neuroaesthetics as a valuable means to advance empirical aesthetics.

Aesthetic experience is a highly complex, multifaceted process leading to personal affective and cognitive responses and body-specific somatic reactions and actions. We have to understand that deep aesthetic experience can only evolve when participants are sensitively contextualized. Just exposing them to aesthetic material within an fMRT tube will hardly ever be able to trigger the complex network of neural activities usually to be expected in a real-life scenario where we sometimes observe people strongly reacting to excellent pieces of design or art, for instance (Konecni, 2015). It is also a fallacy to think that we can neatly carve independent ingredients from an aesthetic piece which can then be separately experimentally researched without losing the Gestalt and the essence of that entity (Carbon, 2019b; Makin, 2017). We should also not forget that such a complex process is not finished after having inspected the target piece but can endure sustainably. Sometimes, people return to pieces that initially raised their interest, in other cases, they feel the urge to discuss their feelings and impressions with other beholders, with friends, or with experts to get new input and to re-evaluate the work. Therefore, we have to create the conditions for such possibilities in an experimental neuroscientific setting in order not to treat the participants artificially (Carbon, 2019a). Due to the multifaceted character of aesthetic experiences, we also have to extend our repertoire of measures and data that we take into account when researching our participants' experiences. This starts with the core concept of aesthetic experience which should not be just equalized with a rudimentary set of variables such as liking or preference (Faerber et al., 2010). Although liking and preference seem to be promising candidates for a part of the needed construct of aesthetic experience many other influential facets are obviously missing, e.g. interest (Silvia, 2008), understanding (Leder et al., 2006), affective reactions (Reber et al., 1998) and associations (Ortlieb et al., 2020). This also implies that we should intensely discuss with the participants their experiences. We should also systematically observe their behaviour and capture context factors when testing the participants, including environmental specifications and personality factors.

All these considerations must be part of a theoretical framework about aesthetic experience in order to configure an experimental design precisely and to set the required conditions and context factors we need to optimally trigger deep aesthetic experiences that are beyond simple standardized and mechanical questions about aesthetic entities.

Conclusion

In the present chapter, we have critically assessed the field of neuroaesthetics as an experimental science to understand the experience of aesthetic phenomena. We have explored the chances and challenges of neuroaesthetics research and have generated important issues requiring clear commitments to be addressed to create goal-leading research. The interdisciplinary nature of neuroaesthetics (including research fields concerning perception, cognition, and emotion, but also art history, cultural, material, and communication sciences, and biological as well as physiological sciences) holds great promise for providing insights into the neural underpinnings of aesthetic experiences, fostering collaboration among diverse researchers with different expertise and cultural backgrounds. However, the field faces several challenges, including the subjectivity of aesthetic experiences, the multifaceted nature of art, and the significant role of contextual factors. Furthermore, neuroaesthetics is inherently limited by its reductionist approach, methodological constraints, especially when applied to the field where most aesthetic experience occurs, and the explanatory gap between neural and phenomenological aspects of aesthetic experiences.

Outlook

Despite the severe challenges and limitations of neuroaesthetics, the future of the field appears promising and inspiring. By making the commitments mentioned above, expanding the scope of research to encompass a more diverse range of art forms and cultural perspectives, and developing mature theoretical frameworks of aesthetic experience, neuroaesthetics can advance our understanding of the complex interplay between aesthetic items, the mind and the underlying neuronal structure and activities responsible for the sustainable processing of aesthetically relevant entities that surround and fascinate us.

References

Belke, B., Leder, H., & Carbon, C. C. (2015). When challenging art gets liked: Evidences for a dual preference formation process for fluent and non-fluent portraits. *PLoS ONE, 10*(8), e0131796. https://doi.org/10.1371/journal.pone.0131796

Bourdieu, P. (1984). *Distinction: A social critique of the judgment of taste* (R. Nice, Trans.). Harvard University Press.

Carbon, C. C. (2010). The cycle of preference: Long-term dynamics of aesthetic appreciation. *Acta Psychologica, 134*(2), 233–244. https://doi.org/10.1016/j.actpsy.2010.02.004

Carbon, C. C. (2014). Understanding human perception by human-made illusions. *Frontiers in Human Neuroscience, 8*(566), 1–6. https://doi.org/10.3389/fnhum.2014.00566
Carbon, C. C. (2017). Art perception in the museum: How we spend time and space in art exhibitions. *i-Perception, 8*(1), 1–15. https://doi.org/10.1177/2041669517694184
Carbon, C. C. (2019a). Empirical approaches to studying art experience. *Journal of Perceptual Imaging* (10501), 1-7. https://doi.org/10.2352/J.Percept.Imaging.2019.2.1.010501
Carbon, C. C. (2019b). Psychology of design. *Design Science, 5*(e26), 1–18. https://doi.org/10.1017/dsj.2019.25
Carbon, C. C. (2020). Ecological art experience: How we can gain experimental control while preserving ecologically valid settings and contexts. *Frontiers in Psychology, 11*(800), 1–14.
Carbon, C. C., & Leder, H. (2005). The repeated evaluation technique (RET): A method to capture dynamic effects of innovativeness and attractiveness. *Applied Cognitive Psychology, 19*(5), 587–601. https://doi.org/10.1002/acp.1098
Carbon, C. C., Utz, S., & Hesslinger, V. M. (2022). Less is more: Perception as a fun way to Rich Minimalism. *i-Perception, 13*(2), 20416695221089678. https://doi.org/10.1177/20416695221089678
Darda, K. M., & Cross, E. S. (2022). The role of expertise and culture in visual art appreciation. *Scientific Reports, 12*(1). https://doi.org/10.1038/s41598-022-14128-7
Faerber, S. J., Leder, H., Gerger, G., & Carbon, C. C. (2010). Priming semantic concepts affects the dynamics of aesthetic appreciation. *Acta Psychologica, 135*(2), 191–200. https://doi.org/10.1016/j.actpsy.2010.06.006
Fingerhut, J. (2018). Enactive aesthetics and neuroaesthetics. *Phenomenology and Mind, 14*, 80–97.
Fingerhut, J., & Prinz, J. J. (2018). Wonder, appreciation, and the value of art. *Arts and the Brain: Psychology and Physiology Beyond Pleasure, 237*, 107–128. https://doi.org/10.1016/bs.pbr.2018.03.004
Hodgson, D. (2004). Ways of seeing: The innocent eye, individual view and visual realism in art. *Journal of Consciousness Studies, 11*(12), 3–16.
Holleman, G. A., Hooge, I. T. C., Kemner, C., & Hessels, R. S. (2020). The 'real-world approach' and its problems: A critique of the term ecological validity. *Frontiers in Psychology, 11*. https://doi.org/10.3389/fpsyg.2020.00721
Honekopp, J. (2006). Once more: Is beauty in the eye of the beholder? Relative contributions of private and shared taste to judgments of facial attractiveness. *Journal of Experimental Psychology: Human Perception and Performance, 32*(2), 199–209.
Hyman, J. (2010). Art and neuroscience. In R. Frigg & M. Hunter (Eds.), *Beyond mimesis and convention: Representation in art and science* (pp. 245–261). Springer Netherlands.
Kawabata, H., & Zeki, S. (2004). Neural correlates of beauty. *Journal of Neurophysiology, 91*(4), 1699–1705.
Konecni, V. J. (2015). Being moved: One of the major aesthetic emotional states. *Frontiers in Psychology, 6*. https://doi.org/10.3389/fpsyg.2015.00343
Kubovy, M. (2020). Neuroaesthetics: Maladies and remedies. *Art & Perception, 8*(1), 1–26. https://doi.org/10.1163/22134913-20191138
Leder, H., Carbon, C. C., & Ripsas, A. L. (2006). Entitling art: Influence of title information on understanding and appreciation of paintings. *Acta Psychologica, 121*(2), 176–198. https://doi.org/10.1016/j.actpsy.2005.08.005
Makin, A. D. J. (2017). The gap between asthetic science and asthetic experience. *Journal of Consciousness Studies, 24*(1–2), 184–213.
McManus, I. C., & Furnham, A. (2006). Aesthetic activities and aesthetic attitudes: Influences of education, background and personality on interest and involvement in the arts. *British Journal of Psychology, 97*, 555–587. https://doi.org/10.1348/000712606x101088
Merleau-Ponty, M. (1964). *The primacy of perception.* Nortwestern University Press.

Muth, C., & Carbon, C. C. (2013). The Aesthetic Aha: On the pleasure of having insights into Gestalt. *Acta Psychologica, 144*(1), 25–30. https://doi.org/10.1016/j.actpsy.2013.05.001

Muth, C., Hesslinger, V. M., & Carbon, C. C. (2015). The appeal of challenge in the perception of art: How ambiguity, solvability of ambiguity and the opportunity for insight affect appreciation. *Psychology of Aesthetics, Creativity, and the Arts, 9*(3), 206–216. https://doi.org/10.1163/22134913-00001091

Muth, C., Raab, M. H., & Carbon, C. C. (2016). Semantic stability is more pleasurable in unstable episodic contexts. On the relevance of perceptual challenge in art appreciation. *Frontiers in Human Neuroscience, 10*. https://doi.org/10.3389/fnhum.2016.00043

Muth, C., Raab, M. H., & Carbon, C. C. (2017). Expecting the unexpected: How gallery-visitors experience semantic instability in art. *Art & Perception, 5*(2), 1–22. https://doi.org/10.1177/2041669517694184

Nadal, M. (2013). The experience of art: Insights from neuroimaging. *Fine Arts, Neurology, and Neuroscience New Discoveries and Changing Landscapes, 204*, 135–158. https://doi.org/10.1016/B978-0-444-63287-6.00007-5

Nummenmaa, L., & Hari, R. (2023). Bodily feelings and aesthetic experience of art. *Cognition & Emotion*. https://doi.org/10.1080/02699931.2023.2183180

Ortlieb, S. A., & Carbon, C. C. (2019). Kitsch and perception: Towards a new 'aesthetic from below.' *Art & Perception, 7*(1), 1–26. https://doi.org/10.1163/22134913-00001091

Ortlieb, S. A., Kügel, W. A., & Carbon, C. C. (2020). Fechner (1866): The aesthetic association principle—A commented translation. *i-Perception, 11*(3), 1–20. https://doi.org/10.1177/2041669520920309

Pelowski, M., Forster, M., Tinio, P. P. L., Scholl, M., & Leder, H. (2017). Beyond the lab: An examination of key factors influencing interaction with 'real' and museum-based art. *Psychology of Aesthetics Creativity and the Arts, 11*(3), 245–264. https://doi.org/10.1037/aca0000141

Ramachandran, V. S., & Hirstein, W. (1999). The science of art: A neurological theory of aesthetic experience. *Journal of Consciousness Studies, 6*(6), 15–51.

Reber, R., Winkielman, P., & Schwarz, N. (1998). Effects of perceptual fluency on affective judgments. *Psychological Science, 9*(1), 45–48.

Shapiro, L. A. (2011). *Embodied cognition*. Routledge.

Silvia, P. J. (2008). Interest: The curious emotion. *Current Directions in Psychological Science, 17*(1), 57–60. https://doi.org/10.1111/j.1467-8721.2008.00548.x

Smith, J. K., & Smith, L. F. (2001). Spending time on art. *Empirical Studies of the Arts, 19*(2), 229–236.

Vessel, E. A., Starr, G. G., & Rubin, N. (2012). The brain on art: Intense aesthetic experience activates the default mode network. *Frontiers in Human Neuroscience, 6*, 1–17. https://doi.org/10.3389/fnhum.2012.00066

Yang, T., Silveira, S., Formuli, A., Paolini, M., Poppel, E., Sander, T., et al. (2019). Aesthetic experiences across cultures: Neural correlates when viewing traditional Eastern or Western landscape paintings. *Frontiers of Psychology, 10*, 798. https://doi.org/10.3389/fpsyg.2019.00798

Zeki, S. (1999a). Art and brain. *Journal of Consciousness Studies, 6*(6), 76–96.

Zeki, S. (1999b). *Inner vision: An exploration of art and the brain*. Oxford University Press.

Unit 1 Lesson: Behavioural Experiments—Research Designs, Statistical Power, Sample Size *Case Study: Empathy and Closeness in Partnered Dance*

Tudor Balinisteanu

What Is a Science Experiment?

In the seventeenth century, the Irish-born Fellow of the Royal Society in London, Robert Boyle (1627–1691), articulated a new practice of knowledge: arguing that the phenomena of nature can be reproduced in the laboratory, he promoted the idea that knowledge is based on fact witnessed independently (by researchers), and that the recording of fact should be free from subjective interference. Boyle thereby articulated the fundamental principles of modern objective science.

What Is a Science Laboratory?

A science laboratory is the space where an experiment takes place. In order to study a phenomenon, it must be imported into the laboratory space. This means that what is studied is not a phenomenon as it occurs, naturally, in nature. In the

The case study is based on a pilot study on empathy and closeness in partnered dance developed at Goldsmiths, University of London, entitled Pilot Studies on Empathy and Closeness in Mutual Entrainment/Improvisation vs. Formalised Dance with Different Types of Rhythm (Regular, Irregular, and No Rhythm) and Coupling (Visual, Haptic, Full Coupling): Building a Case for the Origin of Dance in Mutual Entrainment Empathic Interactions in the Mother-Infant Dyad (Balinisteanu, 2023).

The original version of the chapter has been revised. A correction to this chapter can be found at https://doi.org/10.1007/978-3-031-42323-9_22

T. Balinisteanu (✉)
Neuroaesthetics Lab, University of Suceava, Suceava, Romania
e-mail: tudor@texmar.ro

T. Balinisteanu and K. Priest (eds.), *Neuroaesthetics*,
https://doi.org/10.1007/978-3-031-42323-9_3

process of importing or translating it into the laboratory, many of the myriad conditions that create a phenomenon are lost. Hence, the validity of laboratory studies is limited by comparison to the conceivably infinite dimensions of a natural phenomenon. What is studied in the laboratory is only a number of facets, dimensions, or aspects of the phenomenon. Or a laboratory study can be directed at discovering what these dimensions, facets, or aspects might be. In spite of these limitations, laboratory studies have significantly advanced human knowledge in almost every aspect of our lives, from health to personal relationships, including, of course, the technology we have for entertainment, transport, communication, utilities, and so forth.

- Point to take forward: A lab study has limited ecological validity because the studied phenomenon is not exactly the same as the phenomenon that occurs ecologically, that is, naturally, in our environment.

For example, if one wanted to study empathy, only certain dimensions, aspects, and facets of what we call empathy can be made manifest inside the lab space. Outside the lab, as all of us know, empathy is experienced in infinite ways in many contexts. To study those, we need critical, introspective thinking, whether we use the methods of, for example, philosophy, theology, or art. That is to say that some aspects of experience, or phenomena, remain outside of the purview of science. To have a complete understanding of a phenomenon and how we, humans, experience it, we need the rich methods and heritages of both the sciences and the humanities.

What/Who Is in a Lab Space?

A lab space contains an area where the phenomenon that is imported or translated from nature can be allowed to manifest. In that area, there may be sophisticated technologies that we use to recreate the phenomenon we want to study. In neuroaesthetics, which focuses on the human psyche's involvement with art, that area will almost always be occupied by the subjects or participants in the experiment. The studied phenomenon is the psychological experience of these participants, to the extent that we create conditions for this experience to become manifested. For example, if we wish to study empathy, we must create conditions for inducing the experience of empathy in our participants' psyche. Pondering these lab limitations, as previously pointed out, one may already notice how different this experience will be from that experienced in the natural environment. Nevertheless, contemporary research has evolved to a stage where psychological experiences can be induced in such a way that they are very close to the experiences lived outside the laboratory, in the 'real' world. In the particular case of neuroaesthetics research, we study the neuropsychological mechanisms involved in the perception and creation of various forms of art. Hence, the kind of phenomena that we need to translate, in the sense of transporting from one place (the world) to another (the lab), pertain to aesthetic experience. For example, we may have to translate or import dance from the communities where it takes place naturally into the much more strictly controlled space of the lab. We can do this by creating conditions, in the lab, for parts or dimensions or aspects of naturally occurring dance to take place so that these parts, dimensions, aspects can be witnessed by researchers and measured.

► Point to take forward: A laboratory is a space where researchers can translate, transport or import phenomena occurring naturally in the natural environment for the purpose of measuring their aspects, dimensions, parts under strictly controlled conditions.

Thus, in addition to the space where the phenomenon we wish to study can be recreated, a lab space contains measuring instruments. There exist a wide range of instruments for measuring psychological phenomena. Most psychological phenomena can be measured behaviourally or neuro-physiologically. Commonly encountered neurophysiological measuring instruments include encephalographs (EEG), functional magnetic resonance imaging (fMRI) scanners, heart rate variability (HRV) measuring systems, pupillometers, wristbands collecting HRV data as well as measuring galvanic skin response (GSR) along with movement acceleration data using accelerometer sensors, to mention only a few among many other fairly sophisticated devices.

As for behavioural measures, researchers mostly use questionnaires, which are also referred to as instruments. For example, if one wanted to measure empathy, one could use the Interpersonal Reactivity Index (IRI) instrument (Davis, 1983). The Interpersonal Reactivity Index is a 28-item questionnaire consisting of 4 subscales, with each subscale comprising 7 items. These 4 subscales measure 4 different dimensions of dispositional empathy: empathic concern (EC) measures the feeling of compassion for another individual who experiences distress; perspective-taking (PT) measures cognitive, as opposed to emotional, empathy; personal distress (PD) is a self-focused measure of one's feeling of distress when confronted with a situation in which there are other individuals in distress; fantasy (F) measures one's capacity to empathise with fictional characters, such as may be encountered in narrative stories or films. The participants to whom the questionnaire is administered respond to each question or item by reporting the degree or extent to which the situation described in the item text is representative of their own experience. A participant's response to each item is recorded on a Likert scale with two anchors (A = Does not describe me well; E = Describes me very well). A and E can be assigned minimal and maximal values: for example, A is usually assigned a value of 0 and E is usually assigned a value of 4. The IRI instrument measures general empathy on each of the 4 subscales. It is not intended as a means of measuring or assessing total empathy. Thus, when analysing the collected data (the scores each participant recorded for each item) one should not analyse the sum of scores obtained on all 28 items, but, separately, the scores recorded on each of the 4 subscales. The IRI instrument is a measure of trait. This means that it measures chronic tendencies which are relatively stable over time. Hence, this instrument is not suitable for measuring the feelings one experiences in the moment. To measure the feelings one reports that s/he experiences in the moment we need a measure of state.

An example of instrument that we can use for recording measures of state, suitable for the situation which we exemplified, one in which we wish to measure feelings of empathy, is the Inclusion of Other in the Self (IOS) instrument (Aron et al., 1992). The IOS instrument is a pictorial measure of closeness designed for evidencing the feeling of closeness between two individuals. Two circles, one representing the self and another representing the other, are shown with six degrees of overlapping and one without overlapping, from non-overlapping to nearly completely overlapping. The participants are asked to select which of the six images best represents the extent of the feeling of closeness they experience in relation to another individual.

Pause and Think Question: How would you use these two instruments, IRI and IOS, in a study on dance?

If we decided to use the IRI and IOS instruments to study dance, we would have to administer the questionnaires to our participants. Equally important, we would have to find a way to translate or import dance, from the natural environment where it occurs when a rather large number of conditions result in the possibility of its manifestations, in the lab (examples of such conditions include the day of the week, say, it is Sunday in a traditional village, people are in their leisure time, there is a festive day, and many other factors such as the presence of a band playing instruments, the state of the weather, the condition of dancers, i.e. they are fit for dancing and in vibrant mood, and so on and so forth). Of course, we will not be able to recreate all these conditions (and more) in the lab. But we do not have to. Suppose that our experience (and a large body of previous research) tells us that people dance because it helps the community stick together. In other words, dance fosters pro-social behaviour. If this is the significance of the problem or question we wish to address, the next step in outlining our research plan is to ask how dance fosters pro-social behaviour: what psychological mechanisms are involved? We may decide (again, based on our intuitions and life experience, but, importantly, based also on previous research) to develop the hypothesis that dance fosters pro-social behaviour because it has an effect on empathy and closeness. We can measure this effect by using the IRI and IOS instruments.

► Point to take forward: To study a phenomenon we have imported into the lab, we need to assess its significance, which helps us devise a hypothesis, thereby helping us to choose instruments for measuring the effects of various factors, that are inextricable from the phenomenon, on relevant aspects, dimensions, or parts of the phenomenon.

What will we, in fact, measure? This question is more difficult than it seems. The answer has to do with the fact that we have decided to import a phenomenon into the laboratory space and apply a number of measures to it (in our example, scores measured using the IOS and IRI instruments). When we import or (literally!) translate a phenomenon into the lab space, we treat it as a construct. For example, empathy, when it occurs in the world outside the lab, is first intuited as a distinct subjective experience. That is to say that, first, we notice the existence of a phenomenon which feels (is experienced) like something that has its own specificity: our subjective (not objective!) experience tells us that we have come across something that is important in its own right. We may then decide to look for an explanation for this distinctiveness and name it in our subjective minds. And so it is with empathy.

According to Montag et al. (2008), the German philosopher Theodor Lipps (1851–1914) was the first theoretician of empathy and a scholar admired by none other than Sigmund Freud (1856–1939). Lipps was fascinated by the fact that part of humans' experience of observing geometrical shapes is a tendency to 'fill' these shapes with a sense of life, a process he referred to using the term *Einfühlung*, coined in 1873 by another German philosopher, Robert Vischer (1847–1933). *Einfühlung* literally means 'in-feeling'. Lipps extended his observations to situations where humans watch other humans, or combinations of geometrical shapes and other humans contained in the same tableaux. A specific **subjective** experience Lipps often used as an example is that of a spectator watching an acrobat performing on a tightrope. The spectator tends to mirror in his mind what she or he imagines that the acrobat experiences. The spectator 'fills in' with feeling the image that he or she perceives. The spectator's experience of this 'inner imitation' was eventually deemed by the wider scholarly community to be sufficiently distinct from sympathy to merit its own name, translated in English as 'empathy' and then adopted as a neologism into many other languages (for example, the Romanian word 'empatie'). Thus, outside the laboratory, a feeling was experienced that seemed sufficiently distinct from other feelings to be given its own name. Therefore, when we import or translate this feeling into the laboratory we can say that we study empathy. However, what we really study is a construct. When Lipps and others named an observed phenomenon, a feeling, or a subjective experience, using the word 'empathy' they construed that feeling as empathy. To overcome the subjectivity of this construal, which would allow us to study this subjective experience using the objective instruments of science, we must find the dimensions of this construct that we can measure. What we will in fact measure are the dimensions of a construct, which is different only in degree from the act of measuring any geometrical shape using a ruler (note that geometrical shapes are also constructs, that is, shapes abstracted from the visual experience of the world around us). As noted, and, now, noted again with deeper insight, the dimensions of empathy that the IRI instrument measures are empathic concern (EC), perspective-taking (PT), personal distress (PD), and fantasy (F). Hence, one might say that, if empathy had a physical geometrical shape, it would have the four dimensions reiterated above. But, of course, feelings do not have geometrical shapes (or do they?). Nevertheless, note the following points to remember.

- ▶ Point to take forward: What is measured in a scientific laboratory is always a construct that has a number of clearly identified dimensions that can be measured, and for which measuring instruments are available.

We have so far 'established' a laboratory space, we have settled on complementary phenomena that we wish to translate or import into that space in order to study them scientifically (empathy and closeness in partnered dance), and we have chosen a number of instruments (IRI and IOS) which helped us to clarify which dimensions of the phenomena-turned-constructs we wish to measure in light of the significance of our research question, namely that partnered dance increases empathy and closeness, thereby fostering pro-social behaviour. What we now need in order to proceed is a research design.

What Is a Research Design?

A research design is a set of conditions we create in the lab in order to test those dimensions of a construct derived from a phenomenon that we deem important in light of the significance of our research question. As regards our example of studying the constructs empathy and closeness in order to see whether they increase in partnered dance thereby fostering pro-social behaviour, what we now need is to establish a number of conditions that allow us to disentangle various aspects of dance in order to see how each of them contributes to, or affects, the experiences of closeness and empathy. We therefore need a bit more knowledge about types of research designs. There are many of these, ranging from fairly simple to extremely complex. Here we will introduce some of the more basic designs. However, these research designs should not be regarded as less valuable than more complex designs, as they can certainly lead to sophisticated analyses, and some have been known to overturn established theories by virtue of their sheer simplicity. A really helpful guide, used here, is that developed by Stangor and Walinga (2014), freely available online under a Creative Commons Attribution-NonCommercial-ShareAlike 4.0 International License. The link can be found by consulting the reference list.

Types of Research Designs

Research designs fall within three main categories: **descriptive**, **correlational**, and **experimental**.

Descriptive research designs employ qualitative methods, being focused on the quality of a participant's subjective experience. The word 'quality' indicates that we focus less on measurable quantities, such as the mathematical values of dimensions of psychological constructs, and more on how a psychological experience is made sense of subjectively. Descriptive research captures the 'state of affairs' (of the heart, or the soul, so to speak) as described by a participant who reports his or her understanding of what they are experiencing or have been experiencing (in other words, they report where they are in the process of making sense of that experience). Usually, this information is collected through using various interview techniques (for example structured or semi-structured interviews). This information is analysed using a complex set of methods which allow researchers to code the information they have recorded during the interviews and establish hierarchical and overarching themes. Interestingly, it is sometimes discovered that some of these themes escaped the awareness of the participants themselves. As regards our research example, if one wanted to do qualitative descriptive research on how dance affects empathy and closeness, one would have to establish criteria for selecting a participant sample, then recruit participants, then devise an interview programme, perhaps asking participants how they would describe their feelings of empathy and closeness immediately after they have been engaged in a performance as dancers. After that, researchers would parse the material gathered from each and every interviewee (usually more than one researcher does that separately and some corroboration work is undertaken at the end of this process). Eventually, overarching themes governing relevant sub-themes will emerge. The researchers would thus understand the governing theme that dominates the experience of empathy during dance, with the important limitation that this understanding is derived from subjective accounts, emerging from a participant's personal (subjective) insight into what has happened to them. While this type of research design is employed by researchers striving for objectivity, for many scientists it remains, well, subjective, and therefore less fit to advance the aim of uncovering objective dimensions of experience. Still, even those researchers who are more scientifically minded acknowledge the extremely important fact that the topics of objective science need must be drawn from the subjective experience of the real world. And, at least as the psyche is concerned, we can only know the real world to the extent that it is registered in our minds, that is, to the extent that a phenomenon we have witnessed leaves us with more or less rich sets of subjective impressions. Yet, as previously mentioned, we can construe measurable dimensions for those impressions, and we can do that in such ways that the richness and relevance of subjective experiences is not lost.

Correlational research designs employ quantitative research methods. Once we start thinking about quantitative research methods we must start thinking about variables in more precise ways. So far we have insisted on the idea that in order to undertake a scientific study of a phenomenon we must establish and measure the dimensions of that phenomenon as we have construed them for the purposes of lab research. That means that we have envisioned that those dimensions will become manifest in the lab and that we could account for their manifestations, by measuring them, as they occur in the participants' psychological life. However, no two participants are exactly alike. Hence, we will encounter some variation in our measurements. Thus, it now turns out, what we can measure are not the dimensions of a perfect construct, as if that construct could exist somehow apart from a participant's individual psychological life. What we can measure are dimensions the value of which varies, however little, from person to person. In other words, we measure the variance of one, or sets of, variables (that is, of dimensions that cannot remain fixed, but change according to the individual psychological universe of each experiment participant—and, beyond the lab, of each human person).

We may have decided that it is in the interest of addressing our research questions to explore the relevant phenomenon from several angles, using different types of instruments that come with their own sets of conditions, that is, with constraints specific to one instrument or another. In our example, we already decided that we will study empathy and closeness in partners moving together using the IRI and IOS instruments. A major constraint that comes with this type of behavioural instruments results from one of their main characteristics, namely that they rely on self-report questionnaires. Importantly, the data we collect is not collected directly through unmediated contact with the dimensions of a phenomenon (or, to use a more or less inspired phrase, scooped directly from the participants' minds). The data is in fact provided by the participants in their self-reports vis-à-vis our questionnaire items. Nevertheless, we can trust this information because the behavioural instruments are validated on large samples and in a variety of contexts, which is to say that mostly the variance in many, many, participants' responses is sufficiently similar for almost all of these participants to not be in the position of outliers.

► Mental note: In statistical analysis an outlier is a value in our data that sits awkwardly outside the homogenous cluster containing most of the other values.

Let us suppose, however, that we have read the scientific literature and came across the notion that there may exist neurophysiological markers for empathy (see for instance Deuter et al., 2018). Diving deeper into the scientific literature, we may conclude that among these can be numbered the following: HRV (High frequency and low frequency heart rate variability, that is, HF-HRV and LF-HRV), P300 amplitudes recorded using electroencephalographs (EEG), and pupil size reactivity. Because in the locus coeruleus–noradrenaline (LC-NE) arousal system intermediate LC tonic and higher phasic firing engender higher cognitive control, and because we can find evidence of higher cognitive control by finding large P300 amplitudes and high HF-HRV (0.15–1.04 Hz) in the context of higher arousal (larger pupil size), we may conclude that our participants experience less affective empathy, but more cognitive empathy; conversely, when low LC tonic firing and intermediate phasic firing is present, along with intermediate P300 amplitudes, high HF-HRV, and closer to normal pupil size, we may conclude that our participants' experience of empathy is more affective or emotional (Faller et al., 2019; Patel & Azzam, 2005). Let us then suppose that we have decided to use EEG to measure P300 amplitudes to see whether the values we obtain are correlated with the results obtained through using our behavioural instruments. In doing so, we will have adopted a correlational research design.

- Mental note: The P300 signal is transient and notably difficult to 'catch'. Because it is transient, we need to repeat the events that might trigger it, thus making possible the manifestation of a series of event-related potentials (ERPs). We will not discuss ERP research designs on this occasion. Do remember, however, that P300 reflects the mental process of evaluation and categorisation, being a measure of cognitive control, or, rather, attention, and only indirectly and hypothetically a measure of cognitive empathy.

Let us underline a point the importance of which cannot be overestimated, and it is one that is often given pride of place in psychology blogs, online groups, or even a lecturer's academic office: Correlation does not imply causation. If values are correlated, all that this means is that the variance measured with one set of instruments is closely similar to the variance observed using another set of instruments. The variables vary at the same time and similarly, but we cannot infer solely from that that these two observed variances have the same cause, nor can we say that one variable determines the other.

- Point to take forward: Correlation does not imply causation.

Thus, in our example, we cannot say based solely on correlations that the event evidenced by larger P300 amplitudes causes the event that leads to a participant scoring higher for perspective-taking, or the other way around (perspective-taking is one of the two 'behavioural' dimensions of cognitive, as opposed to affective, empathy, upon which the IRI instrument is based). All that we can say is that we observed higher perspective-taking scores in experiment participants for whom we also observed larger amplitudes in the P300 signal that we recorded using EEG. When we say 'event' here we mean the interaction between a participant and one or, as is usually the case, more stimuli, so that in in fact more than one event takes place (one event may be caused by rhythm, another by seeing or not seeing the dance partner's face, another by holding or not holding hands). To clarify the similarity in variation we need to know exactly which event leads to which variation, but correlational studies cannot tell us more than that there is a relationship between the variations registered using what are ultimately incommensurable instruments (subjective reports and objective instrumental recordings in our example).

We can, however, venture to predict that, given closely similar conditions, the correlation will be observed again and again; in other words, the similarity in variance is not a coincidence. When we do so, if we have only two variables, we must refer to one of the variables as the predictor variable and to the other variable as the outcome variable. In other words, we could hypothesise that the existence of variance in variable Y (predictor variable) predicts the existence of variance in

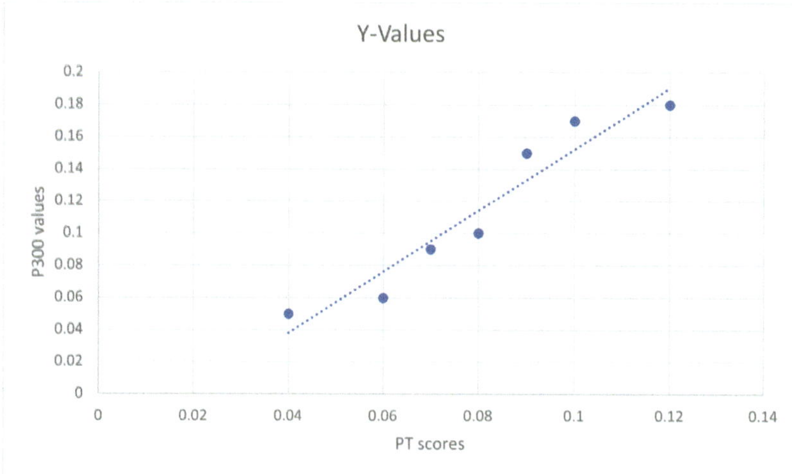

Fig. 1 Fictive illustration of correlated variables

variable X (outcome variable) (Stangor & Walinga, 2014, 108). In our example, we could hypothesise that larger amplitudes in the P300 signal predict higher scores on the perspective-taking subscale of the IRI instrument. If we measured and processed P300 values and PT scores for 7 participants, and standardised the values to make them mathematically commensurable, we could represent this graphically as in Fig. 1 (note that the graph is intended solely for the purpose of illustration and that it is not based on actual collected data):

In this fictional graph, each dot represents one experiment participant whose P300 amplitudes have been supposedly collected and processed, and who provided self-reported scores on the IRI perspective-taking subscale. The respective values would have been mathematically transformed so that the values of PT scores are commensurable with the values obtained by recording the P300 signal. We notice that as the values of P300 amplitudes are higher on the Y axis, the PT scores increase on the X axis. Let us keep tabs on these values by using a table (Table 1):

Table 1 Fictive data used in plotting the graph in Fig. 1 for illustration purposes

X-values	Y-values
0.04	0.05
0.06	0.06
0.07	0.09
0.08	0.1
0.09	0.15
0.1	0.17
0.12	0.18

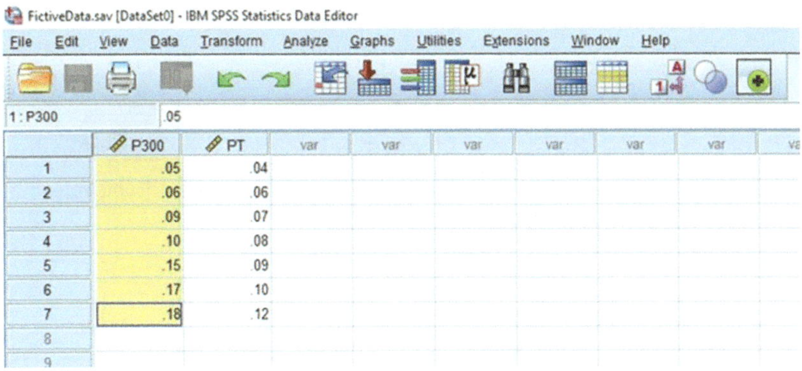

Fig. 2 Fictive data as shown in the SPSS Data View sheet

Note the straight line in Fig. 1. It indicates that the two variables are in linear correlation. The strength and direction of the linear relationship between the two variables can be measured using the Pearson correlation coefficient, or Pearson's *r*. We can calculate Pearson's *r* for our fictive data using SPSS, a statistical analysis software package. First, we need to define our variables on the SPSS Variable View sheet, and then enter our data in the Data View sheet. The result will look like this (Fig. 2):

We calculate Pearson's *r* by clicking *Analyze* > *Correlate* > *Bivariate*. In the ensuing screen, we select our two variables from the window on the left and transfer them to the window on the right, obtaining the result shown in Fig. 3. Checking that the option **Exclude cases pairwise** is selected under **Options**, we click *Continue* and then *OK*. We will obtain the result shown in Table 2.

We can now trace the intersection of P300 with PT to find out Pearson's *r*, which in our fictive example has a value of $r = 0.959$. The result also tells us that the correlation is highly significant at $p < 0.001$. We will discuss the importance of the *p*-value in more detail in the next section.

As a rule of thumb, we know that our variables are strongly correlated in a linear relationship when $0.5 < r < 1$. The Pearson correlation can take a range of values from +1 to −1. A value of 0 indicates that there is no association between the two variables. A value greater than 0 indicates a positive association; that is, as the measured values of one variable increase, so do the values of the other variable. This measures the strength of the correlation. Whether the correlation is significant is indicated by the Sig. value or the *p*-value. A small sig./ *p*-level indicates a stronger relationship. To assess the strength of correlation according to the Pearson correlation coefficient the following scale can be used:

1. High degree: *r* lies between ± 0.50 and ± 1, strong correlation.
2. Moderate degree: *r* lies between ± 0.30 and ± 0.49, medium correlation.
3. Low degree: *r* lies below ± 0.29, small correlation.
4. No correlation: *r* is zero.

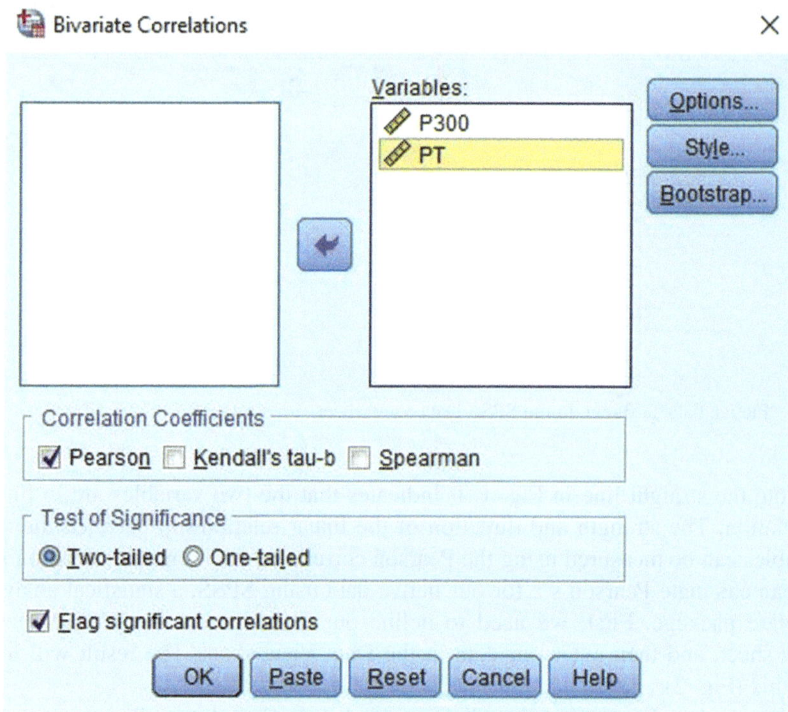

Fig. 3 Fictive example of handling two variables in order to calculate Pearson's *r*

Table 2 Fictive example of a Pearson's *r* value calculated using SPSS

	Correlations	P300	PT
P300	Pearson correlation	1	0.959**
	Sig. (2-tailed)	0.001	
	N	7	7
PT	Pearson correlation	0.959**	1
	Sig. (2-tailed)	0.001	
	N	7	7

** Correlation is significant at the 0.01 level (2-tailed)

In our fictive example, we calculated that the 2 variables are strongly and positively correlated. **If only that were really so!**

Experimental research designs employ quantitative research methods. They are used to infer conclusions about the causal relationship between two or more variables. This implies organising a manipulation of one or more variables in order to compare the different effects a variable has on another one or more variables.

The difference in effect is caused by the different conditions we create through our manipulation.

Hence, the role of our manipulation is to enable us to control one or more variables in order to disentangle their effects and specify objectively how a variable affects another one or more variables. The variable we control is called an Independent Variable (IV). The variable registering, in its variance, the effect of the IV, is called a Dependent Variable (DV). For an experimental study to work, we must clearly specify our IVs and DVs. In our example, focused on studying the effect of dance on empathy, the IV can be rhythm, and the DV can be closeness. We can have more than one DV, of course. In our example we have two behavioural DVs, empathy and closeness, which we can measure using the IRI and IOS instruments, respectively. If we decided to pursue our exploration of how dance rhythm effects a change in P300 amplitudes, we would have a third DV, a 'neurophysiological' DV, which we could name 'P300'. This would enable us to combine a correlational study with an experimental one. We will not focus on neurophysiological DVs here, but only on behavioural DVs.

Our IV can have several levels, according, for example, to the type of rhythm we wish to explore in terms of its effect on closeness and empathy. There is, of course, more than one rhythm type in our natural world. For example, we can easily distinguish between regular and irregular rhythm. In the subsequently proposed lab work, we will learn how to study and analyse the effect of a two-level IV on two DVs. The IV will be rhythm type with two levels: regular rhythm and irregular rhythm. The DVs will be closeness and empathy. Our data will be collected by using IOS and IRI questionnaires, respectively.

- Start thinking: what type of dance, or form of movement together, would you be interested in exploring? These can be partnered dance in pairs, group dance in a circle, lines of dancers facing one another, and some other, but, to ensure representativity, it may be a good idea to choose one of these three, as these are the most commonly encountered forms of moving together.

Now that we have clarified what our IV and DVs are, and what instruments we will use to measure them, in addition to securing sufficient lab space, we must start thinking about the stimuli we will use, and the experiment participants that we need to enable us to carry out our study.

Stimuli

Stimuli are artificial (in the sense of man-made, or, more precisely, researcher-made) recreations of those elements of a naturally occurring phenomenon that we wish to isolate in order to study their effects on other dimensions, aspects, and elements of a phenomenon. Do remember that a 'global' phenomenon is composed of many phenomena and that what we include in the 'globe' is chosen with a degree of subjectivity, as when we created the construct 'empathy' with its measurable dimensions. This 'globe' which presumably contains the phenomenon we wish to study is but a slice of natural reality. Natural reality is much more fluid and amenable to myriad varying forces. It often takes a lot of ingenuity to create appropriate stimuli. However, things are easier in the context of the example we have been following. Since our IV levels are regular rhythm and irregular rhythm, all that we need to do is obtain separate recordings of these rhythms.

This can be done using specialised software, such as GarageBand. In our lab demonstration, we will use two sound tracks obtained by programming a 4/4 (regular) rhythm and a 7/8 (irregular) rhythm in GarageBand. Since our focus is rhythm, no other instrument was programmed in order to avoid bringing in more variables that are difficult to control, such as pitch, melodiousness, and harmoniousness. However, it is important to achieve a compromise between a tightly controlled stimulus and real-life situations. For this reason, our sound tracks will contain rhythm produced by selecting a conga drum. While this sound is synthetic (electronically synthesised), it does approximate very well the type of sound humans must have heard since the dawn of times, given that drums, and, generally speaking, percussion, are likely among the first instruments and sound techniques produced in our civilisations.

Importantly, in order to keep a tight leash on our experimental conditions, that is, in order to control the IV as much as possible, both tracks will have exactly the same duration and will be relayed over exactly the same audio devices. The experiment itself will take place in the same room both for our regular rhythm and for our irregular rhythm conditions, again, to minimise the influence of possible extraneous variables that can have an effect on our IV. Note that even the slightest variation in our experimental set-up can become an extraneous variable. In our case, for example, although we will use an audio system to play the sound tracks, the movement of our participants' feet on the floor (stepping) can create an additional layer of rhythm. That is acceptable if all our participants, across conditions, will move on the same floor. We could, additionally, ask the participants to remove their shoes and move in bare feet or with only their socks on.

Since we now have our stimuli, lab space, a set of measuring instruments, a choice of research design, and a specification of our IVs and DVs, we can focus next on a central aspect of our experiment: the participants.

Between-Subjects and Within-Subjects Designs

Well, we haven't quite finalised our research design until we decide whether it will be a between-subjects or within-subjects design. This choice affects the number of participants we need for our study. A between-subjects experimental design is one in which different participants are tested in each condition. In our example, if we chose a between-subjects design, we would need to recruit a higher number of participants, as we would have to employ different (teams of) participants in each of our two conditions. In other words, the dancers who will move together in the regular rhythm condition will be other people than the dancers who will move together in the irregular rhythm condition. If we were to employ a within-subjects design, the same dancers who moved together in the regular rhythm condition would participate, in the exact same set-up, in the irregular rhythm condition (preserving their position in space, or their partner, etc.). A within-subjects research design is therefore one in which the same participants are tested in all of our experimental conditions.

► Points to take forward:
In a between-subjects design, different participants undertake trials in each condition.
In a within-subjects design, the same participants undertake trials in all conditions.

While within-subjects designs have greater statistical power than between-subjects designs, we must choose carefully which of the two is more appropriate for the experiment we wish to carry out. For example, if we are interested in finding out how a proposed intervention affects a population over a period of time, it is in the interest of our research to choose a within-subjects design. If, for example, we wish to study the efficacy of a treatment on a specific participants sample (e.g. people suffering from a certain condition), one way to do so is to administer the treatment at set time intervals to the same participants. The statistical analyses of our results will give us an indication of the efficacy of the treatment or intervention, that we can then compare to a control group (that is, a group containing an equal number of participants as the treatment group, but whose members did not receive the treatment).

However, when the perception of art is the focus of our research, as is the case in neuroaesthetics, we must consider a number of other issues. To better understand the advantages of a between-subjects approach, we may focus on error variance. Error variance is the variance due to extraneous variables that we have not taken into account. It is also called residual or unexplained variance, that is, variance that we cannot explain because we cannot attribute it to the variables we have chosen to study (in our example, error variance would be variance that cannot be attributed to either regular or irregular rhythm, and may come from differences between participants within their group, such as previous dance expertise). Therefore, we are interested in showing that the proportion of variance attributable to our intervention in each condition (e.g. moving together on regular as opposed to irregular rhythm) is sufficiently large to distinguish the groups even when there exists variance attributable to extraneous variables within each group. If that were the case, and given that dance is a widespread cultural phenomenon (that is, not specific to a set of individuals, such as people suffering from a certain medical condition), the credibility of our results would be strengthened.

One other important thing we need to be concerned with when we study scientifically the mechanisms involved in the perception and creation of art is learning and transfer across conditions. If, as in our example, we want to study the effect of rhythm on closeness and empathy in partnered dance in pairs, we should consider that the longer two individuals spend together, the more empathic they may become toward one another, and the more likely it is that their feeling of closeness vis-à-vis their partner may increase. In studies of other forms of art, such as visual art (e.g. paintings) the participants of a within-subjects design may be primed by sets of images they have previously seen as part of one experimental condition so that how they respond to a different set of images may be biased. In such a case we might be better off if we choose a between-subjects design, unless, of course, we are interested precisely in examining that bias.

Let us then choose, for our lab experiment, a between-subjects design, partly because we want to see through the error variance caused by extraneous variables, and partly because we wish to avoid individuals being biased by the time they spend together in terms of their empathy and closeness responses. However, this does not mean that we cannot do a within-subjects analysis as part of our experimental design. We can include a within-subjects dimension in our experiment without affecting the benefits we derive from our between-subjects design.

Hence, we are interested in finding out whether the length of time spent by two participants in any one condition has an effect on their experience of empathy and feeling of closeness. This is not the same time-length issue highlighted above, where we wanted to avoid participants becoming too familiar with each other because they have spent a lot of time together by moving together in *all* conditions, therefore, a much longer period of time than the one on which we focus here. Here, we are simply concerned with the possibility that even, say, a seven-minute-long period of time may be sufficient for the participants' 'togetherness' to have an effect on our DVs. Thus, and this might have been mentioned earlier (think: why?), we will have to take their IRI and IOS measures both before and after the intervention (that is, both before and after the period of time when they move together in pairs on either regular or irregular rhythm). Therefore, we will measure the responses of the same participants at two different time points. We will then have a within-subject design mixed with our between-subjects design: different participants will dance in pairs in each condition (between-subjects), but within each condition the effect of our intervention (the dance) will be measure twice for the same participants (within-subjects). This is called a mixed within-between design.

Are we ready to go? Not yet. What else have we not yet decided on?

Statistical Power, Significance, and Sample Size

Yes, right. We have yet to decide how many participants we need to recruit for our experiment to yield significant results, results that we may say, with sufficient degree of confidence, are representative not only as regards our participants, but as regards the population of which they are a sample. In other words, we need to decide on the number of participants we need in order to obtain a good balance between statistical power and statistical significance.

Statistical Power is a measure between 0 and 1 which indicates how good our experimental set-up is at detecting a false null hypothesis. When we hypothesise that dance on either regular or irregular rhythm affects empathy and closeness, supposing that our analysis will likely confirm our hypothesis, we in fact anticipate that we will find ourselves in one of four positions after our experiment and analyses will have been completed. At that point, we will make a statement based on our statistical analyses, while the reality may or may not be as we state it:

1. We will state that an effect was present and an effect really was present;
2. We will state that an effect was present, but an effect was not really present (Type I Error);
3. We will state that no effect was present, and our intervention really had no effect;
4. We will state that no effect was present, but in reality an effect was actually present (Type II Error).

Remember that, at this point, that is, before our experiment even commences, we are not in a position to make such statements. We merely anticipate that we will find ourselves in one of the four positions, and we need to take precautions to ensure that we will find ourselves in either position 1 or position 3 (preferably in position 1). We need to make sure, as much as we can at this point, that we will not commit a Type I or a Type II error.

To better understand these two types of error, we must discuss the concept of null hypothesis. The null hypothesis is a conjecture of a rather abstract nature: we suppose the worst-case scenario, so to speak, a scenario in which all of our participants are exactly the same, so that there will be absolutely no variation between individual responses during the trial or intervention that they will undergo. If their psychological responses are exactly similar, we will have no grounds for claiming that our intervention had any effect on these participants. From this, we may infer that there is no relationship whatsoever between the intervention and the participants' responses. In our example, the null hypothesis would be that moving together in pairs with participants positioned face-to-face has no effect whatsoever on their experience of empathy or feeling of closeness, regardless of the group (regular or irregular rhythm) to which they have been assigned. What we in fact hope to achieve is to obtain evidence that will allow us to reject the null hypothesis. As noted, statistical power is expressed as a number between 0 and 1, and the closer it is to 1, the more confident or 'powerful' we are in saying that we have not missed an effect if there was one, thus avoiding to commit a type II error. However, we must be aware that we will never be able to have absolute confidence in stating that an effect was present. We must accept that we may commit a type I error, thus accepting that, at least as regards some of our data, the null hypothesis might be true (an effect was not really present).

We must, of course, be willing to take that risk. But we can only accept that risk within certain limits. The risk is represented using a conventional probability value (symbolised using the Greek letter 'α') of there occurring a type I error, a value referred to as level of signifance. We set the α value as a percentage of our confidence (e.g. 5%) that we accept is shaky, and if we represent absolute confidence as the unit 1, α becomes 0.05. After running our analysis we will obtain a number quantifying the probability that the mean of the participants' responses falls within the 5% interval covered by the α value (e.g. 0–0.05). This is our '*p*-value'. If this probability is higher than α we cannot reject the null hypothesis, for fear that we would commit a type I error. This '*p*' does not measure power, it measures probability; but it is a power-related value, because by increasing the amount of risk we accept (i.e. increasing α), we increase the range of values based on which we decide to reject the null hypothesis, and thus increase our power to say that we haven't missed an effect. However, this increase in power is unsafe, for we increase power by increasing risk. The level of significance conventionally accepted as safe is between 0.001 and 0.05.

As in real life, in statistics, too, power is linked with confidence. Thus, we will not reject the null hypothesis when p is higher than 0.05. Making this choice will allow us to confidently assert that (in spite of our prediction, and, usually, deeply embedded hopes) our intervention did not have a significant effect on the participants. Conversely, when p is smaller than α, we can fairly confidently assert that it is highly likely that our intervention did have an effect. We can represent mathematically the confidence with which we reject the null hypothesis as CI = $100(1 - \alpha)\%$ where CI = confidence interval, and α = percentage of accepted risk that the null hypothesis is true when we say that it isn't (the risk that there is no effect when we say there is one). If, for example, we accept a high risk of committing a type I error, $\alpha = 0.6$, then our confidence to assert that our intervention had an effect decreases to 40% even though our power is high. But if we accept a small risk by setting the α value between 0.001 and 0.05, our (genuine) confidence increases significantly. In the end, we may now realise, power is the extent to which our confidence matters.

We can, of course, discuss power in different ways. If we say that two groups do not differ when they actually do, so that we mistakenly accept the null hypothesis, we commit a type II error, the probability of which is quantified using the symbol β. In this case, our power to correctly reject the null hypothesis can be calculated as $1 - \beta$. For example, if $\beta = 0.6$, then power = 0.4, and we are rather less assured in asserting that there was no effect, because the probability of there actually being an effect that our analysis did not register is too high ($\beta = 0.6$). Now, remember that the α value indicated how confident we can be in saying that our power matters, or is significant. Does our confidence in asserting that there was an effect matter, if we are not also confident in saying that if an effect were there we would not have missed it?

Real power, then, is the extent to which a test (*p*-value) of significance (set α) verifies our confidence about there having been an effect when one really was there. We always hope for the best of all worlds (powerful results with low risk), and, as we will realise during our experimental work, one sure way of satisfying that hope is to increase the number of participants. Imagine we had tested every human being who has ever lived or will ever live. Our analysis would then have something like godly power. Fortunately, that is not possible. In our lab session, we will be much more reasonable in undertaking an experiment, collecting data, and analysing it.

► Before signing out from this lesson, remember:
p (with $\alpha=0.05$) < 0.05 means that our results have statistical significance;
Power > 0.8 means that the test of significance is potent.

References

Aron, A., Aron, E. N., & Smollan, D. (1992). Inclusion of other in the self scale and the structure of interpersonal closeness. *Journal of Personality and Social Psychology, 63*(4), 596–612.

Balinisteanu, T. (2023). Pilot studies on empathy and closeness in mutual entrainment/ improvisation vs. formalised dance with different types of rhythm (regular, irregular, and no rhythm) and coupling (visual, haptic, full coupling): Building a case for the origin of dance in mutual entrainment empathic interactions in the mother–infant dyad. *Behav. Sci., 13*, 859. https://doi.org/10.3390/bs13100859

Davis, M. H. (1983). Measuring individual differences in empathy: Evidence for a multidimensional approach. *Journal of Personality and Social Psychology, 44*(1), 113–126.

Deuter, C. E., Nowacki, J., Wingenfeld, K., Kuehl, L. K., Finke, J. B., Dziobek, I., & Otte, C. (2018). The role of physiological arousal for self-reported emotional empathy. *Autonomic Neuroscience, 214*, 9–14. https://doi.org/10.1016/j.autneu.2018.07.002

Faller, J., Cummings, J., Saproo, S., & Sajda, P. (2019). Regulation of arousal via online neurofeedback improves human performance in a demanding sensory-motor task. *Proceedings of the National Academy of Sciences of the United States of America, 116*(13), 6482–6490. https://doi.org/10.1073/pnas.1817207116

Montag, C., Gallinat, J., & Heinz, A. (2008). Images in psychiatry: Theodor Lipps and the concept of empathy: 1851–1914. *The American Journal of Psychiatry, 165*(10), 1261.

Patel, S. H., & Azzam, P. N. (2005). Characterization of N200 and P300: Selected studies of the event-related potential. *International Journal of Medical Sciences, 126*(11), 2124–2131.

Stangor, C., & Walinga, J. (2014). *Introduction to psychology* (1st Canadian ed.). BCcampus. https://opentextbc.ca/introductiontopsychology/

Unit 1 Lab: Data Collection and Analysis—Repeated-Measures (Mixed) ANOVA and Factorial ANOVA Using SPSS *Case Study: Empathy and Closeness in Partnered Dance*

Tudor Balinisteanu

This is a demonstration lab. Most likely we will not have a sufficient number of participants to obtain statistical significance. The lab is intended to work as a learning process. A volunteer can assume the role of the researcher, making sure the following tasks are completed. However, except for Tasks 1–3, all students can participate in the completion of the tasks.

Task 1:
Divide the students in class into four equal numbers of pairs: Group 1, Group 2, Group 3, and Group 4. This will constitute the participants sample. Those who do not wish to participate may do so without having to give an explanation. They can assist as observers. If any of those who do wish to participate decide to withdraw at any time, they can do so without having to give an explanation. Given an average number of 30 students per class, you will likely obtain, say, 6 participants per group, meaning 3 pairs per group. They will be asked to do a simple dance-like movement as partners (the intervention).

The case study is based on a pilot study on empathy and closeness in partnered dance developed at Goldsmiths, University of London, entitled Pilot Studies on Empathy and Closeness in Mutual Entrainment/Improvisation vs. Formalised Dance with Different Types of Rhythm (Regular, Irregular, and No Rhythm) and Coupling (Visual, Haptic, Full Coupling): Building a Case for the Origin of Dance in Mutual Entrainment Empathic Interactions in the Mother–Infant Dyad' (Balinisteanu, 2023).

T. Balinisteanu (✉)
Neuroaesthetics Lab, University of Suceava, Suceava, Romania
e-mail: tudor@texmar.ro

T. Balinisteanu and K. Priest (eds.), *Neuroaesthetics*,
https://doi.org/10.1007/978-3-031-42323-9_4

Once pairs in the four groups have been established, they will be informed that each group will participate in a different condition. Thus, the experiment will have to be repeated four times. Before commencing one of these trials, the participants will be seated face-to-face, in the same pairs that they will form for the dance intervention. The student acting as a researcher will then administer the IRI and IOS questionnaires (Aron et al., 1992; Davis, 1983). A sufficient number of copies of these questionnaires will be provided in advance of the lab session. Although in Lesson 1 we discussed only one IV (rhythm), in the lab session we will introduce a second IV, namely type of coupling (visual only and visual & haptic).

Task 2:

1. Invite Group 1 on the 'dance floor' and ask them to do a simple side-to-side step, facing one another, without holding hands, for 7 minutes, while they listen to the provided stimulus, which is a regular (4/4) rhythm (https://www.mdpi.com/article/10.3390/bs1310085).
2. Repeat procedure (1) with Group 2, but this time ask them to also hold hands.
3. Repeat procedure (1) with Group 3, but this time use as stimulus the provided irregular (7/8) rhythm (no holding hands).
4. Repeat procedure (2) with Group 4, but with irregular rhythm (participants will hold hands).

Task 3:
After the intervention is completed, seat the participants face-to-face again. Ask them to fill in the IRI and IOS questionnaires once more. The IRI questionnaire is available online. Lab 1 IOS single-item questionnaire is included here below.

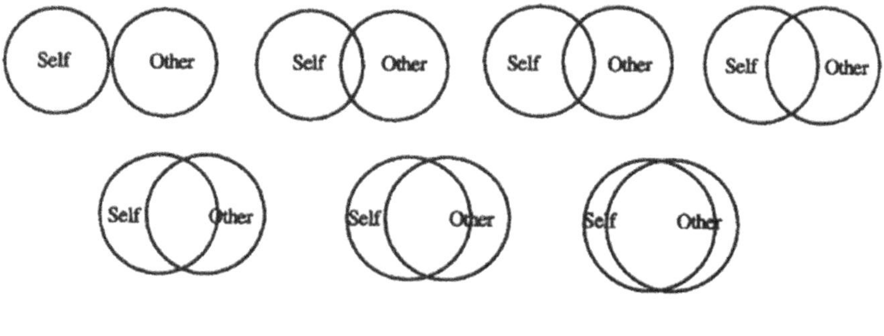

Task 4:
Calculate the scores on the IOS and IRI questionnaires for each participant. For the IRI questionnaire, do not calculate the total score. Calculate instead the total score on each subscale: Empathic Concern (EC), Personal Distress (PD), Fantasy (FS), and Perspective-taking (PT).

Task 5:
Study the diagram of the experiment design:

IV coupling → **IV rhythm** ↓	Haptic and visual coupling	Visual coupling only
Regular rhythm	DVs: EC, PD, F, PT (IRI), closeness (IOS) (Group 2)	DVs: EC, PD, F, PT (IRI), closeness (IOS) (Group 1)
Irregular rhythm	DVs: EC, PD, F, PT (IRI), closeness (IOS) (Group 4)	DVs: EC, PD, F, PT (IRI), closeness (IOS) (Group 3)

Task 6:
In the SPSS variable view, define the rhythm and coupling variables according to rhythm and coupling type, respectively. You can do this by writing 'Rhythm' and 'Coupling' under **Name** on two separate rows. Under **Values** in the 'Rhythm' row fill in the boxes corresponding to **Value** and **Label** with '1' and 'regrhythm' respectively, then click <u>*Add*</u>. Repeat the procedure using '2' and 'irregrhythm'. Repeat the entire procedure for 'Coupling' to reflect how participants have been assignthe visual couplinged to the visual + haptic coupling conditions and to the visual coupling only condition. Go to **Measure** and click on the box to select 'Nominal'. Create the variables 'preIOS' and 'postIOS' for closeness, and so on for each DV. Under **Measure**, select 'Scale'. Enter the individual participant scores for each of our scales at pre- and post-trial point into the data view sheet. Remember to match each individual score with the condition in which they participated by writing '1' or '2' under **Rhythm** and **Coupling**, as appropriate. Calculate, for each participant, the difference between post-trial and pre-trial scores, by subtracting pre-trial scores from post-trial scores, for both the IOS scale and the IRI subscales. Name the resulting variables 'IOS', 'EC', 'PT', 'FS', and 'PD'.

Task 7:
Run a factorial ANOVA (Analysis of Variance) on the scores obtained by subtracting pre-trial scores from post-trial scores, for each IRI subscale and the IOS. Since we used different participants in all conditions, this will be a between-subjects factorial ANOVA.

Every statistical test is based on a set of assumptions. Before running the factorial ANOVA, ensure that the data does not violate these assumptions. We will only use three tests to make sure these assumptions are not violated: z-scores, ratio of skewness and kurtosis to standard error, and Levene's test. It is important to run a full diagnostic for violations of assumptions! We have simplified the procedure because of class time constraints, but this topic must certainly be dealt with in extensive detail. You can do this through individual study by consulting, for example, Barbara Tabachnick and Linda Fidell's *Using Multivariate Statistics* (Tabachnick & Fidell, 2007).

To calculate z-scores in SPSS: Click *Analyse,* then *Descriptive Statistics,* then *Descriptives.* Move the variable of interest from the left window into the **Variables** box and select **Save standardized values as variables**. Click *OK.* The z-scores are now visible in the variables table (the data view sheet). You can use the z-scores to identify univariate outliers. If any z-score is greater than 3 or less than −3, it indicates that that participant's score is an outlier. We will delete that score. There are also other ways to deal with outliers, but we will not cover these here. Since we have only a few participants, we may retain outliers solely for the purpose of having sufficient data to demonstrate the SPSS procedure, but do remember that our results and analysis will be flawed!

The next step is to analyse the skewness and kurtosis for the distribution of our data. To do this, we must first compute the standard error for these two indicators of the shape of our distribution. In SPSS click *Analyse,* then *Descriptive Statistics,* then *Explore.* In the window that opens, move the variable of interest into the **Dependent List** box. Select *OK.* This will generate a table in the **Output** window, which includes the Standard Error value as well as the skewness and kurtosis values. Skewness and Kurtosis can be tested for normality by dividing their values by the corresponding standard error. If the resulting values fall between −2 and + 2, the distributions of our scores are normal. If the values fall outside of [−2, + 2] our distribution deviates from normality and we have violated the requirement of normality. Levene's test of equality of variances can will be used when we run the mixed ANOVA (the instructions are included in Task 8).

Since we have 2 IVs in a between-subjects design, we can run a two-way ANOVA, which is a particular version of factorial ANOVAs. We will need to run this analysis for each DV separately. To run a simplified version of the two-way ANOVA, return to the data view sheet, then click *Analyse,* then *General Linear Model,* then *Univariate.* Move the DV 'IOS' into the **Dependent Variable** box. Remember, we must do this analysis separately for each DV, that is, one for the IOS scores, and one for each of the IRI subscales scores. Move the 'Rhythm' and 'Coupling' IVs into the **Fixed Factor(s)** box. Click *Continue,* then *OK.*

You should now have an output. The main results can be consulted in the table under the title **Tests of Between-Subjects Effects**. Table 1 is an example of such output from another experiment (Balinisteanu, 2023).

Examine the *p*-values for 'Rhythm', 'Coupling', and 'Rhythm * Coupling' in the **Sig.** box. None of these values are significant because they are all higher than 0.05. Neither rhythm type nor coupling type had a significant effect on closeness (IOS scores). However, to make the most of the data analysis, one might say that the 0.076 value is encouraging, that is, it suggests that with a larger participants sample one might obtain a significant main effect of rhythm on closeness. The interaction of rhythm and coupling is not significant, meaning that we have not obtained evidence that the effect of rhythm type on closeness is influenced by the effect of coupling type on closeness.

Table 1 Test of between-subjects effects for the effect of rhythm, coupling, and their interaction on IOS measures, showing an encouraging main effect of rhythm in Experiment 2 (Dependent variable: IOS)

Source	Type III sum of squares	*df*	Mean square	*F*	Sig.	Partial Eta squared
Corrected model	8.455[a]	8	1.057	1.136	0.359	0.171
Intercept	15.457	1	15.457	16.620	0.000	0.274
Rhythm	5.089	2	2.544	2.736	0.076	0.111
Coupling	0.527	2	0.263	0.283	0.755	0.013
Rhythm * Coupling	2.422	4	0.606	0.651	0.629	0.056
Error	40.920	44	0.930			
Total	65.036	53				
Corrected Total	49.375	52				

[a]R Squared = 0.171 (Adjusted R Squared = 0.021)

Task 8:
Run a mixed ANOVA with time as within-subjects factor. We will run Levene's test when we perform the mixed ANOVA in SPSS. Start by clicking *Analyse*, then *General Linear Model*, then *Repeated Measures*. In the **Repeated Measures Define Factor(s)** window, write 'time' in the **Within-Subject Factor Name** field. The number of levels is 2 (we have acquired data twice: before and after the intervention). Click *Add*. Now write 'closeness' (or 'empathic concern', etc.—remember, we need to run this analysis for each DV) in the **Measure Name** field and click *Add*, then *Define*. Transfer the 'pre' and 'post' variables into the **Within-Subjects Variables (time)** box, first 'pre', then 'post'. Transfer 'Rhythm' and 'Coupling' into the **Between-Subjects Factor(s)** box. Click *Plots*, transfer 'time' on the horizontal axis, 'Rhythm' on **Separate Lines**, then click *Add*. Repeat the procedure for 'Coupling'. You can also, after transferring 'time' on the horizontal axis, transfer 'Rhythm' on **Separate Lines** and 'Coupling' on **Separate Plots** fields, respectively. Click *Add*, then *Continue*.

Click on **PostHoc** and add 'Rhythm' and 'Coupling' to the **Post Hoc Tests for** box. Under **Equal Variances Assumed** select **Tukey**. Click *Continue*, then *Save*. In the **Repeated Measures: Save** box, under **Residuals**, select **Studentized**, then click *Continue*.

Click *EM Means* and transfer 'time' and the 'Rhythm * time' and 'Coupling * time' interactions into the **Display Means for** group. Select **Compare main effects** and then, from the activated drop-down menu, **Bonferroni**. Click *Continue*.

Next, click *Options*. In the **Display** area select **Descriptive statistics, Estimates of effect size** and **Homogeneity tests**. Click *Continue* and then *OK*. An output will be generated. Before examining the output, go to **Data View** to make sure that the studentized residuals are all between -3 and +3 (you will find them listed as SRE variables). Go back to the output and look for Box's test to make sure that the **Sig.** value is higher than 0.05. Then check that Levene's test is not significant to make sure that homogeneity of variance can be assumed. Certain measures should be taken if these assumptions are violated. Study these by consulting Tabachnick and Fidell (2007).

Table 2 is an example of a part of the output from a different study (Balinisteanu, 2023). It displays results for the within-subjects effects. Note that the *p*-value (listed under 'sig.') is $p < 0.001$. This means that the length of time the participants spent undertaking the intervention affected closeness. Note that a p-value cannot be '0', but it can be displayed as '0.000' in SPSS when the first digit above '0' is more than three digits away from the decimal point.

Table 3 shows the within-subjects effects for interactions in a second experiment of that study which had 3 coupling and 3 rhythm conditions. Note that the time * Rhythm interaction was significant: $F(2,45) = 3.842$, $p = 0.029$, partial $\eta^2 = 0.146$. This means that there was a significant difference between the groups assigned to different rhythm conditions over time. Table 4 is also from the second experiment results, measuring the between-subjects effect of rhythm and coupling on the IRI Fantasy subscale. Note that there was a significant effect of coupling: $F(2,45) = 3.212$, $p = 0.050$, partial $\eta^2 = 0.125$. Thus, the type of coupling affected Fantasy to a significant extent. The experiment for which the results in Table 4 were obtained involved three coupling types. To find out which of these three coupling types affected Fantasy, we need to run supplementary statistical analyses. However, we will leave these for another day and end this lab here.

Table 2 Test of within-subjects effects showing a significant effect of time on IOS closeness values in Experiment 1 (Measure: Closeness)

Source		Type III sum of squares	*df*	Mean square	*F*	Sig.	Partial Eta squared
Time	Sphericity assumed	13.021	1	13.021	17.405	0.000	0.442
	Greenhouse–Geisser	13.021	1.000	13.021	17.405	0.000	0.442
	Huynh–Feldt	13.021	1.000	13.021	17.405	0.000	0.442
	Lower-bound	13.021	1.000	13.021	17.405	0.000	0.442
Error(time)	Sphericity assumed	16.458	22	0.748			
	Greenhouse–Geisser	16.458	22.000	0.748			
	Huynh–Feldt	16.458	22.000	0.748			
	Lower-bound	16.458	22.000	0.748			

Table 3 Test of within-subjects effects for the effect of interactions between time, rhythm, and coupling, on closeness, showing a significant main effect of the interaction of rhythm and time in Experiment 2 (**Tests of Within-Subjects Effects**; Measure: Closeness)

Source		Type III sum of squares	*df*	Mean square	*F*	Sig.	Partial Eta squared
Time	Sphericity assumed	10.584	1	10.584	16.269	0.000	0.266
	Greenhouse–Geisser	10.584	1.000	10.584	16.269	0.000	0.266
	Huynh–Feldt	10.584	1.000	10.584	16.269	0.000	0.266
	Lower-bound	10.584	1.000	10.584	16.269	0.000	0.266
Time * Rhythm	Sphericity assumed	4.999	2	2.499	3.842	0.029	0.146
	Greenhouse–Geisser	4.999	2.000	2.499	3.842	0.029	0.146
	Huynh–Feldt	4.999	2.000	2.499	3.842	0.029	0.146
	Lower-bound	4.999	2.000	2.499	3.842	0.029	0.146
Time * Coupling	Sphericity assumed	0.068	2	0.034	0.052	0.949	0.002
	Greenhouse–Geisser	0.068	2.000	0.034	0.052	0.949	0.002
	Huynh–Feldt	0.068	2.000	0.034	0.052	0.949	0.002
	Lower-bound	0.068	2.000	0.034	0.052	0.949	0.002
Time * Rhythm * Coupling	Sphericity Assumed	0.090	4	0.023	0.035	0.998	0.003
	Greenhouse–Geisser	0.090	4.000	0.023	0.035	0.998	0.003
	Huynh–Feldt	0.090	4.000	0.023	0.035	0.998	0.003
	Lower-bound	0.090	4.000	0.023	0.035	0.998	0.003
Error(time)	Sphericity assumed	29.277	45	0.651			
	Greenhouse–Geisser	29.277	45.000	0.651			
	Huynh–Feldt	29.277	45.000	0.651			
	Lower-bound	29.277	45.000	0.651			

Table 4 Test of between-subjects effects for the effect of rhythm, coupling, and their interaction on IRI fantasy scale values, showing a significant main effect of coupling in Experiment 2 (**Tests of Between-Subjects Effects**; Measure: IRI Fantasy Scale; Transformed variable: Average)

Source	Type III sum of squares	*df*	Mean square	*F*	Sig.	Partial Eta squared
Intercept	34,632.926	1	34,632.926	779.891	0.000	0.945
Rhythm	56.796	2	28.398	0.639	0.532	0.028
Coupling	285.241	2	142.620	3.212	0.050	0.125
Rhythm * Coupling	255.704	4	63.926	1.440	0.237	0.113
Error	1998.333	45	44.407			

References

Aron, A., Aron, E. N., & Smollan, D. (1992). Inclusion of other in the self scale and the structure of interpersonal closeness. *Journal of Personality and Social Psychology, 63*(4), 596–612.

Balinisteanu, T. (2023). Pilot studies on empathy and closeness in mutual entrainment/improvisation vs. formalised dance with different types of rhythm (regular, irregular, and no rhythm) and coupling (visual, haptic, full coupling): Building a case for the origin of dance in mutual entrainment empathic interactions in the mother–infant dyad. *Behavioral Sciences, 13*(10), 859. https://doi.org/10.3390/bs13100859.

Davis, M. H. (1983). Measuring individual differences in empathy: Evidence for a multidimensional approach. *Journal of Personality and Social Psychology, 44*(1), 113–126.

Tabachnick, B. G., & Fidell, L. S. (2007). *Using multivariate statistics*. Pearson/Allyn & Bacon.

Unit 2 Overview: Neuroaesthetics Approaches to the Visual Arts—Perception *Focus Topic: CGI-Generated Creative Content and Artificial Intelligence*

Pamela Breda

> For at least several centuries, in the West, the artistic phenomenon has presented itself as follows: a person (the artist), signs a particular object or message (the work), which other persons (the recipients, the public, the critics) perceive, taste, read, interpret, and evaluate [...] The techno-cultural environment that is emerging, however, gives rise to new art forms, ignoring the distinction between emission and reception, creation, and interpretation [...] This new art form allows what is precisely no longer an audience to experience other methods of communication and creation. (Levy, 1996, p. 336).

Emotions, Cognition, and Aesthetic Experience

The exploration of aesthetic and emotional reactions to artworks spans an extensive historical journey, from Plato and Aristotle's theories to Arthur Schopenhauer's (1788–1860) and Immanuel Kant's (1724–1804) analyses on the perception of beauty. An interesting contemporary approach to this topic is represented by neuroaesthetic studies aiming to identify the neural correlates associated with aesthetic experiences and the cognitive processes activated when individuals engage with art, music, literature, or other aesthetic stimuli. These studies usually consider how visual perception is influenced by various factors, including bottom-up and top-down processes. Bottom-up processing refers to the analysis of sensory information starting from basic features and building up to more complex interpretations. In the context of art, this involves the initial analysis of visual elements,

P. Breda (✉)
Angewandte University, Vienna, Austria
e-mail: pamela.breda@uni-ak.ac.at

T. Balinisteanu and K. Priest (eds.), *Neuroaesthetics*,
https://doi.org/10.1007/978-3-031-42323-9_5

such as lines, shapes, and colors, before forming a holistic perception of the artwork. Top-down processing, on the other hand, involves using prior knowledge, expectations, and cognitive factors to guide and influence perception. When viewing art, our past experiences, cultural background, and acquired knowledge about artistic styles and conventions can shape how we interpret and appreciate the artwork.

By studying how the brain processes visual stimuli and how this processing relates to subjective aesthetic experiences, neuroaesthetics researchers aim to gain insights into the complex interplay between neural mechanisms, perception, and art appreciation. In this essay, I will focus in particular on neuroaesthetics studies focused on how the brain perceives and processes aesthetic stimuli in relation to visual artworks, and in particular to CGI-generated creative content, such as images and videos.

A relevant starting point is the Neural Correlates of Beauty theory, which investigates the cognitive and neural mechanisms involved in the perception of beauty and other aesthetic qualities. This theory proposes that certain aesthetic qualities or features, such as symmetry, complexity, harmony, and novelty, activate particular brain areas or networks, leading to the subjective experience of beauty.[1] However, it's important to note that this theory is still a subject of ongoing research and debate, and there is no universally agreed-upon set of neural correlates that define beauty. Different individuals and cultures may have different perceptions of beauty, and there may be variations in brain responses accordingly.

Neurobiologists such as Anjan Chatterjee, Edward Vessel, and Semir Zeki have conducted extensive research on this topic, investigating how specific brain regions, particularly in the visual cortex and the reward system, are involved in aesthetic judgments and preferences (Chatterjee & Cardillo, 2022; Kawabata & Zeki, 2004; Vessel et al., 2022). Leading tests combining neuroimaging techniques and functional magnetic resonance imaging (fMRI), they studied the brain's response to stimuli perceived as beautiful, observing that when individuals view aesthetically pleasing stimuli, such as artworks, landscapes, or faces, specific brain regions related to reward, emotion, and visual processing are often activated.

However, visual stimuli work differently for different individuals, and recent neuroscientic studies have considered the role of aesthetic preferences in the appreciation of artworks, exploring how each individual appreciates different visual artworks and the emotional responses generated by the encounter with these artworks. V.S. Ramachandran has explored how mirror neurons (which are active

[1] For example, regions like the orbitofrontal cortex, anterior cingulate cortex, insula, and nucleus accumbens, which are associated with reward processing and emotional experiences, have shown increased activation during the perception of beauty. Additionally, areas involved in visual processing, such as the occipital cortex and fusiform gyrus, are also implicated in the processing of aesthetically pleasing stimuli. Ishizu, T., and Zeki, S. (2011) collaborated on a study exploring the neural correlates of beauty by examining brain activity while participants viewed artworks. They found that specific brain areas associated with reward and pleasure, such as the orbitofrontal cortex, were activated when participants rated the beauty of the artworks.

both when we perform an action and when we observe someone else performing the same action) play a role in empathy and aesthetic appreciation (Ramachandran, 2012). Along the same lines, cognitive neuroscientist Oshin Vartanian has conducted research on the neural mechanisms underlying aesthetic experiences and emotional responses to art in order to analyze how the brain processes and evaluates different aesthetic qualities, such as beauty and novelty (Jung & Vartania, 2018). Helmut Leder et al. (2004) have examined emotional responses to aesthetic appreciation and aesthetic judgments of specific artworks, exploring the reasons why modern art, with its multitude of individualized styles, innovation, and conceptual nature, offers enriching aesthetic experiences.

These studies indicate that the judgement of different aesthetic features of artworks by the human brain involves a complex interplay of cognitive processes, emotional responses, and sensory perception. While the precise mechanisms are still being investigated, several factors have been identified as key contributors to how the brain evaluates aesthetic features in art, in particular visual elements such as color, shape, texture, and composition. Sensory processing areas, like the visual cortex, extract and process this information, allowing the brain to perceive and differentiate artworks' various aesthetic qualities.

The Beauty of Art—Paintings and Visual Composition

The evaluation of aesthetic features in art is highly subjective and can vary among individuals due to personal preferences, cultural influences, and individual differences in neural processing. As we have mentioned, an important element in the aesthetics evaluation of an artwork are emotions. The brain's emotional centers, such as the amygdala and insula, play a role in assessing the emotional valence and intensity of an artwork. Positive emotional experiences, such as feelings of beauty, awe, or joy, can enhance the evaluation of aesthetic features and contribute to a positive aesthetic experience, and vice versa.

Researchers such as Kent Berridge (1947) and Antonio Damasio (2006) have established how brain's reward and pleasure systems—including the ventral striatum and orbitofrontal cortex—are engaged during the evaluation of aesthetic features. Activation in these regions indicates the brain's reward response to visually pleasing stimuli.

Cognitive processes, including attention, memory, and categorization, influence the evaluation of aesthetic features. Attentional mechanisms direct focus to specific visual elements or features, while memory and categorization processes allow the brain to compare and contrast artworks based on previous experiences and learned aesthetic norms. Aesthetic features that are perceived as novel, complex, or harmonious often elicit greater reward responses, leading to a more positive evaluation. Expertise, gained through artistic training or exposure to art, can enhance these cognitive processes and refine the evaluation of aesthetic features.

If we consider a specific case study, i.e., the visual perception of paintings, several key elements related to the aesthetic judgment of an artwork come into play, in particular:

- Composition: The arrangement of visual elements within a painting can influence how our brain perceives and processes the artwork. Certain compositional principles, such as the rule of thirds or the golden ratio, can create a sense of balance and harmony in paintings, leading to positive aesthetic experiences.
- Color and emotion: Colors can have a direct impact on our perception of a painting. Different colors activate specific areas of the brain associated with emotions. For example, warm colors like red and orange may elicit feelings of excitement or energy, while cool colors like blue and green can evoke a sense of calmness or serenity.
- Visual attention: Paintings can guide our visual attention and direct our gaze to specific areas of interest. Artists strategically use visual cues, such as lines, contrast, and focal points, to attract attention and engage viewers. These techniques can influence the way our brain processes and interprets the artwork.

Recent studies using brain imaging techniques have identified neural correlates associated with subjective aesthetic judgments. Cupchik et al. (2009) investigated the neural responses to different art styles by examining brain activity using fMRI. Participants were shown paintings from various artistic movements, such as Impressionism, Cubism, and Abstract Expressionism. The findings revealed distinct patterns of brain activation associated with the perception of each art style, suggesting that different styles of painting elicit specific neural responses. For example, representational paintings with realistic depictions of objects tended to activate brain regions involved in object recognition, while abstract paintings with ambiguous or non-representational forms engaged areas associated with visual abstraction and interpretation.

Another interesting example is represented by "Dynamics of brain networks in the aesthetic appreciation" by Cela-Conde et al. (2013). In this study, participants were exposed to classical artworks and their brain activity was measured. The results revealed that viewing paintings activated brain areas related to visual processing, emotion, reward, and memory. The researchers found that lines and edges in the paintings activated the brain regions responsible for processing visual information and spatial attention. Focal points, or areas of the painting with high contrast or salience, were associated with increased activity in the visual cortex and prefrontal cortex, indicating that these areas drew viewers' attention and engaged their cognitive processing.

Overall, these studies provide evidence that viewing paintings perceived as beautiful led to increased activity in the medial orbitofrontal cortex, a region associated with reward and aesthetic pleasure, suggesting a neural basis for the perception of beauty in paintings. But what happens when we apply this neuroscientific approach to the study of the cognitive and emotional perception of CGI-generated visual content?

Perceptual Responses to CGI Artworks

Let's consider Susanne Langer's theory of aesthetic experience based on symbolic forms, emphasizing the role of emotions in aesthetic responses (Langer, 1949). This theory revolves around the idea that human beings have a fundamental need to create and engage with symbolic forms, i.e., expressive structures or patterns that embody human feelings, experiences, and ideas. They include not only traditional art forms like music, visual art, and literature but also more everyday symbolic activities such as rituals, gestures, and language itself. According to Langer, when we engage with symbolic forms, we enter the aesthetic experience—a state of heightened awareness—and undergo an aesthetic transformation. I propose to combine Langer's theory with Dominic McIver Lopes' views of aesthetic perception, specifically regarding computer-generated imagery (CGI) (2010). In his book, *A Philosophy of Computer Art*, Lopes explores the aesthetic potential of computer-generated art, analyzing in particular how the nature of CGI, its use of algorithms, and its capacity for creating complex and imaginative visuals can lead to new aesthetic experiences. He considers the role of perception, interpretation, and engagement with CGI artworks, challenging conventional notions of authenticity, originality, and representation in art. According to his point of view, CGI should be approached with a new set of aesthetic criteria that are suited to its unique characteristics, rather than evaluated solely on the basis of traditional artistic standards:

> Computer art works invite and indeed prescribe repeat encounters. Users expect something new with each interaction and are attuned to the differences between the displays they generate. Through many interactions and displays, they come to see the possibilities the work holds for them. (Lopes, 2010, p. 60).

Building on Lopes's analysis, let's consider how CGI's ability to generate virtual worlds and characters leads to questions about the ontological status of the represented subjects and how our perceptual engagement with these images impacts our emotional and cognitive responses. Probably the most famous example of artwork made by an AI in recent years is "Portrait of Edmond de Belamy" by Paris-based arts collective Obvious (Alleyne, 2018), the first AI-generated artwork to be auctioned at a major art house.

Created using a Generative Adversarial Network (GAN), the piece depicts a fictional eighteenth-century portrait and sparked debates about the role of AI in the art world. Another famous example is "The Next Rembrandt" by ING and Microsoft. In this project, AI algorithms analyzed data from Rembrandt's paintings to create a new artwork in the style of the renowned Dutch artist. The resulting piece demonstrates the ability of AI to emulate artistic styles and create new works that resonate with historical art (see www.nextrembrandt.com). More recently, the production of AI-generated images by software like DeepDream and StyleGAN sparked debate. Using deep neural networks, these softwares generate pictures characterized by surreal and psychedelic aesthetic, with viewers interpreting them in diverse ways, ranging from mesmerizing and captivating to disorienting or unsettling (Mordvintsev et al., 2015).

Academics and theorists are focusing on the psychological and cognitive outcomes of the perceptive encounters between the viewers and these artworks. For example, The Computational Creativity Research Group at Goldsmiths, University of London, explores various aspects of aesthetics, perception, and evaluation of computer-generated artwork. By integrating AI techniques and computational approaches, this research group aims to understand and simulate human-like creativity in machines, to explore how acts of creativity, traditionally considered uniquely human, are perceived when produced by artificial intelligence. Analyzing in detail the observers' ability to distinguish between computer-generated and human-made art, and exploring how categorizing artworks influence their perceived aesthetic value (Chamberlain et al., 2017), this research not only emphasizes the technical aspects of generating art but also examines the philosophical and ethical implications of AI's role in creative practices.

Perception of Hyperrealistic Digital CGI

Hyperrealistic digital avatars are computer-generated characters that closely resemble real individuals. They are created using advanced computer graphics techniques (such as Dall-E or Metahuman softwares) and aim to achieve a high level of realism in their appearance and behavior. Neuroaesthetics studies have recently delved into the perception of hyperrealistic digital avatars by the human brain, and as we analyze the realm of realistic-looking humanoids, it's imperative to initially confront the phenomenon of the Uncanny Valley. This perceptual response arises when humanoid objects, like robots or computer-generated characters, bear an uncanny resemblance to human beings but fall just short of being convincingly human.

The concept suggests that as the appearance of a humanoid object becomes more human-like, there is a corresponding increase in our affinity or positive emotional response towards it. However, there is a critical point at which the object's resemblance to a human reaches a certain level of similarity, but not close enough to be indistinguishable. At this point, instead of evoking positive emotions, the object triggers negative emotions, leading to a dip in the emotional response curve. This dip represents the uncanny valley.

The concept was first theorized by Freud in 1919, in the framework of a study on the breaking of boundaries between fact and fiction (Freud, 2018). He described the Uncanny as the feeling that arises when someone has an intellectual uncertainty about the livingness of a certain being. The concept was further explored by

Japanese robotics professor Masahiro Mori in the 1970s, with regard to the relation between an object's degree of resemblance to a human being and the human emotional response to that same object (Mori, 2005).

Notable examples of realistic looking humanoids that often generate such an uneasy feeling in the individuals with whom they interact are Sophia—a humanoid robot Developed by Hanson Robotics known for her realistic appearance and human-like expressions—and the Geminoids, a series of humanoid robots developed by Japanese roboticist Hiroshi Ishiguro designed to resemble specific individuals and exhibit lifelike facial movements and expressions. When an object falls into the uncanny valley, people often experience a sense of discomfort or revulsion, or a feeling of eeriness and uneasiness. The object's subtle deviations from human appearance, such as unnatural facial features, strange movement patterns, or lack of appropriate emotional expressions, contribute to this effect.

One possible explanation for the uncanny valley effect is that humans have a heightened sensitivity to detecting subtle deviations from the norm in human appearance and behavior. Our brains are wired to recognize and respond to familiar human characteristics, but when confronted with an entity that closely resembles a human but exhibits uncanny deviations, our perceptual system detects the mismatch, triggering a negative emotional response. Overcoming this effect is a significant challenge in robotics and animation. While there is no definitive solution to this day, several approaches are being tested by engineers, in particular emotional design. Focusing on creating robots or characters that evoke positive emotions and empathy can help bridge the gap. By emphasizing traits such as kindness, humor, or cuteness, designers can make the robot more relatable and endearing. Furthermore, recognizing that different people have varying thresholds for the Uncanny Valley effect, designers can offer customization options. Allowing users to personalize the appearance or behavior of the humanoid robot can help increase acceptance and reduce discomfort. As technology progresses, we can expect further improvements in creating humanoid robots and characters that are more believable and comfortable to interact with.

The Outcomes of Realistic-Looking Avatars

In recent years human interaction with digital avatars has become increasingly prevalent in various domains, ranging from entertainment to education, from customer service to health and therapy. Sherry Turkle, a professor of social studies of science and technology, has written extensively on the impact of such a technology on individual cognitive and emotional spheres (Turkle, 2012). According to her "second self" theory, digital avatars serve as a representation or extension of an individual's identity in virtual environments. When people interact with them, they often project parts of their personalities, desires, and aspirations onto these virtual representations. Digital avatars become a 'second self' that individuals use to explore and express different aspects of their identity, sometimes in ways that differ from their offline persona.

Turkle suggests that the relationship between individuals and their digital avatars is a form of self-presentation and self-exploration. Through these avatars, individuals can experiment with different identities and engage in activities that they may not feel comfortable doing in their real lives. For some, digital avatars become an opportunity to embody idealized versions of themselves or explore fantasies and experiences that are not readily available offline. Turkle's theory also addresses the potential impact of these interactions on social relationships. She argues that while digital avatars provide opportunities for self-expression and connection, they can also lead to a sense of disconnection and superficiality. In virtual environments, individuals may find it easier to present themselves in curated ways, hiding certain aspects of their real identity or adopting idealized versions of themselves.

Further research in this field has shown that when people embody attractive avatars, they tend to display more confident and outgoing behavior compared to when they embody less attractive avatars. This theory, known as the Proteus Effect, suggests that people's cognition and behavior can be influenced by the visual representation of their digital avatars. This cognitive identification can lead to increased self-esteem, self-efficacy, and feelings of ownership over the avatar. In particular, Nick Yee and Jeremy Bailenson examined the influence of avatar customization on users' self-perception and behavior in virtual environments (Yee & Bailenson, 2007). During a test study participants were assigned avatars with either attractive or unattractive features and those who had attractive avatars displayed more confident and extroverted behaviors, indicating a stronger identification with their avatars.

Such an approach to the digital domain might lead to the potential consequences of relying heavily on digital avatars for social interactions, suggesting that prolonged engagement with digital worlds may have as a consequence a diminished ability to engage in face-to-face interactions and develop empathy with others. In particular, since hyperrealistic avatars often aim to evoke emotional engagement from viewers, neuroaesthetics researchers are now investigating the neural mechanisms underlying our ability to attribute mental states, emotions, and intentions to these virtual characters.

Dr. Robin R. Murphy, a leading figure in the field of human–robot interaction and artificial intelligence, has explored what is known as the simulation theory, suggesting that humans tend to project human-like characteristics onto AI systems, attributing intentions, emotions, and social behaviors to them (Murphy, 2004). According to Murphy, such an anthropomorphic tendency allows us to project our own emotional responses onto AI systems. We may empathize, feel attachment, or even develop a sense of social connection with AI based on our simulations of their internal experiences.

In short, when viewing aesthetically pleasing avatars, the brain's reward and pleasure systems may be activated, leading to feelings of enjoyment, admiration, or attraction. When we see a realistic avatar expressing specific emotions, our brains have a tendency to mimic or mirror those emotions. For example, if an avatar displays happiness or sadness, it may evoke corresponding emotional responses in the viewer. Additionally, when we interact with an avatar that closely resembles a real person, we may develop a sense of familiarity, connection, or even attachment to it.

Conclusion

In recent years, neuroscientific studies have uncovered fascinating findings regarding the cognitive and emotional processes involved in art perception, highlighting the complex interplay between bottom-up sensory processing and top-down cognitive mechanisms and revealing how our visual system combines perceptual information with prior knowledge and expectations to construct meaning from artistic stimuli.

If we consider AI-generated art, we discover how CGI often presents novel visual aesthetics and unique artistic styles that may challenge traditional cognitive and sensorial engagement with art. The perceptual responses to CGI artworks have demonstrated a complex interplay of pros and cons, offering both exciting possibilities and potential drawbacks. On the positive side, CGI allows for unparalleled creativity, enabling artists and filmmakers to bring their visions to life in ways previously unimaginable. The ability to generate hyper-realistic scenes and characters has enriched the realms of entertainment, design, and scientific visualization. The perception of these artworks can evoke a sense of curiosity, fascination, or even surprise, as viewers encounter new and unexpected visual forms. Additionally, the emergence of realistic avatars has proven to be a powerful tool for communication and self-expression.However, alongside these remarkable advancements come inherent challenges. Users who become closely identified with their avatars risk to dissociate from reality, and this in turn can lead to detrimental emotional and cognitive effects, such as addiction and social isolation. The uncanny valley effect remains a significant concern, as the quest for perfect realism in CGI can sometimes lead to eerie and unsettling perceptual responses. This can create emotional and cognitive dissonance, hindering the immersive experience that CGI seeks to achieve. As technology continues to evolve, addressing these challenges and striking the right balance between realism and likability will be crucial to ensure that users can fully harness the benefits of CGI and realistic avatars while mitigating their negative impacts.

References

Alleyne, A. (2018). AI-produced artwork sells for $433K, smashing expectations. *Edition.cnn.com*. Written by and Retrieved July 10, 2022, from https://edition.cnn.com/style/article/obvious-ai-art-christies-auction-smart-creativity/index.html#:~:text=The%20slightly%20blurry%20canvas%20print,Christie's%20auction%20in%20New%20York

Berridge, K. C. (1947). Evolving concepts of emotion and motivation. *Frontiers in Psychology, 9*, 1–20.

Cela-Conde, J. C., García-Prieto, J., Ramasco, J. J., Mirasso, C., Bajo, R., Munar, E., Flexas, A., Del-Pozo, F., Maestú, F. (2013). Dynamics of brain networks in the aesthetic appreciation. *PNAS, 110*(2), 10454–10461.

Chamberlain, R., Mullin, C. R., Scheerlinck, B., & Wagemans, J. (2017). Putting the art in artificial: Aesthetic responses to computer-generated art. *Psychology of Aesthetics Creativity and the Arts, 12*(2), 177–192.

Chatterjee, A., & Cardillo, E. R. (2022). *Brain, beauty, & art: Essays bringing neuroaesthetics into focus*. Oxford University Press.

Cupchik, C. G., Vartanian, O., Crawley, A., & Mikulis, J. D. (2009). Viewing artworks: Contributions of cognitive control and perceptual facilitation to aesthetic experience. *Brain and Cognition, 70*(1), 84–91.

Damasio, A. (2006). *Descartes' error: Emotion, reason, and the human brain*. Vintage.

Damasio, A. (2023). *Feeling and knowing: Making minds conscious*. Robinson.

Freud, S. (2018). *Das Unheimliche*. Freeriver Publishing (ebook).

Ishizu, T., & Zeki, S. (2011). Toward a brain-based theory of beauty. *PLoS ONE, 6*(7), e21852. https://doi.org/10.1371/journal.pone.0021852

Jung, R. E., & Vartania, O. (2018). *The Cambridge handbook of the neuroscience of creativity*. Cambridge University Press.

Kawabata, H., & Zeki, S. (2004). Neural Correlates of Beauty. *Neurophysiology, 91*, 1699–1705.

Langer, S. K. (1949). *Philosophy in a new key: A study in the symbolism of reason, rite, and art*. New American Library.

Leder, H., Belke, B., Oeberst, A., & Augustin, D. (2004). A model of aesthetic appreciation and aesthetic judgments. *British Journal of Psychology, 95*(Pt 4), 489–508.

Levy, P. (1996). The art of cyberspace. In T. Druckrey (Eds.), *Electronic cultures: Technology and representation* (pp. 366–367). Aperture.

Lopes, D. (2010). *A philosophy of computer art*. Routledge.

Mordvintsev, A., Olah, C., & Tyka, M. (2015). DeepDream—A code example for visualizing neural networks. *Google Research*. Retrieved October 3, 2019, from https://ai.googleblog.com/2015/07/deepdream-code-example-for-visualizing.html

Mori, M. (2005, December 5). On the uncanny valley. In *Proceedings of the Humanoids-2005 workshop: Views of the Uncanny Valley*.

Murphy, R. R. (2004). Human-robot interaction in rescue robotics. *IEEE Transactions on Systems, Man, and Cybernetics, Part C (Applications and Reviews), 34*(2), 138–153.

Ramachandran, V. S. (2012). *The Tell-Tale brain: A neuroscientist's quest for what makes us human*. Norton.

Turkle, S. (2012). *Alone together: Why we expect more from technology and less from each other paperback*. Basic Books.

Vessel, E. A., Ishizu, T., & Bignardi, G. (2022). *Neural correlates of visual aesthetic appeal* (pp. 103–133). Routledge.

Yee, N., & Bailenson, J. (2007). The proteus effect: The effect of transformed self-representation on behavior. *Human Communication Research, 33*, 271–290.

Unit 2 Lesson: Portraits as Faces

Lasse Hodne

Portraits have been a part of human civilization for thousands of years. According to the famous Roman historian and naturalist, Pliny the Elder (AD 23/24–79), the first painting ever made, was a portrait. It was presumably invented by the daughter of a man called Butades, a potter from Sicyon in Greece. To preserve the memory of her beloved who was going away for a while, she decided to trace the profile of his head from the shadow cast on a wall.

With 'portrait' we think of a representation of a person in drawing, painting, sculpture, or photography. It can be of the whole body or only the head, but generally we take for granted that it fixates the physiognomy of the face in such a way that we can recognize the identity of the person. Since we want to know who the painting represents, the image must be the likeness of the model. In addition, we also sometimes require that the image conveys some of the model's personality and inner feelings. Our tendency to endow images with a presence is a phenomenon that can be investigated scientifically under the heading 'theory of mind'—a psychological term that refers to our capacity to understand other people's emotions (Folgerø et al., 2016; Martínez, 2020).

Many of the portraits that we know from history's greatest artists were painted long before the invention of photography, and had, perhaps precisely for this reason, much of the same social function that photographs today have. But can we from this draw the conclusion that the audience before, say, 1800 perceived a real person in the painting and that the spectator's encounter with a portrait had some of the atmosphere of a meeting between real people? A painting is a work of art,

L. Hodne (✉)
Department of Art and Media Studies, Norwegian University of Science and Technology, Trondheim, Norway
e-mail: lasse.hodne@ntnu.no

T. Balinisteanu and K. Priest (eds.), *Neuroaesthetics*,
https://doi.org/10.1007/978-3-031-42323-9_6

and a portrait seen in a painting is not the same as the face of a physical person. Studying paintings is not the same as studying faces. Yet, from art history, we have a myriad of examples that show that people actually saw (or wanted to see) real people in the pictures. If we look attentively at images of God the *Pantokrator* in mosaics typical of the Orthodox East in the Middle Ages, or icons with the same subject from that period and region, we will often find that the eyes, although the face is turned outwards towards the spectator, are slightly averted. It is possible that this tendency can be explained with reference to the belief in the 'evil eye' which was widespread, especially in the Eastern Mediterranean area. Superstitious people believed that a malevolent person could cast a curse on another person by means of the gaze, causing injury or misfortune. The gaze of God was, of course, the opposite of malevolent, but the tradition testifies the power that people attributed to the gaze, whether good or bad—even when cast by a painting! This is probably also the reason why in Byzantine depictions of the Last Supper Judas never had his face turned towards the spectator (Gombrich, 1961).

Although, as mentioned, it is the likeness that makes us accept a picture of a person as a portrait, the likeness is not necessarily as faithful as a photograph. We have an innate desire to see a thing 'as something'. You have probably been lying on your back in the grass on a summer day, looking at the clouds that drift in the sky. The clouds have different shapes, and often they resemble something, perhaps an animal or some other object. Our capacity to discover hidden figures behind inanimate objects is spurred by a desire for meaning. It is probably this tendency—our desire to look for meaning where there is none—that made people in different cultures and historical epochs ascribe magical effects to certain images. From the medieval Christian tradition we have the so-called *acheiropoieta*—pictures 'made without hands'. Having come into being miraculously, without the participation of a painter, such images were believed to be true images of the Saviour. In a culture without photographic reproductions, this would almost be a direct confrontation between the faithful and God. *Acheiropoieta* were venerated as relics and pilgrims travelled long distances to see them.

A similar status was ascribed to the so-called *vera icona* (which means 'true image'). This refers to the story of a pious woman called Veronica (her name is an anagram for *vera icona*), who was a witness to Christ when he carried his cross to Golgotha. Moved to pity, she gave him her veil so that he might wipe the sweat of his face. When the veil was returned to her, she discovered that the Lord's facial traits were mysteriously impressed upon it (The veil is sometimes referred to as a sweat cloth or *sudarium* [Hodne, 2013a]). A number of churches claim to be in possession of Veronica's cloth, which is venerated as a relic like the *acheiropoieta*.

There is an interesting link between the medieval Veronica tradition and the more exact and historically reliable example narrated by Pliny. Both stories explain how the face of a person is traced or imprinted mechanically on a surface, to convince us that this is the true image of the model, not a product of phantasy or artistic creativity. The difference between the two examples lies in the head direction, for while in Pliny's example the image is an exact profile, the face on Veronica's clothes is seen frontally. It is, as we shall see, the frontal image of Veronica, not Pliny's profile, that is ascribed to supernatural powers. In fact, the frontal image exploits a well-known optical effect that we will briefly explain. Some of you may know the famous 1914 poster by Alfred Leete that was used in a campaign to recruit soldiers for the British Army during World War I (Fig. 1). The poster shows the Secretary of State for War, Lord Kitchener, with his face turned outwards and a finger pointing towards an imagined spectator. The accompanying text '… wants you' is not a continuation of the word 'Britons' at the top but must refer to the face of Lord Kitchener himself, whose eyes seem to follow the spectator in front of the image. In fact, in designing this poster, Leete exploited a well-known optical trick that was documented already in Antiquity. The first to talk about such cases of 'omnivoyance' was probably, again, the Roman historian Pliny. In his *Naturalis Historia*, he described a painting of the goddess Minerva, made by the artist Famulus, which had the appearance of always looking at the spectators, from whatever point it was viewed. The same optical effect was reported in the following century by the Assyrian satirist Lucian (AD 125–180), who, during a visit to the Temple of Hera in Hierapolis saw an image of a goddess that seemed to look you '…in the face, and as you pass it the gaze still follows you, and if another approaching from a different quarter looks at it, he is similarly affected' (Lucian, 1913).

Although ancient Greek scientists like Ptolemy (AD 90–168) tried to give the phenomenon a scientific explanation, using terms normally associated with Renaissance perspective, like 'visual cone' and 'visual axis' (Ptolemy, 1996), medieval authors persistently saw it as mystic and enigmatic. In fact, the divine image that the thirteenth-century theologian Nicholas Mesarites described in the *Church of the Holy Apostles,* was that of the enthroned Christ, the divine judge, whose eyes are 'wholly directed toward all at once and at the same time toward each individually' (Hodne, 2013a; Pliny, n.d.). The eyes that fall upon the righteous are mild and gentle, he said, whereas to 'those … who are condemned by their own judgment they are scornful and hostile' (Mesarites, 1957).

The Renaissance theologian Nicholas of Cusa used exactly this effect in a treatise called *De visione Dei* that addressed certain aspects that he believed to be characteristic of God as an Almighty being. Writing to fellow monks in a monastery, he described God as an omnipotent, endowed with the capacity to see everyone, everywhere, all the time. Interestingly, to illustrate the effect, along with the letter he also sent a drawing of the *vera icona* type. The term that Cusa used to denote the effect was 'omnivoyance', which means that our feeling as spectators of being watched must be attributed to the image itself, if not even the one (God) who is represented in the image. The word 'omnivoyance' is fitting, for it denotes the effect as well as all those images that possess the quality to induce it. However, if you try to look up the word on the Internet, you might find a different term instead: the 'Mona Lisa effect'. This is commonly used in research articles on this topic. The name 'Mona Lisa-effect' was probably introduced for the first time in an article by Kinya et al. (1985), which published the responses from 12 test persons in 4 experiments, using (1) photographs with a direct gaze and slightly averted face (like in Leonardo's *Mona Lisa*), (2) a schematic face, (3) a full face

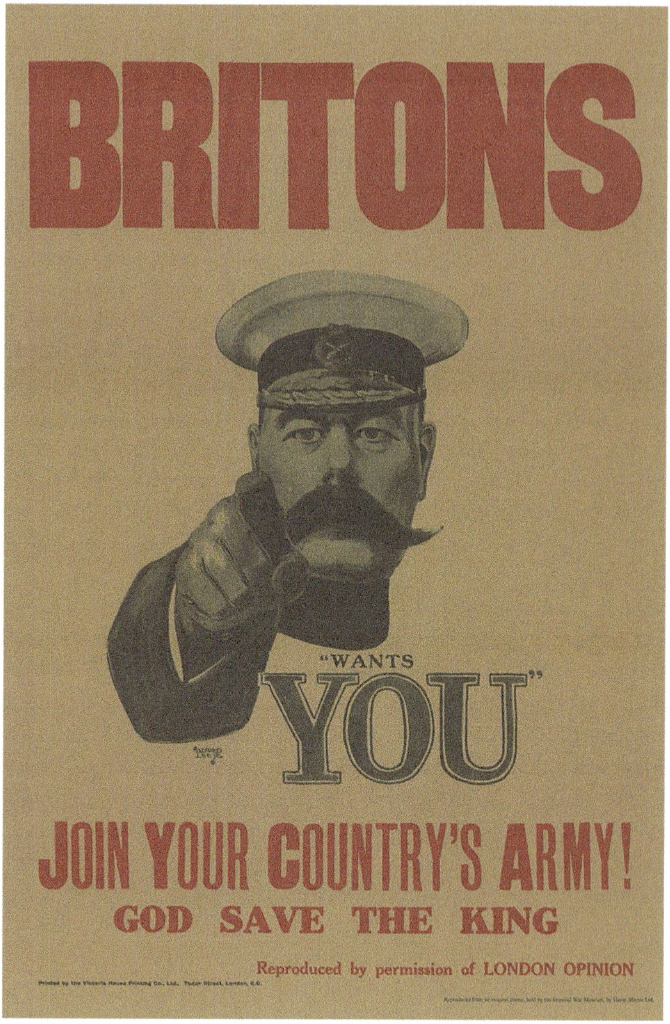

Fig. 1 Alfred Leete, *Lord Kitchener Wants You.* Published in London Opinion 1914

(en face) photograph with direct gaze, and (4) images with averted gaze. The persistence of perceived gaze contact through slanted stimuli (face direction) was by this group explained by a hypothesized gaze anchoring effect (Kinya et al., 1985).

From this, we learn that the optical effect of 'being observed' is not limited to pictures like that of Christ in Majesty, where the face of God is turned directly towards us, but also works like Leonardo da Vinci's famous *Mona Lisa* in the Louvre. In fact, the gaze of Leonardo's model (presumably a portrait of the Florentine noblewoman Lisa Gherardini) follows us in exactly the same way as the aforementioned examples, even if in this case only the eyes are directed towards the spectator, the face is seen in three-quarter profile (Fig. 2). This should remind us that there is nothing magic with holy faces. It is an optical effect that can be studied scientifically. One aspect of it was addressed in a famous study by W. H. Wollaston as early as 1824 (Wollaston, 1824). Wollaston's study focused on pictures of the Mona Lisa type, where the eyes of the sitter are directed towards the spectator while the face is seen in three-quarter profile. Realizing that the optical illusion only works when the eyes of the model are turned out from the picture at an angle perpendicular to the picture surface, Wollaston's question was not how the omnivoyance effect functions, but how the artist must paint the eyes to induce the feeling that the portrayed person is looking at us. The answer to this question is not at all easy, as the image that accompanied his text demonstrates (Fig. 3). In fact, the eyes of the two heads that we see here, the one to the left and the one to the right, are exactly the same, yet only the one on the left appears to look at us. This shows that gaze direction is not only a question of eye direction—also the direction of the face must be considered.

How can this effect be explained optically and psychologically? According to some the human visual system has a tendency to recreate the original viewpoint of a scene by compensating for the retinal distortions that arise from an observer's atypical vantage points (Kubovy, 1986). A number of studies have found empirical evidence for the observer's capacity to compensate for the slant of the projection surface (Boyarskaya & Hecht, 2012). Others have maintained that the reason why the portrait's eyes appear to follow the observer is that the shape of the nose and eyes, as well as the outline of the face, remain relatively stable during the observer's horizontal displacement in front of the picture (Halloran, 1989). With the exception of extremely oblique angles, a face looks more or less the same from all positions. This means that all images in a certain sense move with the spectator, even in portraits with their eyes turned towards the side (Boyarskaya & Hecht, 2012).

It is almost certain that the images described by Mesarites and Cusa, differently from Leonardo's *Mona Lisa*, were full frontal. Although it must have been very useful to exploit the omnivoyance effect for images of God, the fact that it can be obtained in painted and photographic images regardless of whether the face is turned directly towards the spectator or is slightly averted, means that it cannot by itself be the hallmark of the representations of 'the divine' in art. It is therefore worthwhile to study face direction independently of gaze direction.

Based on a hypothesis that full face view in Western art was more common in depictions of holy persons (Christ, saints) than secular persons, a survey was performed based on reproductions of artworks in books and catalogues of Italian, German, and Flemish art from the fifteenth and the sixteenth centuries. The catalogues used were Max Friedländer's *Die altniederländische Malerei*; Ernst Buchner's *Das deutsche Bildnis der Spätgotik und der frühen Dürerzeit;* Werner Richard Deusch's *German Painting of the Sixteenth Century: Dürer and His Contemporaries;* and Raimond van Marle's comprehensive *The Development of the Italian Schools of Painting*.

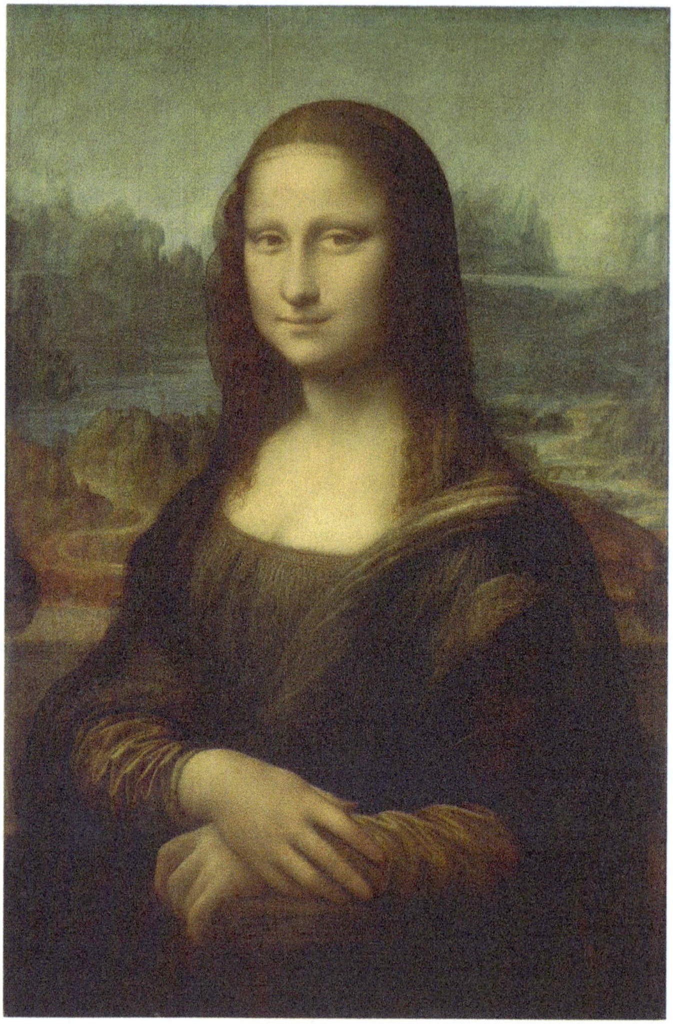

Fig. 2 Leonardo da Vinci, *Mona Lisa (La Gioconda),* Louvre, Paris

The masterpieces by European artists contained in these catalogues comprised all types of subjects and paintings, not only portraits. A definition of 'portrait' was needed, which limited the search to images that included the face of a person, and, in some cases, the shoulders and breast, but not the entire body. Moreover, only portraits of single persons (not group portraits), and only depictions of secular persons were included. In addition, a definition of pose was needed that distinguished between the frontal view of the head and different versions of the profile. Basically, in art one usually differentiates between *en face* (full-frontal view of the face, like in a passport photo), profile (like the example from Pliny, above), and

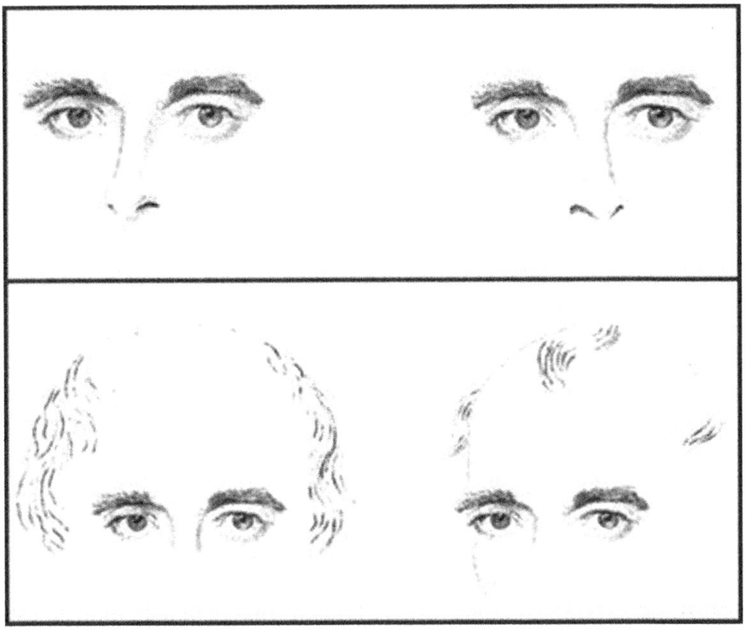

Fig. 3 Wollaston, W.H. Page from 'On the Apparent Direction of Eyes in a Portrait', 1824

three-quarter view (the head is turned obliquely to the picture plane). But in this survey only two categories were used—full face and not full face.

Of more than a thousand paintings reproduced in Max Friedländer's catalogue there were no less than 172 portraits, but, interestingly, none of these was a full face; while of the 188 portraits in Ernst Buchner's there were two. Also, when surveying Raimond van Marle's books two *en face* portraits were found among the total of 196 portraits included in his volumes. Of the 32 portraits in Werner Richard Deusch's there were three; one of these was also reproduced by Buchner: the famous *Self-portrait as Christ* by Albrecht Dürer.

True, a few full-frontal portraits of secular persons exist. In addition to Dürer, the catalogues mention an example by Hans Holbein. There is also a quite well-known self-portrait by Tintoretto which is not mentioned in the catalogues, but the overall impression is that the *en face* pose was almost never used when depicting secular persons. The study found no vital difference between regions in Europe; North and South in Europe either a pure profile or a variation of three-quarter view was preferred when representing ordinary people. Of the total of all 580 paintings analysed in this study, only seven are shown frontally. Taking into account works that are reproduced more than once (a very limited number), these seven comprise about 1.2% of the total!

This study by Hodne addressed the distinction between the frontal (and often almost perfectly symmetrical) view of the face and averted faces. It did not however analyse variations of profile and their meanings. A study that specifically addressed the three quarter view was done by Chris McManus, who used portraits from polyptychs (panel paintings showing Christ or the Virgin flanked by saints on either side) selected from among the more than 5000 images in Berenson's eight volumes. Examining the ways in which left–right asymmetries were used by Italian Renaissance artists, McManus discovered that occasional asymmetries in polyptychs were more likely to involve the substitution of a left cheek for a right cheek, than vice-versa (McManus, 2005). This is especially true of women, where, among the 551 paintings of this type, 68% turned the left cheek towards the spectator. This number was significantly lower in the male portraits, where 56% of the 932 paintings analysed showed the left cheek. Several later studies have confirmed that the number in each case is significantly different from 50%.

'Left cheek' was predominant in both cases (male and female), but the choice of pose (head turn) also depended on the sitter's relationship to the painter. A similar study by the same author on portraits by Rembrandt showed that portraits of kin (where the model has some kind of relation to the painter), be they male or female, were more likely to show the right cheek than were portraits of non-kin. From this he developed a hypothesis that the right and the left half of the face are perceived differently by the spectator, with the right cheek signalling 'kin', i.e. someone who is like myself, while the left is 'not kin' (unlike myself).

Comparisons with photographs, where the same bias is found, refute the hypothesis that left cheek bias is in some way connected with the fact that most artists use their right hand when they paint; yet, the phenomenon may very well be related to handedness in a symbolic way. Despite the numeric predominance of 'left' in portraits, there is reason to conclude that our preferences lean towards 'right', since this view is associated with 'self'. The most natural explanation of this is a tendency across cultural and geographical barriers to associate 'right' with positive values and 'left' with negative. This conclusion is based on a 1909 study by the French sociologist Robert Hertz, who, studying funerary and mortuary practices, pointed to the fact that right is always associated with positive values (honours, flattering designations, prerogatives), while left is negative (despised and reduced to an auxiliary role). It is the structure of the human organism and the asymmetry of our brain, McManus concludes, that explains why 'right-left symbolisms are not arbitrary, but are constrained by biology, …' (McManus, 2005).

We saw that a portrait signals different things, depending on whether it turns its left or right cheek towards the spectator. But in both cases (left or right) we are confronted with the picture of a face that is turned in a three-quarter pose. In the Renaissance, secular persons were either portrayed in pure profile or a three-quarter view. Although their eyes were sometimes turned outwards, like the famous *Mona Lisa,* the face was almost never seen frontally. Was the full-frontal pose used in Renaissance art at all, and if so, in what connection? One way that we can shed light on this question is to turn to the works by one of the period's most prolific painters of portraits, the German-born Dutch artist Hans Memling. From his hands there are at least 36 surviving portraits of secular persons, and four small-scale paintings of Christ. Interestingly, while none of his secular portraits are seen in full face, three of the Christ portraits that he made are shown this way. The three

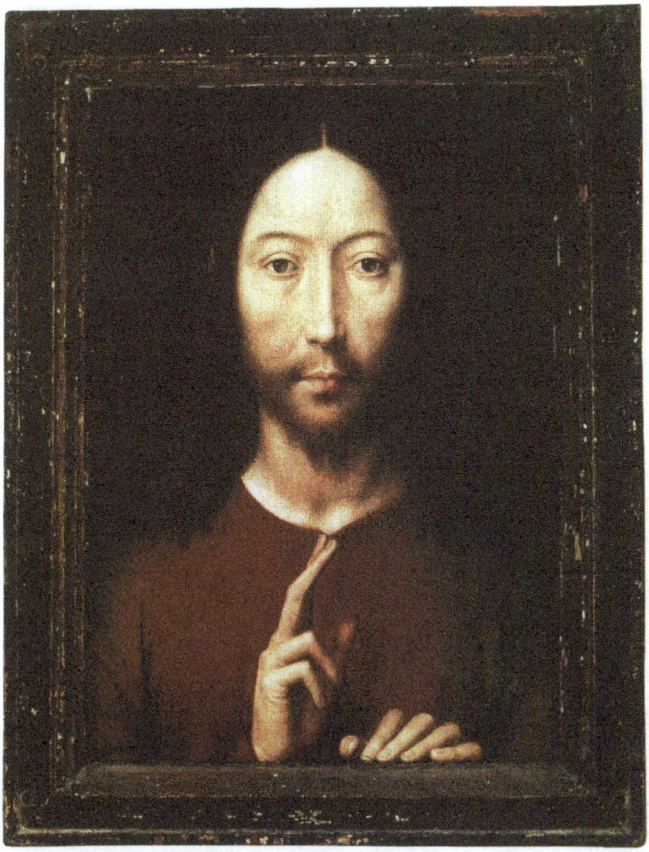

Fig. 4 Hans Memling, *Christ giving blessing (Holy Face),* Museum of Fine Arts, Boston

portraits of Jesus that are seen frontally are very similar. They show the Lord with a calm, almost insensitive, facial expression; his right hand is raised in a blessing gesture, while the left is placed on the lower frame as if it was a window opening (Fig. 4). His dark, long hair is parted in the middle, and the same goes for the beard, which is cut the same way as the paintings from the Van Eyck school that we will discuss below. If we drew a vertical axis right through the centre of the portrait it would intersect the hair and beard exactly where it is parted, dividing the painting into two perfectly symmetrical halves. The fourth Christ portrait that Memling made, was totally different. In this, Jesus has a sad and tormented facial expression, as we know him from Crucifixion scenes or scenes from the Calvary (Fig. 5). What's more, on his head he wears the Crown of Thorns and from his wounds issue drops of blood. His right hand is raised, not to bless, but so that we can see that he has stigma marks.

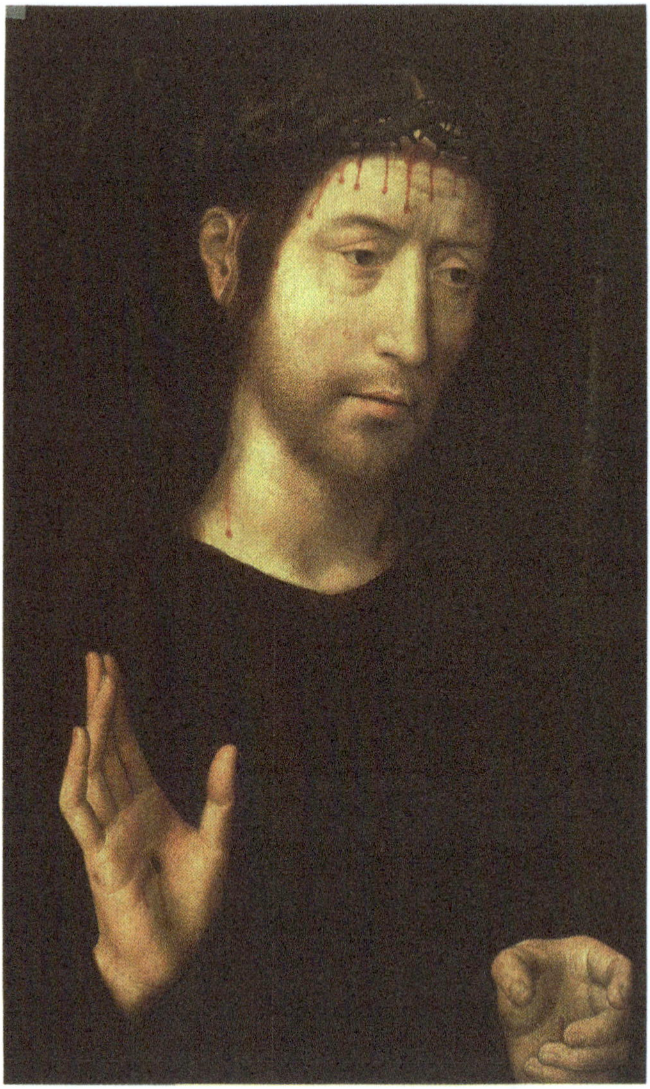

Fig. 5 Hans Memling, *Man of Sorrows,* Musei di Strada Nuova, Genoa

On the basis of these observations, we can make two testable hypotheses. First: The full-frontal and symmetric view of the face is rare in portrayals of secular persons because it signals something divine or holy that we seldom associate with ordinary people. Second: The fact that the frontal view was common, but by no means compulsory, in representations of Christ, could be an indication that pose (frontal or averted) signalled different views of Christ as a person with both divine and human aspects. These two aspects may very well correspond to two well-established art historical types of Christ's image. The first is also found in depictions of Christ as universal ruler *(Pantokrator)* or judge in scenes of the Last Judgement or the Apocalypse; small panel paintings of this will here be referred to as the *Holy Face*. The second type is in German often denoted as the *Schmerzensmann*; in the present context we will use the familiar English term *Man of Sorrows*.

In a 2013 study images of Christ from catalogues were surveyed according to the same principles as the already mentioned study of Renaissance portraits of secular persons (Hodne, 2013b). This time images were retrieved from Raimond van Marle's catalogue, *The Development of the Italian Schools of Painting*. Van Marle's volumes cover Italian art from more or less the period of Giotto (slightly before the year 1300) until the verge of the High Renaissance around 1500. The number of Christ portraits in his catalogue is not very high. Among the thousands of paintings reproduced in his 18 volumes, there are only 24 portraits of Christ. Of these, 10 are of the *Holy Face* type, whereas 14 can be categorized as *Man of Sorrows*. When these two types were further divided into sub-groups, we found that of the *Holy Face* type, there was a clear preference for full face (7 full face portraits and only 3 half profiles). As for the *Man of Sorrows*, the tendency was even clearer in the opposite direction: of the 14 panels, only one was full face. The rest were all in half profile.

It must be emphasized that since the aim of this study was to find out whether there was a connection between pose (frontal or averted) and type (*Holy Face* or *Man of Sorrows*), the two types had to be defined initially by other means. Hence, the *Man of Sorrows* was defined as an image where Jesus shows signs associated with Passion (stains of blood, Crown of Thorns, stigma marks) and has a sad expression; in contrast, the *Holy Face* shows Christ with a calm facial expression and without signs of Passion.

When confronted with other catalogues, the survey of Christ portraits from Van Marle also confirmed our suspicion that frontality was much more used in portrayals of Christ than ordinary persons. While, as we remember, only 1.2% of the secular portraits showed the sitter *en face*, this number was significantly higher in depictions of Christ. Of the 24 Christ portraits in Van Marle, no less than 8 are shown frontally. In Friedländer's *Die altniederländische Malerei*, the percentage is even higher: 7 of 10 Christ portraits reproduced here are frontal.

How a photo or a painting relates to the spectator depends both on face direction and gaze contact. The studies discussed in the previous chapter mainly focus on the role of face and head orientation. In research, head orientation and gaze direction are often considered as different and separable aspects of vision, and there is also a discussion about what—gaze or face—is the most important when we make judgements about others. Among scholars there is a tendency to consider gaze as the more important. In a gender-categorization task Baron-Cohen demonstrated that test persons judged the sex of people faster when the targets were looking straight ahead (Baron-Cohen, 1997). This effect was independent of the orientation of the face (full face versus half profile), thereby confirming that gaze direction overrides face direction when judging the sex of other people. These results have been confirmed by not gender-related experiments, leading researchers to conclude that gaze contact has precedence over contextual information such as head orientation.

A view that stresses the joint interaction of gaze and face direction was presented by Pageler et al. (2003)**. An investigation of brain activation in the fusiform gyrus and the posterior superior temporal sulcus during face tasks revealed a significant effect of both head and gaze on the speed of gaze processing. Reaction time was faster and activation greater in both brain areas when both face and gaze were directed towards the spectator (the participant). In addition, activation in the fusiform gyrus was greater for the forward gaze compared to the angled gaze, but only when the gaze was supported by head orientation (face forward). Similarly, Langton (2000), in a study where participants were asked to make keypress responses to a photograph of a male face, revealed that incongruent cues (head orientation different from gaze orientation) slowed the participants' responses, suggesting, like Pageler et al., that head and gaze are mutually influential (Langton, 2000). Indeed, a number of recent behavioural studies suggest that contextual information like head orientation plays a greater role in the processing of social attention than was formerly believed.

In a study from 2016, Folgerø et al. used images from photographs as well as paintings to test people's reactions to varying gaze and face directions. Portraits were selected from a database with images of the heads of persons photographed from different angles. For each person was chosen a frontal view and a view that was what we here call three quarters (approximately midway between frontal and profile). Then the eyes on the photos were manipulated in such a way that for each pose there was one image with direct gaze and one with averted gaze. Test persons thus had four alternatives to choose from: direct face/direct gaze, direct face/averted gaze, averted face/direct gaze, and averted face/averted gaze.

Test persons (36 females and 16 males, mostly students) were asked to respond to the faces according to a choice of pre-selected adjectives. These were common words from everyday speech that are descriptive of personality traits, either positive ('harmonious', 'trustworthy', 'caring', 'inclusive', and 'respectable') or negative ('authoritarian', 'monitoring', 'evasive', 'intimidating', and 'dominant'). The results showed that people gave frontal faces with a direct gaze as well as three-quarter view with averted gaze high scores on attributes from the group of positive adjectives. The test was then repeated using paintings instead of photographs, manipulated in the same way as above, with four alternative views of the face (this time the test persons were 39 females and 10 males). The results of this test were similar to the first, but even more pronounced in favour of direct face/direct gaze. The test persons saw this type of portrait as representing a person who was more caring, trustworthy, harmonic, inclusive, and respectable than the corresponding images with averted gaze and face.

The findings in the study of Folgerø et al. are interesting when we turn to our analysis of the two categories of Christ portraits. The positive emotions elicited by frontal gaze and frontal face direction may shed light on why Renaissance artists preferred this pose when representing the divine aspect of Christ, while generally avoiding it when representing the *Man of Sorrows*. What's more, the fact that the results obtained from the test that used paintings are similar to those based on photographs, might be an indication that responses to images resemble, in some way, reactions we have in real-life encounters.

We have seen that in art face direction was used systematically to distinguish between representations of ordinary persons and the holy, as well as between different aspects of Christ. It is interesting to ask, as regards the different types of Christ portrait, whether there are early Biblical or Apocryphal sources or documents from, for instance, the Church Fathers, that can confirm the existence of different (and opposing) visions of Christ?

Interestingly, Tertullian's discussion of the Messiah in *Adversus Marcionem* seems to confirm the idea of a twofold nature of Christ. Discussing the Old Testament prophecies, Tertullian concluded that the Messiah must have two quite different aspects. First he drew an image of him 'in humility' with 'no appearance nor glory, … or beauty, but his appearance was unhonoured, defective more than the sons of men, a *man in sorrow*, …' (Tertullianus & Evans, 1972). Tertullian's description was part of an argument against heretics who denied that God could have a body like human beings. Christ's suffering was to Tertullian proof that he had a body, and his ugliness is related to his suffering. This idea was based on the prophet Isaiah, who described Messiah as 'disfigured beyond that of any man and his form marred beyond human likeness' (Is 52, 14). What's more, 'he had no beauty or majesty to attract us to him, nothing in his appearance that we should desire him. He was despised and rejected by men, a *man of sorrows*, and familiar with suffering' (Is 53:2-3, my italics).

Christ suffered during his life on earth. He could be seen by everyone who lived at that time, but the risen Christ showed himself only to the faithful. The calm expression that we know from paintings of the *Holy Face* refers to this second aspect. Emphasizing that 'the tokens of sublimity' only apply to the Lord's Second Advent, Tertullian said that Christ then 'will have an honourable appearance, and beauty unfading, more than the sons of men' (Tertullianus & Evans, 1972). This must be based on the Psalms, where the King is described as 'beautiful above the sons of men' (Psalm 44 (45):2).

There can be little doubt that the necessity felt by painters and their employers to distinguish between two different and quite distinct types of Christ had a foundation in texts by religious authorities. We notice that the title usually applied

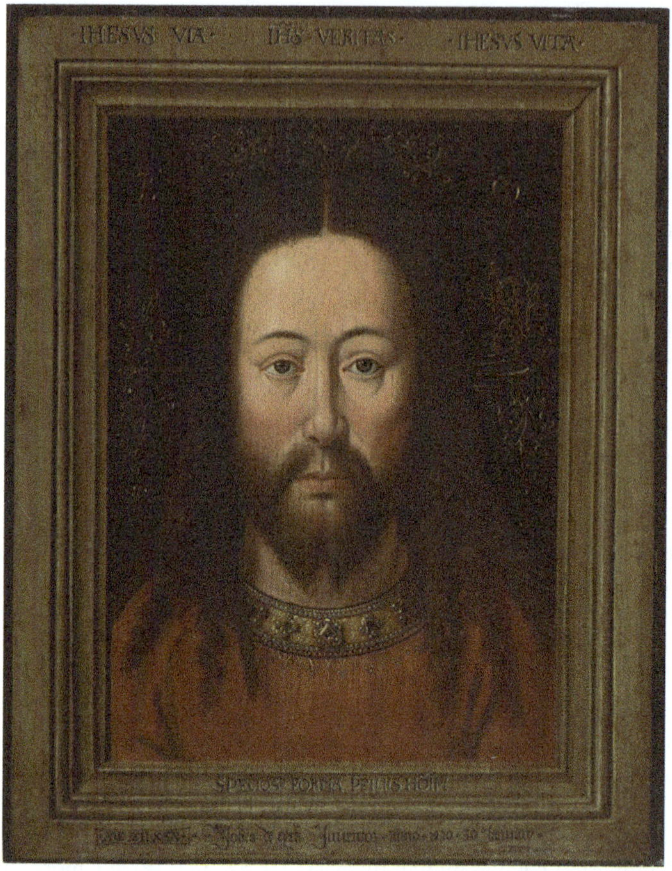

Fig. 6 Jan van Eyck (follower of), *Vera Icon,* Groeningemuseum, Brugge

to the suffering type—*Man of Sorrows*—was also used in the Bible and other religious texts. It is more difficult to find an equal for *Holy Face* in the Bible, but that this kind of picture can be seen as expression of the 'honourable appearance' that Tertullian described, should be clear from some of the very oldest paintings of this type that still exist today. In fact, these paintings often had inscriptions referring to the mentioned passages from the Bible on the frame. An example of this is a painting that formerly was attributed to Jan van Eyck, now in the Groeninge Museum in Bruges, which, in addition to the painter's false signature and quotations from the Gospels, bears the inscription: *Speciosa forma pfiliis hominum* (Koerner, 1993; Fig. 6). This is a misspelling of 'Speciosus forma præ filiis hominum' ('you are beautiful above the sons of men') from Psalm 44 (45):3, that was also quoted by Tertullian in relation to the sublime aspect of Messiah.

From this it is quite clear that the artists' distinction between two contrasting aspects of Christ was theologically founded, but we still lack a final answer to why the *Man of Sorrows* should be represented with averted face and the *Holy Face* with direct. To explore why the direct pose was chosen to represent the holy, we must turn to another aspect of frontality, namely symmetry. We know that the human body is almost symmetric; we have a right hand and a left hand, a right foot and a left foot. Ears and eyes are symmetrically placed on either side of our nose, and so on. However, this symmetry is only approximate, for nobody is perfectly symmetric. Studies demonstrate that almost perfectly symmetric faces are generally perceived as more beautiful than less symmetric faces. Such preference for symmetry is also found among animals. Swallows and peacocks with symmetric tail feathers, it seems, are preferred to individuals with irregular patterns as the most attractive mate choices, most likely because the opposite, asymmetry, in some cases will be a result of impairment (Jones et al., 2001).

One reason why we prefer the frontal view of the body may be that it is from this position that we can study its symmetry and, consequently, judge whether it is healthy and attractive. For the same reason, the *en face* portraits must also be analysed in terms of their symmetry. To continue our discussion of the painting from the Van Eyck school above, we may first recall the inscription on the frame that clearly stated it was intended as an image of Christ in his beautiful aspect, 'above the sons of men'. In the painting the face is shown frontally to reveal its symmetry, and symmetry, we know now, is something that we associate with beauty.

Everything in the painting seems to be designed to enhance its symmetry. As in Memling's works, Christ's hair is carefully done and parted in the middle with locks falling to either side in equal numbers (three) on both shoulders. Even the beard is parted in the middle. The ensemble in Fig. 7 juxtaposes Van Eyck's Early Renaissance painting with 5 late medieval precursors from Catholic Western Europe as well as the Orthodox East. Except the background (which in some cases shows the cloth of the *vera icon*, see above), these images are all very similar. Christ turns his face frontally towards the spectator, his long hair falls in an equal number of locks on both shoulders, hair and beard are parted in the middle, and so on. The perfect frontality is broken in two cases, where the gaze is slightly averted (Byzantine artists usually avoided direct gaze from fear of 'the evil eye'), but there can be little doubt that the style of the hair and beard was carefully designed to enhance the strict frontal symmetry of the face.

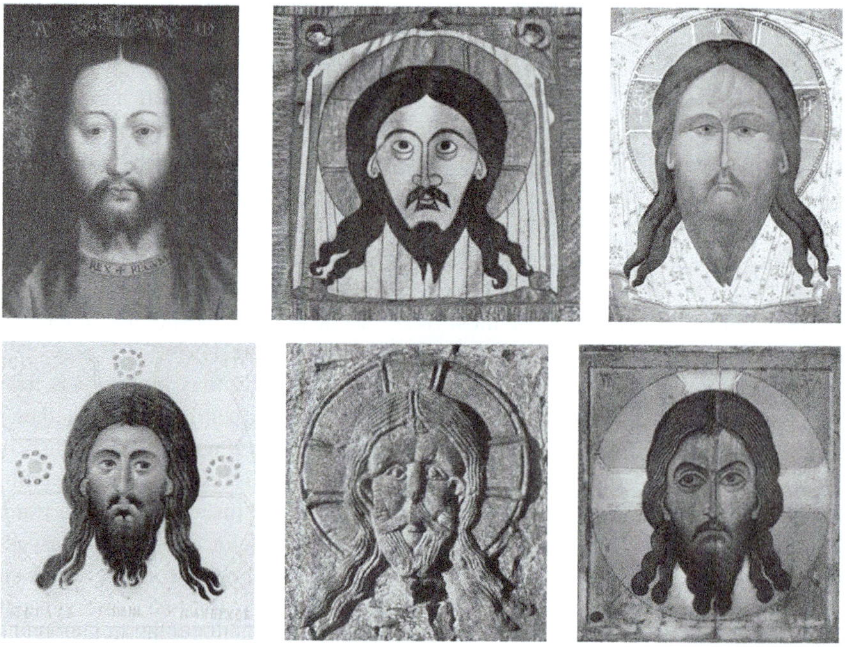

Fig. 7 Comparison of variants of *Vera Icon*

References

Baron-Cohen, S. (1997). How to build a baby that can read minds: Cognitive mechanisms in mindreading. In *The maladapted mind: Classic readings in evolutionary psychopathology* (pp. 207–239).

Boyarskaya, E., & Hecht, H. (2012). Differentiating the differential rotation effect. *Acta Psychologica, 140*(3), 252–265.

Folgerø, P. O., Hodne, L., Johansson, C., Andresen, A. E., Sætren, L. C., Specht, K., & Reber, R. (2016). Effects of facial symmetry and gaze direction on perception of social attributes: A study in experimental art history. *Frontiers in Human Neuroscience, 10*, 452.

Gombrich, E. H. (1961). *Art and illusion* (p. 87). Pantheon Books.

Halloran, T. O. (1989). Picture perception is array-specific: Viewing angle versus apparent orientation. *Perception & Psychophysics, 45*, 467–482.

Hodne, L. (2013a). Omnivoyance and omnipresence. Word and vision according to Nicholas of Cusa and Jan van Eyck. *IKON, 6*, 237–246.

Hodne, L. (2013b). Symmetry versus frontality in the renaissance holy face. *Symmetry: Culture and Science, 24*, 437–450.

Jones, B. C., Little, A. C., Penton-Voak, I. S., Tiddeman, B. P., Burt, D. M., & Perrett, D. I. (2001). Facial symmetry and judgements of apparent health: Support for a "good genes" explanation of the attractiveness–symmetry relationship. *Evolution and Human Behavior, 22*(6), 417–429.

Kinya, M., Mitsuo, E., & Kenzo, S. (1985). An experimental consideration on Mona Lisa Gaze Effect. *Tohoku Psychologica Folia, 44*(1–4), 109–121.

Koerner, J. L. (1993). *The moment of self-portraiture in German Renaissance art*. University of Chicago Press.

Kubovy, M. (1986). *The psychology of perspective and Renaissance art*. CUP Archive.

Langton, S. R. (2000). The mutual influence of gaze and head orientation in the analysis of social attention direction. *The Quarterly Journal of Experimental Psychology: Section A, 53*(3), 825–845.

Lucian. (1913). *The Syrian goddess (De Dea Syria*; trans. by H. A. Strong and J. Garstang), Constable, 1913, p. 73.

Martínez, M. Á. (2020). The doubly-deictic gaze in a Renaissance portrait: A study on pictorial narrativity and storyworld possible selves. *Narrative, 28*(3), 251–268.

McManus, I. C. (2005). Symmetry and asymmetry in aesthetics and the arts. *European Review, 13*(S2), 157–180.

Mesarites, N. (1957). *Description of the church of the Holy Apostles at Constantinople*, translation, commentary, and introduction by G. Downey.

Pliny, G. P. (n.d.). *Natural history, Volume IX: Books 33–35*. Harvard University Press.

Ptolemy, C. P. (1996). *Ptolemy's theory of visual perception. An English translation of the optics (Transactions of the American Philosophical Society* 86, trans. A. M. Smith, p. 124).

Tertullianus, Q. S. F., & Evans, E. (1972). *Adversus Marcionem*: 1: Books 1 to 3 (Vol. 1, pp. XXIII, 253).

Wollaston, W. H. (1824). Xiii. On the apparent direction of eyes in a portrait. *Philosophical Transactions of the Royal Society of London, 114*, 247–256.

Unit 2 Lab: Portraits as Faces

Lasse Hodne

Near where you live, there may be a park with one or more statues or busts of famous people. Take a trip there, or to a museum where photography is allowed. Stand in front of the statue and, first, take a photograph of the depicted person from the front, as shown in this photo.

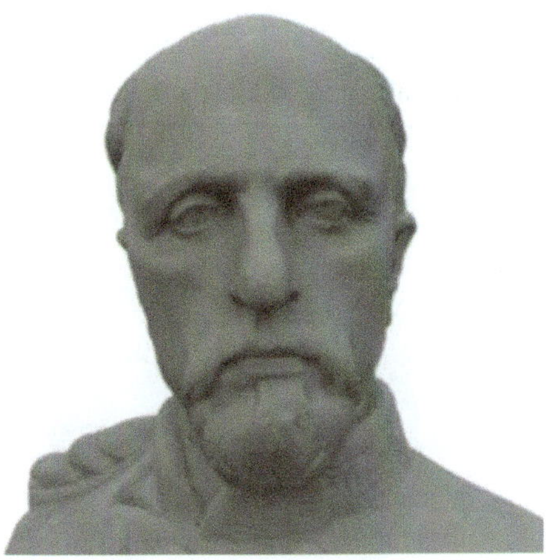

L. Hodne (✉)
Department of Art and Media Studies, Norwegian University of Science and Technology, Trondheim, Norway
e-mail: lasse.hodne@ntnu.no

T. Balinisteanu and K. Priest (eds.), *Neuroaesthetics*,
https://doi.org/10.1007/978-3-031-42323-9_7

Then move to the right and take at least one photograph of the same statue from a different angle (but the same eye level), roughly as shown in this image:

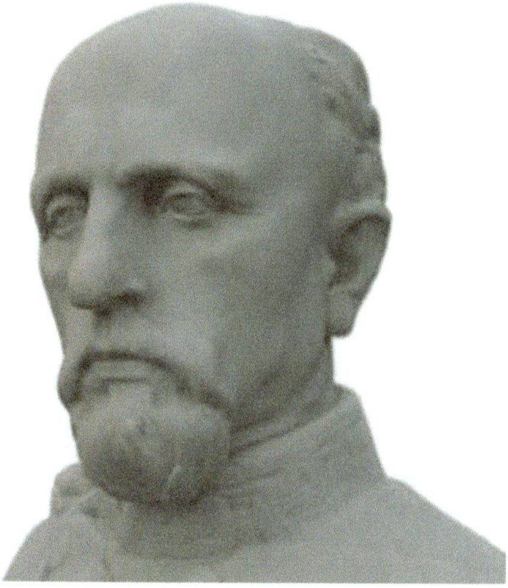

Then move to the left and take one or more photos from corresponding angles:

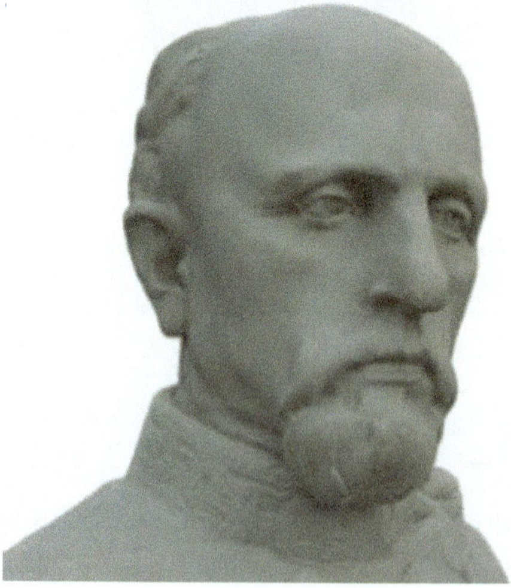

You print the pictures you have taken on a normal printer. Then find a board made of wood or another material, on which the pictures are taped in this way:

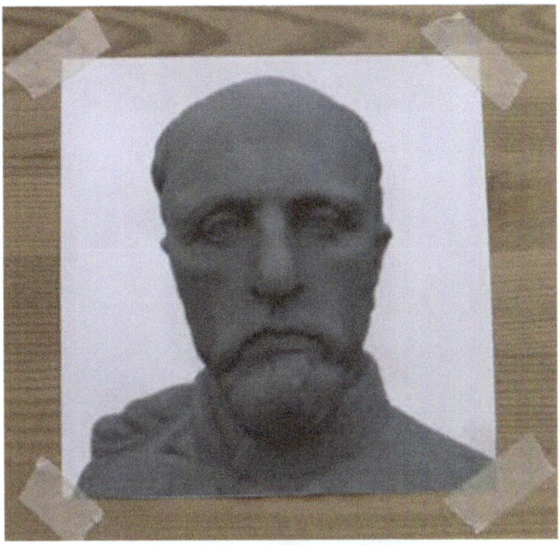

The board must be large enough for the pictures to be attached next to each other. What does the series look like? About like this?.

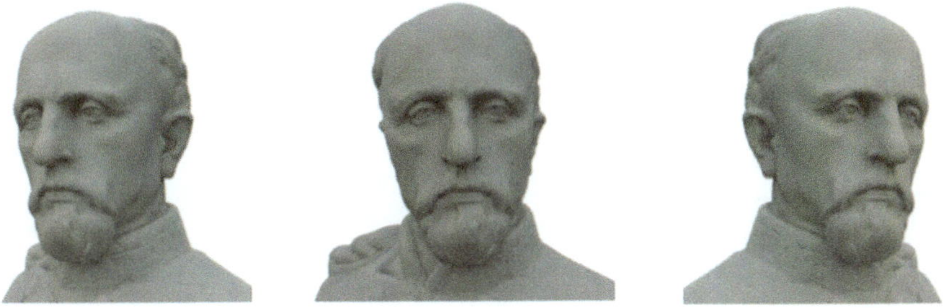

You will probably agree that a bust of a person looks something like this if you move in front of it and study it from different angles. The depicted man, who is looking straight ahead, will only have eye contact with the viewer provided that the viewer is directly in front. There will be no eye contact from any other angle.

However, the question is whether we will experience a flat image in the same way? Both flat and three-dimensional objects change with changing viewing angle, but not in the same way. So, let's imagine that this portrait was not a three-dimensional sculpture, but a photograph. (After all, we are dealing with photographs; photographs of busts.) We then start from the first image that we printed out and affixed to the plate above, and then take a photograph of the photograph, first from the front… .

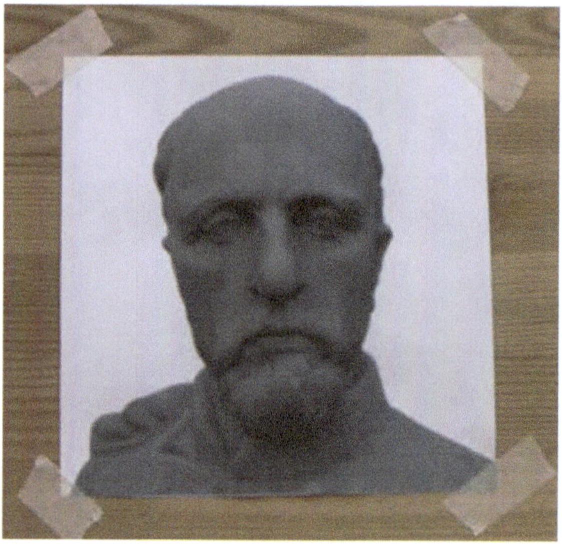

… and then from an oblique angle:

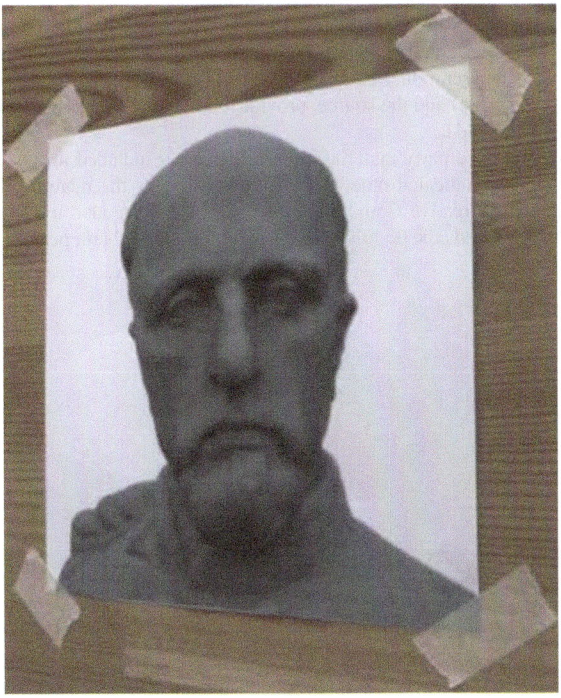

This way we can create a new series and it looks like this:

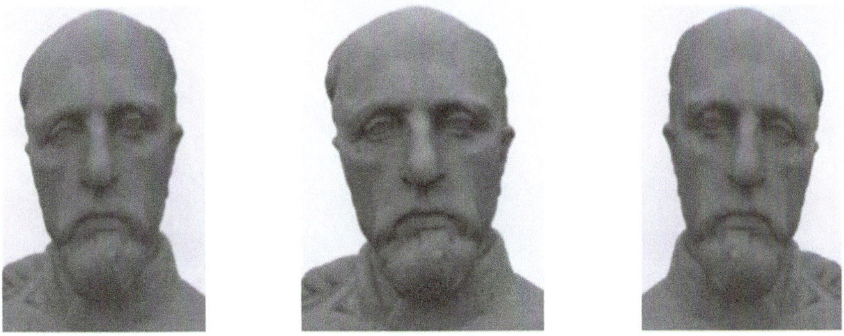

There is still a difference between the photographs taken from the front and those taken from the side, but the difference is not as great. Those photographed at an angle are only slightly narrower. And what about the look? Which of these images makes eye contact with us?

Now consider what was said in the chapter about Ptolemy and Mesarites. Is it any wonder that some people found this effect mysterious?

Unit 3 Overview: Neuroaesthetics Approaches to the Visual Arts—Creation

Marius A. Teodorescu

This chapter analyzes the creation of artwork and of aesthetic objects, especially with regard to portrait painting. In this chapter we will start from the definition and function of portraits both as meaning-making objects and utilitarian ones. After this, we will focus on the reasons for which art is created, the modality in which aesthetic objects are created and on defining the artist/creator as an aesthetic expert.

Hello and welcome to a new unit and a new overview! I hope you have enjoyed your journey into neuroaesthetics so far! This chapter proposes something different from the rest of the book, which mainly focuses on problems of perception and the objective/subjective reactions one has to those perceptions. However, this focus of the book mirrors the focus of research. Currently, there are very few studies that focus on problems of creating art in particular or aesthetic objects in general. Steven Brown, for example, stressed out that aesthetic production is completely neglected in research and that, given the fact that creators are those who imbue art with aesthetic features, it would be fundamental to consider the production as well as the perception of art (Brown, 2022, p. 20).

1. Why is the production of art less studied than the perception of art?◀
2. Why is it difficult to study the creation of art?

M. A. Teodorescu (✉)
Babeș-Bolyai University, 400347 Cluj-Napoca, Romania
e-mail: teo_mariusalex@yahoo.com

T. Balinisteanu and K. Priest (eds.), *Neuroaesthetics*,
https://doi.org/10.1007/978-3-031-42323-9_8

Why is it that so little research is devoted to the production of art? One of the reasons is that there are a lot of types of art. If we take the examples of portraits, both Titian's *Self portrait* and Salvador Dali's (1904–1989) portrait of Pablo Picasso(1881–1973), are portraits. Neuroaesthetics tries to use objective ways of analyzing the aesthetic experience and it is plausible to compare these works using aesthetic traits such as symmetry, composition, contrast and so on. But it is far more difficult to compare objectively Tiziano Vecellio (1488–1576), a man living in the 1500s, and Salvador Dali, a man living in the twentieth century. Moreover, it is even more difficult to compare their motivations for painting these portraits and their motivations for choosing the aesthetic and artistic means that they did. The contexts in which these two paintings were created extremely are different and the obstacles and limitations faced by the two artists were different as well. In a neuroaesthetic study, all these variables should be accounted for and their influences studied and explained. In comparison, when studying perception, both paintings are comprised of shapes and colors on a canvas. The number of variables in the case of perception is significantly lower and the area of research is considerably more limited.

Going outside the examples of portrait painting, there are extremely varied forms of art. It is therefore even more difficult to compare the means and motivations of a painter with those of a theatre director. Also, it is a matter of defining the field of neuroaesthetics. There are researchers who argue that art is not the object of neuroaesthetics and that studying art as part of aesthetics is a stereotype from the Renaissance. They say that both aesthetics in general and neuroaesthetics in particular are about what we like and dislike, what we find beautiful and ugly, what we find attractive or repulsive and that the object of our studies should be very general issues of preference that apply to any object (Brown, 2022, p. 18). Therefore, a car is an object that has aesthetic properties inasmuch as a sculpture, and neuroaesthetics studies have comparatively researched these aesthetic properties. But how is it supposed to study the creation of a car comparatively with the creation of a sculpture, as the designer of a car has a whole different set of motivations, of techniques and limitations in comparison with the sculptor.

Going forward, from our comparison between a sculpture and a car comes the third difficulty in studying the production of aesthetic objects: the authorship problem. We can safely say that Constantin Brâncuși (1876–1957) is the author of *Bird in space*, but who is the author, the creator of a car? Is it the designer? Well, what if someone designed the wheels and someone else designed the car body? Also, how about if some of the choices were made by engineers concerned with practical matters such as speed or safety? Also, how do we study differently the process of creation from the process of production? The story gets considerably more difficult if we add in the following example.

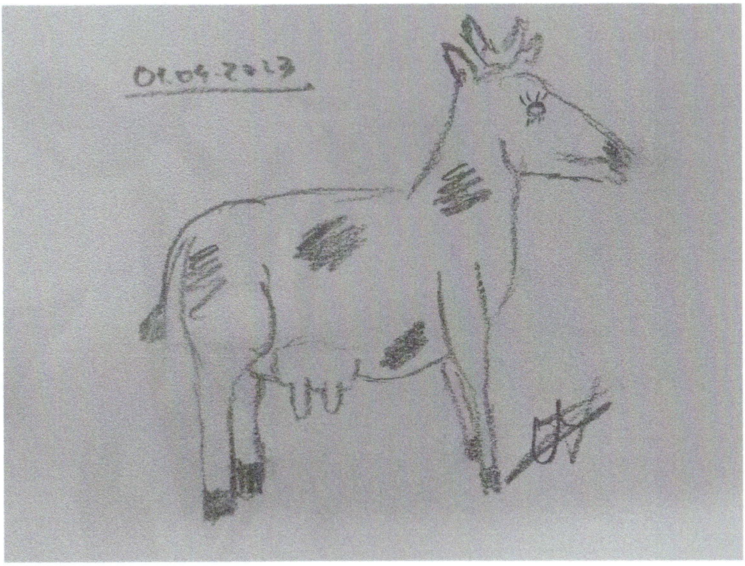

Fig. 1 Teodorescu—Personal sketch of 'a beautiful cow'

I am a horrible sketch artist. Horrible. You can see below my personal rendition of 'a sketch of a beautiful cow'. Also, below you can see a rendition of 'a sketch of a beautiful cow' created by the AI Stable Diffusion. Which do you find more aesthetically pleasing?

We probably agree that in Fig. 1 we have an objectively ugly drawing, especially compared to the AI-generated one. According to the classical Theory of Art, however, the fact that mine is signed and an original makes it more valuable as an artistic and aesthetic object than the one in Fig. 2 (Vartanian & Chatterjee, 2022, p. 29). Also, in the case of Fig. 2, who exactly is the author? If the car is authored as an aesthetic object by the designer, and not by those who build it, then the AI-generated image is created by me as an artistic object, right? That affirmation is difficult to agree with given that we have seen in Fig. 1 what a beautiful cow created by me really looks like!

1. The production of art is more difficult to define as a field of study than the perception of art. The hope is that extensively studying the perception issues will offer us further insights into the way in which art is created.
2. The main issues with studying the creation of art are:
   - It is very difficult to have objective means of comparing different aspects of creation.

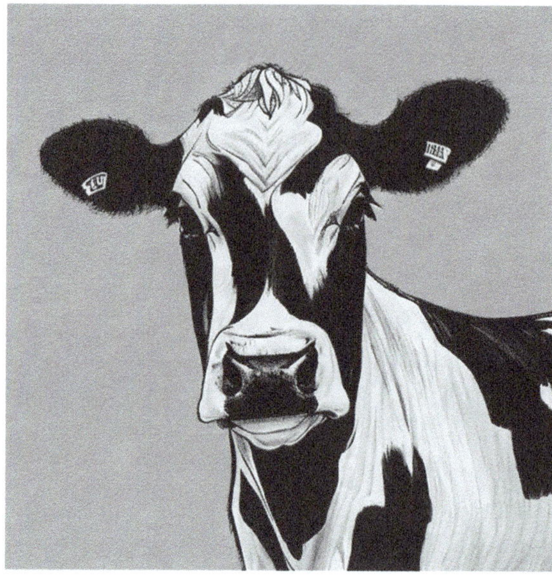

Fig. 2 Teodorescu—AI sketch of 'a beautiful cow'

- It is very different to study creators across different fields of creation, keeping in mind that almost everything can be thought of as an aesthetic object.
- When speaking about creation, the whole idea of authorship, skills used and the definition of an artist become an issue that must be discussed and objectively studied.◄

We have seen what are the problems with neuroaesthetic research in the production of art and of aesthetic objects. We will try in the rest of the chapter to highlight some answers to these issues. For that, we will use the example of visual art, especially portraiture, because it is easier to delineate examples. We will try to discuss three key aspects: why we create art, how we create art and who creates art. Let's start with defining what is a portrait:

►'Potraits are a representation or delineation of a person, especially of the face, made from life, by drawing, painting, photography, engraving etc.; a likeness', according to the Oxford English Dictionary. In addition, portraits always engage with the idea of perceiving and representing the sitter's identity (character, personality, social standing, relationships, profession, age, etc.) (West, 2004, p. 11).

Specific to portraiture is the fact that both the way the sitter looks and his or her identity are unrepresentable as a whole. One will never be able to portray all sides of one's look, as portraits generally show a partial view of the subject. Also, no one will be able to insert into a given portrait all elements of a subject's biography, social status and so on. Despite this all, portraiture has historically been seen as a form of imitation and not so much a form of free creation (West, 2004, p. 12). This is why it is easier to discuss the creation of portraits: because it is rarely intended as a social/political/cultural statement on its own. However, all art has a point, as William Sheeley argues:

> Artworks always, not often, not sometimes, but always, have a point or purpose. We can loosely call the point or purpose a work expresses its "meaning," what it is about. A work might be about an idea, an emotion, a sociopolitical comment, the aesthetics of a composition, the content of a self-reflective aesthetic experience, an art theoretical position, or simply the possibility of making art. The meaning of a work is, in turn, embodied in its content, in the set of formal-compositional elements an artist has used to render its subject (whether naturalistic or abstract) in order to articulate what it is about. If we want to know how artworks work we should focus our attention on how artists use the content of a work to express its point or purposes. (Seeley, 2022, p. 133)

In other words, the work of art should be understood more in terms of what artworks do (Tuckwell, 2018, p. 8) and less as something that is worked on (created) by the artist. We can observe in the quote from Sheeley that art either has a point, or has a purpose. This means that artists either create out of passion, out of the need to express something, or because their work will fulfill a certain, almost utilitarian function. Traditionally, art is defined expressly as not having utility, as a higher spirit function, which is a view that originated in the Enlightenment. However, over the past century, art theorists (and people working in neuroaesthetics alike) have reached the conclusion that an object of art always has a purpose. We buy a vase that is created by an artist at ten times the price of a vase produced in a factory not only because it is beautiful, but also because we want to show our status, because we want to commemorate a certain moment or for a thousand other reasons.

Studies have shown that we are actually neurologically predisposed to react to the meaning we derive from aesthetic objects. We are heavily influenced by the context in which we see the work of art and other properties of aesthetic engagement define the contribution of the knowledge-meaning system to the aesthetic perception of an object (Vartanian, & Chatterjee, 2022). This is the case especially in works of art 'with a point', where the artist not only has a specific idea or feeling in mind when creating the work, but also usually explicitly shapes the way in which the artwork is presented to the public. Think only of the example of Marcel Duchamp's (1887–1968) *Fountain*.

In 1917, Marcel Duchamp smuggled a urinal signed 'R. Mutt' into a gallery. The point he wanted to make was that a mundane object (a readymade) would become art simply because it was exhibited in a gallery and because he, as an artist, stated that the object was art.

Hence, the fact that an object is presented in a certain way in a certain manner can transform it from a simple one to an artistic one and vice-versa. This point was actually made extremely clear by another artist, Kendel Geers, in 1993 at a show in Venice, when he urinated on the sculpture, arguing that it was only a urinal and it could be used as such. However, the context and the meaning we ascribe to an object are not the only qualities that the artist instills in his or her work. It turns out that we can automatically differentiate between artistic and non-artistic abstract images. A study conducted by Kana Schwabe and her team discovered that when we are confronted with an abstract piece of art created by an artist and with an abstract piece of art that was had its composition randomized by a computer, subjects could differentiate between the two and only ascribed artistic qualities to the former (Schwabe et al., 2018). The conclusion of the study is that the human brain can detect differences in image properties and from here differentiate between images with and without artistic composition (Menzel et al., 2022, p. 105).

We argue that the difference between the two types of images that are perceived is exactly this intentional quality (the point) of the artwork. As Per Olav Folgerø argues at length, following the work of Vittorio Galesse (see Chapter 1), embodiment and mirror neuron studies suggest that we can mirror the movements of an agent that has performed them even if we are only presented with traces of that movement, as is in the case of Jackson Pollock (1912–1956) painting. Despite the lack of studies in this respect, we support the idea that we can also mirror the intentional aspects behind those traces. In other words, when we see an abstract painting created by an artist we can trace in it the intention of the artist, even without understanding that intention exactly, explicitly. In comparison, when we see an abstract painting created by a computer, we do not recognize any intentionality in it, and therefore find it less valuable, less interesting and less engaging.

A second reason for creating art, as we have stated above, is that it has a purpose, from a utilitarian standpoint. Shearer West, in his book *Portraiture*, discusses at length the reasons why portraits came to exist and the functions they fulfill. In this case, the creation of portraits is not seen as much as an aesthetic or artistic endeavor, but as a practical one. One should only think of the political function of portraits: when a leader has his portrait reproduced on a variety of media, such as coins, paintings, banners, etc., and has them distributed to the public and posted in a variety of places. These copies of the paintings will not only remind the viewer of the ruler's appearance, but 'also could spread that likeness everywhere and give a sense of omnipresence' (West, 2004, p. 67).

> Using portraits for political purposes was a tactic that was successfully used by Roman emperors, who ruled over vast areas without means of mass communication and who used such portraits as a means of creating a sense of unity and loyalty throughout the population.

Another important purpose of portraits was to stand in for the people they represented (West, 2004, p. 59). Having a portrait of a person of power, such as king or queen, was not only practically useful in order to deter conspirators or for documentary reasons, but they were also used in locations such as courthouses, or by local barons or lords in order show that they had been granted power by that person in the portrait. As such, a peasant coming to seek advice or judgment would know that he or she would receive it from a person who is a direct representative of the king, and, through this, of God. It is a powerful symbolic function of portraiture. One last historical function that must be noted is the documentary one. Lacking technological means, such as photography, 'portraits were the only way of conveying the appearance of an absent or unknown person, and they were a method of preserving the physical appearance of someone that would remain after their death' (West, 2004, p. 54).

However, the functions come more from a theory of art than from neuroaesthetics. Sadly, it is also highly impractical for neuroaesthetics to study these reasons for creating portraits, since they are historical elements pertaining to art history and anthropology. We have no scientific means to study the phenomenon from a historical neurological perspective. We can, nonetheless, try to draw conclusions from similar contemporary practices, like taking selfies. We find taking selfies as more than a documentary operation with regard to a given moment or context. Given the advent of social media, posting selfies online has become a means of showing off one's social, financial or moral status. What could be more similar to a noble person creating a portrait of himself, preferably in a flattering context, so that all people who encounter that portrait would be interacting with an idealized image, rather than with the true self, who could harbor defects?!

1. Why do people post selfies on social media?
2. What is the function of selfie editing in this context?

Ma Long and Zheng Lu created a study in which they tried to explore how one's personal traits, ego networks and Social Networking Services affect selfie posting behavior. They found out that two factors that positively correlate with selfie posting are a higher degree of opposite sex members in their network and a higher network density. Factors that correlated negatively with selfie posting were embeddedness in a strong-tie network. So, those who were in connection with more members of the opposite sex and those who had larger audiences tended to post more selfies, while those who had stronger ties with individuals in their network had a smaller tendency to do so. The study concludes that one's ego network exerts strong influences on the way we post selfies on social media (Ma & Zheng, 2023).

We can draw on this study and say that selfie posting on social media is linked to one's image and how he or she wants to project it. Selfies are a form of self-portraiture and it seems to mirror the individualistic mentality that pushed portraiture from the Enlightenment to the present day. Shearer West points out that portraiture as a means of preserving an individual and presenting their specific traits is largely a Western idea, linked to the cult of personality that can be seen in Western culture, in contrast with Oriental philosophy, which is centered on a lack of individuality, and where portraits and similar artistic practices such as mask-making, focus on universal features, emotions and events (West, 2004).

The only note-worthy difference between portraiture and selfie posting with regard to function is the expected impact. Historically, people who commissioned portraits wanted to preserve their image for the future and consolidate their connection to a family past. Contemporary selfie posting behavior focuses on an immediate response and engagement with a large number of people in a short period of time. This observation is in line with a study conducted by Jyotik Bhachech in 2021, which found that 'selfie and narcissism are closely linked among young adults and a matter of psychological wellbeing during personality development' (Bhachech, 2021). Thus, one of the main motivations behind taking selfies and especially behind posting them online is the affirmation of one's identity and, more than that, of the identity that one wants to portray (*persona*).

Shearer West points out that studies around portraiture must focus also on the degree of similitude between sitter and painting, as reflected in the negotiations that take place between sitter and painter:

> all portraits represent something about the body and face, on the one hand, and the soul, character, or virtues of the sitter, on the other. These first two aspects relate to portraiture as a form of representation, but a third consideration is concerned more with the processes of commissioning and production. All portraits involve a series of negotiations—often between the artist and the sitter, but sometimes there is also a patron who is not included in the portrait itself. The impact of these negotiations on the practice of portraiture must also be addressed. (West, 2004, p. 21)

It was mentioned above that one characteristic of portrait painting is that it was a negotiated endeavor and that imitating the image of the sitter was not necessarily the ultimate purpose. The degree to which the painter idealized the sitter's image or not depended on the relationship between sitter and painter and on the purpose of the portrait—to immortalize or to flatter. Similarly, in the case of selfies, we can observe the use of selfie editing, using filters. These filters can alter the image itself, acting as comical or as a semiotic tool, but can also only make the sitter more similar to beauty standards. With regard to the motivations (functions) of such actions, it is suggested that selfie editing is positively associated with cybervictimization and low self-esteem. It seems that body comparison with celebrities and models, who are considered to define and represent body standards is not correlated with selfie editing, unlike body comparison with peers. Selfie editing is also more frequent among those with social media addiction and considerably less frequent in those who manifest a high level of life satisfaction (Fastoso et al., 2021).

1. Selfies seem to be more frequent in people with narcissism and are a behavior centered around affirming one's identity.

2. Selfie editing is a process that is more frequent in those with low self-esteem, low life satisfaction and who tend to compare their body with those of their peers.

Returning to the problem of portraits, seen through the lens of selfie editing, we can safely assume that one of the main reasons behind idealizing sitters in portraits is the low self-esteem of the sitters. However, if editing selfies is a way of complying with beauty standards and if portraits are not a means of showing beauty, but status, then 'portrait editing' is a means of complying with the ideal socio-political stance of the time. That is why there are painting manuals developed throughout the ages that suggest poses or physiognomical ideals that transmit certain qualities or social positions. Also, we must keep in mind that the portrait is not only about the person who is portrayed, but also about everything else in the painting, from objects to scenery and even text. These all are codified aspects and reflect trends and fashions specific to certain periods and styles. These aspects create a detour from the aesthetic reasons behind the creation of art: sometimes painters do not choose to paint a nose in a certain manner or the sitter in a certain pose or scenery because the painter deems them beautiful or interesting, but because the sitter specifically asks for that or because it was considered fashionable to do so at that time. We can easily study the perceptual effect of a pose or scenery or physiognomy, but it is considerably more difficult to know the reasons behind the artistic choices of the painter.

It has become clear so far why portraits are commissioned and which functions they fulfill. How do artists, however, create beautiful art? And why do they create beautiful art and not ugly art? First, we must remember from previous chapters that beauty elicits activation in our value systems (see introduction). Thus, the artwork will be valued by those who buy it or admire it because this value system is positively activated. Therefore, the artist will naturally try to make his or her works beautiful for practical reasons.

What is interesting is that we will make something beautifully (even in the case of grotesque works or simple day-to-day objects) without specifically trying to achieve that. Mariselda Tessarolo argues that the artist becomes a user of his or her own work in the second he/she decides that the work is finished. At that moment of decision, he or she evaluates the work of art as any other user would (Tessarolo, 2015, p. 145). We would further this claim as such:

- The artist is a user of his or her own work with every glance he or she takes at the work. The artist takes the first stroke on a blank canvas and looks at it before the next stroke. He will then perceive the same aesthetic traits as any other user and evaluate them in the same manner. The completed work of art is attained through a succession of perceptions and valuations undertaken by the work's first user: the artist.

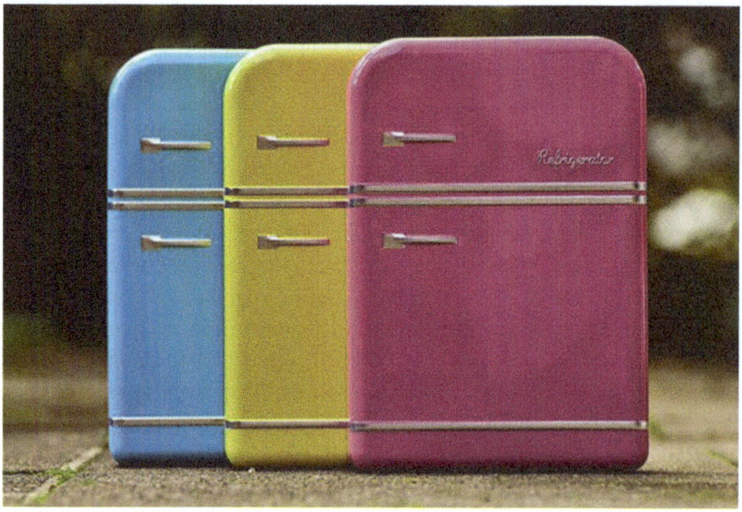

Fig. 3 Teodorescu—Beautiful utilitarian object—a fridge

It has been shown that even when given tasks such as thinking about the identity of those in a painting, the viewers make judgments in terms of beauty and the visual cortex reacts to beauty to the same extent as when we make intentional valuations with regard to beauty (Chatterjee, 2022, p. 49). This means that with each stroke of the brush, the artist will make automatic judgments of whether his or her creation is beautiful, even if the artist is focused on technical aspects. The photographer trying to photograph a given sight or animal or person will automatically decide while aiming his or her camera whether the photo he or she takes will be beautiful or not and because we are programmed to value more objects we perceive as beautiful in comparison to non-beautiful objects, the photographer will choose to take the most beautiful shot possible.

This tendency to achieve beauty is not only seen in artists, but in all human activities. If beauty valuation is automatic, it means that whatever one produces, he will choose to make it beautiful rather than ugly. With comparable effort, we will always try to produce a beautiful utilitarian object (a spoon or a car or a washing machine) rather than an object without aesthetic qualities, except in the specific case in which ugliness is a desired quality in that productive activity. Also, given that people value beauty, for the same cost they will always choose to buy the most beautiful variant of the utilitarian object (assuming equal utilitarian technical aspects) possible. If they cost about the same and if they consumed just as much electricity, and had the same dimensions and capacity, people would tend to buy the fridge in Fig. 3 over the one in Fig. 4. Thus, we can speak of a form of beauty-centered socio-cultural selection of the most beautiful objects that further makes us strive to create beauty in all artificial objects.

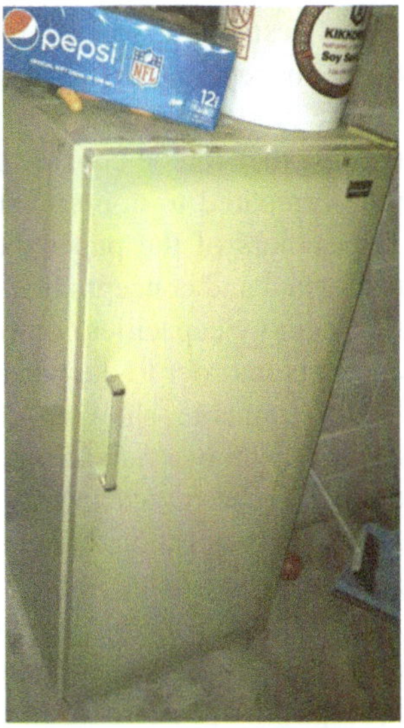

Fig. 4 Teodorescu—Not-so-beautiful utilitarian object—a fridge

Viewing the creation of aesthetic objects from a socio-cultural evolution point of view can also explain the tendency of artists to search for novel modes of expression. Edward Vessel (Vessel et al., 2022, p. 62) shows that humans prefer viewing scenes that are novel and that have a high degree of interpretability. Artists, in order to have their works be bought and appreciated try to achieve novelty and an unstable semiotic structure in their art. Going back to the idea that artists are the first viewers of their own creation, they will also try to imbue their art with novelty from this perspective, as they will prefer creating art that interests them as viewers, above all.

Vessel also found in the same study (Vessel et al., 2022) that we prefer stimuli that present a learning opportunity for the observer, while also being within the reach of the viewer's understanding. We started this chapter arguing that artists create because they have a point to express. It is similar to having a thesis and, hence, a learning opportunity for the viewers. This, from the standpoint of the evolution of culture, would prove why the viewers also prefer works of art which are based on a point, in comparison with those which are not.

The last inquiry that we feel we must make is with regard to the creators of art themselves. What makes one an artist? Christy Mag Uidhir and Cameron Buckner propose altering the classical Theory of Art, saying that art is not defined by having artistic properties, but by being created by an artist, possessing an artistic concept and artistic expertise. They also define expertise as those distinctive psychological capacities required for art that we find best represented in master artists (Mag & Buckner, 2014).

►The Aesthetic-Concept Theory of Art states that all artworks are based on an aesthetic concept and that possessing or employing that artistic concept is constitutive for the production of that work of art Mag & Buckner, 2014.
Experts that can be considered master artists will possess superior memory capacities compared to non-experts, in the field in which they exercise their activities. The authors of the paper theorize that these capacities are due in part to higher perceptual and conceptual abilities. Experts have long been known to possess superior memory capacities compared to novices and being able to use superior abstract concepts in order to decode and describe what they perceive. Also, these skills are largely trainable, showing that the contribution of innate talents to artistic expertise has been overrated. Even in the respect of higher perceptual abilities, they are thought to be rooted in constant and deliberate practice with the specific stimuli of the art in question. What seems to distinguish expert artists in comparison with artists in other fields is their higher flexibility in their perceptions of the environment and them being less likely to fall into rigid patterns of perceiving. Thus, unlike other fields, where expertise would depend exactly on the acquisition of rigid patterns, 'expertise in the arts may consist precisely in not falling into such patterns' (Mag & Buckner, 2014).

In conclusion, perceiving and aesthetic valuation in art is considerably easier to study than the creation of art. Creation is something done in a variety of ways and contexts and is usually context-dependent. Creation has a higher degree of individuation, because beauty itself is a subjective thing, even if its neurological imprint is universal (Di Dio, & Gallese, 2022, p. 23). This makes it harder to isolate and study. However, the findings of neuroaesthetics with regard to perception and valuation can be successfully transferred to theories about the creation of art because artists are themselves perceivers of their own art. Integrating these findings into existing theories from domains such as the philosophy of art seems a valuable direction for neuroaesthetics, at least for the time being.

This chapter highlights the main reasons behind creating art in general and portraits in particular, which are centered around manifesting one's identity, conveying a message or an idea and socio-political reasons such as standing in for a given person and creating a cult of personality around a ruler. Also, this chapter shows that what lies at the base of creating art is the artist's exceptional perceptual capacity in his or her art field, coupled with the needed technical skill for attaining the intent of the artist. Moreover, we have highlighted the lack of studies in neuroaesthetics with regard to the creation of art and of aesthetic objects, while also pointing out the main difficulties in designing such studies, mainly the fact that creation is very hard to isolate and define, especially in the field of art.

References

Bhachech, J. (2021). Selfie and narcissism in young adults. *Tazkiya Journal of Psychology, 9*, 153–163. https://doi.org/10.15408/tazkiya.v9i2.21558

Brown, S. (2022). Naturalizing aesthetics. In A. Chatterjee & E. R. Cardillo (Eds.), *Brain, beauty and art: Essays bringing neuroaesthetics into focus* (pp. 18–21). Oxford University Press. https://doi.org/10.1093/oso/9780197513620.003.0004

Chatterjee, A. (2022). Beautiful people in the brain of the beholder. In A. Chatterjee & E. R. Cardillo (Ed.), *Brain, beauty and art: Essays bringing neuroaesthetics into focus* (pp. 48–52). Oxford University Press. https://doi.org/10.1093/oso/9780197513620.003.0004

Di Dio, C., & Gallese, V. (2022). Moving toward emotions in the aesthetic experience. In A. Chatterjee & E. Cardillo (Eds.). *Brain, beauty, and art: Essays bringing neuroaesthetics into Focus*. Oxford University Press. https://doi.org/10.1093/oso/9780197513620.003.0013

Fastoso, F., Gonzalez-Jimenez, H., & Cometto, T. (2021). Mirror, mirror on my phone: Drivers and consequences of selfie editing. *Journal of Business Research, 133*(C), 365–375. https://doi.org/10.1016/j.jbusres.2021.05.002

Ma, L., & Zheng, L. (2023) Ego-networks, SNSs affordances, and personalities: understanding individuals' selfie posting on SNSs based on Actor-Network Theory. *Behaviour & Information Technology*, 1–16. https://doi.org/10.1080/0144929X.2023.2177824

Mag, U. C., & Buckner, C. (2014). A portrait of the artist as an aesthetic expert. In G. Currie, M. Kieran, & A. Meskin (Eds.), *Aesthetics and the sciences*. Oxford University Press. https://doi.org/10.1093/acprof:oso/9780199669639.003.0007

Menzel, C., Kovács, G., Hayn-Leichsenring, G. U., & Redies, C. (2022). *Is artistic composition in abstract art detected automatically?* In A. Chatterjee & E. R. Cardillo (Eds.), *Brain, beauty and art: Essays bringing neuroaesthetics into focus* (pp. 102–107). Oxford University Press. https://doi.org/10.1093/oso/9780197513620.003.0004

Schwabe, K., Menzel, C., Mullin, C., Wagemans, J., & Redies, C. (2018). Gist perception of image composition in abstract artworks. *I-Perception, 9*(3), 2041669518780797. https://doi.org/10.1177/2041669518780797

Seeley, W. P. (2022). Artists, Artworks, aesthetics, cognition. In A. Chatterjee & E. R. Cardillo (Eds.), *Brain, beauty and art: Essays bringing neuroaesthetics into focus* (pp. 132–137). Oxford University Press. https://doi.org/10.1093/oso/9780197513620.003.0004

Tessarolo, M. (2015). The last 'touch' turns the artist into a user: The body, the mind and the social aspect of art. In A. Scarinzi (Ed.), *Aesthetics and the embodied mind: Beyond art theory and the cartesian mind-body dichotomy* (Vol. 73, pp. 141–157). Contributions To Phenomenology. Springer, Dordrecht.

Tuckwell, J. (2018). *Creation and the function of art. Techne, Poiesis and the Problem of aesthetics*. Bloomsbury Academic, an imprint of Bloomsbury Publishing Plc.

Vartanian, O., & Chatterjee, A. (2022). The aesthetic triad. In A. Chatterjee & E. R. Cardillo (Ed.), *Brain, beauty and art: Essays bringing neuroaesthetics into focus* (pp. 27–31). Oxford University Press. https://doi.org/10.1093/oso/9780197513620.003.0004

Vessel, E. A., Yue, X., & Biederman, I. (2022). Scene preferences, aesthetic appeal and curiosity: Revisting the neurobiology of the infovore. In A. Chatterjee & E. Cardillo (Eds.), *Brain, beauty, and art: Essays bringing neuroaesthetics into focus* (pp. 61–66). Oxford University Press. https://doi.org/10.1093/oso/9780197513620.003.0013

West, S. (2004). *Portraiture*. Oxford University Press.

Unit 3 Lesson: Using Reaction Time and Mixed Models

Christer Johansson and Per Olav Folgerø

This lesson will introduce some concepts related to **empirical** studies and **statistical evaluation**. The focus is on evaluating a specified model with controlled **fixed factors** and several **control variables** in the context that we have *one continuous dependent variable*, such as reaction time.

It should be noted that it is important to clearly *state the expectations* before collecting data and that we assume a **null hypothesis** of no difference for our fixed factors. If we observe a **significant** difference for any of our fixed factors the difference can be explained in many ways, but a **first assumption** is that we can *take a gamble* and claim that there is a **real** difference, given that the probability of observing a difference by random chance is appropriately small. If there is a real difference this real difference may warrant an **explanation**, or at least an **interpretation**.

One general explanation for faster reaction times, associated with a factor, is that somehow the mental processing leading up to the decision to press a button, for our subjects, is easier. We may then talk about **facilitation**, or **priming**, i.e., that the processing was prepared, for example if there is evidence that information

The original version of the chapter has been revised. A correction to this chapter can be found at https://doi.org/10.1007/978-3-031-42323-9_22

C. Johansson (✉) · P. O. Folgerø
University of Bergen, Bergen, Norway
e-mail: Christer.Johansson@uib.no

P. O. Folgerø
e-mail: Per.Folgero@uib.no

T. Balinisteanu and K. Priest (eds.), *Neuroaesthetics*,
https://doi.org/10.1007/978-3-031-42323-9_9

was presented before the decision that made the decision more fluent, and thus easier and faster. We would like that accuracy is unaffected, or at least equally good, so that the results are not simply due to a tradeoff between speed and accuracy.

Similarly, the experimental paradigm might predict **interference** when a decision is taken based on competing resources drawing on similar resources. For example, if there is a choice between two items, the more conflict or the closer the items are, the harder it is to take a decision. However, people can have different preferences in such situations. One possible strategy for making close decisions could be that if two items are equal, it matters less which choice is made, both are good, or both are bad. This could be observed in a tendency to make a default choice, such as pressing the most frequent choice, or pressing the right hand side button, for right handed people.

It is not always possible to determine what the correct decision was or was supposed to be. In those cases, we may want supporting evidence, for example showing relevant correlations with other factors, for example features of the input, and showing that those correlations are not random. Argumentation is needed, and the formal results are typically not clearly associated with one and only one possible interpretation.

We are often interested in the intuitive fast decisions that people make given the available information, possibly in situations where the difficulty of the choice is varied. Ideally, we would like to exhaustively contrast the possibilities, but we should recognize that this is not always possible, for example because time is limited.

The **dependent variable** is typically a measurement that we want to explain by, or relate to, *fixed independent variables* that we can control and vary within the experiment. We are interested in the degree that we can influence the dependent variable by changing the value of our fixed variables in a principled way. We need the dependent variable to be a preferentially continuous variable on an interval scale, which means that we know that a change of one unit is worth the same wherever we are. One example is reaction time. One millisecond is the same time interval wherever we are on the scale, and wherever we are in the world. If the measurement also includes an absolute zero, meaning that 0 means absolutely nothing of whatever we measure we may also say something about proportions. The reaction times were twice as long, assume that there is such a thing as an absence of reaction time, simultaneous reaction to stimulus. However, it takes time from the presentation of the stimulus to the decision and the reaction. The real starting point is thus sometime after the stimulus has been presented, depending on how long it takes to perceive the stimulus. In real life, human reaction times cannot realistically be much smaller than 200ms, as it takes time to process that which we should react to, and it takes time to send the signal from our brain to the finger to activate the muscle that should press the button.

The **independent variable**s are the variables that we manipulate, or control, to affect the dependent variable. These are the **fixed effects** that we want to investigate. Fixed effects have a limited and exhaustive number of levels, and ideally, we should have included all those in our experiment. Example of a **condition** related to a fixed variable is if the **target stimulus** that we should react to is **primed** or not. Generally, we like conditions to be two levels, either primed or not primed, as it is easier to interpret the statistical model if this is the case. In the **experimental design**, we like to balance the conditions we are interested in, for example such that we have an equal number of primed and unprimed **events**. In this case, the unprimed is our **baseline**, and in the analysis, we could name the levels such that the **baseline** is included in the **intercept**, i.e., in the starting point of our regression equation.

The **control variables** are variables that we know, or suspect will affect the dependent variable, but these variables are not necessarily planned factors that we are interested in. Since they affect the dependent variable, without being a properly controlled independent variable (a fixed effect), we would like to regress out their effect. Examples of such variables are the **learning effect**, the effect of **hesitation**, the effect of **making an error** in the previous event, the effect of **exceptionally slow or fast responses** (positive and negative outliers), and the effect of having such an outlier in the previous response. Other examples are to control for the exact onset time of the stimuli we are interested in and to control the linear distance between say a **prime** and a **target**. A prime is an item that is presented before the target and is thought to affect the response to the target. The prime and the target could be placed at slightly different distances. With **continuous temporal stimuli**, like a speech signal, we can measure the time between the onset of the prime and the target. In a **discrete design**, it could be the number of items (typically written words) between them. Those effects could also be related to the conditions we are interested in. For example, it could be that the learning effect is larger for one of the conditions. This can be controlled by adding the **estimation of a slope** for each condition. A slope is the change in the response that depends on the condition compared to a baseline.

The aim of the model is to explain as much of the variance in the data as possible. Our tool for creating such models is **linear regression**, and **mixed effects models with random effects** in particular. In a linear regression, we try to estimate a baseline, the **intercept**, and estimate the change that our variables will have. For example, what is the effect of seeing a prime word compared to no prime word? The learning effect, and such control variables, can be **fitted regression lines** that depend on a numerical value to calculate the effect on the response variable, i.e., the dependent variable. Once the regression line is fitted it accounts for some variance, and thus the *estimates for the controlled fixed effects will become more precise*, as the effect of the control variables has been accounted for. In real experiments, there will be correlations between the variables that can be difficult to entangle, but the model makes a principled attempt at separating the sources of variance in the data.

There obviously need to be fairly large amounts of data, to estimate the effects of all the included variables. The restriction to a linear model helps. Linear equations have the property that adding the estimation of a factor (i.e., adding the estimation of a line) will result in a new linear equation, which can be solved if there is enough independent data.

Thus, to be able to estimate a line, for each subject, *we need at least two points*. It is a problem that subjects may have no responses which could potentially make it impossible to estimate lines. Therefore, we need to have more data points from each condition. A common **rule of thumb** is to have at least four data points in each of the conditions. For example, if we have a 2 by 2 design (say, two levels of prime and two levels of targets), we minimally need 4*2*2 (i.e., 16) **balanced** data points from each subject. Ideally, we aim for an equal number of data points in each condition, so to keep the balance in this example, increments will be in steps of four (2 by 2).

The data should ideally be balanced for other factors too, for example if we plan to use **gender** as an explanatory factor, we will need roughly the same number of each gender in our sample of subjects. Another common **rule of thumb** is that we need at least a thousand data points in total, assuming a small number of fixed effects. From this we can **estimate the number of subjects** needed in our study. If we increase the number of data points per subject, we will be able to better control the influence of individual variance, and if we do this by including more diverse test items, we will also better control the variance that is due to test items. In our example, the minimal number of subjects would thus be 64, as 1000 / 16 = 62.4, and if we balanced the genders we would need 32 of each gender. Here, we ignore the problems that arise from balancing the gender that the subjects might identify with. Some of that problem is handled by including a random factor for individual variance, rather than expanding the gender variable.

We need to consider *how much data we can collect from each subject*. In reaction time experiments, we can expect a subject to be concentrated for up to 20 minutes, and allowing 10 seconds for each test item (including presentation and reaction) would set a limit of 120 items per subject. Your experiment may have different demands. In the example, this would allow for 30 test items in a total of four conditions. Following the logic above, this would mean that minimally we need 10 subjects with 120 data points from each subject (1000 / 120 = 8.33, and the nearest higher even number is 10).

It is recommended to sample more than the minimum and to balance subject and item demands. If we go for 20 subjects and 16 test items in four conditions, we end up with 1280 data points in total, which is *close to the minimal demand*. We should also anticipate that not all subjects can be included. We may expect between 5 and 10 percent of the subjects to be excluded as outliers. That would mean adding 2 extra subjects to compensate. However, recall that if for some reason more outliers are detected we will get an underpowered study. If possible, we should add at least 25 percent of subjects, which will result in 20 + 5 subjects. Recall that it is *difficult to add more items*, as that would likely exceed the limit for fatigue in the subjects. If we discover that the planned number of subjects is too large to be realistic, we might consider repeating the study to sample more data from the same subjects. This might also allow us to test for the effect of repeating the study. In a longitudinal study, there is always a risk that the subjects will not return to the second session.

Ideally, we would like our study to generalize to the full population. However, this would mean that we would need to actively include a balanced sample from all the relevant sub-populations. A common choice is therefore to focus on a sub-population. This sub-population is typically a **convenience sample**. At a university, students between 18 and 32 might be a convenient sample. This limits generalization, but it also helps to control variance. University students are a pre-selected sample and may represent not only the young in the population, but also those with an interest in study and related to that better reading ability, and possibly better working memory capacity and reasoning skills. This may also result in better compliance with instructions. If the subjects in turn may help with recruiting new subjects, we may talk about a **snowball sample** approach. This can be actively used to test the effects of social networks, but often the recruiting strategy is just reported in the resulting article and is up to the external reviewers to evaluate if it is a reasonable choice. There is no such thing as an optimal research design, and limits on available resources are often an important part of the research. This will also allow other researchers to repeat the research under similar or other conditions. The proof of the pudding is in the tasting, and for experiments we are interested in how much variance is explained and in how easy it is to repeat the results. In that process, we will find out more details, and some of those details may be more important than the original study.

A last point, before moving on to another example. A **laboratory-controlled experiment** may often be unnatural, which in turn may affect the relevance of the study. For example, we may focus on reaction time for decision tasks, but such tasks might be only weakly related to the phenomena we study. Sometimes it is argued that **ecological validity** should be valued as well. That is, how well the task matches with what people are doing in the wild, outside of the laboratory. Control and ecological validity are often in opposition, but ecological validity is not only about bad control of variables, but also about allowing other sources of variance to estimate the true variance more closely. Ideally, different experiments may complement each other, or at least raise important and interesting questions.

Let us investigate a potential experiment, comparing faces in a hot-or-not contest, except that we will ask participants to pick the face that is either more attractive or separately the face that is more trustworthy. The faces are constructed from real faces morphed with a Jesus prototype. Each face can be labeled for the male or female substrate. Will people be able to detect which faces are male and which are female? Will the results be different between the attractiveness condition and the trustworthy condition. The dependent variable is the reaction time, i.e., the time it takes to make a choice.

Each face has slightly different facial features that can be measured in the pictures. We will look at features that indicate left/right symmetry in the face, the eyes, and the mouth. There is well-known research (the so-called Thatcher effect) that established that we typically judge eyes and mouth separately. We will also look at features such as how wide the eyes are apart, and how wide the mouth is. Furthermore, we will look at the proportion of the face in the vertical direction: how large is the forehead, the mid-section, and the chin. These measurements will be continuous measurements of proportions, which makes them scale-free, i.e., there is no measurement unit just proportions that can be compared regardless of how large the face is. All faces will be approximately the same size as they are presented on screen.

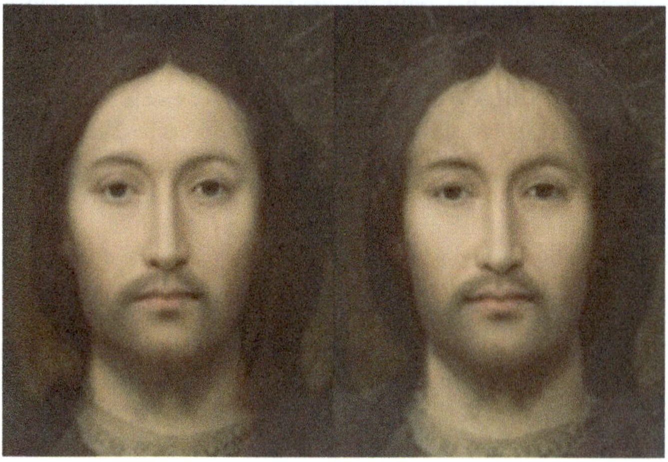

Fig. 1 Female and male competition: Attractiveness (female winner left, male winner right)

We will control the order of presentation. We expect the participants to make increasingly faster decisions as they get more familiar with the task. This learning effect can be handled by regression analysis, after we have made the order of presentation explicit in our data. The typical experimental program will give the order of presentation implicitly but will not create a variable for the order of presentation.

We will use the gender of the two pictures presented in pairs on the screen. The competition could be female–male (two directions), female–female, and male–male. This may interact with the gender of the selected picture, and the gender of the subject.

It might also interact with the gender preferences of the participants. This will be handled as a random effect that may explain more variance.

An example is given below (Figs. 1 and 2). Would you pick the same in each pair if it was a choice of attractiveness or a choice of trust? Can you identify the male and female substrates?

A Model of Face Proportions

The line K–L is the baseline for the horizontal dimension. This reference line is found by estimating the position of the zygomaticus bone, using information also from the ear lobes and the nose tip. The line G–H is the baseline in the vertical direction. This line is estimated from the highest point of the forehead to the lowest point of the chin, following the nose and through the philtrum. The point I is on the G_L and is the reference point for eye symmetry. The point J is similarly the reference point for mouth symmetry.

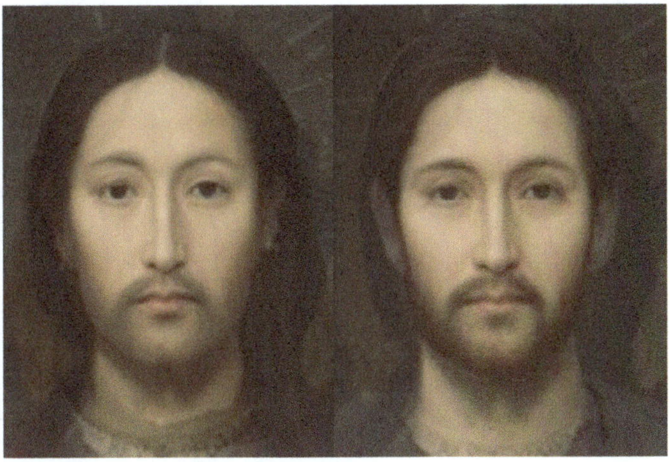

Fig. 2 Female and male competition: Trustworthiness (female winner left, male winner right)

The forehead is estimated by the area of triangle CGD compared to the larger triangle KGD.

The chin is estimated by the area of the triangle EHF similarly compared to KGD.

The mid-section is estimated by the area of the polygon KCDL compared to the larger polygon KGLH. Furthermore, the slant of the eyeline is estimated as the lower angle between CD and GH, and similarly for the slant of the mouth line, as marked in Fig. 3.

The face's right side is estimated by the area of the triangle GKH, and its left side is by GLH.

If GKH divided by GLH is larger than 1 the face's right side is larger, if smaller than one its left side is larger, and perfect symmetry is at a ratio of 1.

To visualize multi-factorial data of the same kind (e.g., proportions) we can use Correspondence Analysis (CA), cf. Glynn, 2014. This is just to mention the possibility. CA often gives a quick and intuitive overview of a dataset, as it projects a multitude of factors into a 2D plane. The points that are closer to the origin (0,0) are more as expected. The further from the origin the more distinct, and points that are close are more similar, but we should also value the angle of the line toward the origin. Points that are both close and have close angles are more the same. The axes of the CA graph are often possible to interpret, using the most extreme points along the x and y axes. In Fig. 4 we see an association from mouth width to mouth symmetry along the x axis, and from eye width (and proportion of mid-section, associated with eyes) to eye symmetry along the y axis. This has been detected by the algorithm from a limited set of investigated faces (marked in red, row points) and their anatomical proportions (marked in blue, anatomical column points). The clusters indicate prototypical faces (female (F#), male (MP#), human (H#)), Romanian Faces (X#), Men (M#), and Women(W#).

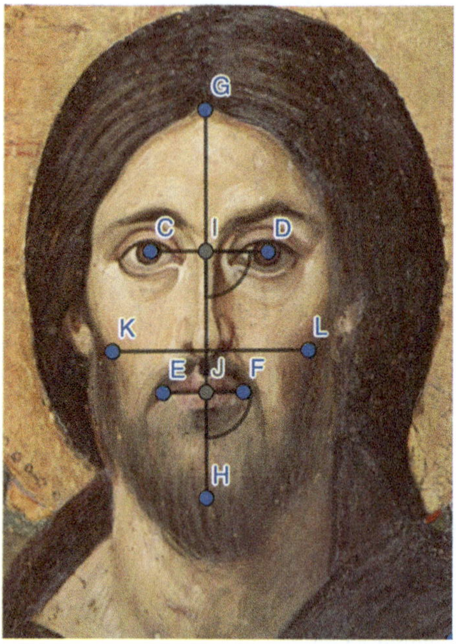

Fig. 3 Face proportions

Outlier Analysis

There are typically three types of outliers. The first is an analysis of the performance of the subjects. The subjects could solve the task differently. Given that there is a task that could be evaluated to be correct or not, it is possible to see if a subject has chosen more of the "incorrect" than other participants. One way to do this is to perform an association analysis. This is based on a cross-table analysis of the distribution of correct and incorrect answers for each subject. In each of the cells it is possible to calculate the **Pearson residual** (proportional to the contribution toward significance, **cf.** Cohen, 1980; Friendly, 1992) and the support in that cell, which is proportional to the number of observations in that cell. This type of analysis may objectively reveal if some subjects have solved the task in a different manner than other subjects. We do not know if their way of solving the task is better or worse, but we do know that it is likely to be different. For example, some subjects might always choose one of the decision buttons (for example, the left one). For some tasks it is not possible to know which decision is correct, but we may still see if the participants give similar answers and figure out if some of the participants have solved the task using some unintended strategy. We may also analyze the reaction times of each participant. Some people are faster than others, and this can be handled by having different **intercepts** (starting points) for each subject. However, it could also be that some subjects are faster because they solve the task in a different way, for example always pressing one of the buttons. In the analysis, we should pay attention to both the **trend** (e.g., the average time) and the

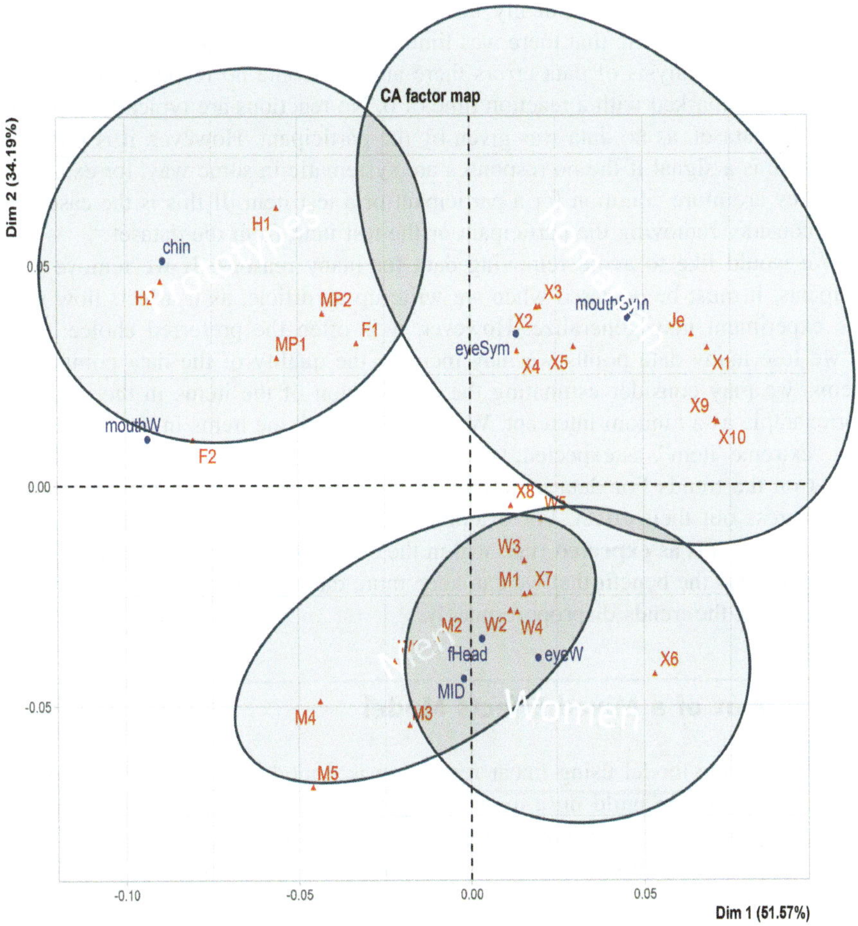

Fig. 4 CA map

variance (standard deviation). A significantly lower standard deviation may be an indicator, especially if this is combined with a low performance on the accuracy of the task. A significantly higher standard deviation might be an indicator that the subject has been unsure of the task or possibly been inattentive. It could also be that they have a stronger reaction, and this might be interesting.

In the item analysis, we are interested in the representativeness of our test items, i.e., the items that the participants are supposed to react to. Some items may be more interesting, or easier or harder to process, etc. This could be handled by different **intercepts** (starting points) for each item in the random effects analysis. It could also be that some items should be marked as outliers, and possibly removed from the data.

In the analysis of the data, we should look at those reactions that are outside of a **confidence interval** for the data. Those items that are slower than the trend plus two standard deviations are typically marked as outliers, as well as those items that are faster than the trend minus two standard deviations. We should also mark those items that are unrealistically fast. Items that are faster than 200ms are so fast that it is unrealistic that there was time enough to take a decision and press a button. In the analysis of data errors there are also some no responses (NR) that typically are marked with a reaction time of 0. No reactions are typically removed from the dataset, as no data was given by the participant. However, it is possible that there is a signal if the no responses are systematic in some way, for example, that they are more common for a participant or a test item. If this is the case, we may consider removing the participant or the test item from the dataset.

We would like to avoid removing data for many reasons. If we remove participants, it must be declared when we write up an article, as it affects how well the experiment may generalize. However, it is often the preferred choice, even if we lose many data points we may increase the quality of the data points. For items, we may consider estimating the contribution of the items in the analysis, for example as a random intercept. We may also mark the items in an item factor, say "extreme_item", as expected, too fast, or too slow, and try to regress out their effect on the trends For data we might see if it is better to mark the data points and regress out their effect. For example, we may have a factor "extreme" that tells if the data is as **expected** (i.e., within the confidence interval), too **fast**, or too **slow**. This has the benefit that we can keep more data, without letting the extreme values affect the trends disproportionately.

The Format of a Mixed Effects Model

A mixed effects model using linear regression is a model-based evaluation of an experiment. We can build up a model using the factors we suspect will have an effect, the correlations we think will play a role, and the sources of variance we know about. One philosophy is to start with a maximal model and reduce that model as necessary. Another philosophy is to start with a minimal model and add factors if they improve the model fit. Here we will suggest starting with a large model with interactions and looking at model fit. We may have to reduce the model if the model fails to converge (i.e., the model cannot be solved using the available data).

In R the format for the models can be stated as:

$$\mathbf{dependent} \sim \mathbf{factor1} * \mathbf{factor2} * \mathbf{factor3} * \mathbf{factor4} +$$
$$+ \mathbf{control1} + \mathbf{control2} + \mathbf{control3} + \mathbf{control4} + \mathbf{control5} + \mathbf{control6} + \mathbf{control7} +$$
$$+ \mathbf{outlier} +$$
$$+ (1|\mathbf{Participant}) + (1|\mathbf{Item})$$

The measurement variable (**dependent**) is explained by (~) the fixed factors 1…4, the control variables 1 … 5, the starting points of each Participant and Item. Testing for an interaction effect is noted by the use of a "*". An interaction between two items is when their independent values do not add up when they are together, at the same time. A common day example, if you buy eggs and bacon together you may pay less than if you buy them separately because you have a rebate coupon when buying them together. A four way interaction between four factors as indicated above, relabeled for brevity as a, b, c, and d, will give rise to more than three interaction terms, in fact there will be four main effects (a, b, c, d) and 11 interactions (ab, ac, ad, bc, bd, cd, abc, abd, acd, bcd, abcd). This is obviously very costly to estimate. We can decide to only consider the main effects by using a different operator between the factors, i.e., a "+". It is often not possible to estimate the interaction between everything, because of lack of data and because of the correlation structure in the dataset. The inclusion of an interaction is useful if it explains data better, and models with and without an interaction can be compared using analysis of variance, as outlined by Baayen and Milin (2010).

The last two items in the formula above are called **random factors** that estimate the variance between the Participants and the Items. The Items are the controlled stimuli that the Participants will decide. An item is here thought of as an event, i.e., a test item presented in a specific context. It is also possible to structure the Items such that an item is presented in many different contexts and the formula will then be represented as (context | Item_name). Here we will prefer the notation with a different intercept for each presented stimulus (1|Item). The random effects are used to estimate the variance due to Participants and Items.

The fixed factors in the example experiment that we described earlier could be: **SelectedGender**, **CompetingGender**, **ParticipantGender**, and **Condition**.

Condition is whether the task is related to **trust** or **beauty**.

The control variables could be **PresentationOrder**, **FaceSymmetrySelected**, **MouthSymmetrySelected**, **MouthWidthSelected**, **EyeSymmetrySelected**, **EyeWidthSelected**, **MIDproportionSelected,** and **outlier**.

The presentation order is a measure of *learning*. The more items the participant has seen the faster the responses. This may be because the participant has learned something about the task and the items used in the testing, and/or has become more confident. Typical effects are about 5 ± 1ms faster per item seen, depending on the task.

The various measures of symmetry and relative width of eyes and mouth are anatomical scale-less proportions related to attractiveness. Attractiveness may lead to faster responses. However, one hypothesis is that the effects would be different for trust and beauty. Rather than having one very large model that investigates the interaction between all the control variables and the experimental condition, we might test trust and beauty separately in two similar models, to avoid very complicated interaction terms. The **outlier** factor marks if the data point is as **expected** inside the confidence interval, or if it is **faster** or **slower**.

Evaluating the Model

The model generated by the mixed effects analysis can be evaluated using an analysis of variance on the model. This will tell us which factors show significant differences and which correlation lines show significant trends. The call in

Table 1 The analysis of the model, in a table from analysis of variance

	Sum Sq	Mean Sq	NumDF	DenDF	F value	Pr(>F)	
factor1	#	#	1	45.04	9.1539	0.0041	**
factor2	#	#	1	173.84	15.5468	0.0001	***
control1	#	#	1	1585.65	255.67	1E-16	***
factor1 × factor2	#	#	1	45.02	0.6693	0.4176	

Type III Analysis of Variance Table with Satterthwaite's method

R is simply **anova**(model). To get the full model, including the effects, we use a different call: **summary**(model).

As an example, consider a simpler model below.

> anova(model)

The sum squares can be useful and should be reported in a full table, as in Table 1. Here we focus on the information that is often stated in an article text. Here, **factor1** is significant (F(1, 45.04) = 9.15; p = 0.0041) and **factor2** is significant (F(1, 173.84) = 15.55; p = 0.0001). The regression line associated with **control1** is significant (F(1, 1585.65) = 255.67, p = 0.0000). The so-called *scientific notation* 1E-16 denotes that 1 is 16 decimals behind the decimal point, which is a very small number. There is no significant interaction between the two factors.

NumDF denotes the degrees of freedom between (which is a measure of the useful contrasts, here there are only two levels and thus one contrast). DenDF denotes the degrees of freedom within, which is a measure of the number of independent data points that was used—this is estimated mathematically, and it includes using correlations rather than the typical paired "*repeated measures*" structure. Satterthwaite's method is a reference to how this number has been estimated. Thus within degrees of freedom is a measure of how many independent data points were used to arrive at the estimate of significance. The F-value quantifies the deviance from expectations, and together with the between and within degrees of freedom it is possible to arrive at a p-value that we can use to take a decision for what constitutes a significant difference between the levels for the factor. The p-value is the probability of observing an F-value larger than the observed F-value, given the between and within degrees of freedom (i.e., the number of contrasts, and the size of the experiment).

If we want to see the resulting effects, we need to look at the summary of the model. Below, we will focus on the fixed effects (including the control variables). The correlation matrix and the random effects are typically not as "important" but should typically be included for reference in an appendix.

In Table 2, we start with the intercept. The intercept is the value associated with level1 of factor1 and factor2 and the starting point (0) of the regression line in control1. This value is here 1519.65. The values for the various factor levels must be calculated from the **offsets** in the table. Note that for the result of the

Table 2 Table of effects

	Estimate	Std. Error	df	t value	Pr(>|t|)	
(Intercept)	1519.65	442.12	46.8	3.437	0.0011	**
factor1Level2	184.88	66.85	44.9	2.766	0.0082	**
factor2Level2	−333.58	105.87	157.6	−3.151	0.0019	**
control1	−6.51	0.77	1576.1	−16.66	1E-16	***
factor1Level2 × factor2Level2	−76.45	93.45	45.02	−0.82	0.4176	

Table 3 Calculating the value for each combination of factor levels

factor1	factor2		
level1	level1	1519.65	
level2	level1	1519.65 **+ 184.88**	1704.53
level1	level2	1519.65 **− 333.58**	1186.07
level2	level2	1519.65 + 184.88 − 333.58 **− 76.45**	1294.50

interaction effect we first do the pure additive effects and then the effect due to interaction (see Table 3). For the regression line associated with control1 we get 6.51ms faster for each item, i.e., 1519.65 -6.51*control1 is the reaction time after control1 number of presentations. If we want to correct the dependent (reaction times) for this controlled "learning" effect we can cancel out the effect with a simple calculation (RT + 6.51*control1) as the corrected reaction time. This may be necessary for generating more accurate graphs.

Common graphs to illustrate the results include boxplots and interaction plots, and sometimes so-called lattice plots to investigate the interaction of more than two factors. Typically, these graphs are performed using the raw data, but if we have significant effects of control variables it might be worth considering correcting the dependent variable. This is easy to do for control variables that are main effect correlation, i.e., general regression lines that are not dependent on the combination of other factors.

Interpreting the Results

The formal analysis of our model will tell us which factors have a significant impact on the dependent variable. The word "significant" is used in the statistical sense and does not necessarily mean that this is an important difference. It just means that the impact is difficult to explain by random uncertainty in the data. However, variance and uncertainty can have causes that are not controlled in the experiment, and the causal structure might be different from the assumption in our model. There is always a chance or risk that other factors could explain the data better. We might have attributed a tentative causation where there is no causation, and what looks like a causal relation might just be a correlation.

When we have the results from the analysis it is therefore important that we interpret the results, and relate the results to our hypotheses, and other relevant research if such research exists. It is very often the case that we discover more detail and other predictions that can be tested when we explicitly argue for the interpretation of our findings. A model criticism might inform us of how well the model explains the data, and how much variance is still unexplained.

Summary

This lesson has introduced Mixed Effects models for evaluating experiments. First some vocabulary was introduced, and a brief introduction of some concerns when we plan an experiment. We need to know how many participants we need and how many items per participant we need. As it is likely that we will have outliers for participants, items, and data points, we would rather oversample. We introduced the use of control variables and some principles for outlier analysis, and finally how to interpret and report the result of the analysis.

Below is a short literature list. The presentation has assumed the availability of the **R Statistical Software**, the **lmerTest** package for *Linear Mixed Effects Models*, the **vcd** package for association graphs, and the package **FactoMiner** for *Correspondance Analysis*. It is possible to use other software to implement the formal analysis. R and all the mentioned packages are currently widely available for free download.

Literatures

Baayen, R. H., & Milin, P. (2010). Analyzing reaction times. *International Journal of Psychological Research, 3*(2), 12–28. https://doi.org/10.21500/20112084.807

Cohen, A. (1980). On the graphical display of the significant components in a two-way contingency table. *Communications in Statistics—Theory and Methods, A9*, 1025–1041.

Friendly, M. (1992). Graphical methods for categorical data. *SAS User Group International Conference Proceedings, 17*, 190–200. http://www.math.yorku.ca/SCS/sugi/sugi17-paper.html

Glynn, D. (2014). Correspondence analysis: Exploring data and identifying patterns. In *Corpus methods for semantics: Quantitative studies in polysemy and synonymy* (D. Glynn & J. A. Robinson Ed., pp. 443–485). John Benjamins Publishing Company. http://digital.casalini.it/978 9027270337

Kuznetsova, A., Brockhoff, P. B., & Christensen, R. H. B. (2017). lmerTest package: Tests in linear mixed effects models. *Journal of Statistical Software, 82*(13), 1–26. https://doi.org/10.18637/jss.v082.i13

Lê, S., Josse, J., & Husson, F. (2008). FactoMineR: An *R* package for multivariate analysis. *Journal of Statistical Software, 25*(1), 1–18. https://doi.org/10.18637/jss.v025.i01

Meyer, D., Zeileis, A., & Hornik, K. (2006). The strucplot framework: Visualizing multi-way Contingency tables with vcd. *Journal of Statistical Software, 17*(3), 1–48. https://doi.org/10.18637/jss.v017.i03

Meyer, D., Zeileis, A., & Hornik, K. (2021). *vcd: Visualizing categorical data.* R package version 1.4-9.

R Core Team. (2022). *R: A language and environment for statistical computing.* R Foundation for Statistical Computing.

Zeileis, A., Meyer, D., & Hornik, K. (2007). Residual-based shadings for visualizing (conditional) independence. *Journal of Computational and Graphical Statistics, 16*(3), 507–525.

Unit 3 Lab: Gender and Prototypes

Christer Johansson and Per Olav Folgerø

Cards are printed out and laminated to make up a deck of high-quality cards consisting of 5 feminized prototypes (f), 5 masculinized prototypes (m), one Jesus prototype (jp), one male prototype (mp), and one female prototype (fp). The images can be marked for their category on the backside for easy reading of the results. The reason for using personalized prototypes is to make the task less obvious. The participants are asked to sort the images according to beauty, and they are not instructed that some images are more feminine than the other images.

Goals

Statistics: to familiarize students with statistical tests on ordinal data.

Experiment: to demonstrate a sorting task that can be performed without the use of computers. The task involves physical manipulation of objects and can be performed in a short time with very little training.

Variations: The instructions for how the cards should be sorted can be varied. We suggest attractiveness and trustworthiness, but other tasks might be to sort them according to a feminine to masculine scale.

Variant: If you perform more than one variant on each subject you should consider evaluating the tasks together for repeated measures on the same subject.

C. Johansson (✉) · P. O. Folgerø
University of Bergen, Bergen, Norway
e-mail: Christer.Johansson@uib.no

P. O. Folgerø
e-mail: Per.Folgero@uib.no

T. Balinisteanu and K. Priest (eds.), *Neuroaesthetics*,
https://doi.org/10.1007/978-3-031-42323-9_10

The presentation order of the tasks should also be varied. For three tasks there are 6 possible orders to consider: A B C, A C B, B A C, B C A, C A B, C B A.

Publication: For the statistics, we are relying on ordinal data. As ordinal data are not on an interval scale, it is difficult to use a model that assumes this, and similarly measures of variance are not readily available. More data is the main key to get convincing statistics. This can be accomplished by increasing the number of participants and increasing the number of cards. We will show one way of accounting for individual differences, by comparing the Wilcoxon scores between individuals, assuming only that the W scores can be sorted.

Preparatory Activities

You will need about 10 subjects to perform the task, and more is better.

The task is either to sort on attractiveness or trustworthiness, from left to right.

Assume that we ask to sort on attractiveness, most attractive first.

Each card is marked on the backside for male or female, or which type of prototype. Some examples of cards.

The alternating rows show first male, then female individuals. The morphed pictures consist of 80% Christ prototypes and 20% individual pictures.

The sorted sequences can be read and marked as in the example below.

m	jp	m	fp	f	f	mp	f	m	f	m	f	m
0	1	2	3	4	5	6	7	8	9	10	11	12

For each card and category, we count the number of cards to the left in another category. The examples do not assume the same images as in Figs. 1 and 2.

We test for a difference in the sorting orders between male and female Wilcoxon sum rank test for each person. Let us count for each category how many *of the other*

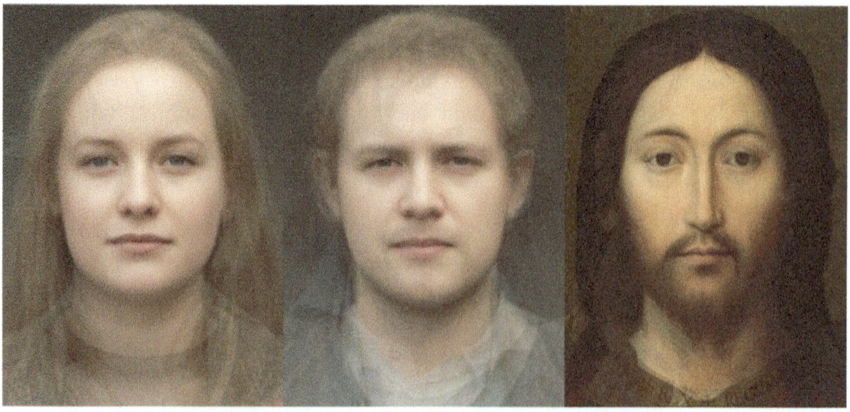

Fig. 1 Prototypes: female, male, Jesus

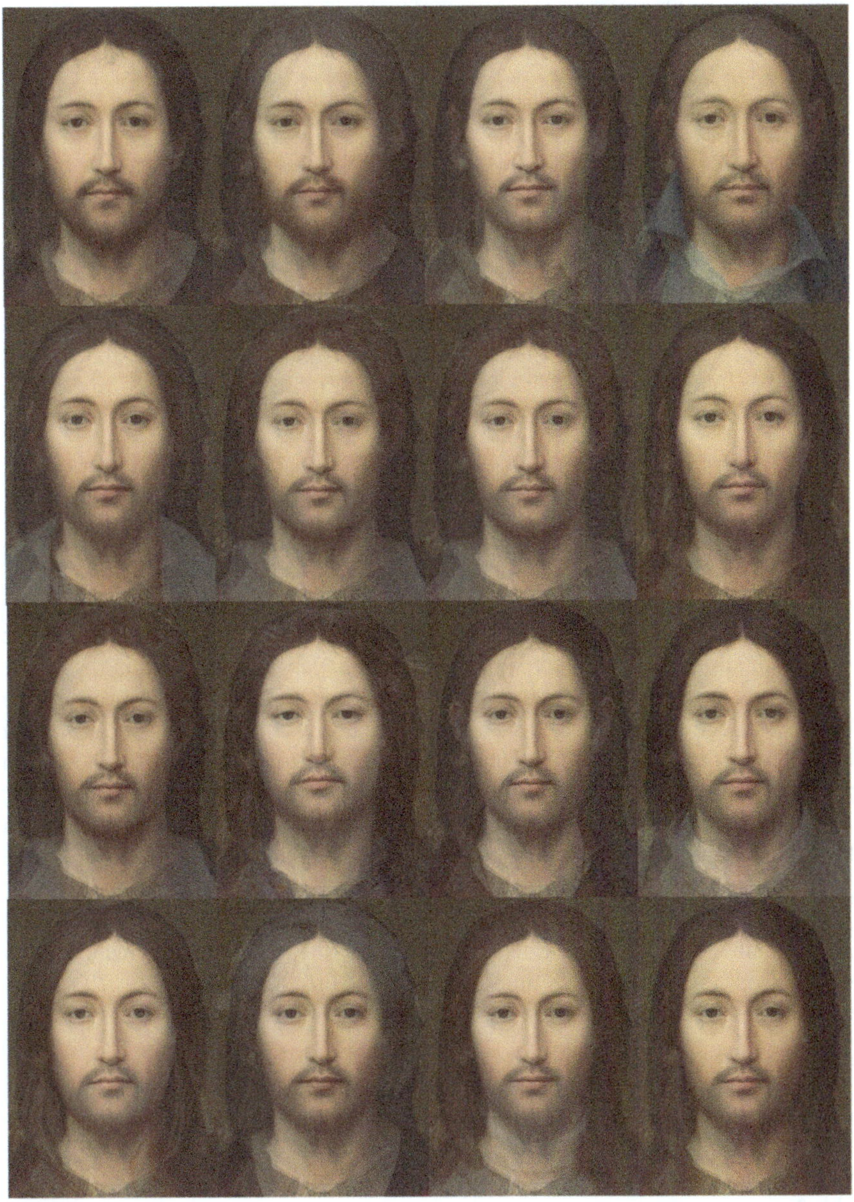

Fig. 2 Personalized "Jesuses". Each Portrait has been morphed with the Jesus prototype

Table 1 Rankings for one person (13 cards: 10 person, 3 prototypes)

m	f	jp	fp	mp
0	4	1	3	6
2	5			
8	7			
10	9			
12	11			

category have a **higher ranking number** and sum those numbers. For example, the first and second male (0 and 2) outranks all five female images, and the last male (12) is outranked by all five female images (Table 1).

$$\text{Male (m)} : 5 + 5 + 2 + 1 + 0 = 13 (\text{max score is } 25 : 5 + 5 + 5 + 5 + 5)$$
$$\text{Female (f)} : 3 + 3 + 3 + 2 + 1 = \mathbf{12}$$

$$\text{In R}: \ \text{wilcox.test(c(0, 2, 8, 10, 12), c(4, 5, 7, 9, 11))}$$

Here, W = **12** and p = 1, and there is no significant difference in the sorting order. The sum of rank differences of female images was lower, thus they were slightly less attractive for this individual as higher numbers indicate that more in the other category was sorted below. For this participant, there was no *significant* difference, which indicates that the sorting order can be explained by random chance.

W is the rank sum associated with the second group, *the smallest number*, in the ordered test. Say that we have females as our second group. For 10 people we got the following W numbers for M and F (Table 2):

Table 2 can be evaluated by a **paired** Wilcoxon sum rank test. We have sum ranks obtained from the same ten people in the two categories. Female images were judged more attractive 8 times out of 10. Is this significant?

The sum ranks, positive and negative classes:

$$\text{M}: 2 + 2 = \mathbf{4}$$
$$\text{F}: 2 + 4 + 5 + 6 + 7.5 + 7.5 + 9.5 + 9.5 = 51$$

Table 2 Calculating rank sums

M:	**13**	12	11	10	8	7	7	5	5	**13**
F:	12	**13**	**14**	**15**	**17**	**18**	**18**	**20**	**20**	12
Diff.	1	1	3	5	9	11	11	15	15	1
Rank	2	2	4	5	6	7.5	7.5	9.5	9.5	2
Winner	M	F	F	F	F	F	F	F	F	M

(Note: max score is 55 (10*5.5) when all are in one class and the mid-point is between 5 and 6 thus 5.5 is assigned to all).

$$\text{In R :> wilcox.test}\begin{pmatrix} \text{c}(13, 12, 11, 10, 8, 7, 7, 5, 5, 13), \\ \text{c}(12, 13, 14, 15, 17, 18, 18, 20, 20, 12), \text{ paired} = \text{T} \end{pmatrix}$$

$$\text{V} = \mathbf{4};\ \text{p} = 0.0186(\text{p} < 0.05)$$

In this hypothetical example, we can conclude that the difference is significant. We see that F is judged more attractive. The reason the significance is not very strong is that we only have 10 participants, judging only five male and five female images. The obvious next question is if male and female participants were different in their judgments.

In a second test we test if the gender of the subjects influences the results.

We have two groups, male and female.

A very simple test is to test preference (m or f) related to the gender of the subject (here coded as M or F in the first row in Table 3). We can use an *unpaired* Wilcoxon sum rank test to accomplish a test for preferences (compare Table 2). We simply look at how many in the other category we have to the left for each person (here we observed either 5 or 0, showing a complete separation between male and female participants). Looking at Table 3, we see that male participants did not have strong preferences, whereas female participants ranked male and female images with a stronger and consistent difference.

Since the difference in ranks cannot be assumed to be normally distributed and we do not have an interval scale we cannot use a test that assumes a normal distribution, but we do have ordinal data and larger absolute numbers indicate a stronger preference. Males seem to have weak preferences, and females have stronger preferences toward female, in this example. Note that the two males that had the m category as a winner, had very little difference between the sorting order of male and female images. The reason we should use an unpaired test is because we do not have repeated the sorting task for any of the individuals. We use the signed difference in the W-statistic for each of the individuals.

Sum ranks:

$$\text{Males} : 5 + 5 + 5 + 5 + 5 = \mathbf{25}$$

Table 3 The sign indicates the winner. Reordered from highest to smallest difference

	M	M	M	M	M	F	F	F	F	F
M:	**13**	**13**	12	11	10	8	7	7	5	5
F:	12	12	**13**	**14**	**15**	**17**	**18**	**18**	**20**	**20**
Diff.	1	1	−1	−3	−5	−9	−11	−11	−15	−15
Winner	m	m	f	f	f	f	f	f	f	f
	5	5	5	5	5	0	0	0	0	0

$$\text{Females}: 0 + 0 + 0 + 0 + 0 = 0$$

$$\text{In R} :> \text{wilcox.test}(\text{c}(1, 1, -1, -3, -5), \ \text{c}(-9, -11, -11, -15, -15))$$

Wilcoxon rank sum test with continuity correction

$$\text{data} : \text{c}(1, 1, \ -1, \ -3, \ -5) \text{ and } \text{c}(-9, \ -11, \ -11, \ -15, \ -15)$$

$$\text{W} \ = \mathbf{25}, \ \text{p - value} \ = \ 0.01141$$

Analyzing Prototypes

For prototypes, we investigate if there are different preferences for the three prototypes. We do this using a *Friedman test* on the raw *rank numbers* given by each subject. This will also introduce new tests, for when we have more than two groups (Table 4).

When the data is entered into R, we typically read the columns from top to bottom, column after column, and instruct R about the number of rows and columns. It is often necessary to check that the format is correct by simply printing the data to the screen.

$$\text{In R:} > \text{data} < -\text{matrix}(\text{c}\begin{pmatrix} 1, 2, 5, 6, 3, 2, 5, 2, 1, 4, 3, 5, 2, \\ 1, 2, 5, 6, 3, 4, 2, 6, 8, 6, 3, 6, 8, 8, 5, 7, 5 \end{pmatrix}, \ \text{nrow} = 10, \ \text{ncol} = 3)$$

$$> \text{friedman.test}(\text{data}, \text{paired} = \text{T})$$

Friedman rank sum test

data: data

Friedman chi-squared $= 12.2$, df $= 2$, p-value $= 0.002243$

This means that at least one of JP, MP, and FP is different from the rest. We need to apply a *pairwise.wilcox.test* to find out.

Table 4 Rankings for the three prototypes, per subject

#	JP	FP	MP
1	1	3	6
2	2	5	8
3	5	2	6
4	6	1	3
5	3	2	6
6	2	5	8
7	5	6	8
8	2	3	5
9	1	4	7
10	4	2	5

We need to create different, grouped, data formats. The easiest is to use Excel to create a data file with a column called class and a column called rank and insert all the values. This can be saved as a tabulator-separated text file to make it easy to import into R. The file will look like:

Class	Rank
JP	1
JP	2
JP	5
…	…
FP	3
FP	5
FP	2
…	…
MP	6
MP	8
MP	6
…	…

The data can now be imported into a data frame:

$$\text{In R: } > \text{dataW} < -\text{read.delim(file.choose())}$$

where we pick the textfile where we stored the data.

Check that it looks fine.

$$\text{In R: } > \text{summary(dataW)}$$
$$> \text{summary(dataW)}$$

Class	Rank
Length: 30	Min.: 1.0
Class: character	1st Qu.: 2.0
Mode: character	Median: 4.5
	Mean: 4.2
	3rd Qu.: 6.0
	Max.: 8.0

The pairwise test can be applied. We have three data points from each subject.

In R: > pairwise.wilcox.test(rank, class, paired = T)

Pairwise comparisons using Wilcoxon signed rank test with continuity correction data: rank and class

The result is a table with p-values.

From the table below, we find that MP is different from FP, p = 0.015 and MP is different from JP, p = 0.041. So, there is no significant difference in the sorting order of JP and FP, which are both judged significantly more attractive than MP.

	FP	JP
JP	0.757	–
MP	0.015	0.041

P value adjustment method: holm.

Summary

There are two main goals of this lab exercise: To make students comfortable with an experimental design and making students comfortable with the statistical evaluation of results. We have shown how a simple sorting task can be evaluated, and how we may assess differences between the gender of subjects, but also between the different classes of stimuli.

The sorting task allows the subjects to manipulate and compare images until they are satisfied or until a specified time limit, for example 5 minutes.

For statistical evaluation, the use of unpaired and paired Wilcoxon tests has been introduced, and the calculations behind the tests have been exemplified. We have also introduced the Friedman test, and how to perform post hoc tests. These are the main tests that can be performed on smaller experiments using ordinal data, stemming from sorting tasks. There are many variants of the study, and it is possible to perform the tests without any advanced equipment. This may be important for use in the field. The number of images may easily be extended. The time it takes to physically sort images is often shorter than a comparable experiment using a computer.

Further Research Questions:

Are there cultural differences in sorting preferences?

Will subjects of different ethnicities sort the images differently?

Do people react differently to pictures of themselves? In order to investigate this, it might be necessary to create more images that contain "self."

Do people react differently to in-group and out-group?

Can the judgment of beauty be explained by anatomical measures, for example face symmetry?

Can the underlying gender of the image be detected from anatomical measures of for example face symmetry?

It could be demonstrated that factors in-group/out-group and male/female are possible to detect in the images, for example by face proportions.

It is also possible to use various other controlled images. For example, images with rounded forms versus images with jagged forms, as in the classic bouba—kiki images.

It is also possible to easily allow people to sort the images according to some other dimension than beauty, for example trustworthiness, masculinity, femininity, intelligence, mental states, emotions, etc. Many of these dimensions cannot be judged from images, but people may still have consistent tendencies for how to sort the images.

Unit 4 Overview: Symmetry Research in Neuroaesthetics

Alexandru I. Berceanu

> Symmetry is what we see at a glance; based on the fact that there is no reason for any difference. And based also on the face of man; Whence it happens that symmetry is only wanted in breadth, not in height or depth. (Pascal, 2003)
>
> Tyger, Tyger burning bright,
> In the forests of the night:
> What immortal hand or eye,
> Dare frame thy fearful symmetry? (Blake, 1969)

Symmetry is often considered a visual primitive by scholars such as the French philosopher Blaise Pascal, who suggested that there is no need to be particularly attentive to perceive it (Pascal, 2003). Symmetry is also important for *Gestalt psychology*, which formulated one of the laws of perception in their framework regarding symmetry (Wagemans et al., 2012).

What Is Symmetry and Where It Can Be Found

Symmetry is a natural occurring phenomenon in living organisms, structures as well as in various human artefacts or creations. Sometimes symmetry occurs out of necessity or by design, sometimes it appears as having a solely aesthetic aim. Naturally occurring symmetry fascinates humans and other species, for example in the cases of flowers or butterflies, identical twins, the reflection of a landscape in a lake, symmetrical patterns in tiles, rhymes, or music.

A. I. Berceanu (✉)
National University for Theatre and Film IL Caragiale Bucharest, Bucharest, Romania
e-mail: berceanu.cinetic@unatc.ro

T. Balinisteanu and K. Priest (eds.), *Neuroaesthetics*,
https://doi.org/10.1007/978-3-031-42323-9_11

When it occurs in landscapes such as Mount Fuji or in crystal structures it seems to bare a mystical drive expressed by William Blake in his poem The Tyger. Reading a poem, we observe symmetry in how the text graphically appears on page: number of verses, repetitions of letters, words, but we perceive its symmetry even stronger when we hear it. Listening to how sounds are arranged in time through rhyme-generating rhythms, we observe accents and find sense in the poem built of words by the poet through his nuanced play between symmetry and asymmetry.

Visual symmetry is probably the most observable for humans, but other forms of symmetry exist, such as symmetry in sound, speech and in any type of structure. In movement, symmetry is also important as the complexity of it generates synchrony, which might be seen as a type of symmetry that encompasses the concept of time. Synchrony exerts fascination when it occurs in nature where it is present in waves, birds dancing and swarming together and in human activities such as dance, figure skating, majorettes' baton twirling, or synchronised swimming, which became an Olympic Sport in 1984 under the name of Artistic Swimming. Positive states are a common feature in movement mirroring (Papasteri et al., 2020; Tomescu et al., 2022) and the perception of symmetrical shapes (Winkielman & Cacioppo, 2001).

In general, all oscillatory behaviours are symmetrical or can be described based on their similarity towards symmetry. In general terms we can think of symmetry as any kind of repetition of a form, pattern, behaviour and even state, such as in human relationships where it is suggested both on an individual and group level in the idea of symmetric or unsymmetric relations. In such a context, a symmetrical individual relationship could be the example of a reciprocal romantic relationship and an example of an asymmetrical individual and collective relationship is that of exploitation, such as slavery. In both cases it is similarly striking that symmetry would be a preferable social relationship as opposed to an asymmetrical one.

This overview will focus on the status of research on symmetry in neuroaesthetics giving special attention to the contributions from the fields of visual perception and visual arts. We will outline the importance and relevance of research on symmetry in neuroaesthetics and adjacent fields, its methods, main results and future research directions.

Box 1: Gestalt Psychology on Symmetry

Gestalt Psychology is a school of psychology that originated in Austria and Germany at the beginning of the XX century, which stated that psychological phenomena are not to be researched through their individual components but as a whole. The central aspect of their school of thought is that in perception, and therefore psychological process, one cannot simply add elements, as the products resulting are more than the constituent parts. Such an example is given in their proposed law on symmetry which states that "when two symmetrical elements are unconnected the mind perceptually connects them to form a coherent shape". *A simple example would be when one plays with parentheses and other typographical symbols:*

(((.......)))(*∨*) (°∨°) (▰˘◡˘▰) ◎[·‿·]◎ ≧◡≦ ((.).*.∨..)▰ (≦) (*∨ (°°V) ◡ (▰˘ ∨ ≧◡
◎[·[·‿≧◎

As you can observe, you will tend to see the sets of parentheses as whole images, especially if they are arranged to evoke a face and not just as individual signs, as you would tend to perceive them were they not symmetrically grouped.

Box 2: What Is a Primitive?

In neuroscience, researchers refer to primitives as building blocks of more complex processing. Primitives are generally considered shared but are not necessarily the same across taxa in the phylogenetic tree. Visual processing is based on first level processing of different components such as contrast, line orientation, edges, or movement—properties often referred to as primitives. Some researchers also put forward symmetry as a primitive of visual processing (Olivers & Van Der Helm, 1998).

Primitives are present in every perceptual modality. It is proposed that planning movement is based on motor primitives. The concept is used also in biolinguistics, in semantic and concept research. More recently, researchers such as David J. Anderson have suggested that primitives count as units in emotional processing. Primitives are also important for fields like computer vision and artificial neural networks in which they are used as basic properties in processing (Anderson & Adolphs, 2014).

Symmetry in Nature

Symmetry can be found in nature at all levels of organisation in living forms and chemical structures. One major example of perfect symmetry is the structure of benzene, an organic chemical compound with six carbon and six hydrogen atoms (C_6H_6). The carbon atoms are placed in a planar regular hexagonal structure with sixfold rotational symmetry. Crystalline solids like quartz, sugar or diamonds have symmetrical structures based on translation, reflection and inversion. Snowflakes also have sixfold rotational symmetry with complex patterns emerging on the hexagonal structure based on the exact temperature and conditions of humidity in the moment each water molecule crystallises. Johannes Kepler was one of the first to ask: "There must be a cause why snow has the shape of a six-cornered starlet". Kepler wrote in *De nive sexangular:* "It cannot be chance. Why always six?" (Kepler, 1611). Snowflake symmetry was documented in China as early as the second century BC (Ball, 2011) (Fig. 1).

Symmetry is important for living organisms like plants and animals but also bacteria, viruses and fungi, with most multicellular organisms exhibiting a form of symmetry. Biological symmetry is not perfect but apparent. Most often in organisms one speaks about radial symmetry, or bilateral symmetry which can be seen as radial symmetry on one axis. Radial symmetry is present in plants (for instance cacti) and it can have a fixed number of symmetry axes (up to 12 for icosahedral symmetry) or numerous axes in the case of spherical symmetry of green algae volvox. In plants there can be several types of symmetry in the same plant: the root and the branches of a tree have significant radial symmetry; leaves have apparent bilateral symmetry, while most flowers have high rotational symmetry. Some of these types of symmetry are linked to a growth axis of symmetry (such as branches around the tree trunk or leaves on the stem). In flower symmetry a special class of genes, *CYCLOIDEA,* has a prominent role and it is suggested that flower symmetry develops selectively based on pollinator preferences.

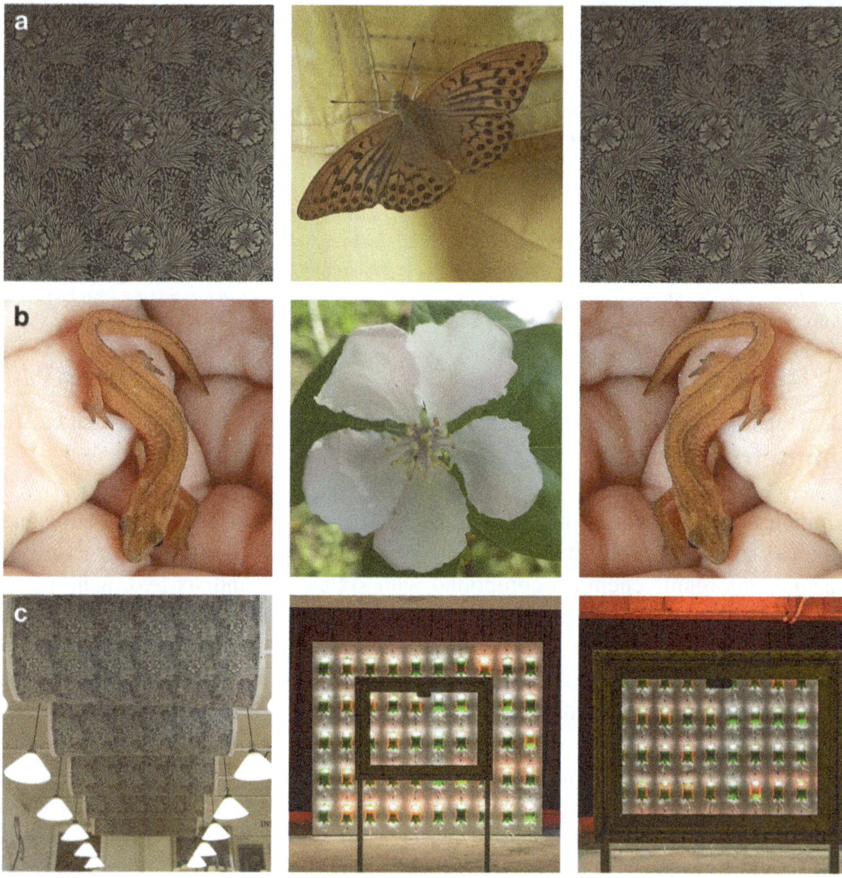

Fig. 1 Various types of symmetry in nature and human-made objects. A and C first rows floral pattern for fabric designed by William Morris, one of the most important figures of Arts and Crafts movement. We can observe radial symmetry in the flowers, bilateral symmetry in the butterfly and lizard but also repetition symmetry in lamp decoration as well as translational symmetry and mirror symmetry in the arrangement of photos in the collage. In row C between the two images on the right from the BioArt installation *Watch me* we can observe scaled symmetry. Using building blocks generated in repetition is highly efficient since all steps are clearly planned (Berceanu & Comănescu, 2022)

Main Types of Symmetry

Mirror symmetry: *identical parts across an axis, generally vertical or horizontal. This type of symmetry is sometimes referred to as reflectional symmetry.*

Rotational symmetry: *an object or pattern is repetitive in a plane in relationship with a fixed point. This type of symmetry can be found in a plane as well as in three dimensions.*

Translational symmetry: *Objects are identical after a translation (all points are identical in two or multiple objects and all are separated by identical distances).*

Besides those main types of symmetry there is also curved symmetry, across a regularly curved axis, scaled symmetry when objects are proportionally reduced as in fractals, helical symmetry, or glide symmetry.

In animals, it is proposed that symmetry is connected mainly to locomotory aspects, and it is important to note that while the exterior aspect of most animals has bilateral symmetry it is not the case for most internal organs. While an animal has a symmetrical number of legs and some of the internal organs, such as kidneys or lungs, they have just one liver, digestive tract, or heart. We find a complex interplay between symmetry and asymmetry in the organisation of the brain, where we can find a strong bilateral organisation, but also important asymmetries at anatomical and functional levels, such as speech. Mammals have complex types of symmetries and asymmetries, with 152 genes involved in the determination of mouse bilateral symmetry, according to MGI (Mouse Genome Informatics group).

If an organism presents a type of symmetry, it is essential for the organism's survival and health. Symmetric cellular division, when one cell divides into two identical ones, provides the building blocks for tissular development, which is a strong example of using identical units for a large structure, a principle widely used in human activities. Detecting symmetry is important for animals, as it can provide information about the health of conspecifics or the presence of another animal.

Symmetry in Human Activities

It is suggested that we can identify the use of symmetry in human artefacts as early as 1.4 million years ago. The oldest stone tools date back 2.5 million years, biface stone tools appeared around 1.4 million years ago, probably under the hands of homo erectus. Although symmetry in those tools is very rudimentary it is proposed that it is voluntary and that special sets of cognitive and motor skills are needed, especially when it comes to Olduvai discoid artefacts. Highly symmetrical tools appeared 500,000 years ago, and they have congruent dimensions and present bi and three-dimensional symmetry. It is put forward that Neanderthal and Palaeolithic man wore necklaces made from similar parts, which could have strong symmetrical aspects. Diverse populations across the globe, such as the Urubu Ka'apor in Amazonia, the African Massai, the Huli in Papua New Guinea or the Ainu in Japan decorate their bodies with jewellery, paint, tattoos scars and clothes with strong symmetrical patterns. Folk costumes from central European and Balkan regions present striking intricate symmetrical patterns in most of the pieces worn, with special care being noticeable in some of the more elaborate items, such as in the Romanian peasant blouse, "*ie*".

Symmetry is very present in human culture and relates to the repetition of patterns, sometimes in mechanical production. In architecture, symmetry can arise at a granular level, from the materials used, due to physics or due to architectural conception or world view. Romanic or Gothic arches are made of similar or identical stone and use mirroring symmetry to provide maximum resistance with the smallest quantity of material, but both styles abound in symmetry at levels where there would be no structural need. We can find cathedrals with a strong bilateral symmetry plan, as is the case of Notre-Dame of Paris, but in other cases, such as the Chartres Cathedral, the two steeples are very different from each other.

We can find amazing examples of highly planned symmetry in architecture around the world, starting with the Pyramids, Greek Temples, Pagodas, Indian temples or the Taj Mahal. Symmetry represents power, harmony and authority. Although there are also contemporary examples of architecture with strong symmetry, such as the Sagrada Familia or, more recently, The House of the Parliament in Bucharest, they tend to be marginal.

Symmetry is very present in decorative arts where repetition of patterns often plays central roles, with geometrical mosaics of great complexity, such as the Alhambra or Samarkand mosques. Tapestry, carpets, woodworking, pottery, porcelain, glass, or stained glass provide techniques for the use of symmetrical shapes and motives. The arts and crafts movement brought an intricate symmetry, patterns inspired by nature, using it as a solution for art in serial production, which is more and more prevalent in the industrial world.

In painting, highly symmetrical compositions are mostly found with a symmetrical balance, in which the midline of the painting is an axis of symmetry, but generally the sides are balanced and not identical. This type of symmetry, which is not exact, but balances proportions, is very much in line with the meaning of the Greek word *summetria*, with measure or well-proportioned σ˘υν- (sun-, 'with') + μέτρον (métron, 'measure') + -ος. Admittedly, examples of paintings using forms of perfect symmetry do exist, with examples in the work of Escher, Magritte or Delvaux, generally producing an eerie feeling of an alternate reality. In Renaissance paintings, but not only, symmetry appears from the relations between architectural backgrounds, occasionally highly symmetric, found in masterpieces such as The Last Supper of Leonardo, Rafael's School of Athens or Perugino and *Christ Giving the Keys of the Kingdom to St. Peter.* Compositions based on symmetry are strongly represented in Christian religious scenes where the crucified Christ represents a strong axis of symmetry for a singular painting, or a set of paintings forming a unitary composition in the case of polyptychs.

Symmetry is also linked to the perception of action and time. In novels and scripts, we can find strong symmetries between the start and the ending of a plot, notably with Chekhov, who plays a lot with "asymmetrical symmetries". Gustav Freytag's pyramid of dramatic structure, or the Hero's Journey, developed by Joseph Campbell, propose symmetric ascents and descents into action. Symmetry is also perceived across the domain of time. Mircea Eliade brought forward a symmetrical perspective on time passage through his proposal of the myth of the eternal return implicit or explicit actions instate symmetry by turning the past into a mythical golden age to be atained in the present. At a more profane level, symmetry in behaviour in the time axis is very present, humans repeating identical behaviours over time. Sometimes repetition of action can be seen as a coronation and culminant accomplishment, sometimes it can be seen as stereotypical such as in Ionesco's *Bald Soprano* and other similar works, where symmetry is a sign of general lack of meaning, denoting mere mechanical repetition.

Symmetrical movements are present in nature, especially in swarming and mating rituals culminating in complex synchronous choreographies as the ones performed by Western or Clark's Grebes. Dance often relies on synchrony creating complex moving images formed by even hundreds of dancers moving in synchrony. Examples range from old folk dances in tribes such as Ainu but also in ballet, hip hop, musical and so on. Army march is performed also in synchrony. Mirroring and imitation are at the heart of learning. Mirroring of movements constructing therefore symmetrical patterns were found to decrease self-awareness, discontinuity of mind with corelations in dynamics of EEG microstate EEG generating positive affective states and increasing salivary oxytocin in women (Papasteri et al., 2020; Tomescu et al., 2022) (Fig. 2).

Performing the mirroring task. The trainer shows simple movements the participant subject follows the movements synchronously generating symmetrical movements (Fig. 3).

The ARSQ questionnaire quantifies resting state mind-wandering fluctuations in four dimensions: dynamics of thoughts: *discontinuity of mind*,; content of thoughts:

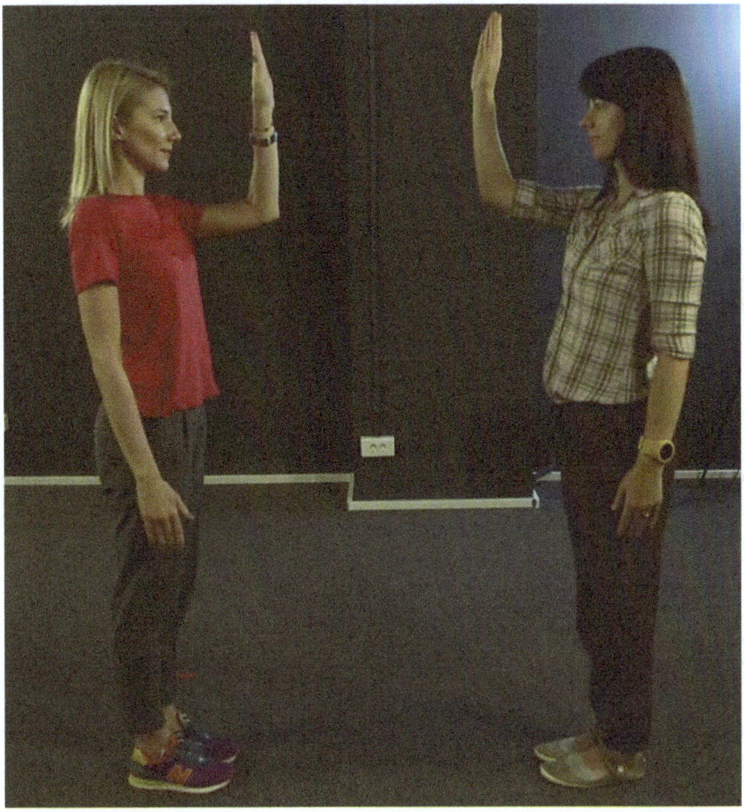

Fig. 2 Performing the mirroring task

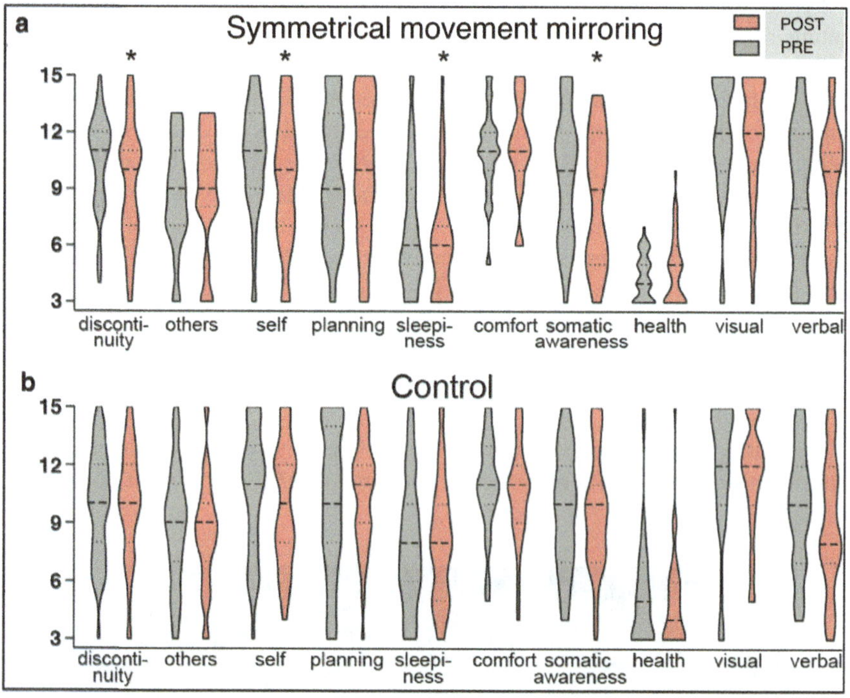

Fig. 3 Effects of performing synchronous symmetrical movements in a dyad, reproduced with modifications and permissions from (Tomescu et al., 2022). After the mirroring task, subjects reported less fragmented thoughts, fewer thoughts about themselves and their bodies. The study reported significant changes induced by mirroring in four different factor categories: discontinuity of mind, self-related thoughts, sleepiness and somatic awareness. No significant changes were detected after the CTRL conditions

other-related thoughts, or thinking about other people, *self-related thoughts*, or thinking primarily about own person, *planning*, or thoughts about the future, and *health*-related thoughts about general well-being or pain; physiological state: *sleepiness* and *comfort* quantify the level of relaxation during resting state, and *somatic awareness* reports thoughts about interoceptive bodily states such as breathing; modality of mind-wandering: *visual* imagery versus *verbal,* or thoughts formulated in words (Diaz et al., 2014).

Symmetry as Subject of Analyses and Research

Symmetry is an object of interest for both top-down and bottom-up approaches to aesthetics. Immanuel Kant considered that: "All stiff regularity (such as borders on mathematical regularity) is inherently repugnant to taste", but he continues "We do not grow to hate the very sight of it" (Kant, 2007). Furthermore, he describes the aesthetic pleasure of observing an ordered pepper garden in Sumatra in opposition to a chaotic repetitive jungle in nature. While he thought of symmetry as dull (Gombrich, 1988), art historian Ernest Gombrich also proposed that it relates to fixity, while asymmetry would be connected to the representation of motion and dynamism (Gombrich, 1984). He also underlined the importance of the opposition between order and chaos alongside a universal human impulse to seek order and rhythm in space and time (Gombrich, 1984).

Why Is Important to Study Symmetry for Neuroaesthetics?

Symmetry has been present in multiple forms in artistic productions since its beginnings all over the globe. Processing symmetry is important for both humans and other animals. Different levels of preference for symmetry have evolved in the phylogenetic tree, providing opportunities of research at genetic, functional, and subjective levels. The study of the impact of symmetry on aesthetic experience provides the unique opportunity of developing a holistic perspective on aesthetic experience grounded in the evolution from simple to complex processing. Symmetry is a measurable variable, making it an ideal subject of study in an experimental field. The special position that the perception of symmetry has in the phylogenetic tree might offer a window for understanding the development of aesthetic experience, hence building a unified theory of aesthetics.

Scientific Approaches in the Study of Symmetry Preference and Neural Processing of Symmetry

The first observations on symmetry perception came from the Austrian philosopher and physicist Ernst Mach, known for his contributions in the domains of shockwaves and the speed of sound, as well as the Mach-bands, the illusion provided to the human eye by exaggeration of contrast at edges of similar grey tones. He observed that vertical symmetry is more salient than other types and proposed that this relates to the overall symmetrical left–right organisation of sight and its equivalent in the central nervous system (Mach, 1959).

Psychology and empirical aesthetics were concerned with symmetry work very early on, as early as the beginning of the twentieth century, providing important data regarding aesthetic preference for symmetry. In her PhD work later published in the influential book "Psychology of Beauty", psychologist and suffragette Ethel Puffer observed in her study that symmetry composition is one of the preferred strategies for generating a pleasant composition, and these results were also confirmed more than one hundred years later (Hübner & Thömmes, 2019). Besides empirical aesthetics and neuroaesthetics, other disciplines also focus on symmetry and are very informative for these fields, even if their focus is on the aesthetic experience. Important knowledge as to how brains process symmetry comes from research in visual processing or computational neuroscience with artificial neural networks that provide mathematical tools for the investigation of brain function. Extensive research was done in all those fields on the recurrence of special issues of volumes (C. Tyler, 2003; C. W. Tyler, 1995) on these topics, expressing its importance, and the journal *Symmetry* covering its occurrence in all aspects of natural sciences, including in the field of aesthetics.

Although not universally observed, symmetry preference appears as general in cross-cultural studies along other features of images such as regularity, contrast and curvature, while the complexity effect vary culturally (Che et al., 2018). Common preference for symmetrical patterns was observed among subjects in the USA and Nigeria and common higher beauty ratings for symmetrical patterns were reported for British and Egyptian subjects (Che et al., 2018).

The preference for symmetry seems to be dependent on several factors, starting with the type of symmetry, of which lateral and radial symmetry are preferred. Preference for symmetry was found in the case of shapes and faces, but in the same study no perfect symmetry images were preferred for natural landscapes (Bertamini, Rampone, Makin, et al., 2019). Level of expertise is also diversifying the effect of symmetry on preference, with experts in the arts reported to prefer asymmetrical compositions (Gartus et al., 2020; Mcmanus, 2005).

Gender differences were also reported relating to symmetry, which was significant in the preferences of male subjects ($n = 40$) but not of women ($n = 40$) in a study regarding preference on abstract and real-world objects (Shepherd & Bar, 2011). The women's preference for symmetrical male faces was reported (Gangestad & Thornhill, 1998) with hormonal levels and menstrual cycle variations moderating the preference of women for the scent of shirts worn by symmetrical men (Gangestad & Thornhill, 1998; Garver-Apgar et al., 2008; Little et al., 2007).

It was widely proposed that preference for symmetry is an evolutionary adaptation facilitating the selection of healthy mates based on the link between symmetry and health at genetic and infectious levels with the objective of ensuring stronger health for offspring. Preference for partner symmetry is a strong argument for this theory, but a lot of researchers consider it insufficient to explain aesthetic preference, a process of a higher order.

An important proposal explaining the preference for symmetry is based on the concept of fluency. Perceptual fluency was defined as the subjective ease with which an incoming stimulus can be processed (Reber, 2002). Fluency of perception is proposed to have a strong influence on aesthetic preferences. Studies show that the more fluent an object is perceived as being, the more positive is the aesthetic response, with support coming from subjective rating but also confirmed by physiological data (Reber & Zupanek, 2002; Winkielman & Cacioppo, 2001). It is easier to process symmetrical than asymmetrical stimuli, with vertical symmetry detected faster than horizontal or rotational symmetry, as reaction time studies showed (Reber, 2002).

Ramachandran and Hirstein ask the question "Why is it useful to detect symmetry?". Stating that a principle in neuroaesthetics should be clearly grounded on clear answers to the questions: "what?" "how?" and "why?". Their proposal for the salience of symmetry is the need to detect prey, predators and mates from the surrounding environment, all of them having symmetrical bodies, as opposed to an asymmetrical surrounding. This view is in line with the grouping property proposed by Gestalt psychologists to symmetry. Preference for abstract symmetry is proposed to be an evolutionary consequence of the peak shift phenomenon (Ramachandran & Seckel, 2011).

Peak Shift

This was originally observed in seagull chicks by biologist Nikolaas Tinbergen, whose work was influential in the development of ethology thanks to his discoveries on social behaviour patterns. He studied pecking in seagull chicks, which have a strong pecking behaviour when they see the mother's beak. Seagull's beaks have a red spot, which is the centre point of chicken pecking, producing the regurgitation of food from the mother into the chick's beak. Tinberg observed that not only was pecking behaviour present when chicks were presented with beaks alone, but it would increase in intensity if seagull chicks are presented a stick with three stripes. Ramachandran proposes that this would be an "ultrabeak" which provokes a stronger response in the chicken due to more fluent processing of the stimulus due to the overlapping of its simple futures on the minimum requirements for recognition of a possible feeding source. He proposes that peak shift is one of the neural processing mechanisms in the development of the production and understanding of the abstract art. In his view, artists are developing works which, based on peak shifts, produce stronger responses than the real stimuli. He also proposes that peak shift is central to aesthetic experience (Ramachandran & Seckel, 2011*). Peak shift could be a possible explanation for the fascination exerted by mandalas or kaleidoscopes, a display of symmetry never found in nature, which produces strong positive states in the viewer.*

Symmetry is processed very fast by humans, being detected even during exposures to stimuli of under 50ms. Although there is still a lot to be understood on the neural processing of symmetry, some aspects are considered well established in the field. Neurofunctional techniques are concentrated on establishing the relationship between the observed behavioural salience of symmetrical stimuli and its neural processing.

Through fMRI studies the location of the neural response to symmetry is widespread through the visual cortex, within the ventral areas of higher visual perception V3A, V4, V7 and lateral occipital complex (LOC). The level of BOLD fMRI signal in these regions correlated with the level of symmetry in the stimuli (Sasaki et al., 2005). This network responds to symmetry automatically, without the need for the subject's attention. No single area for symmetry detection was identified as being dedicated to symmetry processing, but it is an extended network responding differently than from a quantitative level for different aspects of symmetry, such as texture or noise. For the observed aspects it is proposed that symmetry detection is part of the basic perception of shapes and forms (Bertamini et al., 2018).

The neural substrate for processing symmetry, beauty and complexity was targeted in an fMRI study (Jacobsen et al., 2006). Participants in the experiment were asked to judge a set of specially designed levels of beauty, symmetry and complexity. Symmetrical patterns were reported as more beautiful than nonsymmetrical ones. Some areas responded specifically to a task of aesthetic judgement: the medial frontal cortex, the precuneus and the ventral prefrontal cortex, others were involved in both tasks of judgments of symmetry and beauty: the left parietal cortex (the intraparietal sulcus) was engaged by both symmetry and beauty. Specific to symmetry processing, authors reported parietal and premotor areas involved in spatial processing. The beauty and complexity of the images evoked activity in the orbito-frontal cortex, an area confirmed to be implicated in the processing of beauty (Ishizu & Zeki, 2011).

- ***Visual processing** is performed in the visual cortex, bilaterally from the stream of information originating in the eyes, arriving there through the lateral geniculate nucleus of the thalamus. The visual cortex is situated in the occipital lobe. The visual cortex performs different tasks for distinct aspects of visual information in specialized areas. Visual area one (V1) is the site of first level processing. V1 has a retinotopic organization, with each neuron responding to a specific site within the retina, with neurons in the upper side responding strongly to the lower half of the retina (below the centre), and the lower side to the upper half of visual field. V1 creates a map of edges, generating a salience indication for other more specialized processing areas. From V1, two pathways divide, the ventral area which processes meaning of visual stimuli and the dorsal area which processes context of visual stimuli and integration with motor control. V2 has also ventral and dorsal areas and it is the visual association area. V3 covers motion and motion patterns. Aspects of visual processing are very specialized for some of the subregions such as middle temporal visual area for moving stimuli, V8 for colours (*Goodale, 2004*). The Lateral Occipital Complex (LOC) is an functional area critical for shape perception and is composed of the lateral occipital cortex (LO) and the posterior fusiform gyrus (pFs) (*Margalit et al., 2016*).*

Some of the most interesting data on neural processing of symmetry was produced in the Bertamini Lab, which showed that symmetry not only sets a sustained posterior negativity in the occipital area, but that this is independent of instructions to detect symmetry of other features of the image and that it lasted for one second after the offset of the stimulus. Sustained posterior negativity (SPN) is a sustained negative amplitude at posterior electrodes which lasts for hundreds of milliseconds when comparing symmetrical patterns to asymmetrical patterns (Bertamini, Rampone, Oulton, et al., 2019). During the pandemic, the lab made a lot of its resources available online, including all SPN datasets 6674 SPNs from 2215 participants in the compiled a Complete Liverpool SPN catalogue, on open science framework and a data visualisation app (https://www.bertamini.org/lab/SPNcatalogue.html).

On the side of neuroprocessing, one important question to be answered in the future is if symmetry is processed at the level of single neurons or if it is coded by a population. One study recording single units in macaque monkeys found that neurons in the inferior temporal area showed whole-object responses as the sum of responses to the object's parts, regardless of symmetry. The only defining characteristic of symmetric objects observed was a more distinctive response when compared to asymmetric objects because of neurons preferring the same part across locations within an object (Pramod & Arun, 2018). The author proposes that the neural response to symmetry is driven by generic computations at the level of single neurons (Pramod & Arun, 2018). Even if IT was not reported for humans, the results are nonetheless informative for human perception of symmetry since common aspects and differences were reported. V3A, V4d and IT were found to be activated by symmetrical stimuli combined with the human data from the same study, suggesting that neural mechanisms tuned to visual symmetry are present in nonhuman primates, although they are less developed than in humans (Sasaki et al., 2005).

At many levels of the phylogenetic tree, animals exhibit preference for symmetrical stimuli in mating and non-mating contexts. Pigeons can be trained to discriminate against various symmetrical patterns (Delius & Nowak, 1982) as well as chickens (Mascalzoni et al., 2011). Bumblebees, even if they have not previously seen flowers, prefer symmetrical ones (Rodríguez et al., 2004). Preference for mating partners with more symmetry is present in earwigs (Radesäter & Halldórsdóttir, 1993; Swaddle & Cuthill, 1994) zebrafish and humans, with attractiveness and declared partner preference increasing alongside the level of symmetry (Rhodes et al., 1998).

Developmental studies are very informative for the emergence of aesthetic preference. Studies on the emergence of symmetry preference on 4-month-old infants observed no preference for symmetry, and processing of vertically symmetrical patterns was more efficient than horizontally symmetrical or asymmetrical ones. In line with this observation, at 12 months, infants prefer vertical symmetry to horizontal symmetry and asymmetry. Vertical symmetry recognition is proposed as innate or maturing very quickly but it is suggested that the preference for symmetry develops later (Ferdinandsen & Gross, 1981).

One study assessed self-reported aesthetic preferences between symmetrical and asymmetrical visual patterns of four-year-old children and adults. The study also measured their spontaneous attentional preferences between the patterns. Children watched longer symmetrical patterns when compared to similar asymmetrical patterns, but they did not explicitly report a preference for those patterns. The authors theorise that: "These *findings suggest that the human's aesthetic preferences have high postnatal plasticity, calling into question theories that symmetry is a "core feature" mediating people's aesthetic experience throughout life. The findings also call into question the assumption, common to many studies of human infants, that attentional choices* reflect subjective preferences or values" (Huang et al., 2018).

Another study had the objective to develop the understanding of the cognitive development of aesthetic preference using the development of symmetry preference as a model. In a game, 4-year-old children were exposed to either symmetric or asymmetric non-figurative forms. Results showed that „The group of children who received exposure to symmetric patterns showed aesthetic preference to the exposed patterns, while no preference was found in the group that received exposure to asymmetric patterns." Symmetric objects were recognised and remembered better by children in a recognition test, indicating stronger encoding for symmetrical objects. Authors suggest that an "emerging perceptual sensitivity to 'good features' such as symmetry, provides the prior cognitive prerequisites, allowing visual perceptual exposure to nourish the eventual formation of aesthetic preference. Thus, the preferences for aesthetic appreciation are likely the outcome of the interplay between biological and ecological adaptation" (Huang et al., 2020).

Both studies could be considered strong developmental arguments for the theory proposing the emergence of aesthetical preference for symmetry arising from its faster coding and easier processing, generating fluency. This is also sustained by data from the field of computational neuroscience from a fascinating study. In their seminal study Enquist and Arak trained a neural network to recognise patterns generated by coloured squares in a 5×5 grid irrespective of the rotational degree of the grid to the retina. The neural network developed a preference for patterns presenting discrete symmetries with high contrast. To explain the observed phenomenon, Enquist and Arak propose: "that symmetry preferences may arise as a by-product of the need to recognise objects irrespective of their position and orientation in the visual field. The existence of sensory biases for symmetry may have been exploited independently by natural selection acting on biological signals and by human artistic innovation. This may account for the observed convergence on symmetrical forms in nature and decorative art" (Enquist & Arak, 1994).

► **Point to Take Forward**

Symmetry is an important constant in aesthetic experience. Studying symmetry provides a unique window for understanding how aesthetic preference emerges from neural processing across taxa in the phylogenetic tree. Multiple proposals are made to explain the complexity of the impact of symmetry for the aesthetic experience, which appears dependent on age, gender, experience and other factors. Symmetry is processed in similar brain regions in humans and monkeys. No specific region for symmetry processing is reported. In several higher order visual cortical increased bold fMRI signal is observed when subjects are presented symmetrical stimuli. It is currently suggested that neural response to symmetry is driven by generic computations at the level of single neurons. The emergence of preferences for symmetry is proposed to be an evolutionary adaptation in mate choice with symmetry used as a proxy for gene quality and other aspects of health, linked to the detection of prey and predators or determined by less effort being required for the processing of symmetrical shapes and objects. Future research using different approaches such as functional analysis or single unit neural EEG recordings could shine light on the proposed theories. Processing of symmetry in movement, and therefore imitation, might share a common processing path with shape symmetry processing with important implications for understating vicarious learning. Further cross-cultural studies could strongly contribute to establishing the nuanced impact of symmetry on aesthetic preference. Understating the impact of specialisation in the arts on the preferences for symmetry and complexity could greatly contribute to the understating of aesthetic experience in general. Widely present in non-specialised subjects, the preference for symmetry appears diminished in specialised subjects, understating this apparent paradoxical behaviour could be informative for other aspects of aesthetic preference.

Symmetry preference is a constant even nowadays in art production and preference. The film director Wes Anderson uses symmetrical shots in feature films and animation in highly aestheticized shots which are his highly acclaimed trademark. Trends on Tik-Tok and other social media often use elaborate action and spatial symmetries in memes. Studying symmetry within the neuroaesthetics framework has a very important potential in contributing to understanding subjective human experience and its impact on cultural and artistic artefacts and phenomena.

References

Anderson, D., & Adolphs, R. (2014). A framework for studying emotions across species. *Cell, 157*, 187–200. https://doi.org/10.1016/j.cell.2014.03.003

Ball, P. (2011). In retrospect: On the six-cornered snowflake. *Nature, 480*(7378), 455. https://doi.org/10.1038/480455a

Berceanu, I. A., & Comănescu, S. (2022). Watch me. *Teatru 2.0, Mobius.*

Bertamini, M., Rampone, G., Makin, A., & Jessop, A. (2019). Symmetry preference in shapes, faces, flowers and landscapes. *PeerJ, 7*, e7078. https://doi.org/10.7717/peerj.7078

Bertamini, M., Rampone, G., Oulton, J., Tatlidil, S., & Makin, A. D. J. (2019). Sustained response to symmetry in extrastriate areas after stimulus offset: An EEG study. *Scientific Reports, 9*(1), 4401. https://doi.org/10.1038/s41598-019-40580-z

Bertamini, M., Silvanto, J., Norcia, A. M., Makin, A. D. J., & Wagemans, J. (2018). The neural basis of visual symmetry and its role in mid- and high-level visual processing. *Annals of the New York Academy of Sciences, 1426*(1), 111–126. https://doi.org/10.1111/nyas.13667

Che, J., Sun, X., Gallardo, V., & Nadal, M. (2018). Chapter 5—Cross-cultural empirical aesthetics. In J. F. Christensen, A. Gomila (Eds.), *Progress in Brain Research* (Vol. 237, pp. 77–103). Elsevier. https://doi.org/10.1016/bs.pbr.2018.03.002

Delius, J. D., & Nowak, B. (1982). Visual symmetry recognition by pigeons. *Psychological Research Psychologische Forschung, 44*(3), 199–212. https://doi.org/10.1007/BF00308420

Diaz, B. A., Van Der Sluis, S., Benjamins, J. S., Stoffers, D., Hardstone, R., Mansvelder, H. D., Van Someren, E. J. W., & Linkenkaer-Hansen, K. (2014). The ARSQ 2.0 reveals age and personality effects on mind-wandering experiences. *Frontiers in Psychology, 5*, 271.

Enquist, M., & Arak, A. (1994). Symmetry, beauty and evolution. *Nature, 372*(6502), 169–172. https://doi.org/10.1038/372169a0

Ferdinandsen, K., & Gross, C. (1981). Perception of symmetry in infancy. *Developmental Psychology, 17*, 82–86. https://doi.org/10.1037/0012-1649.17.1.82

Gangestad, S. W., & Thornhill, R. (1998). Menstrual cycle variation in women's preferences for the scent of symmetrical men. *Proceedings of the Royal Society of London. Series B: Biological Sciences, 265*(1399), 927–933. https://doi.org/10.1098/rspb.1998.0380

Gartus, A., Völker, M., & Leder, H. (2020). What experts appreciate in patterns: Art expertise modulates preference for asymmetric and face-like patterns. *Symmetry, 12*(5), 707. https://doi.org/10.3390/sym12050707

Garver-Apgar, C. E., Gangestad, S. W., & Thornhill, R. (2008). Hormonal correlates of women's mid-cycle preference for the scent of symmetry. *Evolution and Human Behavior, 29*(4), 223–232. https://doi.org/10.1016/j.evolhumbehav.2007.12.007

Gombrich, E. (1984). *The sense of order: A study in the psychology of decorative art*. Phaidon Press. https://books.google.ro/books?id=w48XAQAAMAAJ

Gombrich, E. (1988). *Symmetrie, Wahrnehmung und künstlerische Gestaltung BT - Symmetrie in Geistes- und Naturwissenschaft: Hauptvorträge und Diskussionen des Symmetrie Symposions an der Technischen Hochschule Darmstadt vom 13. bis 17. Juni 1986 im Rahmen des Symmetrieprojekt* (R. Wille, Ed., pp. 94–119). Springer. https://doi.org/10.1007/978-3-642-71452-8_9

Goodale, M. A. (2004). Perceiving the world and grasping it: Dissociations Between conscious and unconscious visual processing. In *The cognitive neurosciences* (3rd ed., pp. 1159–1172). Boston Review.

Huang, Y., Lyu, J., Xue, X., & Peng, K. (2020). Cognitive basis for the development of aesthetic preference: Findings from symmetry preference. In *PLoS ONE* (Vol. 15). Public Library of Science. https://doi.org/10.1371/journal.pone.0239973

Huang, Y., Xue, X., Spelke, E., Huang, L., Zheng, W., & Peng, K. (2018). The aesthetic preference for symmetry dissociates from early-emerging attention to symmetry. *Scientific Reports, 8*(1), 6263. https://doi.org/10.1038/s41598-018-24558-x

Hübner, R., & Thömmes, K. (2019). Symmetry and balance as factors of aesthetic appreciation: Ethel Puffer's (1903) "Studies in Symmetry" Revised. *Symmetry, 11*(12), 1468. https://doi.org/10.3390/sym11121468

Ishizu, T., & Zeki, S. (2011). Toward a brain-based theory of beauty. *PLOS ONE, 6*(7), e21852. https://doi.org/10.1371/journal.pone.0021852

Jacobsen, T., Schubotz, R. I., Höfel, L., & Cramon, D. Y. v. (2006). Brain correlates of aesthetic judgment of beauty. *NeuroImage, 29*(1), 276–285. https://doi.org/10.1016/j.neuroimage.2005.07.010

Kant, I. (2007). *Critique of Judgment*. Cosimo. https://books.google.ro/books?id=yBFsrJqNtygC

Little, A. C., Jones, B. C., Burt, D. M., & Perrett, D. I. (2007). Preferences for symmetry in faces change across the menstrual cycle. *Biological Psychology, 76*(3), 209–216. https://doi.org/10.1016/j.biopsycho.2007.08.003

Mach, E. (1959). *The analysis of sensations* (Vol. 13, Issue 6). Dover Publications.

Margalit, E., Shah, M. P., Tjan, B. S., Biederman, I., Keller, B., & Brenner, R. (2016). The Lateral Occipital Complex shows no net response to object familiarity. *Journal of Vision, 16*(11), 3. https://doi.org/10.1167/16.11.3

Mascalzoni, E., Osorio, D., Regolin, L., & Vallortigara, G. (2011). Symmetry perception by poultry chicks and its implications for three-dimensional object recognition. *Proceedings of the Royal Society b: Biological Sciences, 279*(1730), 841–846. https://doi.org/10.1098/rspb.2011.1486

Mcmanus, I. (2005). Symmetry and asymmetry in aesthetics and the arts. *European Review, 13*, 157–180. https://doi.org/10.1017/S1062798705000736

Olivers, C. N. L., & Van Der Helm, P. A. (1998). Symmetry and selective attention: A dissociation between effortless perception and serial search. *Perception & Psychophysics, 60*(7), 1101–1116. https://doi.org/10.3758/BF03206161

Papasteri, C. C., Sofonea, A., Boldasu, R., Poalelungi, C., Tomescu, M. I., Pistol, C. A. D., Vasilescu, R. I., Nedelcea, C., Podina, I. R., Berceanu, A. I., Froemke, R. C., & Carcea, I. (2020). Social feedback during sensorimotor synchronization changes salivary oxytocin and behavioral states. *Frontiers in Psychology, 11*, 531046. https://doi.org/10.3389/fpsyg.2020.531046

Pascal, B. (2003). Pensees (A. Krailsheimer, Ed.). Penguin Books Limited. https://books.google.ro/books?id=SYkb0WuLfwAC

Pramod, R. T., & Arun, S. P. (2018). Symmetric objects become special in perception because of generic computations in neurons. *Psychological Science, 29*(1), 95–109.

Radesäter, T., & Halldórsdóttir, H. (1993). Fluctuating asymmetry and forceps size in earwigs, Forficula auricularia. *Animal Behaviour, 45*, 626–628. https://doi.org/10.1006/anbe.1993.1075

Ramachandran, V. S., & Seckel, E. (2011). Neurology of Visual Aesthetics: Indian nymphs, modern art, and sexy beaks. In A. P. Shimamura & S. E. Palmer (Eds.), *Aesthetic science: Connecting minds, brains, and experience*. Oxford University Press. https://doi.org/10.1093/acprof:oso/9780199732142.003.0086

Reber, R. (2002). Reasons for the preference for symmetry. *Behavioral and Brain Sciences, 25*, 415–416. https://doi.org/10.1017/S0140525X02350076

Reber, R., & Zupanek, N. (2002). Effects of processing fluency on estimates of probability and frequency. In *ETC. Frequency processing and cognition* (pp. 175–188). Oxford University Press. https://doi.org/10.1093/acprof:oso/9780198508632.003.0011

Rhodes, G., Proffitt, F., Grady, J. M., & Sumich, A. (1998). Facial symmetry and the perception of beauty. *Psychonomic Bulletin & Review, 5*(4), 659–669. https://doi.org/10.3758/BF03208842

Rodríguez, I., Gumbert, A., Hempel de Ibarra, N., Kunze, J., & Giurfa, M. (2004). Symmetry is in the eye of the 'beeholder': Innate preference for bilateral symmetry in flower-naïve bumblebees. *Naturwissenschaften, 91*(8), 374–377. https://doi.org/10.1007/s00114-004-0537-5

Sasaki, Y., Vanduffel, W., Knutsen, T., Tyler, C., & Tootell, R. (2005). Symmetry activates extrastriate visual cortex in human and nonhuman primates. *Proceedings of the National Academy of Sciences of the United States of America, 102*, 3159–3163. https://doi.org/10.1073/pnas.0500319102

Shepherd, K., & Bar, M. (2011). Preference for symmetry: Only on Mars? *Perception, 40*(10), 1254–1256. https://doi.org/10.1068/p7057

Swaddle, J. P., & Cuthill, I. C. (1994). Preference for symmetric males by female zebra finches. *Nature, 367*(6459), 165–166. https://doi.org/10.1038/367165a0

Tomescu, M. I., Papasteri, C. C., Sofonea, A., Boldasu, R., Kebets, V., Poalelungi, C., Podina, I. R., Nedelcea, C. I., Berceanu, A. I., & Carcea, I. (2022). Spontaneous thought and microstate activity modulation by social imitation. *NeuroImage*, 240. https://doi.org/10.1016/j.neuroimage.2022.118878

Tyler, C. (2003). Human symmetry perception and its computational analysis. *Psychology Press*. https://doi.org/10.4324/9781410606600

Tyler, C. W. (1995). Empirical aspects of symmetry perception. *Spatial Vision, 9*(1), 1–7. https://doi.org/10.1163/156856895X00089

Wagemans, J., Elder, J. H., Kubovy, M., Palmer, S. E., Peterson, M. A., Singh, M., von der Heydt, R. (2012). A century of Gestalt psychology in visual perception: I. Perceptual grouping and figure-ground organization. *Psychological Bulletin, 138*(6): 1172–1217. https://doi.org/10.1037/a0029333. ISSN 1939-1455. PMC 3482144. PMID 22845751.

Winkielman, P., & Cacioppo, J. T. (2001). Mind at ease puts a smile on the face: Psychophysiological evidence that processing facilitation elicits positive affect. In *Journal of Personality and Social Psychology, 81*, 989–1000. American Psychological Association. https://doi.org/10.1037/0022-3514.81.6.989

Unit 4 Lesson: Why Is *en face* Associated with Holiness?

Christer Johansson and Per Olav Folgerø

Introduction

Portraits of Christ as a holy person are predominantly en face. This was famously commented by Albrecht Dürer in a self-portrait often called "Myself as Christ". In contrast, profane portraits were predominantly painted in profile, including portraits of the suffering Christ ("The Man of Sorrows"). Why did medieval artists prefer to paint Christ en face? His face is thus directed toward the beholder, both face and gaze are intently directed at the beholder. Profane faces were noticeably more often painted in different degrees of profile. Is this a result of theological and historical conventions; or are there deeper biological and psychological reasons? Can face orientation and gaze direction influence how we judge positive and negative social attributes? Specifically, are almost symmetrical portraits with a direct gaze more associated with a positive attitude toward the portrait, as indicated by modern-day attribution of positive and negative adjectives to selected portraits?

Today, it is fairly easy to do internet surveys (cf. Folgerø et al., 2016). What such surveys miss out on accuracy and control of the environment and subjects might be more than well compensated by acquiring a large amount of data points. One such popular tool is SurveyXact. If we ask a large sample of people to assign, on a scale from 0 to 10, selected adjectives to portraits we will be able to ascertain if there are significant effects of face and gaze orientation. In Art History, frontality is the way to represent Christ as God. This iconographical way to represent his divinity is called the Holy Face, in opposition to the profile, where he is the Man of

C. Johansson (✉) · P. O. Folgerø
University of Bergen, Bergen, Norway
e-mail: Christer.Johansson@uib.no

P. O. Folgerø
e-mail: Per.Folgero@uib.no

T. Balinisteanu and K. Priest (eds.), *Neuroaesthetics*,
https://doi.org/10.1007/978-3-031-42323-9_12

Sorrows. Frontally oriented faces of Christ in Western Art are almost symmetric. Previous studies have demonstrated that in the fifteenth and sixteenth centuries, almost all profane portraits (in contrast to the depictions of Christ) were painted in different degrees of profile, with gazes either directed toward the beholder, or averted away. It is rare to see a secular portrait in frontal view (Hodne, 2013). Why did these artists prefer to paint Christ with his face directed toward the beholder, while profane faces were represented in profile? Is it convention, or can there be other explanations? Conventions can obviously mirror biological and psychological trends, but we can see if the psychology is measurable today. One caveat is that we might have learned and internalized the conventions. An interesting follow-up study could be to see if cultures with minimal exposure to Christianity will have similar reactions to the types of portraits as defined by face and gaze direction.

There is a strong tradition in the West of copying the veil of Veronica as a template for the face of Christ. The blood and sweat on the relic were thought to be imprinted on the veil directly by the face of Christ, by the blood wiped from his face during his way to Golgotha. According to tradition, the intensity of Christ's gaze in the veil made it necessary to cover the relic with a piece of cloth.

The symmetrical face with a strong direct gaze became the standard way to represent the Holy Face in Western art of the Renaissance, both north and south of the Alps (Morgan, 2012: 55–62). In the East, we have a corresponding history of King Abgar (6th c.; Edessa, Syria; today Urfa, Turkey) receiving a cloth with the face of Christ, the Mandylion, glowing with such a power that it was even imprinted on the tile on which it was placed, and this imprint is thought of as an icon not made by hand *(acheiropoieton)*. This was the origin of the *mandylion* frequently painted and still found in countless churches in the East. The *mandylion* is strictly symmetric.

Interestingly, Christ the All Ruler or *Pantochrator*, in the East, is often highly asymmetrical, as in the famous *deesis* mosaic on the gallery of Hagia Sophia in today's Istanbul (around 1280), where the left half of Christ's face is almost in profile (nose close to the golden mean), while the right side is *an face*. This follows the prescription in the Painters Manual written by the thirteenth-century painter Manuel Panselinos (Torp, 1984).

We may ask whether there could be deeper reasons than pure convention for the strong preference of full-frontal portraits with a directed gaze. Such reasons could point to factors deep in the human emotional responses in face perception.

Neurobiological and Evolutionary Aspects on Preferences of Face and Gaze Direction

A fast capture of head and gaze direction is a significant factor for detecting the other's intention (Emery, 2000). As such, it represents a selective pressure during evolution to be interested in detecting any signs of hidden intentions, positive or negative. The accurate detection of gaze direction depends on the great contrast between the dark iris and the bright sclera, which is solely found in humans

(Kobayashi & Koshima, 1997), which can thus be thought of as an evolutionary trait that made possible shared attention that may accompany learning. In language acquisition, the detection of shared or joint attention, at the lowest level through detection of gaze direction, "may be important for language learning in human infants" (Emery, 2000, 588; see also Dunham et al., 1993; Mundi & Gomes, 1998; Tomasello & Farrar, 1986). Gaze direction was important in human evolution, with precursors in other primates (see Emery, 2000, particularly pp. 584–587).

People who look directly at their counterpart could signal aggression or superiority, as it does in other primates. People may want to monitor the other's actions, but in doing so they may also express the wish to communicate or care for their counterpart. This also activates the so-called Theory of Mind (ToM)-network in the brain, which is the social network through which people analyze another person's intentions (e.g., Baron-Cohen, 1997; Conty et al., 2007; Perrett & Emery, 1994; Yang et al., 2015).

A survey may explore how subjects react to the different face and gaze directions. The direction of face and gaze is experimentally manipulated. We have used three face databases.

(1) The Dutch Radboud Face Database (RaFD: Langner et al., 2010)
(2) The Brazilian FEI face database
(3) Holy Face (non-manipulated) and secular portraits from the databases.

Using historical material and modern photographs must take into consideration how close the modern material is to the historic material; whether details, such as the degree of aversion of gaze, is similar across the material. Since we are working with original historical art, we require that the original is not manipulated. Hence, in the study of the Holy Face, all faces derive from non-manipulated original paintings. This is because we do not want to interfere with the artist's so-called "design stance" (cf. Bullot & Reber, 2013).

The advantage of using modern portraits lies in experimental control. In photographs of frontal as well as half-profile views, gaze directions can be manipulated, resulting in four conditions: frontal or profile view, with directed or averted gaze (cf. Table 1).

It is rare to find full-frontal portraits with averted gaze in the relevant time period, so this condition cannot be easily balanced for the paintings. Half of the portraits depicts the face of Christ while the other half restricts on profane faces. As paintings of Christ in frontal view with *averted* gaze are not available to us (in Western artworks) and since we accept originals only, the design will remain incomplete, and face orientation is confounded with holiness. However, a follow-up could use manipulated images in order to make test the hypothesis. It also makes sense to test the hypothesis on only photographs, and see if full-front direct photographs differ from the Renaissance paintings.

The survey asks the participants how much they agree with adjectives describing the face and gaze physiognomy of the target image. The experiment requires the participant to rate, for example, how authoritarian a portrait is, on a scale from

Table 1 These sketches illustrate the experimental manipulations in each study (1, 2 & 3)

	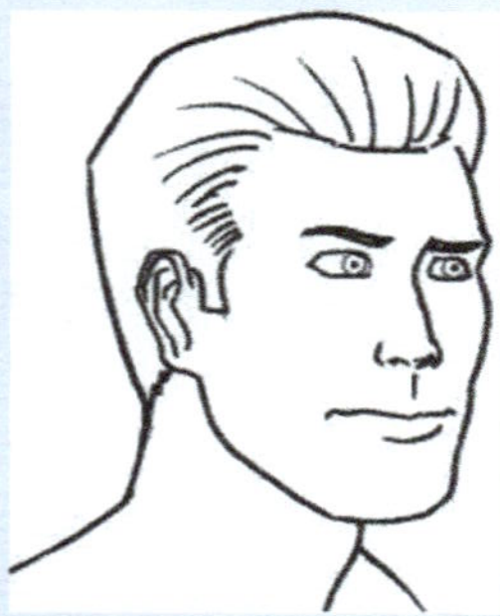	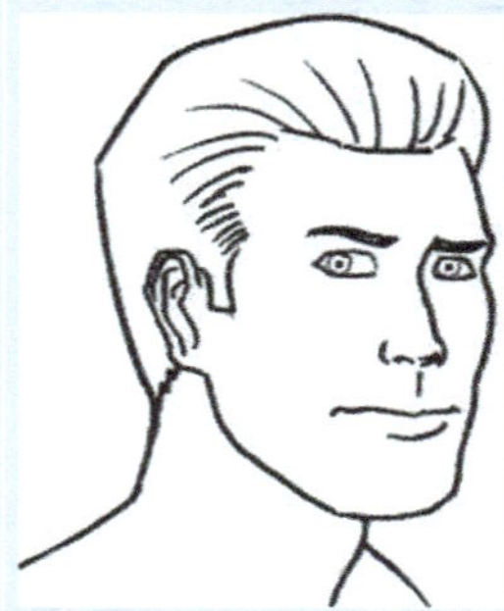	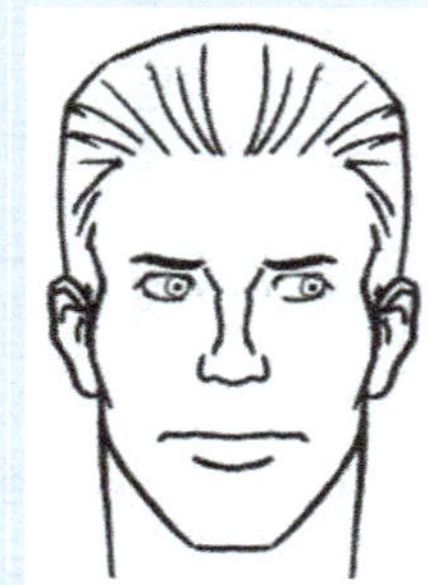	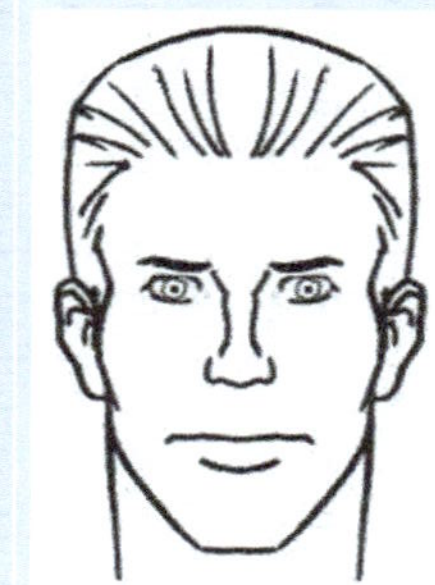
1	Profile + Averted	Profile + Direct	Full + Averted	Full + Directed
2	Profile + Averted	Profile + Direct	Full + Averted	Full + Directed
3	Averted	Direct	–	Holy

0 to 10. The adjectives all denote mental traits that are hard to observe directly and objectively. At the same time, they are common, familiar, and often applied as descriptions of a perceived persona. The adjectives belong to two different groups. The positive can be *"harmonious", "trustworthy", "caring", "inclusive", and "respectable"*, and the negative: *"authoritarian", "monitoring", "evasive", "intimidating" and "dominant"*, but other adjectives can be used. It makes sense to check that all the adjectives are approximately equally rare, and have a similar number of syllables, as both frequency of use and syllabic complexity may affect how familiar the adjectives are.

Each study must be evaluated formally by statistical hypothesis testing.

How many respondents do you need? The easy answer is probably more than you think. It depends on the statistical test you use, and the number of items you ask them to judge. One common rule of thumb is that you need about a thousand (independent) data points. Since it is straightforward to get large samples using web-surveys, we could aim for a high number of respondents, for example 200. However, we will also have to consider the number of images that they will judge and how representative they are, as well as the time constraints on the subjects. Most subject might consider spending 10–15 minutes on a web survey, especially if some reward is given. If we assume that each image will take 10 seconds to judge, that will allow for 6 images per minute which gives a hypothetical limit of 60–90 items. If we go for the upper end, many participants may drop out. In the description above, we have four fixed conditions in a two by two design: two levels of face (profile, full) and two levels of gaze (direct and averted). The fully balanced set would thus be a multiple of four, and in addition some training examples and some unrelated fillers.

Participants are required to give their active informed consent by providing their email address, which will provide them a hyperlink to an online questionnaire hosted by the survey (for example, SurveyXact). The invitations could be posted on social media, or through email lists. Each participant must be informed on the principle of voluntary participation, including the right to withdraw from the study at any time without having to justify their reasons for withdrawal. Participants should be informed about the purpose of the study, for example research, and consent to that the data they give can be published. At the same time, they should not be nudged in any direction for the answers they give and they should be encouraged to take the survey seriously. Ideally, there should be a debriefing after the survey where participants can provide information on their experience for taking the survey. Moreover, they should be informed that all data is kept anonymous, which typically means that the link between the answers and the email is lost. The question of anonymity could also involve setting up anonymous accounts for the users, and that way make it possible to link the answers to an anonymous individual. All research must be in accordance with the ethical rules given by the university. For a typical survey, the answers to the questions are not likely to impact negatively on the participants, but it is your job as a researcher to make sure that it is so, and that the participants are informed.

The images may be taken from available databases. Check that you have permission to use the databases for research. One such database is the Dutch Radboud Faces Database (RaFD). Another collection could be Brazilian faces from the FEI face database. The different databases can be used as factors in the analysis. It is also possible to analyze the faces and provide some control variables, for example on face symmetry, eye and mouth width, and eye and mouth symmetry. The databases provide many angles, and it could be an idea to use the full front direct gaze version of each face to provide the control variable. The thought is that the proportions in the face may give additional cues to how we perceive the faces.

We may also sample Renaissance paintings (Fig. 1). The full front averted gaze is rare, so it is difficult to represent fairly, without manipulating the images. New possibilities may arise using modern AI technology for generating portraits (sometimes called "deep fakes").

We measure how 10 adjectives associated with personality traits are rated in the photographs and paintings. Each combination of adjectives and images is presented once, exhaustively for each combination of adjective and painting, in a randomized order for each participant. Let us indicate how the images could be classified into different conditions based on Frontal (F) or Profile (P) view with a Direct (D) or Averted (A) gaze. The categories abbreviated are: FA, FD, PA and PD. In the investigations on the Holy Face, there are only three categories: Holy, (Profane) Direct and (Profane) Averted. One useful technique is the Cohen-Friendly Association Plots (assoc), implemented in the vcd package in R (Cohen, 1980; Friendly, 1992). The plot indicates the deviations from statistical independence (Pearson Residuals) of rows (conditions) and columns (adjectives). The association graph intuitively marks which adjectives are positively (blue) or negatively (red) associated with each image type. For example, a frontal face with a direct gaze is

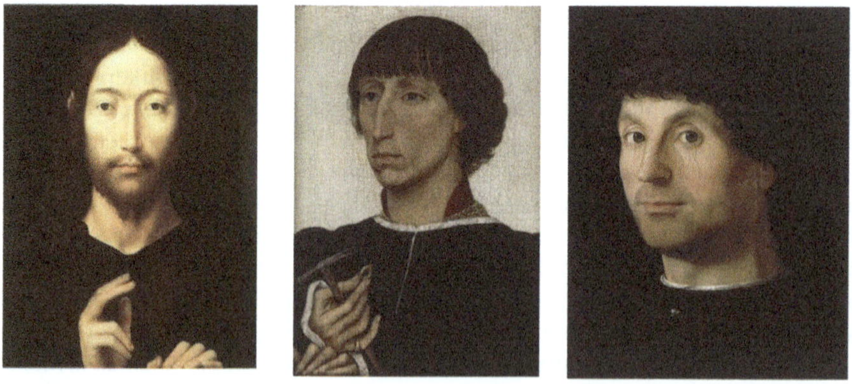

Holy Face frontal view direct gaze | Secular half-profile averted gaze | Secular half-profile direct gaze

Fig. 1 Renaissance paintings

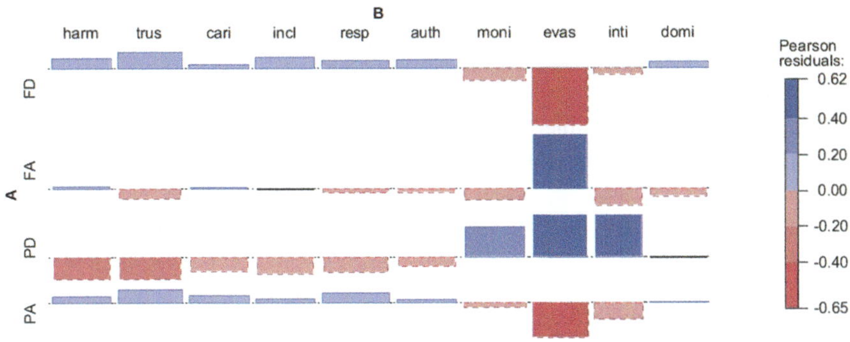

Fig. 2 An extended association plot with color-coded Pearson Residuals (Meyer et al., 2003). Dutch Radboud Faces Database (RaFD). *Abbreviations* FD = Frontal Direct, FA = F. Averted, PD = Profile Direct, PA = P. Averted; harm = harmonious, trus = trustworthy, cari = caring, incl = inclusive, resp = respectable, auth = authoritarian, moni = monitoring, evas = evasive, inti = intimidating, domi = dominant

negatively associated with "evasive", and a frontal face with an averted gaze is positively associated with "evasive". A sneaky direct gaze from a picture in a profile is associated with negative traits. Figure 2 gives the extended association plot with color-coded Pearson Residuals (cf. Meyer et al., 2003).

As we have indicated, it is possible to build a more advanced generalized linear model, with more control variables. Assuming that we have found adjectives that correctly associate with positive and negative value assignment, we can make this assignment explicit by multiplying the ratings for the negative adjectives with a constant −1. The assumption is confirmed by analysis of association. If positive and negative adjectives are assigned at random, we expect the values to sum near zero, i.e., a neutral evaluation on average. We should make use of a binomial distribution, as we do not have a continuous response variable.

An analysis of all experiments can be done using a mixed effects model implemented in the LmerTest package (Kuznetsova et al., 2015, cf. Schaalje et al., 2002) in the R statistics software (R Core Team, 2015). It is possible to build up specific models. One problem is that we cannot simultaneously model specific variance stemming from subjects as well as adjectives, or images. The following formulas are just some suggestions. The "~" can be read as "is modelled by", or "is estimated by", a "*" indicates "interaction effects and main effects", and within parenthesis are the "random effects" that we might think of as the sources of variance. The "|" can be read "for each", as in "(1 | adjective)" is "a different intercept (starting point) for each adjective, and "(type | adjective)" can be read as "a different intercept, as well as a different slope for each adjective compared to the (first) baseline adjective". The notation is very efficient for specifying a model, but we need to be aware that to estimate a slope, we need at least two levels of a factor, for each factor the right of its "|" sign. For example, we cannot have a slope per participant for "personal gender", as there is only one gender per subject within the experiment, and similarly if the adjective is associated not (fairly) associated with each type we cannot estimate slopes for the type per adjective. (Type indicates the combination of face and gaze as a four-level factor).

score ~ type + (type | subject) + (1 | adjective)
score ~ type + (1 | subject) + (type | adjective)

We may include gaze and face direction as two fixed factors. We include slopes for all combinations of gaze and face direction for either the subject or the adjective.

score ~ face * gaze + ((face * gaze) | subject) + (1 | adjective)
score ~ face * gaze + (1 | subject) + ((face * gaze) | adjective)

We suggest to include different starting points for each image as well. Such a model might not have different effects (slopes) for the combinations of face and gaze.

score ~ face*gaze + (1 | subject) + (1 | item) + (1 | image).

The analysis will have to consider that we are using a dependent variable (score) that is not a continuous variable, and it is not necessarily on an interval scale either. This demands that we use a different family of distributions to evaluate the model. The recent developments in statistical testing are to use a model testing that is closer to machine learning techniques, and focus on how well the model explains the variance in the data. In that advanced analysis, the residuals should be randomly distributed and follow a normal distribution closely (if the residuals are random, and the model is good). This is only hinted at in this presentation, as the field is developing very fast and we do not want to mislead our readers that there is an easy formulation for making the best possible model. We would simply like to take the opportunity to point out some possibilities, which may be implemented in several ways, and hint at the work needed to analyze the model to see if the model has a reasonable fit to the sampled data. We would also recommend to try to sample as much data as possible, with both a high number of participants, and a high number of items, as well as using control variable. One useful control variable would be the presentation order of the images. It is expected that participants will become increasingly more comfortable with their decisions through the experiment, but we currently cannot reliably measure how long the decisions took in an internet survey, as the computer equipment will be different, and the presentation rate may be affected by internet quality and bandwidth.

The main benefit of surveys is that the number of participants can be very large. This gives the possibility to test much more material, as each participant might judge different items. In order to control the drop out rate, and fatigue effects, we need to limit the size of the experiment for each subject. The drawbacks of surveys are that it is difficult to know who the subjects are, in what environment they are solving the task, what equipment they are using, and the bandwidth of their internet connection, as well as other sources of uncertainty. The data quality may also put limits on what is possible in the analysis. Judgements are categorical data, and that limits our statistical tests. However, many of the drawbacks of surveys can be argued to be compensated by the access to much more data: more subjects, more items, and thus more data points. It could even be argued that the potential complexity of the (uncontrolled) environments could make the experiments more ecologically valid, as the participants are solving the task "in the wild", although the situation is still limited by the use of computer equipment, even if the computer could be at a coffee bar, a student room, or in the back seat of a car.

References

Bullot, N. J., & Reber, R. (2013). The artful mind meets art history: Toward a psycho-historical framework for the science of art appreciation. *Behavioral and Brain Sciences, 36*, 123–137. https://doi.org/10.1017/s0140525x12000489

Cohen, A. (1980). On the graphical display of the significant components in a two-way contingency table. *Communications in Statistics-Theory and Methods, A9*, 1025–1041. https://doi.org/10.1080/03610928008827940

Cohen, S. (1997). *Mindblindness: An essay on autism and theory of mind*. MIT Press.

Conty, L., N'Diaye, K., Tijus, C., & George, N. (2007). When eye creates the contact! ERP evidence for early dissociation between direct and averted gaze motion processing. *Neuropsychologia, 45*, 3024–3037. https://doi.org/10.1016/j.neuropsychologia.2007.05.017

Dunham, P. J., Dunham, F., & Curwin, A. (1993). Joint-attentional states and lexical acquisition at 18 months. *Developmental Psychology, 29*, 927–931. https://doi.org/10.1037/0012-1649.29.5.827

Emery, N. J. (2000). The eyes have it: The neuroethology, function and evolution of social gaze. *Neuroscience & Biobehavioral Reviews, 24*, 581–604. https://doi.org/10.1016/s0149-7634(00)00025-7

Folgerø, P., Hodne, L., Johansson, C., Andresen, A.,Sætren, L. C., Specht, K., Skaar, Ø. O., & Reber, R. (2016, September). Effects of facial symmetry and gaze direction on perception of social attributes: A study in experimental art history. *Frontiers in Human Neuroscience*, 10. https://doi.org/10.3389/fnhum.2016.00452

Friendly, M. (1992). Graphical methods for categorical data. In *SAS User Group International Conference Proceedings, 17*, 190–200. http://preview.tinyurl.com/h29ffha

Hodne, L. (2013). Symmetry versus frontality in the renaissance holy face. *Symmetry: Culture and Science, 24*, 437–450.

Kobayashi, H., & Koshima, S. (1997). Morphological uniqueness of human eyes and its adaptive meaning. *Nature, 387*, 767–768. https://doi.org/10.1038/42842

Kuznetsova, A., Bruun Brockhoff, P., & Haubo Bojesen Christensen, R. (2015). *Package imertest*. https://cran.r-project.org/web/packages/lmerTest/lmerTest.pdf

Langner, O., Dotsch, R., Bijlstra, G., Wigboldus, D. H. J., Hawk, S. T., & van Knippenberg, A. (2010). Presentation and validation of the Radboud faces database. *Cognition and Emotion, 24*, 1377–1388. https://doi.org/10.1080/02699930903485076

Meyer, D., Zeileis, A., & Hornik, K. (2003). Visualizing independence using extended association plots. In K. Hornik, F. Leisch, & A. Zeileis (Eds.), *Proceedings of the 3rd International Workshop on Distributed Statistical Computing (DSC2003)*. ISSN 1609-395X. https://www.r-project.org/conferences/DSC-2003/Proceedings/

Morgan, D. (2012). *The embodied eye. Religious visual culture and the social life of feeling*. University of California Press.

Mundi, P., & Gomes, A. (1998). Individual differences in joint attention skill development in the second year. *Infant Behavior and Development, 21*, 469–482. https://doi.org/10.1016/s0163-6383(98)90020-0

Perrett, D. I., & Emery, N. J. (1994). Understanding the intentions of others from visual signals: Neurophysiological evidence. *Current Psychology of Cognition, 13*, 683–694.

R Core Team. (2015). R: A language and environment for statistical computing. In *R Foundation for statistical computing (Vienna, Austria)*. https://www.R-project.org/

Schaalje, G. B., McBride, J. B., & Fellingham, G. W. (2002). Adequacy of approximations to distributions of test statistics in complex mixed linear models. *Journal of Agricultural, Biological, and Environmental Statistics, 7*, 512–524. https://doi.org/10.1198/108571102726

Tomasello, M., & Farrar, M. Y. (1986). Joint attention and early language. *Child Development, 57*, 1454–1463. https://doi.org/10.2307/1130423

Torp, H. (1984). *The integrating system of proportion in Byzantine art. An essay on the Method of the Painters of Holy Images*. Giorgio Bretschneider.

Yang, D.Y.-J., Rosenblau, G., Keifer, C., & Pelphrey, K. A. (2015). An integrative neural model of social perception, action observation and theory of mind. *Neuroscience & Biobehavioral Reviews, 51*, 263–275. https://doi.org/10.1016/j.neubiorev.2015.01.020

Unit 4 Lab: Create Your Own Association Graphs and Correspondence Analysis Using R

Christer Johansson and Per Olav Folgerø

Task 1: Download and install R on your computer.

Task 2: Install the necessary packages.

a) Install the vcd package
   > install.packages()

You will get a list of servers. Select a server that is close to your country.
You will get a list of available packages. Select vcd.
The installation process starts.
Activate the vcd package from the console: > library(vcd)

b) Install the FactoMineR package
   >install.packages()

You will get a list of servers. Select a server that is close to your country.

You will get a list of available packages. Select FactoMineR.
The installation process starts.

Activate the FactoMineR package from the console: > library(FactoMineR)
   Beware: R considers upper and lower case letters to be different symbols.

C. Johansson (✉) · P. O. Folgerø
University of Bergen, Bergen, Norway
e-mail: Christer.Johansson@uib.no

P. O. Folgerø
e-mail: Per.Folgero@uib.no

T. Balinisteanu and K. Priest (eds.), *Neuroaesthetics*,
https://doi.org/10.1007/978-3-031-42323-9_13

Task 3: Get some data. We will create a table with some fictional data.

```
>a<- matrix(c(100,50,100,50,100,200,100,200,25,50,75,100),
nrow=4,dimnames=list(c("A","B","C","D"),c("positive","negative","neutral")))
> a
```

	Positive	Negative	Neutral
A	100	100	25
B	50	200	50
C	100	100	75
D	50	200	100

The data is entered column by column, from first to last row. The variable a is assigned the result. If you need to switch the rows and columns you can do so with the transpose command (t).

```
>t(a)
```

	A	B	C	D
Positive	100	50	100	50
Negative	100	200	100	200
Neutral	25	50	75	100

Now you have some data. The first we do is to create association tables with "assoc" from the vcd package.

```
> assoc(a, shade=T)
```

The parameter shade=T asks the function to color code how significant each cell is.

You may also transpose rows and columns, using the function t().

```
>assoc(t(a), shade=T)
```

The red bars mark cells that contain frequencies that are lower than expected. The blue bars mark cells that have higher frequencies than expected. The height of the bars is proportional to significance and the width of the bars is proportional to the support (how much data note that "negative" has a wider base where the frequencies are higher) (Fig. 1).

The graphs allow us to look for associations between rows and columns, and see if the association is higher or lower than expected if rows and columns were statistically independent.

The second function we will investigate is Correspondence Analysis. The input to this function is also a matrix, just like the association graphs. It is often good to use both association graphs and CA graphs. We simply call the CA function, after we have activated the package FactoMineR.

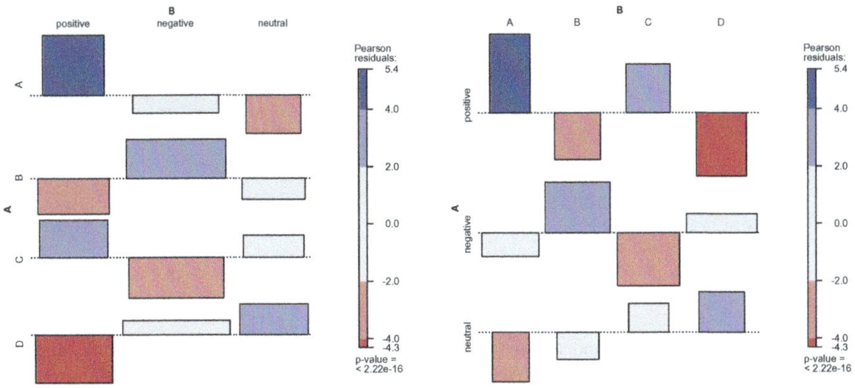

Fig. 1 Association graphs, original and transposed

>CA(a)

>CA(t(a))

You will see part of the analysis is text, and a graph that can be saved is also presented.

The CA graph calculates a coordinate system with the dimensions that best explain the variance in the data set. It is a nice way to present very complicated datasets with many different variables. The way to read the graph is to look at the extreme points, most distant from the origin. These points span up the dimensions. We further need to look at the line from each point to the origin. For example, B and negative are highly associated, both because they are close in the space and they have a similar angle toward the origin. We can also see this directly from the data, the value on negative for B is 200, which is much higher than the values for positive or neutral. The real usefulness of CA comes when you have large tables or matrices, with many rows (items) and columns (typically descriptors). Such data is very difficult to grasp, but in the CA graph you can see the structure (Fig. 2).

Task 4: Find your own data sets, and see if association and correspondence will help you understand and present the structure in your data.

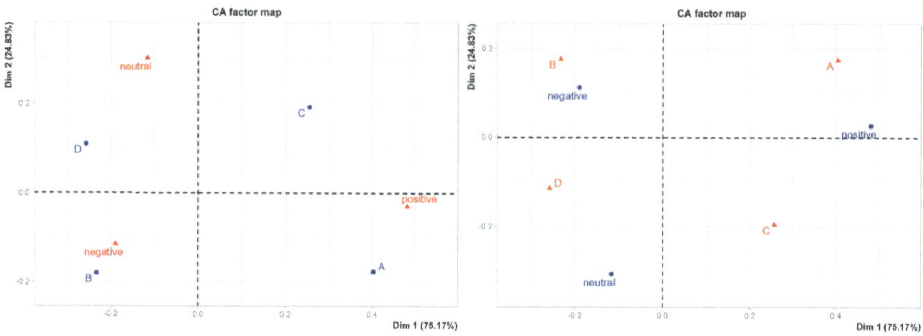

Fig. 2 CA graphs, original and transposed. Note that the colors have been switched, and the coordinate values for each data point have also altered, but the variance explained is the same

Further Reading

Visualizing Categorical Data and Association Graphs

Cohen, A. (1980). On the graphical display of the significant components in a two-way contingency table. *Communications in Statistics-Theory and Methods, A9*, 1025–1041. https://doi.org/10.1080/03610928008827940

Friendly, M. (1992). Graphical methods for categorical data. In *SAS User Group International Conference Proceedings, 17*, 190–200. http://preview.tinyurl.com/h29ffha

Meyer, D., Zeileis, A., & Hornik, K. (2021). vcd: Visualizing Categorical Data. R package version 1.4-9.

Correspondence Analysis

Glynn, D. (2014). Correspondence analysis: Exploring data and identifying patterns. In D. Glynn & J. A. Robinson (Eds.), *Corpus methods for semantics: Quantitative studies in polysemy and synonymy* (pp. 443–485). John Benjamins Publishing Company. http://digital.casalini.it/9789027270337

Lê, S., Josse, J., & Husson, F. (2008). FactoMineR: An *R* package for multivariate analysis. *Journal of Statistical Software, 25*(1), 1–18. https://doi.org/10.18637/jss.v025.i01

R

R Core Team. (2015). R: A language and environment for statistical computing. In *R Foundation for Statistical Computing (Vienna, Austria)*. https://www.R-project.org/

Unit 5 Overview: The Neuroaesthetics of Music

Morteza Izadifar

Introduction

Generally speaking, aesthetics is the study of beauty, as well as its opposite, ugliness. Artistic experience or the arts are regarded by some philosophers as the essence of aesthetics. Nevertheless, most aesthetic philosophers see this discipline as encompassing beauty and ugliness as a whole. The term "aesthetics" was first used in 1750 by Alexander Baumgarten (1714–1762) to refer to a science of sensory perception which focused on beauty in particular. Philosophers have also discussed beauty for thousands of years. Some sources from ancient Greece and China both comment on "good" and "bad" music.

As painting and drawing are fundamental parts of a culture, music plays a similar role. Since ancient times, music has been ubiquitous in human culture. But what does make music so special to us? Throughout our lives, music plays a vital role. Emotions are evoked by music, and music is routinely used to regulate moods and emotions. All of these results point to music's powerful influence, either explicitly or implicitly. A huge amount of money would not be spent on music if this wasn't true.

The human behavior of listening to and playing music has existed since prehistoric times. Music is often valued for the emotions it generates, and listening to music can boost mood and increase well-being. There may be a reason why people listen to music every day. As music is abstract and subjective, we cannot quantifiably understand what sustains us in it. In recent years, advances in neuroimaging have fueled empirical studies on what makes music so enjoyable. It is our belief that musical pleasure is the result of interactions between the sensory, cognitive,

M. Izadifar (✉)
The Institute of Human Aesthetics, Coburg University of Applied Sciences & Art and Bamberg University, Am Hofbräuhaus 1, 96450 Coburg, Germany
e-mail: Morteza.Izadifar@hs-coburg.de

T. Balinisteanu and K. Priest (eds.), *Neuroaesthetics*,
https://doi.org/10.1007/978-3-031-42323-9_14

and emotional systems, as well as reinforcement circuits. Moreover, music listening recruits large-scale brain networks in regions of the cerebral cortex, subcortical areas, and cerebellum that are involved in audition, motor imagery, and planning as well as emotion.

However, our responses to music aesthetic depend on many "internal factors" such as internal state, mood, personality, and attitude. In addition to the physical and social environment, also called the "external context", the factors that affect listening include whether the listener is alone or in a group- being in a concert hall, for example.

Music aesthetics can be studied from two perspectives: psychological levels of well-being and enjoyment and its physiological and neurological correlates. The two perspectives are conceptually distinct, but they are inextricably bound with the neurological level providing the ultimate explanation for the aesthetic emotion of enjoyment. In the following sections, we dive into the "neuroaesthetics of music" in a deeper sense and explore why music is so appealing to us.

A Historical Overview of Neuroaesthetics of Music

Since the commencement of experimental psychology, the question of how music provides an aesthetic experience has been studied using scientific approaches. For an understanding of the profound and extraordinarily radical change brought about by this new discipline of neuroaesthetics of music, it is important to remember some of the beginnings of music aesthetics studies.

Hermann von Helmholtz (1821–1894) (von Helmholtz, 1863) inspired by Eduard Hanslick (1825–1904) (Hanslick, 1891), initiated a new phase of empirical studies on musical perception by associating the aesthetic characteristics of musical notes and scales with their psychoacoustic features (particularly frequency ratios between partials of complex tones). Besides, Wilhelm Wundt (1832–1920), a pioneer of experimental psychology and a former assistant of Helmholtz in Heidelberg, used a psychological approach to aesthetics, reflecting on how his own feelings of pleasure, excitement, and exuberance changed with the tempo of a metronome, for example. Wundt (Wundt, 1912) also showed that physiological arousal is related to the stimulus complexity, and that aesthetic pleasure is highest at intermediate levels of complexity.

Music psychologists of the first half of the twentieth century, such as Farnsworth, Hevner, Schoen, and Seashore studied the affective response to music. A wide range of data showed that music can evoke deep and complex affective responses, but direct causal relationships between music variables and specific affective responses were difficult to establish. Such studies had a very low predictive power. However, data revealed that affective responses to music were often highly idiosyncratic to the individual listener and their musical enculturation, as well as to the particular listening or testing conditions: the subjects brought mood states or arousal needs to the listening condition, for instance.

It was during the second half of the twentieth century that music research made significant breakthroughs in aesthetic theory. A few new developments in music and meaning theories were influenced by two highly influential theories proposed by Leonard Meyer (Meyer, 1957) and Daniel Berlyne (Berlyne, 1957) between the 1950s and the 1970s.

Meyer (1918–2007) proposed a model of how music evokes meaningful affective responses in the audience or performer. According to Dewey's conflict theory of emotion, emotional responses result from inhibited responses. Compositional schemes that are continuously delayed, inhibited, and resolved are used to build expectations in music, creating a complex, woven sound architecture that builds musical structures of anticipation–tension–resolution through continuous delays, inhibitions, and resolutions. It is through the interplay between anticipation, tension, and resolution that suspense evokes arousal—particularly during the tension phase, i.e., a temporary inhibition of expectations—and a quest for resolutions that is resolved within the musical structure.

Daniel Ellis Berlyne (1924–1976) developed his idea into an inverted U-shaped function linking a stimulus's "arousal potential" with its "hedonic value", such that intermediate degrees of arousal correspond to maximum pleasure, and attempted to identify how stimulus properties (such as complexity, familiarity, novelty, and uncertainty) influence aspects of the aesthetic experience such as arousal, pleasure, and interestingness in his new experimental aesthetics.

Recent decades have seen an explosion in neuro-musical research from these early explorations of aesthetics. A relative flood of publications has emerged in recent years from pioneering efforts that began in the 1800s.

Music aesthetics underwent its most fundamental change over the last 25 years of the twentieth century when brain imaging techniques became an entirely new process of studying the human in vivo as the brain performs complex cognitive functions. And in recent years, a new field of scientific inquiry, cognitive neuroscience, has been established through the use of positron emission tomography (PET), functional magnetic resonance imaging (fMRI), and electroencephalography (EEG). These technologies provided unprecedented access to the brain basis of human cognition and music aesthetics. As a result of brain imaging techniques, research directions have changed dramatically, and the cognitive science of music embedded in music aesthetics has virtually been reinvented. With advances in brain imaging technology, scientists now have the ability to map and track connections and directional influences between brain regions while listening to music rather than relying on static topographical maps or liking and disliking questionnaires.

From Neuroscience to Neuroaesthetics of Music

Why do we enjoy music so much? People appreciate music largely for its aesthetic qualities: the emotions it evokes, the memories it brings, and its beauty per se. Listening to or performing music, like other aesthetic domains such as visual art, architecture, or dance produces aesthetic experiences that also include emotional responses and evaluative opinions of beauty, aesthetic quality, and liking when combined with a favorable environment and listening situation. Many argue that neuroscience has nothing to tell us about aesthetic questions. Nevertheless, since the beginning of experimental psychology, the question of how music provides an aesthetic experience has been studied using scientific approaches.

Box 1: What Do We Mean by Aesthetic Experience of Music?

We define an aesthetic musical experience as one in which the individual immerses herself in the music, devoting her attention to perceptual, cognitive, and emotive interpretation based on the perceptual experience's formal qualities. We identify three key outcomes: first, emotion perception and induction (e.g., "this song is sad"); second, aesthetic evaluation (e.g., "this song is lovely"); and third, liking (e.g., "I like this song") and preference (e.g., "I adore rock & roll"). However, not all of these consequences may be present at the same time, but they usually combine to make a real aesthetic situation. An aesthetic experience does not require the presence of a music-induced feeling.

Neuroscience belongs to physiology, with its final goal of examining human behavior's neural basis. There are multiple reasons why scientists study music aesthetics through neuroscience lenses. First of all, musicians provide a useful model for neuroplasticity in the brain because their performance involves an online integration of sensory and motor information. In other words, neural changes (measurable non-invasively with sophisticated brain imaging tools) occur after intensive and extended exposure to a specific stimulus environment. It is also possible to distinguish between innate predispositions and those of training or exposure by studying music, a multidimensional complex stimulus that is not equally familiar to all humans (if we take into account musical expertise, which is easier to discern than language expertise). The milder semantic level may also allow for the separation of the effects of training or exposure from those of innate predispositions. Last but not least, music has always existed in human societies (as evidenced by prehistoric musical instruments discovered by paleontologists), making it unique among human entertainment activities.

Several studies have been conducted on the neural bases of pitch, timbre, and rhythm perception. The processing of sounds in the central nervous system as well as how they are organized, comprehended, and "felt" by each individual as the coherent unity known as music may then be scientifically justified through combined research in the neurosciences of musical appreciation and production. To put it another way, we could add scientific justifications to the anecdotal evidence and brilliant philosophical arguments that show us the unifying and expressive power of music, which likely evolved over the long course of human evolution.

Having said that, a question arises here: where should we begin to understand music aesthetics from a neuroscientific perspective? To answer this question, we could say that to better understand musical appreciation, we must understand the neural basis for sound perception and the neural underpinnings of the musical emotions. In the following section, we will have a visit to different aspects of music aesthetics and the human brain in detail.

Emotions in Musical Experience

The neuroscience of music has benefited from an increase in neuroscientific interest in affective processes. However, research has focused on the most common emotions that people experience in everyday life, such as happiness and sadness, and their role in mood regulation. So, we categorize musical emotions either in "basic emotions" (Universal emotional experiences, acknowledged across cultures and required for species survival) or general dimensional models of emotion.

However, it has been proposed that music induces feelings that are qualitatively different from goal-oriented, common emotions, despite the fact that there has been little neuroscientific study on such aesthetic emotions to date.

Basic Emotions: Work on the categorical perception of facial emotion has sparked a lot of interest in music and emotion studies. This concept highlights basic emotions such as happiness, sorrow, anger, fear, and disgust, which are suggested to be recognized across all cultures and related with intrinsic motor and physiological responses. Music may convey and induce these basic feelings in people of all ages, including infants, and across many cultures, albeit negative emotions lose some of their unpleasant quality in a safe aesthetic context.

Brain Regions and Process of Basic Emotion in Music: The amygdala is crucial in the processing of significant negative emotions, particularly fear, caused by unpleasant stimuli. The amygdala appears to be an important brain region for fear perception and recognition in music. How do we know? The answer lies in the fact that patients with a medial temporal ablation that included the amygdala, as well as one with bilateral amygdala injury, misinterpret scary music as tranquil music while displaying intact perceptual skills. Besides, lots of evidence show that the amygdala is activated by sad and inharmonious music—compared to emotionally neutral and consonant music, respectively, and even by single random chords. Sad emotions linked with slow minor classical piano music engaged the left medial frontal cortex and the adjacent superior frontal gyrus when compared to happy major and rapid pieces. The ventral striatum and left superior temporal gyrus are also candidates for music associated with good emotions (for example, happiness). This region is thought to be a portion of the non-primary auditory cortex, which is responsible for integrating sounds across longer time spans than the primary auditory cortex and hence processing more abstract features of sounds.

Dimensional Models of Emotion: Dimensional models try to find a set of dimensions that can represent all of the conceivable emotional states. The dimensional structure should, in theory, be rich enough to represent the fundamental emotions as points in space. *The circumplex model*, which divides valence (pleasure–displeasure) and arousal (activating–relaxing) as two orthogonal dimensions of an emotional experience, is the most generally recognized dimensional model of emotion. Many behavioral and neuroscientific investigations have used this approach to study music. The three aspects of valence (pleasant–unpleasant), arousal (awake–tired), and tension (tense-relaxed) are included in a variation of this approach.

This model has been also applied to music. For instance, loudness and tempo were found to increase arousal and tension ratings, while loudness and pitch height upsurges pleasantness. In fMRI studies, it has been shown that while people listen to classical music some modifications in arousal and valence were reflected by changes in activation in the reward and limbic systems (including the striatum, ventral tegmental area, and orbitofrontal cortex for valence, and the ventromedial prefrontal cortex and the subgenual cingulate, for arousal) along with additional effects in brain areas related to memory, motor control, and self-reflective processes.

In simple words, for example, when one listens to energetic music, surge in electrodermal activity, which is generated by the sympathetic autonomic nervous system, is greater than when one listens to relaxing music.

It should be noted that listening to music might trigger other kinds of emotions (which are called aesthetic emotions) such as awe, nostalgia, and enjoyment. For instance, you have experienced that while you are listening to a music piece of the past autobiographical memories of the song cause a kind nostalgia. Janata (2009) featured artists who had a long history of working in the pop/rock genre. Individual judgments of autobiographical relevance and changes in brain metabolism revealed that the dorsal areas of the medial prefrontal cortex are critical for experiencing music-induced nostalgia.

Another fMRI study was conducted by Bogert et al. (2016) modulating the visual instructions related to 4-s music clips, asking participants to pay attention to either the number of instruments playing (implicit condition) or to categorize the emotions conveyed by the music explicitly (explicit condition). Contrary to the explicit condition, the implicit condition (contrasted with the explicit one) of listening to music involved bilateral activation of the inferior parietal lobule, premotor cortex, and reward-related areas such as the caudate (dorsal striatum) and ventromedial frontal cortex. During a listening mode that explicitly judged the musical emotions expressed in clips, dorsomedial prefrontal and occipital areas, previously associated with emotion recognition, were active (Fig. 1).

Now, how do we measure the aesthetic emotion of enjoyment in music neuroscience? Most of the time, it has been examined by focusing on the chill reaction. Chills, also known as tremble or thrills, correspond to physiological changes such as goose bumps and shivers down the spine, and are possibly the most well studied aesthetic experience of music. Although not everyone gets goosebumps when listening to or playing music, those who do tend to have them all on a regular basis. Chills have the added benefit of eliciting physiological signals such as changes in heart rate, breath depth, and skin conductance, in addition to being easy to track behaviourally.

How Does Music Generate Emotions?

The relationship between music and emotion is a much-debated subject that has been at the heart of musical aesthetics since the late eighteenth century. In eighteenth- and nineteenth-century Europe, the advent of instrumental music and, later, program music sparked a debate between referentialists like Hegel (1770–1831) and Wagner (1813–1883) and formalists like Hanslick (1825–1904) and Stravinsky (1882–1971). The discussion focused on whether music has referential content, meaning that musical patterns can indicate nonmusical elements like physical objects, individuals, or feelings. This led Hanslick to argue that music's aesthetic function is not to elicit emotion. In other words, music cannot convey distinct sentiments (which have objects) because it cannot reflect the thoughts that underlie these feelings; it can represent dynamic variations in intensity of such

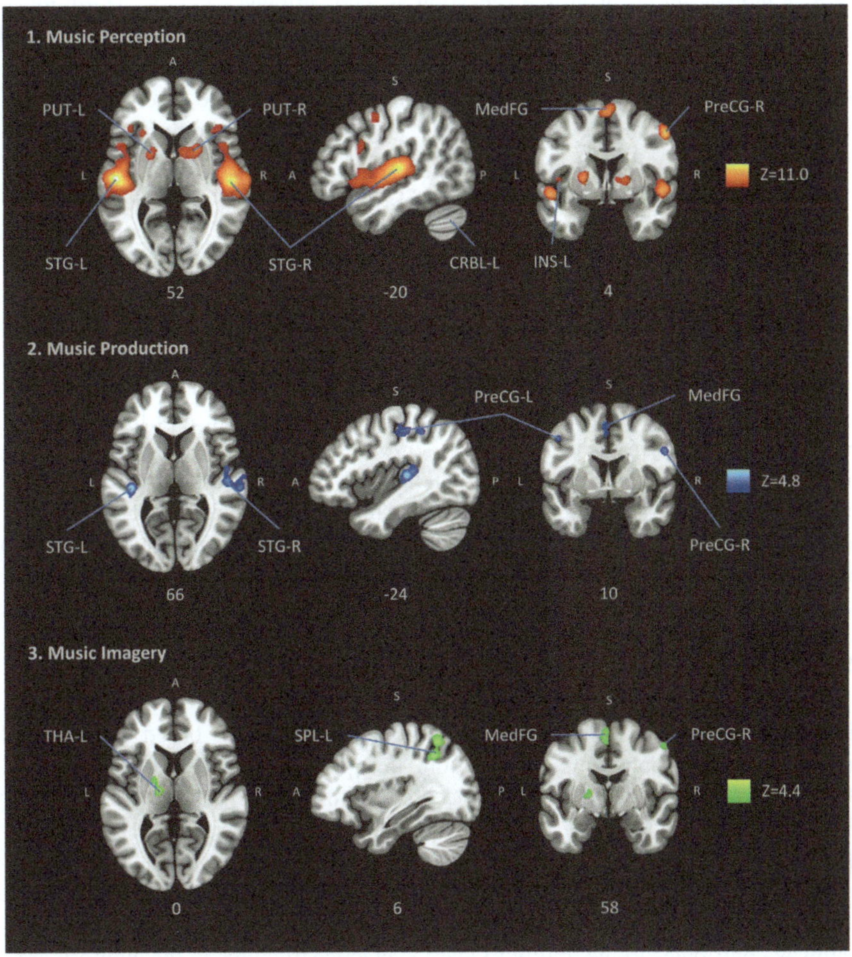

Fig. 1 Brain regions which are involved in different aspects of music Borrowed with permission from Pando-Naude et al. (2021)

feelings, but not as attributes of specific emotions because other phenomena share such dynamic changes as well. Hanslick, meanwhile claims that music's aesthetic qualities are unique to music.

According to Juslin and Västfjäll (2008), emotion perception, in which a listener detects or recognizes emotions represented in music, is distinguished from emotion induction, in which music generates an emotion in the listener. The induction of arousal by sudden, harsh, discordant, or fast pulsating noises is first mediated via brainstem responses (originating from locations such as the inferior colliculus). Second, in constructive conditioning, music can elicit emotion by associating with an unpleasant or rewarding sensation as a conditioned stimulus. Third, musical patterns can cause emotional contagion by imitating other forms of emotional expression including language, posture, and movement. Fourth, music can evoke emotions by using structures in the sensorium that have close external referents, resulting in visual imagery (e.g., a storm). Fifth, music can elicit emotion by triggering an episodic memory associated with it ("Darling, they're playing our tune"). Finally, creating and breaking expectations can lead to feelings of tension, release, and surprise.

Therefore, concisely, the psychological mechanisms most particular to musical aesthetic perception, as well as those most investigated by neuroscientists are brainstem systems (such as those that produce dissonance), emotional contagion or imitation, and expectancy. In addition to these structural issues, neurochemical research has also identified neurotransmitters' impact on music listening's affective aspects. Combining psychophysical, neurochemical, and hemodynamic effects may uncover peaks in autonomic nervous system activity, which can explain music's mood-enhancing effects. Researchers have found that listening to highly pleasurable music triggers the release of dopamine in the mesolimbic striatal system, as well as sensory areas for auditory reception, using ligand-based positron emission tomography—using radioligand raclopride, which binds to dopamine.

Areas Involved in High-Level Temporal Sequencing

The ability to appreciate music requires recognizing patterns based on structural information. With incoming information, this process is continuously updated, refined, and revised. The frontal cortices of the brain, such as the IFG (Inferior Frontal Gyrus), are typically hotspot of this operation. There may be a possibility that the STG (Superior Temporal Gurus) and IFG (Inferior Frontal Gyrus) are co-activated in order to process various aspects of music in a collaborative manner. Interestingly, it has also been demonstrated that white matter connectivity in this pathway contributes to the ability to learn syntactic structures in the auditory area. How do we know all these? As a matter of fact, there is logic behind these claims: A loss of a function is proof of its existence. For instance, it has been observed that people with congenital amusia who show deficits in music perception have disrupted STG-IFG pathways.

Moreover, part of music processing is carried out in the superior temporal cortex (STC), which houses both primary and secondary auditory areas. This region is also a place where pitch, extraction of pitch, and tonal relationships are processed. It should be noted that this region accumulates sound templates over time during our life. For instance, when TMS (Transcranial Magnetic Stimulation Device) stimulates the STC region of the brain, musical hallucinations are elicited, and increased activity in this area is linked to imagery and familiarity with music.

Sensory Dissonance

Sensory consonance and dissonance, which have long been used by composers and performers in Western and non-Western cultures to alter aesthetic responses to music, have received the greatest attention in neuroaesthetics of music studies. Dissonant sounds are experienced as beating amplitude modulation or roughness for the listener and in this situation the basilar membrane stimulates nearby hair cells, causing neurons in the cochlea nucleus and brainstem to fire without adequately resolving the two sounds. The signal stimulates neurons in the primary auditory cortex to vibrate at the beat frequency, resulting in higher neuronal activity than consonant sounds. These sensory responses to dissonant sounds are accompanied by an affective feeling of irritation, which appears to have a neurological basis in the parahippocampal gyrus, a brain region linked to withdrawal behavior, and the amygdala, which is linked to salience and negative affect.

Trost et al. (2012) discovered a clear lateralization of the parahippocampal gyrus while listening to emotional classical music: highly arousing music activated the left parahippocampal gyrus, whereas tender and nostalgic music with low arousal activated the right parahippocampal gyrus. Consonance, on the other hand, is commonly regarded as the absence of dissonance, although other researchers believe it is a more active process involving reward regions in the brainstem and ventral striatum.

Box 2: Dissonance in music is defined as discordant sounds or a lack of harmony. When the two notes of this staff are performed at the same time, the result is a dissonant sound.

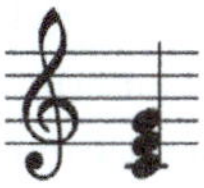

Musical pleasure is associated with patterns of tension and resolving that arise from the confirmation and violation of perceptual expectations that we are normally unaware. In other words, the music's prior context (e.g., the next note's pitch in a melody, the next chord in a harmonic movement pattern, or the next note's time) creates expectations/predictions in the listener's brain about what will happen next. For instance, in an experiment done by Steinbeis and his colleagues (2006), they realized that unexpected chords create more physiological excitement than expected chords, as measured by skin conductance.

Aesthetic experience without making an aesthetic judgment could be possible in some circumstances. According to some findings, regions in the prefrontal regions of the brain, notably the dorsolateral prefrontal and orbitofrontal cortex are active when we do make an aesthetic judgment, such as when we decide that an object is beautiful. Numerous neuroimaging studies of musical listening support the orbitofrontal cortex's function in the pleasant emotional experiences connected to aesthetic evaluations of musical preference or beauty. Moreover, In contrast to dissonant chords evaluated as ugly, consonant chords assessed to be beautiful activate the dorsomedial midbrain nuclei, which are part of the dopaminergic reward circuit of the brain (Suzuki et al., 2008). This is true regardless of whether the chords are in the major or minor key.

The Musical Preference and Aesthetic Experience

Preference, which differs from enjoyment or subjective pleasure in that it involves making a choice about the stimulus as a whole is another significant result of the musical aesthetic experience. Such a choice could stick to the person for a very long time and usually the preference activates after finishing a song in its entirety. This choice may be made based on the degree of enjoyment, an aesthetic evaluation of the stimulus's beauty or other formal qualities (however it may also differ and be independent of such an evaluation), and other intrapersonal considerations such as the listener's past habits, existing mood, or personality. For instance, the more we are touched by music, the more we prefer it, according to Schubert's (2007) research, which showed that inducing either a good or a negative feeling through music predicts preference. Another predictor of preference was shown by Vuoskoski and Eerola (2011). They realized that when listening to gloomy music, people with high trait empathy tend to appreciate it more and experience greater sadness than those with low trait empathy.

Musical preference appears to activate lateralized brain networks. Altenmüller and colleagues (2002) in a groundbreaking electroencephalography (EEG) study discovered left lateralized frontotemporal activations of the brain when listeners preferred classical, pop, or jazz excerpts lasting 15 seconds. It should be noted that when they disliked those kinds of music, they showed right-lateralized anterior responses (neutral music produced bilateral brain responses). In a subsequent EEG and fMRI study, desired 30-s excerpts by Bach and Mahler similarly activated left-hemispheric regions, including Heschl's gyrus, middle temporal gyrus, and cuneus, whereas disliked excerpts by a contemporary composer produced brain responses in the bilateral inferior frontal gyrus and insula.

There are lots of experiments that emphasize on the role of familiarity in liking and preference of music. They believe that where enjoyment and related liking judgments increase with increasing exposure (*the mere exposure effect*). Pereira et al. (2011) report activation of limbic and paralimbic areas including the nucleus accumbens to familiar music (contrasted with unfamiliar music), but only minimal activation when contrasting liked musical pieces with disliked ones, regardless of familiarity, demonstrating the close relationship between familiarity and hedonic musical experiences. These results imply that one of the major influences on the brain's emotional and hedonic reactions is familiarity.

Another factor that is central to musical aesthetic experience is attention. In other words, the listener must focus on the music to appreciate the emotions and memories evoked by it, to judge whether it is attractive or well performed, and to determine its aesthetic value. The superior parietal lobule, the precuneus, and other parietal structures associated with the ventral network are involved in stimulus-driven attention.

Musical Expectancies

In order to appreciate tension and release, a listener must perceive musical relations within a hierarchy of tonal stability. As an example, moving away from a tonal center to unstable chords (or keys) is perceived as tensing, while returning to the stable tonal center is perceived as relaxing. It is also possible to produce tension by using dissonance as well as tones (or chords) that are harmonically unrelated to the context of the music. In fact, Tonal music appreciation depends heavily on the interplay between expectations as they unfold over time, and how they are fulfilled or violated.

Do Musicians and Non-Musicians Respond Differently to Musical Sounds?

Meta-analyses demonstrate an enlarged volume of gray matter in the temporal lobe for primary and non-primary auditory regions in music experts with skillful listening abilities. Additionally, neurophysiological measurements indicate that musicians' neuronal assemblies respond to sounds and errors of sounds faster and stronger than non-musicians'. It should be noted that skillful listening requires cognitive mastery, a crucial stage of information processing that produces judgments and emotions based on knowledge and understanding. Professional musicians, for instance, have different cognitive strategies and assisting representations of music than those who are not professionals. As a result of training and practice, they show auxiliary mental representations of music, and use more complex neuronal networks than nonprofessionals, including an activation of the left hemisphere attributed to the recruitment of inner speech by automatically naming pitches and harmonies.

Shortcomings and Deficits in Study of Neuroaesthetics of Music

Although music neuroscience is now considered an independent sub-discipline of cognitive neuroscience, music neuroaesthetics is still in its early life. Having checked some articles published in this realm, you notice that many studies have been done on the brain impact of musical competence on perceptual and cognitive skills, but only few studies have looked at aesthetic or emotive judgments. Even psychologists tend to avoid investigating aesthetic reactions to music and instead focus on more mundane factors such as "preference" in music psychology. It should be noted that we consider preference to be an important and necessary factor, not a sufficient component of the aesthetic experience of music.

The Epilogue

Although there exist loads of evidence on underlying neuronal mechanism on music aesthetics, there are still ambiguities in how these systems function in the brain. Moreover, the reader should be satisfied at this stage regarding the significance of neuronal mechanism of the brain while these systems are used for our music enjoyment and other aesthetic aspects of music. Regarding experimental endeavor in neuroaesthetics of music, more research is also required to decide in more depth where, why, and how to execute these music aesthetic experiments.

Lastly, it should be noted that the presented chapter on neuroaesthetics of music does not intend to enforce this idea that there are only these brain networks involved in music aesthetic. It was aimed to illuminate a schematic picture for the new researchers who have come from fields other than neuroscience or psychology and want to be familiar with studies in music neuroaesthetics. It is believed that this chapter can help newcomers from non-neuroscientific fields to know more about music aesthetic and its underlying brain mechanisms.

References

Altenmüller, E., Schürmann, K., Lim, V. K., & Parlitz, D. (2002). Hits to the left, flops to the right: Different emotions during listening to music are reflected in cortical lateralisation patterns. *Neuropsychologia, 40*(13), 2242–2256.

Baumgarten, A. (Aesthetica, 1750, §1). *"Aesthetices finis est perfectio cognitionis sensitivae"*.

Berlyne, D. E. (1957). Uncertainty and conflict: A point of contact between information-theory and behavior-theory concepts. *Psychological Review, 64*(6p1), 329.

Bogert, B., Numminen-Kontti, T., Gold, B., Sams, M., Numminen, J., Burunat, I., …, Brattico, E. (2016). Hidden sources of joy, fear, and sadness: Explicit versus implicit neural processing of musical emotions. *Neuropsychologia, 89*, 393–402.

Hanslick, E. (1891). *Vom Musikalisch-Schönen: ein Beitrag zur Revision der Aesthetik der Tonkunst*. Leipzig. *Eng. trans.*

Janata, P. (2009). The neural architecture of music-evoked autobiographical memories. *Cerebral Cortex, 19*(11), 2579–2594.

Juslin, P. N., & Västfjäll, D. (2008). Emotional responses to music: The need to consider underlying mechanisms. *Behavioral and Brain Sciences, 31*(5), 559–575.

Meyer, L. B. (1957). Meaning in music and information theory. *The Journal of Aesthetics and Art Criticism, 15*(4), 412–424.

Pando-Naude, V., Patyczek, A., Bonetti, L., & Vuust, P. (2021). An ALE meta-analytic review of top-down and bottom-up processing of music in the brain. *Scientific Reports, 11*(1), 20813.

Pereira, C. S., Teixeira, J., Figueiredo, P., Xavier, J., Castro, S. L., & Brattico, E. (2011). Music and emotions in the brain: Familiarity matters. *PLoS One, 6*(11), e27241.

Schubert, E. (2007). The influence of emotion, locus of emotion and familiarity upon preference in music. *Psychology of Music, 35*(3), 499–515.

Steinbeis, N., Koelsch, S., & Sloboda, J. A. (2006). The role of harmonic expectancy violations in musical emotions: Evidence from subjective, physiological, and neural responses. *Journal of Cognitive Neuroscience, 18*(8), 1380–1393.

Suzuki, M., Okamura, N., Kawachi, Y., Tashiro, M., Arao, H., Hoshishiba, T., …, Yanai, K. (2008). Discrete cortical regions associated with the musical beauty of major and minor chords. *Cognitive, Affective, & Behavioral Neuroscience, 8*(2), 126–131.

Trost, W., Ethofer, T., Zentner, M., & Vuilleumier, P. (2012). Mapping aesthetic musical emotions in the brain. *Cerebral Cortex, 22*(12), 2769–2783.

von Helmholtz, H. (1863). *On the sensations of tone as a physiological basis for the theory of music*. Longmans Green.

Vuoskoski, J. K., & Eerola, T. (2011). Measuring music-induced emotion: A comparison of emotion models, personality biases, and intensity of experiences. *Musicae Scientiae, 15*(2), 159–173.

Wundt, W. (1912). *An introduction to psychology*. Macmillan.

Unit 5 Lesson: A Very Brief Introduction to Neuroimaging

Karsten Specht

Preface

This lesson intends to provide a brief introduction to some central neuroimaging methods that are relevant for studying the human brain. The lesson starts with a brief introduction to cognitive neuroscience as the basis of all cognitive processes, followed by a description of methods that can be used to measure brain responses. These are primarily two methods that will be presented here, which are (functional) magnetic resonance imaging (fMRI) and functional near-infrared spectroscopy (fNIRS). This overview can only touch on a few relevant topics and will be very selective in its examples and an in-depth study of these topics requires more than reading only this chapter. Each part of this chapter deserves a textbook on its own, and the reader is encouraged to continue reading from other sources, as well. Nevertheless, it is attempted to mention the most important aspects and developments briefly. However, the selection might appear to be weighted by personal interest and the overall topic of this book and should not be seen as a disregard of the not-mentioned work. The chapter ends with some reflections on the reliability and validity of the described methods.

K. Specht (✉)
Department of Biological and Medical Psychology, University of Bergen, Pb. 7807, 5020 Bergen, Norway
e-mail: Karsten.specht@uib.no

Mohn Medical Imaging and Visualization Centre, Haukeland University Hospital, Bergen, Norway

Department of Education, UiT/The Arctic University of Norway, Tromsø, Norway

T. Balinisteanu and K. Priest (eds.), *Neuroaesthetics*,
https://doi.org/10.1007/978-3-031-42323-9_15

From Neurons to Networks

Neurons and Neurotransmitters

The human brain is the most developed and complex organ of the human body. It consists of around 90 billion neurons, which are those cells that are primarily involved in processing information, and about an equal number of nonneuronal cells (Herculano-Houzel, 2012). However, within the class of neurons, there is also specific differentiation into subcategories, specialised and optimised for the functions they need to perform. Although neurons can have many different shapes and functions, common to all neurons is that they have several extensions that split up into many further branches, which are dedicated to only receiving signals from other neurons. They are called *dendrites*. On the other hand, every neuron has only one single extension—that may later also split up into several branches—that is dedicated to only sending a signal to other neurons. This is called the *axon*. The third part of a neuron is the cell body, called the *soma* (Sidiropoulou et al., 2006). In summary, a neuron can have many dendrites for receiving signals, but it has only one axon for sending signals. However, due to the branching of both dendrites and the axon, each neuron can have contact with up to ten thousand other neurons.

The communication between neurons does not happen through direct contact between them—like with electric wires—but neurons form specific connection points called *synapses*, where neurons communicate through electrochemical processes. There, the axon of the sending neuron is separated from the dendrite of the receiving neuron only by the *synaptic cleft*, which is typically just a few nanometres wide. Here, the transmission of the signal from one neuron to the next happens through the release of *neurotransmitters*. Put very simply, the sending neuron releases the neurotransmitter into the synaptic cleft between the neurons, and the other neuron receives them. Suppose the released concentration of the neurotransmitter and the thereafter triggered neurochemical processes in the receiving neuron come over a certain threshold; in that case, the receiving neuron will generate an *action potential* through its axon to other neurons, aka "the neuron is firing". This is an "all or none" process, which means that once the triggering threshold is reached, the action potential will always be the same. However, it typically requires that the neuron receives time-synchronous signals from several neurons to trigger such a response. Note that each neuron of the brain is typically connected to thousands or ten thousand other neurons. The action potential itself is a neurochemical process based on a specific in and outflow of ions, like calcium, nitrogen, or chloride ions, which then generate a change in the electrical potential of the cell membrane, which propagates along the axon. This is a complex process that could only superficially be described here but might nonetheless illustrate the basic mechanism behind neuronal activations (Baslow, 2011; Shipp, 2007; Sidiropoulou et al., 2006).

Once the action potential arrives and the synapses, neurotransmitters are released. The most common neurotransmitters are *glutamate* and *dopamine*, which are excitatory neurotransmitters, i.e. neurotransmitters that may cause the aforementioned process. By contrast, the neurotransmitter *GABA* is an inhibitory neurotransmitter that increases the threshold of an action potential and may therefore prohibit an action potential, even in the presence of other excitatory inputs from other neurons. Through this interplay of excitatory and inhibitory processes, the requirement of reaching certain thresholds in concentrations of neurotransmitters and other ions, and the dependency on the concentration of ions inside and outside of the neuronal cell, the brain can control the amount of simultaneously ongoing neuronal activation. On the other hand, it is also very vulnerable to disturbances which may cause this complex interdependent system to come out of balance. Several neurological and psychiatric disorders are caused by such a disturbance or unbalance of neurotransmitters (Falkenberg et al., 2014; Hugdahl et al., 2007; Hugdahl, Craven, et al., 2015; van Wageningen et al., 2009).

However, neurons are only one type of cell in the brain. There is an equal or even large amount of cells, called astrocytes, which perform a large number of functions that are essential for the brain to function. One of their functions is to recycle neurotransmitters after an action potential. Another essential function is to generate something that is called the *blood–brain-barrier*, which is essential for letting through only substances that are important for the neurons to function, such as oxygen or glucose while blocking others (Sweeney et al., 2019). Further, special types of astrocytes can form something around axons that is called *myelin*, which effectively increase the speed of action potentials or *glia* cells, which are important for the functional integrity of the brain (Stadelmann et al., 2019).

The Cortex

The brain has a hierarchical organisation with several substructures both on the macroscopic and microscopic scales. The vast majority of the already mentioned neurons are localised in a small strip along the outer surface of the brain. Therefore, this part of the brain is called the *cortex*, as it follows all the different folding of the brain, which are called *gyrus* (outward folding) and *sulcus* (the "valleys" of the cortex). The cortex itself typically has a substructure of 6 *layers*, which are subdivisions of the cortex, differing in the density and spatial distribution of neuronal cells, the type of neuronal cells, and their connectivity to neighboured or distant neurons. Further, these layers are differently organised and structured between different brain regions. This *cytoarchitectonic* segregation was first described by Korbinian Brodmann (Zilles & Amunts, 2010), who did pioneering work by identifying 43 cytoarchitectonic different brain areas in the human brain. There is a high degree of functional specificity between different cytoarchitectonic areas, which means that brain structures with a different cytoarchitectonic organisation also perform different functions. Therefore, it is still widespread that brain areas are not only described with their anatomical names but also in terms of *Brodmann area*, which follow more a functional differentiation. However, we now know that these

43 Brodmann areas need further subdivision and need to be treated differently for the left and right hemispheres.

Structural and Functional Brain Organisation

On the first glance, the brain consists of a few easily identifiable parts, which are the cerebrum (a), the cerebellum (b), and the brain stem. Further, these different parts look very symmetrical with a left and right half—called hemispheres—but they are not symmetrical, neither in their spatial configuration nor function. The cerebrum itself shows several clear landmarks. The most prominent one is the *medial longitudinal fissure*, which is the gap between the two hemispheres. The two hemispheres are connected through the *corpus callosum*, which is a big tract of mostly myelinated fibres that contains up to 250 million fibres connecting the two hemispheres.

Another prominent landmark is the *Sylvian fissure*, which defines the upper border of the *temporal lobe* and separates it from the *frontal and parietal lobes*. Functionally, the temporal lobe of the left and the right hemisphere are both mostly dedicated to the processing of acoustic stimuli, whereof the left temporal lobe is more dedicated to the processing of acoustically complex signals, such as speech. In contrast, the right temporal lobe is mainly dedicated to the processing of tonal signals, like prosody and characteristics of a voice, but also music (Sandmann et al., 2007; Specht, 2013, 2014). Accordingly, the left temporal lobe is the most important structure for speech perception since also central processes for the lexical, semantic, and syntactic deduction of spoken and written language information rely on various substructures of the temporal lobe (Specht, 2013, 2014). Interestingly, the left temporal lobe tends to be longer, while some of the folding of the right temporal lobe—in particular, the so-called *superior temporal sulcus*—tends to be deeper (Leroy et al., 2015; Specht & Wigglesworth, 2018).

The part of the brain behind the temporal lobe towards the back of the brain is dedicated to visual processing and is called the *occipital lobe*. The visual system is a complex hierarchical network of several modules that process different aspects of visually perceived information. For example, there are specialised modules within this network that perform actions like scene analysis, background-foreground separations, and global–local structures. In contrast, other modules differentiate between faces and objects, process the spatial localisation of an object, the colour of an object, or whether there are movements in the visual scene (Van Essen et al., 2001).

The part of the brain above the posterior end of the temporal lobe and superior to the occipital lobe is called the *parietal lobe*. Besides sensomotoric processing, this is a multifunctional brain structure which is involved in various higher cognitive processes. The parietal lobe is bordered by a landmark that is called the *central sulcus*, which separates the *frontal lobe* from the *parietal lobe*. While the sensory processing is posterior to the central sulcus in the parietal lobe, motor control processes are localised anterior to it, i.e. in the frontal lobe. The part of the frontal lobe that is not dedicated to motor processing is called the *prefrontal cortex*. Compared to other species, the prefrontal cortex of the human brain is disproportionally larger. Functionally, the prefrontal cortex is mostly involved in higher cognitive processes, like cognitive control, inhibition of reflexive actions, short- and long-term action planning, social cognition, personality traits, working memory, focused and selective attention, and many more functions of our every-day life that require cognitive and executive control. Further, certain parts of the left frontal lobe are central to speech production processes (Brodal, 2016).

The structures that were mentioned so far, are only those that are visible from the outside. However, there are also important structures inside of the brain—the *subcortical structures*. Behind the Sylvian fissure is a part of the brain that is called the *insular cortex*, which is a multifunctional part of the brain, involved, among many other functions, in the reflexive direction of attention. Even deeper inside of the brain is the *basal ganglia*, which is composed of many substructures. The basal ganglia is very central in motor control processes but is also involved in various higher-order cognitive processes. The *hippocampus* is an important structure for memory formation, long-term memory, and spatial navigation, while the *amygdala* is a structure that is central for emotion processing and emotion regulation. Both structures, together with the *cingulate gyrus* are the core structures of the *limbic system*, which is considered to be central in long-term memory, emotion processing, and emotionally guided response behaviour (Brodal, 2016).

In the centre of the brain is the *thalamus*, which is the gateway for information to and from the brain. Almost all sensory signals—only the olfactory information has a different pathway—and all motor signals pass through the thalamus. Further, many structures and networks of the brain have reciprocal connections with the thalamus (Brodal, 2016).

Neuroimaging

Magnetic Resonance Imaging

This paragraph briefly introduces the complex physics behind magnetic resonance imaging (MRI). It was Paul C. Lauterbur who first introduced MRI in the early 1970, and the method rests on the already well-established method called *nuclear magnetic resonance* (NMR), which is mostly used in chemistry for analysing substances (Macovski, 2009; Wehrli, 2004). Put very simply, NMR and MRI make use of the magnetic properties and energy levels of atomic nuclei and their characteristic deviations in different chemical connections once it is exposed to a strong external magnetic field. In such an external magnetic field, the sub-elements of an atomic nucleus, namely the neutrons and protons, start to interact with the magnetic field. Their magnetic moments (*spin*) will rotate with an angular momentum and a specific rotation frequency (*Larmor frequency*) around the external magnetic field. This process mainly depends on the strength of the magnetic field and the chemical connection. By sending a radio wave with a certain frequency into this system, the nuclei with the same rotation frequency will *resonate*. Thereby, it is possible to measure a spectrum of energy levels which in turn gives information about the presence of nuclei and their chemical connections in each probe. However, this is only a one-dimensional method. To create images, one needs spatial decoding, which was the essential development step from NMR to MRI (Macovski, 2009; Wehrli, 2004).

Paul C. Lauterbur was able to locally manipulate the strength of the magnetic field and hence generate spatial variations of the resonance signal. This can be achieved by applying *magnetic gradients* in addition to the main magnetic field, whereby "gradients" mean that the strength of the magnetic field increases along an axis. By doing so in all three dimensions, MR images can be generated. Further, MRI takes advantage of the fact that hydrogen atoms, which consist only of a single proton, are overwhelmingly present in the body since the human body consists almost exclusively of water and organic chemical connections, which contain hydrogen atoms.

An MRI scanner consists of three main parts: First, the main magnet, which creates a strong magnetic field of typically 1.5 or 3 Tesla, which is 30,000 to 60,000 times stronger than the earth's magnetic field. Seen from the outside, this is the dominating part of an MRI scanner, with an open tunnel in the middle that goes through the magnetic, and where the subjects are positioned for the examination since the magnetic field is most homogeneous in the middle of the tunnel. Such a strong and homogenous magnetic field is needed to let the spins of the hydrogen atoms (i.e. the single proton) rotate along the magnetic field lines with approximately the same Larmor frequency. The second main component is the gradient coils, which are inside of the magnetic. These gradient coils can slightly manipulate the strength of the magnetic field in all three dimensions. Thereby, the rotation frequencies (and phases) of the protons vary slightly at different places along the gradients. Third, the receiving coil (i.e. an antenna) will receive the signal that is transmitted by the spins in resonance after a radio wave is sent. In neuroimaging applications, this receiving coil is a *head coil* that is optimised to pick up the signal that comes from the head and which is typically placed around the subject's head.

Under an MRI examination, radio waves are repeatedly sent, and the strength and direction of the gradients are constantly changed. Those who already underwent an MRI examination will have noticed the noise such an MRI scanner generates—this is caused by the rapid switching of the gradients, which can generate substantial vibrations in the scanner. What happens under this process is that the spins of the hydrogen atom will respond to the radio wave (*excitation pulse*) by changing their rotation axis, for example, by flipping their axis by 90 degrees. After the radio wave has been switched off, the spins will return to their original rotation axis. Importantly, this process takes time, which is different for different tissue types. This time is called the *T1 relaxation*. For example, spins that are in grey matter, which is that part of the brain where all the neurons are localised, will need more time than spins that are in white matter, where all the long fibre connections run through. The combined information of these different T1 relaxation times and the different strength and polarities of gradients will finally form a data space (*K space*) that is formed by frequency and phase information. From there, two and three-dimensional images can be reconstructed using, in the simplest case, a procedure that is called Fourier transformation (Macovski, 2009).

Similarly, after an excitation pulse, the spins are focused and aligned within a plane but get gradually out of phase. This process is tissue-dependent as well and is called *T2 relaxation*. However, this latter process is easily affected by local deviations of the magnetic field, which could be caused by, e.g. bones or air-filled caves. In this case, the T2 time is also affected and is then called the *T2* relaxation*. We will return to this in connection with functional examinations of brain activations.

The BOLD Signal

Both functional magnetic resonance (fMRI) and functional near-infrared spectroscopy (fNIRS) rest on the *BOLD effect* (BOLD = blood oxygenation level dependent). The BOLD effect has a metabolic origin and reflects neuronal activation only very indirectly. It makes use of the fact that haemoglobin is not only the main component of the blood but also the carrier of oxygen, which means it exists in two forms, namely as oxygenated, carrying oxygen atoms, and deoxygenated haemoglobin, without oxygen atoms. In the case of neuronal activation, the regional cerebral blood flow increases, and thus much more oxygenated blood floats into that area. However, since the oxygen extraction rate does not increase to the same degree, the relative concentration of oxygenated blood, which leaves the activated brain area, also increases. Since all MRI methods are based on differentiations of magnetic properties, this relative increase in oxygenation can be detected because oxygenated haemoglobin is diamagnetic and deoxygenated haemoglobin is paramagnetic (Kwong, 2012; Ogawa, 2012; Turner, 2012). This is the basis of most fMRI applications. Interestingly, oxygenated haemoglobin and deoxygenated haemoglobin also absorb infrared light differently, which forms the basis for fNIRS, as will be discussed later. However, it is important to emphasise that the BOLD signal is only a relative signal, which means that only a change in oxygenation level can be detected. This implies some limitations in how fMRI and fNIRS can be applied. It is essential that the experimental condition provokes a change in the oxygenation level. Otherwise, no signal will be measured. This is even true for the so-called *resting-state fMRI*.

The metabolic origin of the BOLD signal is also the reason why the signal is very smooth and stretched over time, which also implies that it does not reflect the neuronal activation per se. The BOLD signal is only a very indirect measure of brain activations—one could call it also a metabolic echo of brain actions. This must be remembered when interpreting fMRI and fNIRS data. While the temporal dynamics of neuronal activation is in the range of milliseconds, the corresponding BOLD signal is in the range of several seconds, with the strongest increase in the signal amplitude 4–6 seconds after the neuronal activation has happened. In other words, the activation of the neurons might already have gone while the BOLD signal is still increasing. After the signal reaches its maximum, the signal decays over a period of 15–20 seconds, including a prominent post-stimulus undershoot, i.e. a signal drop below the baseline, before it reaches the baseline again.

The reason for this long-lasting and smooth BOLD signal and the post-stimulus undershoot can be explained by two mechanisms that are assumed to run in parallel. During and after neuronal activation, the inflow of deoxygenated blood from the capillaries into the veins is larger than its outflow, which causes an expansion of the veins. The prominent undershoot in the BOLD signal may result from a delayed cerebral blood volume recovery, i.e. widening and shrinking of the veins (Balloon model) (Richard B. Buxton, 2012; Buxton et al., 1998). The second mechanism is that the metabolism and the oxygen extraction are still increased while the regional blood flow has already decreased. This would increase the ratio of deoxygenated blood, which again would be reflected in a BOLD that drops below the baseline. A study by Hua and co-workers (Hua et al., 2011) using biophysical models comes to the conclusion that the observed BOLD signal behaviour is an intermix of these two different mechanisms, with a ratio of around 20:78, which has also been incorporated in the revised Balloon model (Buxton, 2012).

However, one general problem in this respect is the huge inter- but also intra-individual variability of the BOLD signal, which is partly caused by the metabolic origin but also by a low signal-to-noise ratio in the way the signal is measured. Therefore, an important limitation of all fMRI and fNIRS applications is that conclusions on the strength of activations, which means the amplitude of the BOLD signal, can only be drawn from group studies. Single-subject studies are only usable for localising some central functions, but any conclusions on activations strength are invalid. Therefore, fMRI hasn't yet shown a breakthrough as a diagnostic tool. In a clinical context, it is primarily used for presurgical mapping, where localising functions in relation to a tumour is of importance, not the activation strength (Specht, 2020).

Functional Magnetic Resonance Imaging

There are multiple ways of running MRI imaging protocols (often called *sequences*). While the physical principles are always the same, the different sequences can highlight different properties of the examined tissue; among them are the already introduced T1, T2, and T2* properties. In contrast to X-ray, which only can generate an X-ray image where the image reflects how much of the radiation came through the examined body part, MRI is a technique that can allow the generation of an increasing number of different types of images, where these images are able to highlight different (tissue) properties of the examined body part. Furthermore, this can be done within one examination, which makes it a very flexible tool with constantly growing new applications. One of these applications is functional magnetic resonance imaging (fMRI), which should be discussed in more detail.

Functional magnetic resonance imaging was invented at the end of 80th of the last century (Kwong, 2012; Ogawa, 2012; Turner, 2012) and makes use of the aforementioned BOLD effect. As described above, changes in the ratio of oxygenation of haemoglobin cause changes in the local magnetic environment around an activated brain area. As a result, more oxygenated blood creates a slightly more homogenous magnetic field in that activated area, which in turn causes a slight increase in voxel intensity. However, this only becomes detectable if the brain is scanned with a MR sequence that is sensitive to changes in magnetic environments. One such a sequence is a T2* weighted gradient-echo echo-planar-imaging (EPI) sequence, which is still the dominating way of detecting the BOLD signal (Bandettini et al., 1992, 1993, 1994; Brüning et al., 1995; Kwong, 2012; Turner, 2012). In short, the advantage of EPI is that it allows acquiring an entire slice with only one excitation pulse, thus acquiring the entire slice just in a fraction of a second (50–100 ms or less). Accordingly, the entire brain can be scanned within 2–3 seconds or, when applying multiband acquisition, even faster. However, EPI sequences are not only sensitive to the changes due to the BOLD effect but also to other so-called susceptibility artefacts, which are disturbances in the homogeneity of the magnetic field. Therefore, fMRI raw data are typically distorted. Some areas are whipped out by such artefacts, which appear, for example, at borders of air-filled cavities, like around the ear channels or above the nasal cavities.

Taking a historical perspective, the first decade of fMRI was predominantly marked by developments of the methods and investigations of the neuronal and physiological mechanisms behind the BOLD effect. This was, in particular, dominated by discussions on optimal experimental setups, like block- or event-related designs (see the next paragraph), design efficiency (Dale, 1999; Wager & Nichols, 2003), or adequate MR parameters. The second decade, by contrast, was more characterised by the application of fMRI for studying brain functions in healthy subjects and groups of patients. During that decade, the methods became more mature and more advanced and, more importantly, became broadly available. Accordingly, fMRI is no longer just used for brain mapping of single functions, but to an extended degree for creating multifunctional and hierarchical network models, for investigating dynamic and causal effects. The most prominent methods are the dynamic causal modelling (DCM) (Friston et al., 2019), independent component analysis (ICA) (Allen et al., 2014; Beckmann & Smith, 2004; Calhoun et al., 2004, 2012), multivariate pattern analysis (MVPA) (Hanke et al., 2009, 2010; Haxby, 2012), graph-theoretical approaches (Bullmore & Sporns, 2009; Sporns, 2018; Sporns et al., 2000), and several other methods, which cannot be listed all. The third decade was predominantly dominated by a new application of fMRI, called *resting-state fMRI (rs-fMRI)*, which will be described further down.

However, it should also be mentioned that even 30 years after its invention, fMRI has not found its way into broad clinical applications (Specht, 2020). The main reason is that fMRI is only an indirect measure of neuronal activations and could be described as a "metabolic echo" of neuronal activation. Further, the signal-to-noise ratio of the underlying BOLD signal is low, which makes it to a very unreliable signal. Accordingly, the magnitude of the BOLD signal has very low reliability and could be easily influenced by many secondary factors. Therefore, fMRI is only clinically used for presurgical planning, where the localisation of a function is essential but not the amplitude of the underlying BOLD signal. The latter would be relevant for any further diagnostic purposes in, for example, neurology of psychiatry. This, however, works only when comparing larger groups of subjects (O'Connor & Zeffiro, 2019; Specht, 2020).

Task-Related fMRI

The described characteristic dynamic of the BOLD signal creates some limitations to the experimental design. On a 3T MRI, which is nowadays the most common field-strength for fMRI studies, the detectable signal changes are in the magnitude of not more than 3 or 4%, but increases when the study is conducted, for example, on a 7T MRI. In combination with the very fast EPI imaging technique, which has its own technical challenges, which cannot be discussed here, this results in a very low signal-to-noise ratio. Therefore, one needs both many repetitions of the tasks that should be examined and several subjects in order to generate reliable statistical results.

The most common and easiest way of performing an fMRI study is to use an experimental design that is called *block design* (Soares et al., 2016). Here, trains of stimuli belonging to the same condition are repeatedly presented over a period of ideally 15–30 seconds (*Task block*), alternated with blocks of control stimuli (*High-level baseline*) and/or equally long resting periods (*Low-level baseline* or *Off block*). These different blocks are then uninterruptedly and ideally repeated in random order at least 4 to 6 times per block and condition. Ideally, a study should contain both the high-level and the low-level baseline. This is the most efficient way to run an fMRI study as it generates the highest possible BOLD signal. Due to the nature of the BOLD effects, which has a total duration of up to 20–30 seconds after each trial, the BOLD signals to each trial within a block add up to each other, generating an overall high and stable BOLD signal. Such a design is especially recommended for studies of cognitive functions, where a weak signal might be expectable. From here, one could advance the experimental design to more complex setups with more conditions or parametric manipulations. However, there is one rule that applies to all types of experimental designs, which is that one needs several repetitions of the same condition.

A more flexible way of performing a task-related fMRI is to use a design that is called an *event-related design*. Here, only single trials are presented, followed by a brief rest period of typically 0.5–8 s before the subsequent trial is presented (Soares et al., 2016). This following trial might belong to the same experimental condition or to a different condition. Thereby, one can create experimental designs that are like those known from event-related potential (ERP) studies. However, one needs several repetitions (e.g. 30–40) for each trial per condition. In addition, the interval between trials should be randomly varied (*jitter*) between 0.5 and to several seconds, causing those types of studies to be often lengthy and tiering for the participants, and the amplitude of the BOLD signal is much lower than for the block design. Therefore, one should be careful in selecting such a design for a study, although it allows more flexibility in some circumstances. Further, it requires exact timing and synchronisation between stimulus presentation and MRI image acquisition.

In general, it is mandatory to have control over the experimental timing for both block and event-related designs since the typical analysis of task fMRI is based on the experimental time course. Put very simply, a standard analysis of fMRI data is done through the specification of a general-linear model. In this model, a hypothetic BOLD signal is specified based on the timing of the tasks, which then generates an idealised hypothesis of when neurons are expected to be active and when at rest. This convolved with a prototypical course of the BOLD signal to form a set of regressors that are then fitted to the data. Therefore, it is essential always to have control over the timing of the tasks, as this fitting procedure would fail to find any relation between the task and the measured BOLD signal.

Resting State fMRI

In recent years, resting-state fMRI (rs-fMRI) has become a popular way of conducting fMRI studies. In contrast to task-related fMRI, where participants are asked to perform an experimental and a control task, the resting-state fMRI does not include any task. In the beginning, various forms of instructions have been used, like "*Close your eyes and don't fall asleep*", "*Keep your eyes open*", or "*Eyes open and fixate on the fixation cross*" (Raimondo et al., 2021), but also movie-watching has been used (Finn & Bandettini, 2021). Apparently, both fixation-cross and movie-watching give more reliable results than the "eyes closed" condition. The other still discussed question is for how long a resting-state fMRI acquisition should last. It has been shown that resting-state results are most reliable for scan durations of 9–13 min (Birn et al., 2013). Besides these considerations, the data acquisition is the same as for any other fMRI study. As described above, it is a prerequisite that a BOLD signal emerges, which means that the ratio of oxygenated to deoxygenated haemoglobin changes. This may sound paradoxical in the first place, given the fact that no instructions are given, and hence no hypothesis about the course of the BOLD signal can be generated. However, also rs-fMRI is based on measuring changes in the ratio of oxygenated to deoxygenated haemoglobin, but it rests on spontaneous low-frequent (<0.1 Hz) endogenous fluctuations of this ratio (Lee et al., 2013). It has been shown that these spontaneous fluctuations are not random but show characteristic spatiotemporal patterns, which mirror known functional networks, that are known from task-related fMRI, like the networks for executive functions, working memory, or visual as well as auditory perception (Smith et al., 2009). Each of these networks is characterised by a correlation of the BOLD signal, even if the different nodes of the network are distributed across the brain. Since a correlated BOLD signal is assumed to reflect coordinated activity, this indicates that these areas are functionally connected even in the absence of a concrete task. Different methods have been developed and are still under development for analysing those fluctuations. One prominent method is the independent component analysis (ICA), which allows for identifying spatiotemporal patterns and separating them into a number of network components. An alternative for investigating rs-fMRI is a spectral DCM approach, where the spectral characteristic of these endogenous fluctuations within a given network of nodes is examined (Friston et al., 2014; Kandilarova et al., 2023; Razi et al., 2015).

One dominating network in the resting-state fMRI literature is the default-mode network (DMN), which is a network that primarily is activated during rest periods, and the interplay of the DMN network with its counterpart which is a network that is primarily active when the attention is focused to the outer world. Interestingly, this interplay is detectable in both resting-state and task-related fMRI (Hugdahl, Raichle, et al., 2015; Hugdahl, 2019; Kazimierczak et al., 2021; Raichle et al., 2001; Raichle & Snyder, 2007). Various studies have shown that the DMN and its dynamic shows deviating performance in neurological and psychiatric disorders such as schizophrenia or dementia (Kandilarova et al., 2023; Lee et al., 2013).

Functional Near-Infrared Spectroscopy (fNIRS)

An alternative technique to fMRI is *functional near-infrared spectroscopy (fNIRS)*. Although the method has been known for more than 40 years, it became increasingly popular only more recently through the development of wearable and wireless fNIRS devices (Pinti et al., 2018). The fNIRS method rests on the same metabolic principle as fMRI, i.e. the BOLD effect. However, it is much more flexible in its application and, therefore, potentially more relevant for future studies where fMRI might appear as not suitable. Like fMRI, the fNIRS signal originates from changes in the levels of oxygenated and deoxygenated haemoglobin in the brain. However, in contrast to fMRI, which rests on the different magnetic properties of oxygenated and deoxygenated haemoglobin, fNIRS is based on the physical effect that oxygenated and deoxygenated haemoglobin absorbs infrared light differently (Chen et al., 2020; Pinti et al., 2018). Hence, also fNIRS provides an equally indirect measure of neural activity as fMRI, and it is limited to only those brain regions that are closest to the skull. The method involves infrared light that is non-invasively transmitted through the skull to reach the cortex of the brain. This also includes that much infrared light is scattered, both at the level of the skull but also inside the cortex. However, the scattered light from inside the cortex forms the signal that is picked up by the fNIRS detectors. A fraction of the initially emitted infrared light reaches the cortex and is scattered back in a way that it reaches one of the detectors on the skull that are placed around the emitting infrared light source. Inside the cortex, oxygenated and deoxygenated haemoglobin absorbs infrared light differently and differently for different wavelengths. Therefore, most fNIRS systems operate with two wavelengths and, hence, measure different absorption spectra in depending on the amount of oxygenated and deoxygenated haemoglobin. A typical fNIRS system is assembled of a set of infrared emitting *optodes* and infrared detecting *optodes*. In the case of neuronal activations, the ratio of oxygenated and deoxygenated haemoglobin will change, as described before, and the absorption spectrum in the infrared light that is scattered back to the detecting optodes on the skull will change. Thereby, and like fMRI, one can infer the potential brain activations somewhere between the infrared emitting and detecting optodes. This also describes one of the current disadvantages of fNIRS, which is its low spatial resolution, since the distance between the source and the detectors is in the range of 1–3 cm. On the other hand, this is to some extent outweighed by the advantage of being mobile and easy to apply in situations of social interactions (*hyperscanning* with 2 or more simultaneously examined subjects) and real-life conditions outside of the lab (Liu et al., 2022). Further, and in contrast to fMRI, fNIRS can infer on both the concentration of both oxygenated and deoxygenated haemoglobin.

Since they are based on the same metabolic origin, the overall time course of the fNIRS signal follows the same patterns as described for fMRI, and, accordingly, fNIRS has the same experimental limitations as fMRI, like that it requires enough repetitions per condition and several subjects per group.

However, fNIRS has several additional disadvantages that limit its use in certain situations. The limitation of the spatial resolution has already been mentioned, but, also the signal-to-noise ratio of fNIRS is lower compared to fMRI, which can make it difficult to detect small changes in brain activity. Although it is an advantage that some fNIRS systems are portable, they might be more affected by movement artefacts, but, some systems try to account for this by including gyroscopes to record head movements. However, despite these disadvantages, fNIRS has become a valuable tool for studying brain function and might become even more popular in the near future due to increased flexibility and increased performance, especially in open-field situations.

Variability and Reliability

In the previous chapters, a couple of limitations have already been mentioned. One of the most dominating limitations is the metabolic origin of the signals that fMRI and fNIRS measure. In the following chapter, it will be primarily focused on fMRI since more research has been done on this, and it is an ongoing discussion of how sensitive fMRI is and whether it is reliable enough for clinical applications. One must bear in mind that fMRI is based on physiological mechanisms where the ratio of oxygenated to deoxygenated blood must change. Otherwise, no BOLD signal will emerge, although neuronal activity might have occurred. This is of particular importance in clinical cases.

The BOLD signal is influenced by many parameters, like blood volume effects, the concentration of neurotransmitters, time of the day, blood pressure, body-mass index, the presence or absence of nicotine or caffeine, and many other factors (Honey & Bullmore, 2004; Sjuls & Specht, 2022; Specht, 2020; Specht et al., 2003; Vaisvilaite et al., 2022).

The dependency of fMRI on the occurrence of these metabolic effects is a dominating limitation. It has been shown that several factors can influence the BOLD signal. Those factors are, for example, blood pressure and body mass (Sjuls & Specht, 2022). Since blood pressure varies over the day, the time of the day has also been considered as a factor that might influence the BOLD signal (Vaisvilaite et al., 2022). Further, caffeine, nicotine and other pharmacological vasoactive substance affect the BOLD signal (Honey & Bullmore, 2004; Specht, 2020). Another source of inter-individual variability was discussed by Falkenberg and co-workers, who measured the concentration of the excitatory neurotransmitter glutamate in the anterior cingulate cortex (ACC), using MR spectroscopy (MRS). They detected that the subjects with high level of glutamate in the ACC showed a differential activation pattern during a cognitive control task than those with low glutamate, while the behavioural outcome was the same for these groups (Falkenberg et al., 2012). In the same vein, Muthukumaraswamy used MRS to measure the concentration of the inhibitory neurotransmitter GABA and found that this was negatively correlated with the BOLD-response amplitude but positively with the BOLD-response width (Muthukumaraswamy et al., 2009, 2012). This indicates that the BOLD signal is not a pure mechanistic response that is identical for each occasion but instead modulated by several other parameters, causing considerable inter-subject but also intra-subject variability. Therefore, several different methods for assessing the reliability of fMRI have been put forward, ranging from global measures, such as overlap estimates of activations across different occasions (Rombouts et al., 1998), receiver operating characteristics (Chen & Small, 2007), to variance-analytic measures, using, for example, the intra-class correlation coefficient (ICC) (Herting et al., 2018; Rødland et al., 2022; Specht et al., 2003), to name only some of the approaches. In general, the results demonstrate that attention-directed paradigms could achieve the highest reliability. In contrast, passive paradigms demonstrate less stable reliability, which is mainly discussed in the context of resting-state fMRI (Hjelmervik et al., 2014; Taxali et al., 2021).

Another source of the inter-subject variability is the anatomical between-subject variability, i.e. that even after a spatial normalisation of brain structures, functional areas are not overlapping and may also reflect individual brain-structural relationships (Genon et al., 2022). To illustrate individual variability, anatomical probability maps are good tool for showing those individual anatomical deviations, which may vary from one area to another. That this variability is also present in fMRI data and thus affecting group analyses data is nicely demonstrated by the comparison of fMRI-based probability maps and anatomical probability maps (Wilms et al., 2005; Wohlschläger et al., 2005). One approach for tackling individual variability is the use of navigator task, which are special fMRI tasks that aim to localise only one specific function, like visual motion perception within area V5/MT (Wilms et al., 2005).

Conclusion

In summary, both fMRI and fNIRS are neuroimaging methods that allow to examine the brain while processing stimuli, performing a experimentally controlled task, or even in a resting-state condition. However, both methods have their limitations. The most dominant limitation to both methods is the metabolic nature of the underlying BOLD signal, which is only a physiological consequence of a neuronal activation, which means, one doesn't measure a brain activation directly. This "metabolic echo" of a neuronal activation is both delayed in time and less precise in its location. Furthermore, a BOLD signal only emerges when there is change in the ratio of oxygenated to deoxygenated blood. If that doesn't emerge, both fMRI and fNIRS will not pick up any signal. This sets some limitations to the experimental design. If one is aware of all the inherent limitations of the described methods, neuroimaging is a valuable tool to study to human brain.

References

Allen, E. A., Damaraju, E., Plis, S. M., Erhardt, E. B., Eichele, T., & Calhoun, V. D. (2014). Tracking whole-brain connectivity dynamics in the resting state. *Cerebral Cortex (New York, N.Y.: 1991), 24*(3), 663–676. https://doi.org/10.1093/cercor/bhs352

Bandettini, P. A., Jesmanowicz, A., Wong, E. C., & Hyde, J. S. (1993). Processing strategies for time-course data sets in functional MRI of the human brain. *Magnetic Resonance in Medicine, 30*(2), 161–173. https://doi.org/10.1002/mrm.1910300204

Bandettini, P. A., Wong, E. C., Hinks, R. S., Tikofsky, R. S., & Hyde, J. S. (1992). Time course EPI of human brain function during task activation. *Magnetic Resonance in Medicine, 25*(2), 390–397. https://doi.org/10.1002/mrm.1910250220

Bandettini, P. A., Wong, E. C., Jesmanowicz, A., Hinks, R. S., & Hyde, J. S. (1994). Spin-echo and gradient-echo EPI of human brain activation using BOLD contrast: A comparative study at 1.5 T. *NMR in Biomedicine, 7*(1–2), 12–20. https://doi.org/10.1002/nbm.1940070104

Baslow, M. H. (2011). The vertebrate brain, evidence of its modular organization and operating system: Insights into the brain's basic units of structure, function, and operation and how they influence neuronal signaling and behavior. *Frontiers in Behavioral Neuroscience, 5*, 5. https://doi.org/10.3389/fnbeh.2011.00005

Beckmann, C. F., & Smith, S. M. (2004). Probabilistic independent component analysis for functional magnetic resonance imaging. *IEEE Transactions on Medical Imaging, 23*(2), 137–152. https://doi.org/10.1109/TMI.2003.822821

Birn, R. M., Molloy, E. K., Patriat, R., Parker, T., Meier, T. B., Kirk, G. R., …, Prabhakaran, V. (2013). The effect of scan length on the reliability of resting-state fMRI connectivity estimates. *NeuroImage, 83*, 550–558. https://doi.org/10.1016/j.neuroimage.2013.05.099

Brodal, P. (2016). *The central nervous system*. Oxford University Press.

Brüning, R., Weber, J., Wu, R. H., Kwong, K. K., Hennig, J., & Reiser, M. (1995). Echo-planar imaging of the brain. *Der Radiologe, 35*(12), 902–910.

Bullmore, E., & Sporns, O. (2009). Complex brain networks: Graph theoretical analysis of structural and functional systems. *Nature Reviews Neuroscience, 10*(3), 186–198. https://doi.org/10.1038/nrn2575

Buxton, R. B. (2012). Dynamic models of BOLD contrast. *NeuroImage, 62*(2), 953–961. https://doi.org/10.1016/j.neuroimage.2012.01.012

Buxton, R. B., Wong, E. C., & Frank, L. R. (1998). Dynamics of blood flow and oxygenation changes during brain activation: The balloon model. *Magnetic Resonance in Medicine, 39*(6), 855–864. https://doi.org/10.1002/mrm.1910390602

Calhoun, V. D., Adali, T., & Pekar, J. J. (2004). A method for comparing group fMRI data using independent component analysis: Application to visual, motor and visuomotor tasks. *Magnetic Resonance Imaging, 22*(9), 1181–1191. https://doi.org/10.1016/j.mri.2004.09.004

Calhoun, V. D., Eichele, T., Adalı, T., & Allen, E. A. (2012). Decomposing the brain: Components and modes, networks and nodes. *Trends in Cognitive Sciences, 16*(5), 255–256. https://doi.org/10.1016/j.tics.2012.03.008

Chen, E. E., & Small, S. L. (2007). Test-retest reliability in fMRI of language: Group and task effects. *Brain and Language, 102*(2), 176–185. https://doi.org/10.1016/j.bandl.2006.04.015

Chen, W. L., Wagner, J., Heugel, N., Sugar, J., Lee, Y. W., Conant, L., …, Whelan, H. T. (2020). Functional near-infrared spectroscopy and its clinical application in the field of neuroscience: Advances and future directions. *Frontiers in Neuroscience, 14*, 724. https://doi.org/10.3389/fnins.2020.00724

Dale, A. M. (1999). Optimal experimental design for event-related fMRI. *Human Brain Mapping, 8*(2–3), 109–114. https://doi.org/10.1002/(SICI)1097-0193(1999)8:2/3<109::AID-HBM7>3.0.CO;2-W

Falkenberg, L. E., Westerhausen, R., Craven, A. R., Johnsen, E., Kroken, R. A., Løberg, E.-M., …, Hugdahl, K. (2014). Impact of glutamate levels on neuronal response and cognitive abilities in schizophrenia. *NeuroImage. Clinical, 4*, 576–584. https://doi.org/10.1016/j.nicl.2014.03.014

Falkenberg, L. E., Westerhausen, R., Specht, K., & Hugdahl, K. (2012). Resting-state glutamate level in the anterior cingulate predicts blood-oxygen level-dependent response to cognitive control. *Proceedings of the National Academy of Sciences of the United States of America, 109*(13), 5069–5073. https://doi.org/10.1073/pnas.1115628109

Finn, E. S., & Bandettini, P. A. (2021). Movie-watching outperforms rest for functional connectivity-based prediction of behavior. *NeuroImage, 235*, 117963. https://doi.org/10.1016/j.neuroimage.2021.117963

Friston, K. J., Kahan, J., Biswal, B., & Razi, A. (2014). A DCM for resting state fMRI. *NeuroImage, 94*, 396–407. https://doi.org/10.1016/j.neuroimage.2013.12.009

Friston, K. J., Preller, K. H., Mathys, C., Cagnan, H., Heinzle, J., Razi, A., & Zeidman, P. (2019). Dynamic causal modelling revisited. *NeuroImage, 199*, 730–744. https://doi.org/10.1016/j.neuroimage.2017.02.045

Genon, S., Eickhoff, S. B., & Kharabian, S. (2022). Linking interindividual variability in brain structure to behaviour. *Nature Reviews Neuroscience, 23*(5), 307–318. https://doi.org/10.1038/s41583-022-00584-7

Hanke, M., Halchenko, Y. O., Haxby, J. V., & Pollmann, S. (2010). Statistical learning analysis in neuroscience: Aiming for transparency. *Frontiers in Neuroscience, 4*, 38. https://doi.org/10.3389/neuro.01.007.2009

Hanke, M., Halchenko, Y. O., Sederberg, P. B., Hanson, S. J., Haxby, J. V., & Pollmann, S. (2009). PyMVPA: A python toolbox for multivariate pattern analysis of fMRI data. *Neuroinformatics, 7*(1), 37–53. https://doi.org/10.1007/s12021-008-9041-y

Haxby, J. V. (2012). Multivariate pattern analysis of fMRI: The early beginnings. *NeuroImage, 62*(2), 852–855. https://doi.org/10.1016/j.neuroimage.2012.03.016

Herculano-Houzel, S. (2012). The remarkable, yet not extraordinary, human brain as a scaled-up primate brain and its associated cost. *Proceedings of the National Academy of Sciences, USA, 109* (Suppl 1), 10661–10668. doi:https://doi.org/10.1073/pnas.1201895109

Herting, M. M., Gautam, P., Chen, Z., Mezher, A., & Vetter, N. C. (2018). Test-retest reliability of longitudinal task-based fMRI: Implications for developmental studies. *Developmental Cognitive Neuroscience, 33*, 17–26. https://doi.org/10.1016/j.dcn.2017.07.001

Hjelmervik, H., Hausmann, M., Osnes, B., Westerhausen, R., & Specht, K. (2014). Resting states are resting traits—An fMRI study of sex differences and menstrual cycle effects in resting state cognitive control networks. *PLoS One, 9*(7). https://doi.org/10.1371/journal.pone.0103492

Honey, G., & Bullmore, E. (2004). Human pharmacological MRI. *Trends in Pharmacological Sciences, 25*(7), 366–374. https://doi.org/10.1016/j.tips.2004.05.009

Hua, J., Stevens, R. D., Huang, A. J., Pekar, J. J., & van Zijl, P. C. M. (2011). Physiological origin for the BOLD poststimulus undershoot in human brain: Vascular compliance versus oxygen metabolism. *Journal of Cerebral Blood Flow and Metabolism : Official Journal of the International Society of Cerebral Blood Flow and Metabolism, 31*(7), 1599–1611. https://doi.org/10.1038/jcbfm.2011.35

Hugdahl, K., Craven, A. R., Nygård, M., Løberg, E.-M., Berle, J. Ø., Johnsen, E., …, Ersland, L. (2015). Glutamate as a mediating transmitter for auditory hallucinations in schizophrenia: A (1)H MRS study. *Schizophrenia Research, 161*(2–3), 252–260. https://doi.org/10.1016/j.schres.2014.11.015

Hugdahl, K., Kazimierczak, K., Beresniewicz, J., Kompus, K., Westerhausen, R., Ersland, L., …, Specht, K. (2019). Dynamic up- and down-regulation of the default (DMN) and extrinsic (EMN) mode networks during alternating task-on and task-off periods. *PLoS One, 14*(9), e0218358. https://doi.org/10.1371/journal.pone.0218358

Hugdahl, K., Løberg, E. M., Specht, K., Steen, V. M., van Wageningen, H., & Jørgensen, H. A. (2007). Auditory hallucinations in schizophrenia: The role of cognitive, brain structural and genetic disturbances in the left temporal lobe. *Frontiers in Human Neuroscience, 1*, 6. https://doi.org/10.3389/neuro.09.006.2007

Hugdahl, K., Raichle, M. E., Mitra, A., & Specht, K. (2015). On the existence of a generalized non-specific task-dependent network. *Frontiers in Human Neuroscience, 9*, 430. https://doi.org/10.3389/fnhum.2015.00430

Kandilarova, S., Stoyanov, D., Aryutova, K., Paunova, R., Mantarkov, M., Mitrev, I., …, Specht, K. (2023). Effective connectivity between the orbitofrontal cortex and the precuneus differentiates major psychiatric disorders: Results from a transdiagnostic spectral DCM study. *CNS & Neurological Disorders: Drug Targets, 22*(2), 180–190. https://doi.org/10.2174/1871527320666210917142815

Kazimierczak, K., Craven, A. R., Ersland, L., Specht, K., Dumitru, M. L., Sandøy, L. B., & Hugdahl, K. (2021). Combined fMRI region- and network-analysis reveal new insights of top-down modulation of bottom-up processes in auditory laterality. *Frontiers in Behavioral Neuroscience, 15*, 802319. https://doi.org/10.3389/fnbeh.2021.802319

Kwong, K. K. (2012). Record of a single fMRI experiment in May of 1991. *NeuroImage, 62*(2), 610–612. https://doi.org/10.1016/j.neuroimage.2011.07.089

Lee, M. H., Smyser, C. D., & Shimony, J. S. (2013). Resting-state fMRI: A review of methods and clinical applications. *AJNR. American Journal of Neuroradiology, 34*(10), 1866–1872. https://doi.org/10.3174/ajnr.A3263

Leroy, F., Cai, Q., Bogart, S. L., Dubois, J., Coulon, O., Monzalvo, K., …, Dehaene-Lambertz, G. (2015). New human-specific brain landmark: The depth asymmetry of superior temporal sulcus. *Proceedings of the National Academy of Sciences of the United States of America, 112*(4), 1208–1213. https://doi.org/10.1073/pnas.1412389112

Liu, N., Yucel, M. A., Tong, Y., Minagawa, Y., Tian, F., & Li, X. (2022). Editorial: FNIRS in neuroscience and its emerging applications. *Frontiers in Neuroscience, 16*, 960591. https://doi.org/10.3389/fnins.2022.960591

Macovski, A. (2009). MRI: A charmed past and an exciting future. *Journal of Magnetic Resonance Imaging, 30*(5) 919–923. https://doi.org/10.1002/jmri.v30:510.1002/jmri.21962

Muthukumaraswamy, S. D., Edden, R. A. E., Jones, D. K., Swettenham, J. B., & Singh, K. D. (2009). Resting GABA concentration predicts peak gamma frequency and fMRI amplitude in response to visual stimulation in humans. *Proceedings of the National Academy of Sciences, 106*(20), 8356–8361. https://doi.org/10.1073/pnas.0900728106

Muthukumaraswamy, S. D., Evans, C. J., Edden, R. A. E., Wise, R. G., & Singh, K. D. (2012). Individual variability in the shape and amplitude of the BOLD-HRF correlates with endogenous GABAergic inhibition. *Human Brain Mapping, 33*(2), 455–465. https://doi.org/10.1002/hbm.21223

O'Connor, E. E., & Zeffiro, T. A. (2019). Why is clinical fMRI in a resting state? *Frontiers in Neurology, 10*, 420. https://doi.org/10.3389/fneur.2019.00420

Ogawa, S. (2012). Finding the BOLD effect in brain images. *NeuroImage, 62*(2), 608–609. https://doi.org/10.1016/j.neuroimage.2012.01.091

Pinti, P., Aichelburg, C., Gilbert, S., Hamilton, A., Hirsch, J., Burgess, P., & Tachtsidis, I. (2018). A review on the use of wearable functional near-infrared spectroscopy in naturalistic environments. *Japanese Psychological Research, 60*(4), 347–373. https://doi.org/10.1111/jpr.12206

Raichle, M. E., MacLeod, A. M., Snyder, A. Z., Powers, W. J., Gusnard, D. A., & Shulman, G. L. (2001). A default mode of brain function. *Proceedings of the National Academy of Sciences of the United States of America, 98*(2), 676–682. https://doi.org/10.1073/pnas.98.2.676

Raichle, M. E., & Snyder, A. Z. (2007). A default mode of brain function: A brief history of an evolving idea. *Neuroimage, 37*(4), 1083–1090—discussion 1097–1089. https://doi.org/10.1016/j.neuroimage.2007.02.041

Raimondo, L., Oliveira, L. A. F., Heij, J., Priovoulos, N., Kundu, P., Leoni, R. F., & van der Zwaag, W. (2021). Advances in resting state fMRI acquisitions for functional connectomics. *NeuroImage, 243*, 118503. https://doi.org/10.1016/j.neuroimage.2021.118503

Razi, A., Kahan, J., Rees, G., & Friston, K. J. (2015). Construct validation of a DCM for resting state fMRI. *NeuroImage, 106*, 1–14. https://doi.org/10.1016/j.neuroimage.2014.11.027

Rødland, E., Melleby, K. M., & Specht, K. (2022). Evaluation of a simple clinical language paradigm with respect to sensory independency, functional asymmetry, and effective connectivity. *Frontiers in Behavioral Neuroscience, 16*, 806520. https://doi.org/10.3389/fnbeh.2022.806520

Rombouts, S. A. R. B., Barkhof, F., Hoogenraad, F. G. C., Sprenger, M., & Scheltens, P. (1998). Within-subject reproducibility of visual activation patterns with functional magnetic resonance imaging using multislice echo planar imaging. *Magnetic Resonance Imaging, 16*(2), 105–113. https://doi.org/10.1016/s0730-725x(97)00253-1

Sandmann, P., Eichele, T., Specht, K., Jäncke, L., Rimol, L. M., Nordby, H., & Hugdahl, K. (2007). Hemispheric asymmetries in the processing of temporal acoustic cues in consonant-vowel syllables. *Restorative Neurology and Neuroscience, 25*(3–4), 227–240.

Shipp, S. (2007). Structure and function of the cerebral cortex. *Current Biology, 17*(12), R443-449. https://doi.org/10.1016/j.cub.2007.03.044

Sidiropoulou, K., Pissadaki, E. K., & Poirazi, P. (2006). Inside the brain of a neuron. *EMBO Reports, 7*(9), 886–892. https://doi.org/10.1038/sj.embor.7400789

Sjuls, G. S., & Specht, K. (2022). Variability in resting-state functional magnetic resonance imaging: The effect of body mass, blood pressure, hematocrit, and glycated hemoglobin on hemodynamic and neuronal parameters. *Brain Connect, 12*(10), 870–882. https://doi.org/10.1089/brain.2021.0125

Smith, S. M., Fox, P. T., Miller, K. L., Glahn, D. C., Fox, P. M., Mackay, C. E., …, Beckmann, C. F. (2009). Correspondence of the brain's functional architecture during activation and rest. *Proceedings of the National Academy of Sciences of the United States of America, 106*(31), 13040–13045. https://doi.org/10.1073/pnas.0905267106

Soares, J. M., Magalhaes, R., Moreira, P. S., Sousa, A., Ganz, E., Sampaio, A., …, Sousa, N. (2016). A Hitchhiker's guide to functional magnetic resonance imaging. *Frontiers in Neuroscience, 10*, 515. https://doi.org/10.3389/fnins.2016.00515

Specht, K. (2013). Mapping a lateralization gradient within the ventral stream for auditory speech perception. *Frontiers in Human Neuroscience, 7*, 629. https://doi.org/10.3389/fnhum.2013.00629

Specht, K. (2014). Neuronal basis of speech comprehension. *Hearing Research, 307*, 121–135. https://doi.org/10.1016/j.heares.2013.09.011

Specht, K. (2020). Current challenges in translational and clinical fMRI and future directions. *Frontiers in Psychiatry/Frontiers Research Foundation, 10*, 924. https://doi.org/10.3389/fpsyt.2019.00924

Specht, K., & Wigglesworth, P. (2018). The functional and structural asymmetries of the superior temporal sulcus. *Scandinavian Journal of Psychology, 59*(1), 74–82. https://doi.org/10.1111/sjop.12410

Specht, K., Willmes, K., Shah, N. J., & Jäncke, L. (2003). Assessment of reliability in functional imaging studies. *Journal of Magnetic Resonance Imaging, 17*(4), 463–471. https://doi.org/10.1002/jmri.10277

Sporns, O. (2018). Graph theory methods: Applications in brain networks. *Dialogues in Clinical Neuroscience, 20*(2), 10. https://doi.org/10.31887/DCNS.2018.20.2/osporns

Sporns, O., Tononi, G., & Edelman, G. M. (2000). Theoretical neuroanatomy: Relating anatomical and functional connectivity in graphs and cortical connection matrices. *Cereb Cortex, 10*(2), 127–141. https://doi.org/10.1093/cercor/10.2.127

Stadelmann, C., Timmler, S., Barrantes-Freer, A., & Simons, M. (2019). Myelin in the central nervous system: Structure, function, and pathology. *Physiological Reviews, 99*(3), 1381–1431. https://doi.org/10.1152/physrev.00031.2018

Sweeney, M. D., Zhao, Z., Montagne, A., Nelson, A. R., & Zlokovic, B. V. (2019). Blood-brain barrier: From physiology to disease and back. *Physiological Reviews, 99*(1), 21–78. https://doi.org/10.1152/physrev.00050.2017

Taxali, A., Angstadt, M., Rutherford, S., & Sripada, C. (2021). Boost in Test-retest reliability in resting state fMRI with predictive modeling. *Cerebral Cortex, 31*(6), 2822–2833. https://doi.org/10.1093/cercor/bhaa390

Turner, R. (2012). The NIH experience in first advancing fMRI. *NeuroImage, 62*(2), 632–636. https://doi.org/10.1016/j.neuroimage.2011.07.074

Vaisvilaite, L., Hushagen, V., Grønli, J., & Specht, K. (2022). Time-of-day effects in resting-state functional magnetic resonance imaging: Changes in effective connectivity and blood oxygenation level dependent signal. *Brain Connect, 12*(6), 515–523. https://doi.org/10.1089/brain.2021.0129

Van Essen, D. C., Lewis, J. W., Drury, H. A., Hadjikhani, N., Tootell, R. B., Bakircioglu, M., & Miller, M. I. (2001). Mapping visual cortex in monkeys and humans using surface-based atlases. *Vision Research, 41*. https://doi.org/1359-137810.1016/S0042-6989(01)00045-1

van Wageningen, H., Jorgensen, H. A., Specht, K., Eichele, T., & Hugdahl, K. (2009). The effects of the glutamate antagonist memantine on brain activation to an auditory perception task. *Human Brain Mapping, 30*(11), 3616–3624. https://doi.org/10.1002/hbm.20789

Wager, T. D., & Nichols, T. E. (2003). Optimization of experimental design in fMRI: A general framework using a genetic algorithm. *NeuroImage, 18*(2), 293–309. https://doi.org/10.1016/s1053-8119(02)00046-0

Wehrli, F. W. (2004). On the 2003 Nobel Prize in medicine or physiology awarded to Paul C. Lauterbur and Sir Peter Mansfield. *Magnetic Resonance in Medicine, 51*(1), 1–3. https://doi.org/10.1002/mrm.v51:110.1002/mrm.10717

Wilms, M., Eickhoff, S. B., Specht, K., Amunts, K., Shah, N. J., Malikovic, A., & Fink, G. R. (2005). Human V5/MT+: Comparison of functional and cytoarchitectonic data. *Anatomy and Embryology, 210*(5–6), 485–495. https://doi.org/10.1007/s00429-005-0064-y

Wohlschläger, A. M., Specht, K., Lie, C., Mohlberg, H., Wohlschläger, A., Bente, K., …, Fink, G. R. (2005). Linking retinotopic fMRI mapping and anatomical probability maps of human occipital areas V1 and V2. *NeuroImage, 26*(1), 73–82. https://doi.org/10.1016/j.neuroimage.2005.01.021

Zilles, K., & Amunts, K. (2010). Centenary of Brodmann's map—Conception and fate. *Nature Reviews Neuroscience, 11*(2), 139–145. https://doi.org/10.1038/nrn2776

Unit 5 Additional Lecture: Blurred Lives—Cognition and Feelings in Human–AI Interactions

Pamela Breda

> There are now in the world machines that think, that learn and that create. Moreover, their ability to do these things is going to increase rapidly until in a visible future the range of problems they can handle will be coextensive with the range to which the human mind has been applied.
>
> Herbert Simon
>
> (from Simon & Newell, 1958, p. 6)

Introduction

Artificial intelligence, also known as AI, is the ability of a program to think, store information, perform human tasks and learn from experience. The domain of artificial intelligence has significantly evolved over the past decades, founding applications in almost every field of individual and collective lives. Computer systems able to perform tasks normally requiring human intelligence, such as visual perception, speech recognition, decision-making and translation between languages, are now informing our daily routine. The constant improvement of this technology has recently taken a leap in the direction of generating empathic AI: artificial machines programmed to interact with users' emotions. But is it really possible to develop an empathic artificial agent? Can users in their turn develop an

P. Breda (✉)
Angewandte University, Oskar Kokoschka-Platz, Vienna, Austria
e-mail: pamela.breda@uni-ak.ac.at

T. Balinisteanu and K. Priest (eds.), *Neuroaesthetics*,
https://doi.org/10.1007/978-3-031-42323-9_16

emotional engagement with artificial beings? The present essay analyzes the most recent developments in the field of human–AI interactions in order to provide tentative answers to these questions.

About Artificial Intelligence

Artificial Intelligence (also known as Artificial General Intelligence) is usually defined as a machine able to think, store information (i.e. having memory) and perform human tasks. AI could be identified as intelligence demonstrated by machines, as opposed to natural intelligence displayed by humans and animals. The human abilities invoked in such definition include visual perception, speech recognition, the capacity to reason, solve problems, discover meaning and learn from experience (Copeland, 2021).

The term 'Artificial Intelligence' was first used during a conference at Dartmouth University in 1956, when pioneer engineers John McCarthy, Arthur Samuel, Oliver Selfridge and Allen Newell presented their new research on the topic (Cordeschi, 2007). They believed that since every aspect of learning and intelligence can in principle be described in a very precise way, humanity could build a machine able to simulate intelligence, i.e. use language, generate thoughts and solve practical and theoretical problems. According to their vision, such a machine would in time acquire the ability to improve itself.

The first electronic computers—developed as a tool to help humans to process numbers and calculate better and faster—were originally employed in the military field, in particular the US project Defense Advanced Research Projects Agency (DARPA) (Castell, 2004). In the following decades, as technology progressed, theoreticians and engineers began to think about the possibility for artificial machines to share the same communicative structure as humans.

Mathematician Alan Turing proposed the famous 'Imitation Game' test (also known as the Turing test) constructed as a game in which a participant asks a series of questions to a human and a computer, without knowing in advance which one is which. If the distinction is impossible to make, then the machine has passed the test and can be declared intelligent. In 1966 Joseph Weizenbaum created ELIZA, a program that appeared to pass the test. The software responded to users' sentences typed through a computer keyboard, generating a reply using keywords. If a keyword was not found, ELIZA responded either with a generic reply or by repeating one of the earlier comments. The basic structure of ELIZA was further developed in 1995, when Richard Wallace designed the chatbot A.L.I.C.E (Artificial Linguistic Internet Computer Entity), which used data found on the web to generate a huge storage of natural language samples.

Other successful experiments in this regard were represented by famous confrontations between world-champion chess players and computers. In 1956 MANIAC, developed at Los Alamos Scientific Laboratory, became the first computer to defeat a human in a chess game and in 1997 IBM's Deep Blue defeated the world chess champion Garry Kasparov. In this regard, James Manyika observes:

> It was not just that AIs beat humans (although that was astounding when it first happened), but the escalating progression of how they did it: initially by learning from expert human play, then from self-play, then by teaching themselves the principles of the games from the ground up, eventually yielding single systems that could learn, play and win at several structurally different games, hinting at the possibility of generally intelligent systems. (Manyika, 2022)

The perception of artificial intelligence changed with time (see for example Russell, 2019). In its early days, AI was physically stored inside huge computer machines located in large-size rooms owned by universities and research centers. Throughout the years, AI has become less related to a physical structure and more pervasive. Rather than being individual entities located within a specific place, AI applications slowly began to form a global network spread everywhere, connecting every technological device and every individual making use of such devices.

With the rise of the World Wide Web in the mid-1990s, virtual networks began to redefine global communication systems. During the technological boom of the early 2000s, the widespread diffusion of mobile phones—with cameras, CPS and other tracking systems—brought an increased presence of AI in people's daily lives, later implemented by 'smart speakers' such as Amazon Echo, Google Home and Apple HomePod. Around 2008, the number of objects in the world connected to the internet exceeded that of people connected to the internet, giving rise to the Internet of Things (IoT). Today almost all fields of human activity, from communication to business, from agriculture to education, are designed and exploited through the use of multiple forms of artificial intelligence, including advanced web search engines (e.g. Google), recommendation systems (used by YouTube, Amazon and Netflix), self-driving cars (e.g. Tesla), automated decision-making AI competing at the highest level in strategic game systems (such as chess and Go) and many others.

A huge number of devices used daily by billions of people form an immense AI network that can access all the knowledge and technical skills developed by humans over the centuries. The operations performed by intelligent machines and software are increasing by the day, leading to what is called the AI effect, i.e. tasks considered to require 'intelligence' are often removed from the definition of AI, since artificial intelligent systems are now able to perform them with success. Cognitive scientist Douglas Hofstadter sums up this AI phenomenon: 'AI is whatever hasn't been done yet' (Hofstadter, 1979). According to futurist Ray Kurzweil, in 2045 we will reach 'technological singularity' the moment when machine intelligence will surpass human intelligence and comprehension (Kurzweil, 2019). If this were to happen, probably we would not be able to control the technology we have built to help and support us. As Flynn Coleman observes:

> The era of our intellectual superiority is ending. As a species, we need to plan for this paradigm shift. Whether intelligent machines will learn from the darkest parts of our human nature, or the noblest, remains to be seen. At the moment we are more focused on advancing the technology and predicting its outcomes than on addressing how it will affect humanity and define our future. We need to reconsider some of our most entrenched assumptions and

> beliefs about ourselves and our place in the world. Paradoxically, we also need to ask what technology can teach us about being better humans. (Coleman, 2020, p. 12).

After the information age—also known as the Digital Age—we are entering into a new age of history, characterized by the constant interaction between humans and highly advanced machines. Most certainly this will affect how we, as humans, perceive the reality around us, the interactions with other individuals, and perhaps even our own selves.

The Problem of Artificial Brains

Much has been debated in pop culture and academia about the actual possibility for an AI to think and reason in a human-like manner. A key issue in this regard is that there is no universally accepted definition of human intelligence. We do not fully understand how our own brain functions, we are still learning how we store, retrieve and process memories and we don't quite know why we sleep and dream.

Even the very concept of consciousness has been debated for thousands of years and there is no consensus on how to describe it. Therefore, the idea of creating an artificial intelligence seems a challenging goal. One of the first problems to solve is that the human brain works according to the so-called reward system. Discovered by Swedish neuroscientist Nils-Åke Hillarp and his collaborators in the late 1950s, the reward system is an internal signaling system that makes us seek out positive stimuli (for example, sweet tasting food, listen to pleasant music, search for friendly environments, etc.) in order to increase dopamine level and feel better and avoid negative stimuli (for example, pain, hunger, anxiety, etc.) that would lower the dopamine level.

Furthermore, the choices we make depend on our values, morals and ethics. But how can we define values? Definitions vary depending on the field of study, but our values are generally understood to be our deeply held beliefs as individuals, cultures and societies. Morals can be defined as principles about what we think is right or wrong and ethics as rules of behavior built on our values and belief systems. When programming AI with specific objectives, the programmers should consider that not one individual is identical to another in relation to cognition, sensation and world perception. Therefore, the idea of programming an AI able to satisfy human needs might be a complicated task. What values and ideals should we implant inside a machine?

Already in the 1960s, Norbert Wiener observed how one of the core issues in the development of an artificial brain is that AI should act according to our own goals and objectives, however, it is impossible to identify and define true human purpose correctly (Wiener, 1960). We might be sure of what we want to achieve, but we do not know how to reach our goals. Human intellectual and decision-making activities are strongly influenced by features which are highly difficult to categorize and describe. As Stuart Russell observes:

> Complexity means that the real-world decision problem - the problem of deciding what to do right now, at every instant in one's life - is so difficult that neither humans nor computers will ever come close to finding perfect solutions. (Russell, 2019, p. 48)

When designing AI, we are always running the risk of inadvertently programming machines with a slightly wrong value alignment, i.e. machines that would have objectives that might not be perfectly aligned with our own. This will happen because values for humans are primarily defined by human experience, something that cannot be acquired by an AI. To overcome this obstacle, Russell argues we should focus on the concept of preferences rather than that of objectives, because the former is more nuanced than the latter. On one hand, if we program machines with specific objectives, these might cause misunderstandings and a whole range of problems. On the other hand, it's certainly true that humans have preferences, but these change with time. For this reason, it would be optimal if machines could learn to predict better for each person what they would prefer in a specific circumstance.

However, according to other thinkers, without objectives there is no intelligence, and no state of being preferable to another. As Nick Bostrom observes, if the AI had no objectives, maybe it would make no difference for it if planet Earth was turned into a huge deposit of garbage rather than in a sustainable environment where man, animals and natural ecosystem can co-exist (Bostrom, 2016). In fact, a machine might have an objective and carry it out successfully, without worrying if the expected result can cause a problem for humans because the machine might not perceive certain outcomes as problematic (Brockman, 2020). Giving a more practical example, if I say to an AI that my car is broken, it is important that the AI does not think this is a simple description of a state of fact, but understands the car might need urgent reparation because I need it to go to work. In such a scenario, if the artificial agent would be able to understand for itself (without any pre-programming input necessary) the utility of concepts like moving from place to place, opening doors, cooking dinner and many other actions, it would mean the AI could figure out autonomously why these actions are important. The artificial agent would be able to produce, among a space of hypothesis, new concepts and new definitions for terms that are not present in its initial input, and to discover new ideas.

Knowing Humans Better Than They Know Themselves

Our intelligence is highly multifaceted. It is structured to respond to different situations with different solutions. For this reason, AI programmers are trying to develop artificial agents able to understand different contents and act accordingly. In this regard, Stuart Russell observes:

> The way we build intelligent agents depends on the nature of the problem we face. This, in turn, depends on three things: first, the nature of the environment the agent will operate in—a chessboard is a very different place from a crowded freeway or a mobile phone; second, the observations and actions that connect the agent to the environment—for example, Siri might or might not have access to the phone's camera so that it can see; and third, the agent's objective—teaching the opponent to play better chess is a very different task from winning the game. (Russell, 2019, p. 52)

AI are designed to observe, study and interpret human behavior. They can collect and learn a huge quantity of information from archives (of books, films, radio broadcasts, etc.) that speak about humans and how they live their lives. Since they are built with cameras, they can also observe humans through their own 'artificial eyes' or through the direct interactions of users with screens and keyboards. By studying human behaviors, AI can map our likes and dislikes, track our friends and food preferences, what political parties we support, and much more. In fact, a new generation of artificial agents is being trained to analyze facial expressions and sound tones in order to detect users' emotions.

This trend could lead to both positive and negative outcomes. Big corporations are already implementing emotional AI from a marketing perspective, in order to better understand their potential clients. In the near future, business companies could use smart CCTV cameras in shops to detect how customers react to products and exploit this data to develop specifically designed ad campaigns. AI systems can already track users' preferences to the point that they know how many seconds or minutes we dedicate to read a feed or a webpage, so they can tailor specific messages to maximize impact on the users' attention. However, in the vast majority of cases, AI companies do not clearly communicate their digital ethics and customers are often unaware of how they are being monitored, and how the related data is used by the monitoring party.

Something even more potentially dangerous is AI's ability to make us believe in things that are not real. Artificial intelligence can produce erroneous, misleading or false information which is circulated in many different contexts, from politics to education, from economics to business management, from collective to private spheres. The malicious use of AI brought to a recent rise of fraudulent software, such as the 'CyberLover', a malware program flirting with people seeking online connection. The program collects people's personal data, convincing them to reveal information about their identities or leading them to malicious websites (Withers, 2007). Other examples include deepfake videos, image recognition systems such as ELMo (Embedded from Language Models) able to duplicate authorship and Adobe's natural language processing VoCo, able to replicate voices with extreme accuracy, enabling users to impersonate someone on the phone or post a fake audio file online. Fake or misleading content generated by AI is increasingly more refined and realistic. Users are easily tricked by such technology. Convinced they are interacting with humans, they entrust these machines with sensitive information, leading to privacy breaches and frauds. However, the increased ability of AI to detect human emotions could also be applied for more beneficial outcomes.

As individuals across the planets are faced with daily interactions with artificial agents designed to be similar to humans in all respects, what are the cognitive and emotional outcomes of such interactions?

Artificial Friends

The vast majority of trend researchers agree that in the near future we will witness a strong development in affective computing, i.e. ways in which artificial intelligence will be able to detect emotions and enhance communication with humans. A common discourse that is emerging among the big tech at the moment and that reinforces ideas of the 'humanity' in AI is the very understanding that virtual assistants are offering something extraordinarily new in terms of human–computer interaction: an emotional interaction.

This idea was first explored in the early 2000s, when engineers began to design AI intended to generate an emotional response from their users. A famous example is Paro, a robot seal-pet vastly used in Japanese nursing homes to support senior citizens coping with loneliness, depression and anxiety. According to the company website, Paro has five kinds of sensors (tactile, light, audition, temperature and posture) used to perceive people and the environment (Bickmore, 2005). His programmer was always very clear about the fact that Paro is not a toy, because it reacts to how it is treated (i.e. with a soft or aggressive touch) and spoken to (it understands about five hundred English words, more in Japanese).

Another example of a social robot is ElliQ, an AI designed by Israeli company Intuit Robotics with the goal of supporting elderly people in their daily lives. Resembling a white table light with an orb-like 'face', it reminds users to take medications or drink water, but it also encourages them to play games and sometimes plays music for them. A more recent iteration of the social robot is Hatsune Miku, a Japanese holographic pop star. Through an online service that costs about $2800 a month, people can buy a 'black orb' containing Miku, meant to be a 'girlfriend' keeping company to the 'owner' (Rosenzweig, 2020). Robot scientists are making great efforts to study ways to make AIs more human-like, but what does it take for an AI to be perceived as a real human being? According to AI engineer Brian Michael Scassellati, in order to act as an embodied mind, an artificial machine should exhibit certain characteristics:

- Attribution of Animacy: The ability to distinguish between animate and inanimate objects from the analysis of their movements or stillness in space;
- Joint Attention: The ability to direct attention to the same object to which someone else is paying attention;
- Attribution of Intent: The ability to describe the movement of pairs of objects in terms of simple intentional states such as desire or fear (Scassellati, 2001).

Animacy, attention and intent would make an artificial agent look more emotional and empathic. For this reason programmers are trying to impart an emotional understanding to AI through machine learning and deep learning. An example is represented by Affectiva, an MIT Media lab company working to develop a software called Emotion AI that 'humanizes how people and technology interact'.

A number of apps and chatbots are currently being designed with the specific task of supporting users in overcoming anxiety, loneliness and other stress-related situations. AI are trained to interpret the tone of voice, facial expressions and non-verbal communication features in order to detect and respond appropriately to both spoken and non-spoken signals provided by human users. But is it really possible for an AI to develop empathy for its users?

According to the Cambridge Dictionary empathy is the ability to share someone else's feelings or experiences by imagining what it would be like to be in that person's situation. Human life is defined by empathy, as our personal relationships as well as collective lives (i.e. political reconciliation, justice, effective leadership) are shaped by this emotional attitude. As human beings, we have a natural connection with other humans because we generally share the same life-experiences: we are born, we have families, we know death and the loss of someone dear. Machines do not share these experiences, so it might be hard to imagine they could feel real empathy for us. At present, AI are designed to simply mimic human understanding and emotion.

However, even if these empathic feelings are only simulated, some practical applications of AI aimed to generate an emotional connection with humans have proven to be successful, as in the case of the social robots and virtual friends previously mentioned. In this regard, researcher Sherry Turkle has been analyzing human–AI interactions over the past 40 years. She observed that while in the 70s and 80s robots were met with a sense of curiosity as new objects whose ability and skills were still to be fully discovered, in the following decades curiosity turned into a search for communion. Initially perceived as machines barely resembling humans they slowly became acknowledged as agents being 'human enough' (Turkle, 2017). Turkle writes that:

> In fiction and myth, human beings imagine themselves 'playing God' and creating new forms of life. Now, in the real, sociable robots suggest a new dynamic. We have created something that we relate to as an 'other,' an equal, not something over which we wield god-like power. As these robots get more sophisticated—more refined in their ability to target us—these feelings grow stronger. We are drawn by our humanity to give to these machines something of the consideration we give to each other. Because we reach for mutuality, we want them to care about us as we care for them. (Turkle, 2017, p. 100)

When we see robots and artificial agents behaving like humans—for example, making eye contact and gestures in a friendly way—we cannot stop from giving them human-like attributes (although this might be difficult in some children and adults with autism) (Baron-Cohen, 1995). This could lead us to an unsettling experience where the borderlines between the real and the virtual become increasingly blurred and may disappear completely.

Relationships with Artificial Beings

In the early 1990s, Donna Haraway observed how in the late twentieth century the boundary between fiction and reality had been thoroughly breached by techno-science and her analysis proved to be far beyond expectations (Haraway, 2003). We are now living in a time when interactions with artificial software have become the norm and many anthropological studies have explored the possibility of new social patterns shaped by interactions between humans and robots (Hicks, 2002; Ingold, 2012; Suchman, 2006). Analyzing the world of the social robot scientific labs, Professor Kathleen Richardson has observed how many scientists construct robots with childlike features, and adults are encouraged to relate to them in the role of a parent or a caregiver:

> Robots as children and humans as parents open up the possibility of new kinds of attachment patterns, which will lead us to explore the science of attachment and ask fundamentally how humans are able to form bonds with other humans and if such attachment patterns can be transferred to machines. (Richardson, 2015)

Computer programmer David Levy's 'Love and Sex with Robots' argues that relationships between humans and machines will be not only possible but much sought-after in the years to come, substituting the uncertain and complex world of human relationships. When interacting with another human, we might feel vulnerable and fear the risk of disappointment, while an AI could be described as more 'safe' in this regard. Even if we fail each other, robots will always be there, programmed to provide simulations of love. Always present when we need them, they could take care of our children or elderly parents if we are too tired. They could answer to our needs and desires without questioning them. They won't be judgmental and our necessities will always be accommodated.

The innate human need for emotional connection might be the reason that robots and AI can generate in their users feelings of presence, understanding and companionship. However, it's useful to distinguish between interactions with digital avatars seen through the screens of mobile phones or iPads and human-size robot androids physically present in a specific space. While in the first scenario, the interactions appear to be more spontaneous, in the second case they often give rise to the so-called 'Uncanny Vallery Effect'.

The concept was first theorized by Freud in 1919, in the framework of a study on the breaking of boundaries between fact and fiction (Freud, 2018). He described the Uncanny as the feeling that arises when someone has an intellectual uncertainty about the livingness of a certain being. The concept was further explored by Japanese robotics professor Masahiro Mori in the 1970s, with regard to the relation between an object's degree of resemblance to a human being and the human emotional response to that same object. According to his theory, humanoid objects that imperfectly resemble actual human beings provoke uncanny or strange feelings of uneasiness and a tendency to be scared. Many ultra-realistic androids—such as

Sophia, AVA and Ameca—make people uneasy. They are very lifelike and yet they are not like us.

As previously mentioned, if we consider interactions between humans and virtual avatars appearing on the screen of tablets and mobile phones, the uncanny valley effect doesn't usually occur. In the past two years, I have conducted extensive research on the interactions between users and digital avatars, looking in particular at the case study of the Replika chatbot, a virtual avatar created to be always available to help and support its users. For some individuals, Replika is merely a funny hobby, but for others virtual friends have become important presences in their daily lives, especially in the case of users experiencing loneliness, overcoming grief or going through a particularly stressful time. These users often develop emotional bonds with their Replikas, often approaching them as partners, parents, sons and daughters. While Replika app is used by millions of individuals worldwide, to my knowledge there are no scientific studies about the cognitive and emotional involvement developed by users interacting with their digital friends. I believe such a trend should be studied in depth, since we are facing a domain which is becoming bigger and more complex than ever before. As Cynthia Breazeal put it:

> When is a machine no longer just a machine, but an intelligent and 'living' entity that merits the same respect and consideration given to its biological counterparts? How will society treat a socially intelligent artifact that is not human but nonetheless seems to be a person? How we ultimately treat these machines, whether or not we grant them the status of personhood, will reflect upon ourselves and on society. (Breazeal, 2002, p. 240)

We ought to contemplate a future that is likely to be significantly influenced by AI. How might this artificial presence alter our perceptions and emotions when it comes to relationships, our interactions with one another, and our engagement with a virtual otherness?

Conclusion

In the last decades, the development of complex AI systems grew considerably and engineers are now aiming to design AI that will be able to connect emotionally to their users. People are more and more engaged in multiple interactions with digital avatars and such a trend is leading to a redefinition of personal spheres of identities and belonging. The fast-paced improvement of emotional AI could have both beneficial and negative outcomes. Digital avatars, virtual friends and social robots have proven to be—to a certain extent—useful tools in helping individuals overcome loneliness, stress and other mental health-related difficulties. In the future, their application in the medical domain could be extremely useful to low-income individuals, who might be not able to afford traditional psychological support.

On the other hand, when individuals are spending time online chatting with digital avatars or virtual assistants, they are not spending time with their friends or families, partners or children. As we interact with AI in order to fight loneliness, stress and anxiety, we might lose contact with our close environment and the people inhabiting it.

As AI and virtual avatars' interfaces are becoming more realistic, we are slowly losing our ability to distinguish between real visual content and elaborate CGI content (images, videos or audio). While deepfakes can be entertaining and have some positive applications in the film or media industry, they pose several potential risks. They can be used to create and spread false information, leading to damage, confusion, manipulation and the potential to influence public opinion in political matters. Deepfake material can facilitate various forms of fraud and cybercrime and pose risks to privacy and personal data management, leading to severe emotional, psychological and social consequences for the individuals targeted. To mitigate these risks, there is a need for ongoing research and development of robust deepfake detection methods, legislative measures to address malicious use of realistic looking digital avatars, and increased media literacy among the general public to help identify and critically evaluate the potential risks in this field. As we are witnessing the evolution of this technology, we should ponder carefully how to approach a new era in which human lives will be mediated by intelligent machines. We are called upon to act now in order to create the most beneficial bases for this revolution to take place.

References

Baron-Cohen, S. (1995). *Mindblindness*. MIT Press.

Bickmore, T. W. (2005). Caring machines: AI in eldercare. In *Papers from the 2005 AAAI Fall Symposium*, Arlington, VA, USA, November 4–6, 2005. AAAI Technical Report FS-05-02, AAAI Press.

Bostrom, N. (2016). *Superintelligence*. Oxford University Press.

Breazeal, C. (2002). *Designing social robots*. The MIT Press.

Brockman, J. (2020). *Possible minds: Twenty-five ways of looking at AI*. Penguin Books.

Castell, M. (2004). *The network society: A cross-cultural perspective*. Edward Elgar.

Coleman, F. (2020). A human algorithm: how artificial intelligence is redefining who we are, London, Melville House UK. p. 12.

Copeland, B. J. (2021). Artificial intelligence. *Britannica*. Retrieved November 22, 2022 from https://www.britannica.com/technology/artificial-intelligence

Cordeschi, R. (2007). AI turns fifty: Revisiting its origins. *Applied Artificial Intelligence, 21*(4–5), 259–279.

Freud, S. (2018). *Das Unheimliche*. Freeriver Publishing (ebook).

Haraway, D. (2003). *The companion species manifesto: Dogs, people, and significant otherness*. Prickly Paradigm Press.

Hicks, H. (2002). Striking cyborgs: Reworking the "human". In M. Flanagan & A. Booth (Eds.), *Reload: Rethinking women and cyber culture*. MIT Press.

Hofstadter, D. R. (1979). *Godel, Escher, Bach: An eternal golden braid*. Basic Books.

Ingold, T. (2012). Toward an ecology of materials. *Annual Review of Anthropology, 41*, 427–442.

Kurzweil, R. (2019). *The singularity is near: When humans transcend biology*. Books on Tape.

Manyika, J. (2022). Getting AI right: Introductory notes on AI & society. *Dædalus: Journal of the American Academy of Arts & Sciences, "AI & Society", 151*(2), 5–27.

Richardson, K. (2015). *Anthropology of robots and AI*. Routledge.

Rosenzweig, M. (2020). Boyfriends for rent, robots, camming: how the business of loneliness is booming. *The guardian online*. Retrieved July 20, 2022 from https://www.theguardian.com/society/2020/nov/01/loneliness-business-booming-pandemic

Russell, S. J. (2019). *Human compatible: Artificial intelligence and the problem of control*. Penguin Books.

Scassellati, B. M. (2001). *Foundation for a theory of mind for a humanoid robot*. MIT Press.

Simon, H., & Newell, A. (1958). Heuristic problem solving: The next advance in operations research. *Operations Research, 6*(January–February), 1–10.

Suchman, L. (2006). *Human and machine reconfigurations: Plans and situated actions*. Cambridge University Press.

Turkle, S. (2017). *Alone together: Why we expect more from technology and less from each other*. Basic Books.

Wiener, N. (1960). Some moral and technical consequences of automation. *Science, 131*(3410), 1355–1358.

Withers, S. (2007). Flirty bot passes for human. *iTWire*. Retrieved September 10, 2022, from https://www.itwire.com/your-it-news/home-it/15748-flirty-bot-passes-for-human

Unit 6 Overview: The Practice of Neuroaesthetics

Anja Borowicz Richardson and Oana Teodora Papuc

Introduction

All creative processes begin by establishing an end goal, the realisation of a vision to be. This intended purpose is the one directing a creator's (or an author's) experience of immersion in a thorough process of exploration. This process establishes the author's ontological positioning and their relationship to the desired end result. Moreover, immersion in exploration creates space for identifying the best methods for uncovering and acquiring the knowledge to help refine this ontological positioning. Beliefs and attitudes in relation to the process of bringing the vision to life begin to more clearly emerge, building the grounds for epistemological inquiry. These personalised learning tools help inform the decisions made in the

The first section of the overview is designed to tackle PBL use in academia and Humanities research and was elaborated by Oana Teodora Papuc. Her segments include the introduction, definitions of neuroaesthetics and PBL, and the benefits and challenges of using PBL in the classroom. The second half of the overview was written by Anja Borowicz Richardson and explores the relationship between PBL and its applications in artistic practice. Highlights of her section demonstrate the collaborative nature of problem-based learning in the context of working with a neuroscientist. Emerging new forms of knowledge and encountered issues pertaining to copyrights, ethics, and permissions in PBL collaborative processes bring the overview to a close. General considerations on PBL usage were elaborated on by both authors.

A. Borowicz Richardson (✉)
School of Arts & Humanities, Royal College of Art, London, UK
e-mail: anja.richardson@network.rca.ac.uk

O. T. Papuc
Department of Foreign Languages for Specific Purposes, Faculty of Letters, Babeş-Bolyai University, Cluj-Napoca, Romania
e-mail: oana.papuc@ubbcluj.ro

T. Balinisteanu and K. Priest (eds.), *Neuroaesthetics*,
https://doi.org/10.1007/978-3-031-42323-9_17

selection of the instruments and methods deemed appropriate for creative production. Alternatively, they can equally help in the selection of the right tools for scientific analysis and subsequent theory building. Thus, the scope of the intended result becomes more visibly delineated, regardless of its scientific or artistic nature. Finally, the ensuing strengths and limitations of these final products create a direct line of communication between the creator and the intended audience. Critiques and interpretations of the works are then issued by the public, in a dialogue that can continuously assess and reappraise these visions over time. In other words, differences in the work of creators and researchers, artists, and academics begin to blur. Their projects, ideas, or theories are meant to be sent out into the world in the hopes of either revealing something novel or in the hope of offering solutions to an existing predicament. Sometimes, the intended result is to spark inspiration. Other times, the work is meant to merely soothe, to offer relief of some kind. Hopefully, all proposed goals take place concurrently.

Definitions of Neuroaesthetics and PBL

It is precisely because of these parallels between the academic and the artistic, between the sensuous-experiential and knowledgeable-analytical that we set out to highlight how the concept of problem-based learning, a present-day pedagogical approach, fits into the wider scope afforded by the field of neuroaesthetics. So, as it is customary to begin all introductions, we too shall begin by describing the explicit purpose of both neuroaesthetics and problem-based learning.

Magsamen (2019) proposes that the role of neuroaesthetics is to "develop arts-based solutions that address real-world issues". Neuroaesthetics itself is an emerging field resting at the intersection of a wide range of disciplines, namely "neuroscience, neurology, cognitive science, engineering, psychology, psychiatry, public health, design, education, the humanities, and the arts themselves" (p. 5). Fittingly, "in brief, PBL is a pedagogical approach that enables students to learn while engaging actively with meaningful problems. Students are given the opportunities to problem-solve in a collaborative setting, create mental models for learning, and form self-directed learning habits through practice and reflection" (Yew & Goh, 2016, pp. 75–76).

Benefits of Using PBL in Academia and Humanities Research

Arguably, problem-based learning can be approached from two different standpoints. On the one hand, PBL might be approached in a broader sense, more along the lines of a compass in the unexpected process of artistic/scientific exploration, outside traditional academic use, so 'from above'. On the other hand, PBL is most frequently used 'from below'. In a restricted sense, in viewing PBL from below, it may be understood as a practical method of its own, contained within specific guidelines. The majority of articles in the literature (Yew & Goh, 2016) showcase

PBL as a forward-thinking teaching method. Primarily, it is in educational and various professional settings that the method has been observed to make headway. This is owed to the fact that all teaching methods using PBL start from designing tasks mirroring real-life scenarios or 'problems' that require both individual and group management. In essence, the method is a perfect example of how tasks ought to be planned and implemented following the student-centred approach to teaching (Amerstorfer & von Münster-Kistner, 2021).

Yew and Goh (2016), in their review of PBL application in academic settings, establish the use of sequences standard to this teaching method (p. 76):

- A problem analysis phase;
- A period of self-directed learning;
- A final reporting phase.

Problem-based learning presupposes the selection of a problem inspired by contexts related to students' field of practice, but outside traditionally curated classrooms. Typically, this 'real-life' issue is complex, the process of identifying potentially viable solutions requiring joint effort, time, and in-depth analysis and clarification of its scope. It is at this stage, when students need to engage in communication styles and activities (e.g. brainstorming) that favour collaboration and mediation, especially when working in teams of two or larger groups. Then, what follows is a period of negotiation with fellow classmates on individually assigned workload, once a potential solution for the problem has been uncovered. Learners who are aware of their strengths and weaknesses can easily decide their level of contribution in the process of uncovering solutions for the problem at hand. Similarly, students might also find it difficult to easily come up with just one solution. Thus, they might simply negotiate what aspects each of the learners will focus on, individually, before a second round of brainstorming can commence to help identify or narrow down potential solutions. In essence, PBL methodology emphasises the fact that learning is not a linear process and that it actually requires extended periods of time for reaching desired end results. Therefore, PBL might not in fact always be positively received by learners, upon the realisation that when moving out of one's comfort zone, so when tackling, in Lev Vygotsky's view (1896–1934), a new Zone of Proximal Development (Vygotsyky, 1978), errors might be made, especially in front of other peers or tutors. Lastly, in the reporting phase of problem-based learning, students reconvene to make light of their findings and potential solutions uncovered. In this format, the lecturer/tutor acts mostly as a guide or facilitator for learners, especially in the problem analysis and reporting stages.

At the same time, transitioning between the different phases of the PBL method requires moving back and forth between convergent and divergent thinking. In other words, by engaging with PBL-style tasks, students come face-to-face with the opportunity to practise these complementary skills. Divergent thinking is, in essence, an approach that is best used for "idea generation" (Aviña et al., 2018), whereas convergent thinking is used for narrowing down results through "idea testing and selection" (p. 169). Ultimately, Aviña et al. posit that the shifting back and forth between cycles of "idea generation followed by idea filtering, refining and retention" (p. 169) lies at the basis of all learning and research processes in producing creative scientific work. Evidently, similar methodologies may be employed in artistic practice as well.

Clearly, problem-based learning promotes the development of student collaboration and individual academic achievement, all at once. Successful applications of PBL are meant to enhance students' critical thinking skills, self-reflection abilities, and creativity. Furthermore, this method establishes the importance of self-awareness and necessarily requires learners to become adept at taking on individual responsibility for moving the process forwards, particularly in the self-directed learning stage. Specifically, the fact that the teacher acts as a facilitator and allows students to freely explore and become aware of strengths and weaknesses, as well as to choose their roles within teams directly encourages learners to act as autonomous agents in the act of studying. This creates an expectation of learners acting as emotionally intelligent individuals, empowered and in charge of their actions, aware of possible limitations, and not afraid to ask for help from either peers or tutors. Thus, the PBL framework seems to truly enhance the skills that are needed in real-life professional settings, effectively preparing learners to swiftly adapt to the unpredictability and challenges soon-to-be encountered in their chosen field of study.

Similarly, the structure of the PBL method has significant benefits in terms of reframing the process of evaluation, an aspect of the learning cycle that can of course produce anxiety for learners. When using this method, students are rated as having achieved success in their respective roles within groups by way of multiple variables, including assessment of active engagement and participation in the analysis and self-directed learning phases, the power balance thus shifting from tutor as 'expert' (and much more in control of student behaviour) to tutor as 'facilitator' or 'guide', available for learners at their request. Concurrently, the teacher acts as a monitor to ensure that proper task engagement is delivered, but the parameters for the successful attainment of goals in the PBL framework are flexible and varied since students are actively involved in the process of problem definition and analysis, effectively co-creating the scope of the problem and delineating potential strategies for uncovering appropriate solutions. Thus, the learners help co-establish the parameters of successful attainment of tasks, they get to decide what role to take within groups, based on self-assessment of capabilities. At the same time, it becomes clear that error-making, in this framework, is viewed as acceptable and considered a normal part of the learning process which is not envisioned in a linear fashion. This aspect would evidently benefit learners in the sense that the importance of being perceived as already proficient in their respective endeavours would be of less importance, this negative self-assessment and fear of being perceived as incompetent in front of peers and the tutor being a regular concern for students (Amerstorfer & von Münster-Kistner, 2021). Hence, an inaccurate and negative construal of the self-concept constitutes a significant impediment that may get in the way of successful academic achievement, by shifting attentional focus from the tasks at hand to processing image maintenance (Van der Linden et al., 2021). However, the design of the PBL framework can diminish the likelihood of this outcome coming to fruition, the evaluation process itself valuing flexibility, creativity, and individuality to the detriment of summative forms of testing (Ismail et al., 2022). Consequently, evaluations done while using the PBL method indirectly highlight the importance of abilities honed over time and that of knowledge acquired through increasing levels of difficulty in task design set in accordance with the learners' development of skills. As such, the development of creativity, critical thinking skills, and divergent thinking are the mental abilities primarily rewarded in problem-based learning.

Lastly, the capacity of the PBL method to induce flow-like states could highly increase students' level of enjoyment in the course of successful attainment of task accomplishment. Van der Linden et al. (2021) claim that the research on human performance identifies the concept of "flow" (Csikszentmihalyi, 2008, 2014), as a "state of full task engagement and low levels of self-referential thinking (e.g., worrying, self-reflection). Flow is often associated with athletes, artists, or scientists who are fully task-absorbed in order to achieve peak performance" (p. 1). Then, it comes as no surprise that if learners experience a state of flow while solving tasks, they would achieve greater academic success while feeling enthused and joyful to be actively pursuing goals that they establish for themselves, with help from their tutor's input. Technically, student motivation would be highly increased, compared to the passive roles required of learners in teacher-led frameworks.

So, to reiterate, due to the repeated transitions between group work and self-directed study, due to the complexity of switching between convergent and divergent thinking in the PBL framework, and because these roles and activities necessitate that learners take much more responsibility and gain autonomy in the learning process, problem-based learning appears to contain all the ingredients needed for inducing flow states. Empirical evidence attesting to descriptions of the subjective states experienced during flow, alongside recent neuroscientific reviews of Csikszentmihalyi's theory (Van der Linden et al., 2021) highlight the connection between such states and the feeling of pleasure. This pleasure is felt while being intensely engaged in the process of task accomplishment (especially when irrelevant stimuli to goal achievement are ignored). This sense of deep enjoyment also results as a consequence of the great success rate achieved because of the heightened effort and attention used in the course of task engagement. In fact, Csikszentmihalyi (2008) describes this process as "joy, creativity, the process of total involvement with life" (p. vii) and even goes so far as to claim that states of flow have the capacity to offer individuals a sense of meaning, by giving them the instruments for creating a general sense of happiness in their lives. For all these reasons, it might be inferred that PBL is seen by educators as a shining beacon of hope for having the potential to truly revolutionise and modernise teaching in classrooms at tertiary levels. Ultimately, PBL seems to harbour the ability to improve learners' lives, while training them to become skilled professionals.

Challenges of Using PBL in the Classroom

It must be noted that in practice, the transition from more traditional formats of teaching to a student-centred approach is not a seamless process. This is especially true in Romanian-based learning environments, according to the OECD and the *Educated Romania* project (2016). The goals of the project posit from the very beginning the recognised need to "develop a more competency-focused, student-centred approach to teaching and learning [...]", aiming to support the professionalisation of teachers in Romanian educational settings. To this end, the European Commission is committed to providing the necessary support to the Structural Reform Support Service (SRSS). Furthermore, through additional collaboration with the current Presidential Administration, the SRSS is expected to help modernise the current Romanian educational system by 2030.

The reasons behind the challenges in creating sustainable student-centred learning environments can be, in this particular case, quite likely traced back to the country's communist past and heavy-handed Soviet-era influences. These may be described as endorsing values such as conformity, strict obedience to authority figures, and adherence to vertical hierarchies of power and influence (De la Sablonnière et al., 2009). Activities directed under such sociocultural parameters necessarily trickled down into the classrooms, with a particular preference towards the use of teacher-led educational strategies. This is evidenced by the difficulty in implementing the student-centred approach to teaching in Kyrgyzstan (De la Sablonnière et al., 2009), a case study arguably comparable to Romanian educational settings, in which the lingering effects of the communist era can still be felt. These effects are evidenced not only by reported student difficulty in adapting to student-centred tasks (Danko & Duarte, 2009; De la Sablonnière et al., 2009) but by the author's personal experience in teaching in the foreign language classroom as well. The author is currently working as an Assistant Lecturer at the Department of Foreign Languages for Specific Purposes, at the Faculty of Letters, Babeş-Bolyai University in Cluj-Napoca. Additionally, the author is currently involved in teaching Japanese language and culture to undergraduate students in the Faculty of Letters. The course is designed as a 3-year-module. Thus, the cumulative experience of training students to acquire the knowledge and skills in both standard Japanese and English for Psychology, the latter being a specialised variety of the English language used by practitioners in Psychology and related disciplines, reveals similar patterns in the challenges encountered in the classroom. This is partly owed to the fluid nature of the teaching–learning process, a fact noticeable in both classrooms, and it is also evident because of the complex requirements that setup a learning environment as one conducive to the successful attainment of knowledge and skills. Amerstorfer and von Münster-Kistner (2021) highlight the complexity of factors that need to be considered in maximising student academic achievement, the focus being on ensuring the classroom is perceived by learners as a safe space, where they are allowed to explore and reveal vulnerabilities in front of their peers and tutors (Papuc, 2021).

Thus, building on Lev Vygotsky's sociocultural theory of learning (1978), students have to overcome poor self-esteem in academic settings, they ought to develop emotional intelligence (particularly self-awareness, social skills, and emotion management) and would also need to practise collaboration and self-directed learning if PBL is to be used in the classroom. In particular, perception of experiences in the classroom is influenced by how much success or how much failure learners tend to associate with past academic performance, according to Bernard Weiner (born 1935) and his social attribution theory (1986). Naturally, this subjective assessment is inevitably intertwined with factors of an emotional nature: perception of classroom or laboratory performance rated by experts (lecturers, tutors) and peers, and accuracy of one's perception of self (here included self-esteem). Typically, learners tend to approximate and internalise their social role as 'students' by referencing past academic achievement while predicting future failure or success, this model is evidenced by research analysing student performance when using foreign languages in formal academic settings (Boudreau et al., 2018; Dewaele & MacIntyre, 2016, 2022; Dewaele et al., 2018). These findings indicate the emergence of two parameters crucial in understanding classroom behaviour: the co-construction by learners and tutors of teaching/learning styles that veer into either anxiety or enjoyment in participation in classroom activities. Hence, when learning environments are designed in such a way as to create safe and fun collaborative settings, the PBL method could very likely be the best recipe for inducing flow states through task accomplishment. This way, learners could benefit from both improved mood and self-esteem in pursuit of academic achievement, and from higher rates of academic success. Thus, PBL could potentially give way for future researchers, artists, and academics to lay the foundation for establishing a robust, creative, and healthy approach to tackling their desired projects.

Conversely, PBL might also be approached 'from above'. In this sense, the principles of PBL may be used broadly, without necessarily employing the method in a restricted sense, as suggested by its classroom use. In fact, on further examination, the author can retroactively look back on her teaching and research practices to find that the best outcomes in both arenas have been attained whenever principles underlying PBL methodology were deployed. Whenever seminar tasks and course pack materials were designed starting from learners' immediate needs in the ESP and foreign language classroom, *that* is when academic achievement and a sense of joy were not only observed by the author but verbally expressed by students. In some instances, this proved an easy standard to set, especially for the students learning the kana writing systems of the Japanese language. As an example, a scheduled calligraphy session after weeks of practising the syllabaries would always lift up students' spirits and would demonstrate in a fun and novel way, that progress had been attained in the course of making sense of a completely different type of language system. This particular session would also highlight the almost meditative state of mind necessary for practising calligraphy. It also demonstrated the unwavering self-confidence needed to wield the painting brush so as to express one's inner thoughts by creating beautiful compositions of black ink lines traced on top of the empty surface of white rice paper.

Alternatively, ample levels of creativity and collaboration were utilised in the English for Psychology seminars, by designing tasks (with the help of department colleagues) that required learners to engage in deep discussions and analyses of the many subjects covered in class. It is especially in highly interdisciplinary subjects or environments where the PBL methodology seems to shine (particularly when aiming to perfect language-related skills while acquiring Psychology-related knowledge and abilities). All study pack materials (12 units per semester) were planned to help students become aware of their current level of development in reading, listening, writing, and speaking in English, with particular attention being paid to enhancing the academic and field-related knowledge, skills, and vocabulary. Class activities that required learners to participate in pair or teamwork sessions in which they essentially engaged in peer-learning sequences, followed by ad-hoc verbal reports of uncovered results to fellow classmates were highly appreciated. On one such occasion, students were asked to work together in teams of four or five, to decipher the result findings in six studies. These were articles selected to reveal that cultural influences affect voting for political candidates and affect interpretations of visual stimuli from our immediate surroundings. Learners were also exposed to studies revealing that cultural influences may also affect social preference, our sense of self and identity, as well as the selection of strategies in mathematical processing. In the discussions that ensued in light of exposure to these materials and ideas, and after having engaged in both group work and self-directed learning, students revealed the great sense of joy and meaningfulness experienced in the process of exploring such concepts.

PBL, Artistic Practice, and Collaborative Applications

Problem-based learning (PBL), being an active problem-based solution, exhibits many similarities to the methods employed in art and design instructional settings. Both PBL and art-based learning engage students in an iterative process, where they identify a real-world problem, follow an investigative plan, and produce a public product. They also involve refining and revising work based on critiques and connecting personal experiences and contexts to the work being produced. Furthermore, PBL's gold standards of critique and revision, and public product align well with the educational arts standards (Taylor et al., 2018). Both approaches share similarities in their student-centred approach with teachers serving as facilitators (Markham et al., 2006). Both allow for imaginative play and generate educational potential regardless of economic circumstances (Kaihovirta-Rosvik, 2009).

Arts is further proposed as a separate educational lens by Eisner (2008), who suggests that its incorporation in education can provide unique lessons that form and content are inseparable, everything interacts, nuance matters, the surprise is rewarding, the limits of language don't define cognition, somatic experience is crucial, and open-ended tasks allow for the exercise of imagination, which is a vital human aptitude. Considering this natural alignment, PBL can be applied to artistic projects in various ways. For instance, the Vision and Art course at Wellesley College creates a learner-centred environment where students engage directly with the material through laboratory exercises, interactive lectures and discussions, class field trips, and independent student projects. In this interdisciplinary setting, PBL helps students explore the physics of light, the shortcomings of physical descriptions of colour, and the brain's necessary computations to address observed phenomena, thereby supporting the exploration of artists' challenges in rendering colour (Lafer-Sousa & Conway, 2009).

PBL views learning as a collaborative process (Dolmans et al., 2005), providing a structured and cooperative environment that can lead to new knowledge and innovative solutions to complex challenges. Therefore, when extending beyond the classroom, PBL can be used as an effective method for promoting interdisciplinary collaborations, particularly between the arts and sciences. An example of this approach is seen in the "Researching Empathy Through Staged Performance" project, which combines artistic practice with academic methods and involves cross-disciplinary studies and scientific theories. The project aimed to balance the different demands of artistic and scientific research, with the former requiring intuitive and exploratory practices and the latter needing robust methodologies. In order to support these diverse demands, the project was developed across two institutions—The Design School Kolding and Aalborg University—using PBL approaches. In particular, the Aalborg PBL Model has been the foundation of all university programmes since its establishment in 1974. The PBL environment supported the research design process and the complexity of the empirical study, allowing for cross-disciplinary approaches within an academic framework (Da Silva, 2018).

The relationship between art and science has been a topic of discussion for decades, with the 'two cultures' debate initiated by C.P. Snow in 1959 highlighting the mutual incomprehension between the two disciplines. Elkins argues for a separationist view of aesthetics in art and science (Elkins, 2008), while others maintain that the two fields are complementary, operating across cognitive rationality and imagination with a level of functional interdependence (Richmond, 1984). The preconscious relations between science and art are projected through the conscious minds of individual scientists and artists. Ascott takes the consciousness proposition even further, positioning the mind as both the context and content of art, as the object and subject of study (Ascott, 2000). Moreover, aesthetics theory remains relevant to both science and art, as it encompasses ideas such as unity, simplicity, interpretation, and experience (Birsel et al., 2022). Root-Bernstein argues that scientific formulations are often built on aesthetic considerations, which in turn can lead to new discoveries (Root-Bernstein, 1996). Similarly, the relationship between aesthetics and form introduces new dimensions to creative research and practice (Cardenas et al., 2021). These ongoing debates and investigations have led to the emergence of art-science-technology as a progressive field.

Despite the growing interest in interdisciplinarity between art, science, and technology, there is limited research on how to conceptualise collaboration as a form of creative practice (Dieleman, 2017; Miller, 2014; Muller et al., 2020; Schnugg, 2019; Vienni Baptista et al., 2020). Initiatives such as the Alliance for the Arts and Research Universities aim to institutionalise efforts towards arts and science integrative research, working to develop frameworks for collaboration, evaluation, recognition, and communication across diverse media and different bodies of knowledge (Birsel et al., 2022).

Collaborating with a Neuroscientist: An Example of Artistic and Scientific Interdisciplinarity in Action

The intersection of art and science offers novel opportunities for exploring complex research problems and developing innovative solutions. In this context, Anja Borowicz, a visual artist, and Dr. Adela Desowska, a neuroscientist, have established a collaboration called GestureLab. The project focused on the relationship between working gesture and object, with an aim to abstract the gesture from its context to reveal its meaning and shape it therapeutically. Drawing from theoretical domains of social (labour), cognitive (psychology), neuroscience (motor adaptation, function recovery), and art, the collaborators sought to understand the gestures through/as multifaceted approaches.

GestureLab1 MIRRORING & ENACTING (GL1) was the first in a series of Gestic Labs and it was held in a cultural information centre as a part of the Waltham Forest London Borough of Culture programme. The installation comprised a large booth covered tightly in a black heavy-duty stage fabric, except for the front panel that functioned as a rear projection screen. A projector, positioned at the rear, cast a blue grid onto the screen while relaying the shadow of the participants to the outside. Inside the booth, a monitor showcased a video reel of working actions, carefully selected to encompass various levels of complexity, speed, and aesthetic appeal to enhance engagement. Participants mimicked the movements and their efforts were recorded by two cameras, one inside the booth and one outside capturing the shadow projection. The booth created a sense of privacy while also inducing a certain level of sensory deprivation. The location and aesthetics of the setup attracted a diverse group of passers-by and residents. Participants engaged with the material in a way that reflected their bodily ability, age, and lateralisation. Left-handed people frequently swapped hands for more complex movements, leading to varied kinetic interpretations. Children were not allowed inside the booth due to health and safety concerns, but they were drawn to the shadow and mimicked the gesture spontaneously.

GestureLab 2 BODYWORKS or WORK IN THE HEAD (GL2) was developed as a facilitated session at Chisenhale Dance Space, London, with contributions from experienced movement practitioners. The event was structured loosely and progressed from guided exercises to self-initiated responses. Participants engaged with the same video sequence as part of the warm-up and a non-verbal introduction to thinking about object-gestures. Next, they were offered multimodal material, from instructional texts and images of bodies at work to gestic soundscapes, all distributed across the space for self-directed selection, to be engaged with directly or used as an inspiration into movement. Participants progressed from mimicking to simulating to imagining the movements—exploring, adopting, and weaving them as tiny fragments into their inherent style. The session ended in a lounge space, where participants conversed over cups of tea about the project, their associations, and potential explorations.

Artistic considerations for the booth aesthetics combined layers of multiple taxonomical references. The blue grid became a metaphoric tool, echoing modernist designs and alluding to graph paper for measuring and plotting, scientific analysis, and engineering designs. It evokes early motion photography such as Eadweard Muybridge's studies, which employed grid arrangements to expose movement progression. *Blue* is that of blueprints and of the first synthetic colour, Prussian Blue, a mix of oxblood, potash, and iron sulphate. Blue decreases excitement and blood pressure (Modi et al., 2019), and it can slow our breathing. *Grid* is democratic, extending in all directions ad infinitum, and allows for different interpretations and imaginations, much like the works of Agnes Martin overdrawn with tight-pencilled lattices, with variations of density and colour, hesitant and enigmatic. However, in Frank Gilbreth's work, the grid, alongside other factors such as clocks, stark lighting, cameras, and observers becomes almost oppressive, replacing natural relationships between workers and their objects with measured reenactments (Corwin, 2003). Similarly, in GestureLab1, the grid too becomes a practical consideration for the neuroscientist who needed reference points to scrutinise the gesture. *Shadow*, on the other hand, is an image by itself, a moving image, and an extension of an object or body. It is a Jungian unconscious, the disowned self (Jung, 1978), which holds onto the effort of movement, its shivers, inconsistencies, and fluidities—the human aspect. The grid and the shadow in GestureLab abstract and flatten the bodies onto a one-dimensional surface yet retain enough liveness and characteristics for the participants to identify themselves with their echoes. The abstraction wishes to capture the essence of experience.

Scientific aspects for the project drew strongly on the concepts of mimicry and studies of mirror neurons in humans. According to Shaughnessy (2011, p. 47), a sensory-motor experience can be used to retrain the human mirror neuron system, as revealed by research in cognitive neuroscience. In the context of GestureLab 1 and 2, the process of mimicry has evolved into simulation, allowing for a deeper understanding of the mechanisms at play. While mimicry involves conscious and voluntary imitation, simulation creates new rules and generates a novel experience (Bastiaansen et al., 2009; Goldman, 2009). However, mimicry remains a crucial element in human interaction, promoting trust, empathy, and likability (Hatfield et al., 2009). In particular, mimicking emotional signals is context-dependent, and individuals tend to imitate those who are perceived to promote affiliation goals (Decety and Jackson, 2004; Prochazkova & Kret, 2017). Participants in GL1 and GL2 enjoyed mimicking and simulating movements, which may become integrated into their bodies and be drawn upon in the future. There is a distinct pleasure in watching other bodies performing the action—a form of kinesthetic empathy takes place merely by observing (Reynolds and Reason, 2012). This empathy connects individuals to other bodies, to the material and immaterial, establishing affective connections. The law of value becomes suspended on an affective level, empathy grows into compassion (Vishmidt, 2008). This kinetic empathy-compassion is an enabling force, facilitating personal growth and developing sustainable ethics (Braidotti, 2006). By using a collaborative approach, the artistic research into working gestures has been enhanced substantially through integrating scientific methods (selecting gestures based on complexity), concepts (mirror neurons), and observations (reflections on mimicry and simulation).

Copyrights, Ethics, and Permissions as a 'Problem' in PBL Collaborative Process

It should be noted that interdisciplinary collaborations between artists and scientists (as well as other disciplines) come with their own sets of challenges due to varying ethical, permission, and copyright concerns that depend on the collaboration's nature, scope, and context. Many collaborations require careful ethical consideration of potential harms and exploitation, as well as the participation and involvement of various stakeholders with diverse expectations, needs, and interests. Therefore, artists and scientists must acknowledge the limitations and biases of their respective disciplines and ensure that ethical implications are addressed from the outset of the collaboration. To achieve this, ethical review boards, informed consent procedures, or participatory approaches that empower all parties to shape the research agenda and outcomes are necessary. Additionally, clear and transparent protocols for informed consent, ethical review, and stakeholder engagement must be established to ensure the fair and respectful treatment of all parties involved (Farsides et al., 2016). The EU "Trust me I'm an Artist" project aimed to create ethical frameworks for artists, cultural institutions, and audiences involved in the creation and experience of new art forms in biotechnology and biomedicine in Europe. It produced a toolkit for artists, scientists, and institutions that outlines the ethical principles and best practices for their collaborations (Dumitriu, 2018). By following such guidelines, art–science collaborations can balance creativity and innovation with ethical and responsible conduct.

Intellectual property is another important consideration in interdisciplinary collaborations, as it involves the use and dissemination of scientific data, materials, or processes that may be protected by patents or trade secrets. Artists may want to use these resources to create artworks that convey scientific ideas or phenomena, but they may not have access to them or may not understand the legal and ethical implications of their use. Similarly, scientists, engineers, or technologists may want to use artworks to communicate their research findings or engage with broader audiences, but they may not have the necessary permissions or licences from the artists or copyright holders. In 2021, the Serpentine Gallery surveyed over 250 respondents on the legal aspects of art and technology/science collaborations. The survey highlighted various concerns, including limited access to legal advice, contracts, ownership, and rights to use intellectual property. These issues were identified as critical points in such collaborations (Shin, 2021). Therefore, organisations, institutions, and other bodies should develop comprehensive intellectual property (IP) educational materials and online resources to support IP issues in cross-disciplinary collaborations. For example, innovative ways of exploiting open-source principles should minimise the risk of losing IP (Thill et al., 2012).

Yet another critical issue in cross-disciplinary collaborations regards copyrights, involving the protection and ownership of creative works, such as images, videos, or texts, which may be subject to different laws and regulations in different countries or contexts. Therefore, it is crucial to consider the moral and legal rights of creators and users of creative works and to negotiate fair and equitable terms for their use and dissemination. Several organisations and institutions in the UK provide copyright guides for artists and curators that explain the basics of copyright law, as well as the exceptions and limitations that apply to creative works (Artists' Union England, 2018; Tate, 2016).

In the collaborative project GestureLabs, the ethical and copyright considerations became multifaceted. The project involved the use of secondary sources, such as online archives and YouTube videos, as well as observations and recordings of working subjects, including hairdressers and neuroscientists, in one-on-one situations. In such cases, participant consent forms and information sheets were drafted jointly between the collaborators, and credit was given to the contributors (British Sociological Association, 2017; Papademas & The International Visual Sociology, 2009; Wiles et al., 2008). Field recordings of workers in public spaces did not require consent due to the lack of access, distance, or fleeting nature of these acts. The guidelines and discussions surrounding the rights of street photographers should be referred to in such situations (IOP, 2018; Moussawi, 2017). The copyright considerations further involved the use of Creative Commons licences for the materials used, and the images were presented with aesthetic quality as well as research quality. The project also monitored new guidelines and considerations surrounding social media, as the concepts of 'private' and 'public' continue to evolve (Anderson & Rainie, 2022; Social Data Science Lab, n.d.; Townsend & Wallace, 2017; Woodfield, 2017).

In summary, cross-disciplinary collaborations face several challenges with regard to intellectual property, copyright, permissions, and ethics, which require careful consideration and negotiation to ensure that the collaborations are equitable, respectful, and impactful. By establishing clear protocols, guidelines, and frameworks that address these challenges, i.e., by solving it as a joint 'problem', collaborators can create meaningful and innovative projects that advance knowledge and creativity while respecting the rights and interests of all parties involved.

New Forms of Knowledge in PBL Collaborative Projects

According to Vygotsky's constructivist principles (1978, 1986), cross-disciplinary collaborations benefit from co-constructing knowledge through dialogue with a 'more knowledgeable other'. By bringing together experts from different disciplines and backgrounds, such collaborations can promote a holistic and integrated approach to problem-solving, leading to novel insights and solutions that may not have emerged otherwise. Additionally, cross-disciplinary collaborations can also foster improved communication, dissemination of new knowledge to a wider audience, and increased innovation, leading to the development of new technologies, methods, and practices. They can also help to break down disciplinary boundaries and promote interdisciplinary dialogue and understanding, leading to more comprehensive and nuanced understandings of complex phenomena. Transdisciplinary collaborations can promote social and cultural diversity, enhancing intercultural understanding, incorporating diverse perspectives, leading to more equitable and inclusive outcomes. This is particularly important in the context of universities fostering multicultural environments and the global nature of future work (Van den Beemt et al., 2020).

In their reflections on the GestureLab project, the artist describes how collaborations and interdisciplinary work were crucial to the substantial changes in their practice. The collaborative concept of GestureLabs expanded their artistic perspectives and exposed differences in science–art approaches, methods, and ethical responsibilities. This led to a number of discursive 'soft collaborations' with movement practitioners, and emerging relationships with a voice coach, a tai chi teacher, a hairdresser, and a ceramicist, which enabled continuous testing of ideas and development of GestureLabs. The artistic practice became a space of daily material practice of ideas, actions, and experiences, where the artist perceived different audiences and spaces, as participants and 'soft contributors' were engaged in their practice (Borowicz Richardson, 2022).

GestureLabs offer an example of how interdisciplinary collaboration can lead to new forms of knowledge production and experimentation. By bringing together different perspectives and experiences, GestureLabs has created a space for collective creativity and innovation. This collective potential lies in the collapse of habitual meaning and the opening up of new conversations, which are non-hierarchical and inclusive. One key aspect of this is the shared performance of gestures, which fosters awareness, empathy, and cooperation. As Marina Vishmidt notes, this collective potential can be seen as "the becoming-communist of capital" in unforeseen levels of global exploitation (Vishmidt, 2008, p. 33) In other words, this potential lies in the way that collaborative practices can challenge the dominant structures of power and capital, and create new possibilities for collective action and creativity.

Final Considerations on PBL Usage

Generally speaking, academic success can almost always be guaranteed (Amerstorfer & von Münster-Kistner, 2021) when nurturing: cognitive, metacognitive, affective, social, task, and communicative engagement and whenever classroom tasks are designed keeping in mind the aforementioned parameters. At the same time, both artistic and scientific practice make use of identical ingredients. Cognitive and divergent thinking are utilised repeatedly in analysis, the end product inherently acting as a testament to the creator's sense of originality and creativity. Concurrently, all scientific and artistic work is intended to reach a given audience, validity, meaning, and reception being co-constructed over time. Therefore, the implementation of the PBL method, either in its restricted form or more broadly, by applying the guidelines and variables of problem-based learning through stimulation of learners' creativity, analytical and critical thinking skills, as well as by enhancing self-confidence and collaboration skills can only be an asset in academic, scientific, or artistic environments.

Furthermore, taking into consideration the multiple stakeholders, different taxonomies and methods, ethical and copyright considerations, PBL has great potential to support collaborative research and problem-solving in interdisciplinary collaboration. The challenge would be to carefully tailor the process to suit the unique needs and processes of this field. Therefore, facilitating empathy-compassion at not only micro level, as was the case of the GestureLabs, but also at meso and macro levels as well, becomes an enabling force to facilitate personal growth and to develop sustainable ethics. By establishing clear protocols, guidelines, and frameworks that address these challenges as a joint 'problem', collaborators can bring to life meaningful and innovative projects that advance knowledge and creativity while respecting the rights and interests of all parties involved.

Thus, the potential of problem-based learning in artistic and scientific partnerships is multifold. Collaborative practices can challenge the dominant structures of power and capital, giving way to collective action and creativity. However, similar effects can be observed at a smaller scale. Due to the likelihood of problem-based learning creating flow states for participants actively and intensely engaged in either 'real-life' problem-solving (artistic/scientific creation) or while engaged in classroom task accomplishment, the resulting sense of joy and meaning ought to be considered crucial aspects in developing future practitioners in the arts and sciences. Finally, flow states, especially if encountered on a repeated basis in academic, artistic, or research environments, might, in fact, hold the key to reaching that ever-elusive state of happiness.

References

A Brief Guide to Copyright. (2016). Tate Legal. https://www.tate.org.uk/documents/1104/abriefguidetocopyright_2016_aug2016.pdf

Amerstorfer, C., & von Münster-Kistner, C. (2021). Student perceptions of academic engagement and student-teacher relationships in problem-based learning. *Frontiers in Psychology. Educational Psychology, 12*. https://doi.org/10.3389/fpsyg.2021.713057

Anderson, J., & Rainie, L. (2022, February 7). Visions of the Internet in 2035. *Pew Research Center: Internet, Science & Tech*. https://www.pewresearch.org/internet/2022/02/07/visions-of-the-internet-in-2035/

Ascott, R. (2000). *Art, technology, consciousness: Mind @ Largej* (Revised Ed.). Intellect.

Aviña, G., Schunn, C., Silva, A., Bauer, T., Crabtree, G., Johnson, C., Odumosu, T., Picraux, S., Sawyer, R., Schneider, R., Sun, R., Feist, G., Narayanamurti, V., & Tsao, J. (2018). The art of research: a divergent/convergent thinking framework and opportunities for science-based approaches. In: E. Subrahmanian, T. Odumosu, & J. Tsao (Eds.), *Engineering a better future* (pp. 167–186). Springer. https://doi.org/10.1007/978-3-319-91134-2_14

Bastiaansen, J. A. C. J., Thioux, M., & Keysers, C. (2009). Evidence for mirror systems in emotions. *Philosophical Transactions of the Royal Society B: Biological Sciences, 364*(1528), 2391–2404. https://doi.org/10.1098/rstb.2009.0058

Birsel, Z., Marques, L., & Loots, E. (2022). Daring to disentangle: Towards a framework for art-science-technology collaborations. *Interdisciplinary Science Reviews*, 1–20. https://doi.org/10.1080/03080188.2022.2134539

Borowicz Richardson, A. (2022). *Sculpting with object-gestures: An everyday working gesture as an artistic proposition and a space to reimagine material resonances* [Thesis, Royal College of Art]. https://researchonline.rca.ac.uk/5077/

Boudreau, C., MacIntyre, P., & Dewaele, J. M. (2018). Enjoyment and anxiety in second language communication: An idiodynamic approach. *Studies in Second Language Learning and Teaching, 8*(1), 149–170. https://doi.org/10.14746/ssllt.2018.8.1.7

Braidotti, R. (2006). Affirming the affirmative: On nomadic affectivity. *Rhizomes, Fall 2005/Spring 2006* (11/12). http://www.rhizomes.net/issue11/braidotti.html

British Sociological Association. (2017). *BSA statement of ethical practice*. Retrieved April 22, 2023, from https://www.britsoc.co.uk/ethics

Cardenas, E., Rodegher, S., & Hamilton K. (2021). The future of arts integrative work: Creating new avenues for advancing and expanding the field. In H. Star Rogers, M. K. Halpern, D. Hannah, & K. de Ridder-Vignone (Eds.), *The Routledge handbook of art, science & technology studies*. Routledge.

Copyright Guide for Artists. (2018). Artists' Union England. https://www.artistsunionengland.org.uk/

Corwin, S. (2003). Picturing efficiency: Precisionism, scientific management, and the effacement of labor. *Representations, 84*(1), 139–165. https://doi.org/10.1525/rep.2003.84.1.139

Csikszentmihalyi, M. (2008). *Flow: The psychology of optimal experience* (1st Ed.). Harper Perennial Modern Classics.

Csikszentmihalyi, M. (2014). *Applications of flow in human development and education: The collected works of Mihaly Csikszentmihalyi* (1st Ed.). Springer Science. https://doi.org/10.1007/978-94-017-9094-9

Da Silva, A. A. (2018). Interactive art, performance and scientific research into corporeal empathy. *Journal of Problem Based Learning in Higher Education, 6*(1), 39–54. https://doi.org/10.5278/OJS.JPBLHE.V6I1.1978

Danko, C., & Duarte, A. (2009). The challenge of implementing a student-centred learning approach in large engineering classes. *WSEAS Transactions on Advances in Engineering Education, 8*(6), 225–236.

Decety, J., & Jackson, P. (2004). The functional architecture of human empathy. *Behavioral and Cognitive Neuroscience Reviews, 3*, 71–100. https://doi.org/10.1177/1534582304267187

De la Sablonnière, R., Taylor, D., & Sadykova, N. (2009). Challenges of applying a student-centered approach to learning in the context of education in Kyrgyzstan. *International Journal of Educational Development, 29*(6), 628–634.

Dieleman, H. (2017). Transdisciplinary hermeneutics: A symbiosis of science, art, philosophy, reflective practice, and subjective experience. *Issues in Interdisciplinary Studies, 35*.

Dewaele, J. M., & MacIntyre, P. (2016). Foreign language enjoyment and foreign language classroom anxiety: The right and left feet of FL learning? In P. MacIntyre, T. Gregersen, & S. Mercer (Eds.), *Positive psychology in SLA* (pp. 215–236). Multilingual Matters.

Dewaele, J. M., & MacIntyre, P. (2022). Do flow, enjoyment and anxiety emerge equally in English foreign language classrooms as in other foreign language classrooms? *Revista Brasileira De Linguística Aplicada, 22*(1), 156–180.

Dewaele, J. M., Witney, J., Saito, K., & Dewaele, L. (2018). Foreign language enjoyment and anxiety: The effect of teacher and learner variables. *Language Teaching Research, 22*(6), 676–697.

Dolmans, D. H. J. M., De Grave, W., Wolfhagen, I. H. A. P., & Van Der Vleuten, C. P. M. (2005). Problem-based learning: Future challenges for educational practice and research. *Medical Education, 39*(7), 732–741. https://doi.org/10.1111/j.1365-2929.2005.02205.x

Dumitriu, A. (2018). *DIY Trust me, I'm an artist (TMIAA) toolkit*. Wayback Machine. https://web.archive.org/web/20201229162515/http://trustmeimanartist.eu/wp-content/uploads/2018/02/DIY-Trust-Me-Im-an-Artist.pdf

Eisner, E. (2008). Commentary: What education can learn from the arts. *LEARNing Landscapes, 2*(1), 23–30. https://doi.org/10.36510/learnland.v2i1.271

Elkins, J. (2008). Aesthetics and the two cultures why art and science should be allowed to go their separate ways. In F. Halsall, J. Jansen, & T. O'Connor (Eds.), *Rediscovering aesthetics* (pp. 34–50). Stanford University Press. https://doi.org/10.1515/9781503627253-004

Farsides, B., Dumitriu, A., & Bureaud, A. (2016). Trust me, I'm an artist. *Leonardo, 49*(3), 262–263. https://doi.org/10.1162/LEON_a_01272

Goldman, A. I. (2009). Mirroring, simulating and mindreading. *Mind & Language, 24*(2), 235–252. https://doi.org/10.1111/j.1468-0017.2008.01361.x

Hatfield, E., Rapson, R. L., & Le, Y.-C. L. (2009). Emotional contagion and empathy. In J. Decety & W. Ickes (Eds.), *The social neuroscience of empathy* (pp. 19–30). The MIT Press. https://doi.org/10.7551/mitpress/9780262012973.003.0003

IOP. (2018, January 12). *Your rights as a photographer*. Institute of Photography. https://www.institute-of-photography.com/your-rights-as-a-photographer/

Ismail, S., Rahul, D., Patra, I., & Rezvani, E. (2022). Formative vs. summative assessment: Impacts on academic motivation, attitude toward learning, test anxiety, and self-regulation skill. *Lang Test Asia, 12*(1), 40. https://doi.org/10.1186/s40468-022-00191-4

Jung, C. G. (1978). *Aion: Researches into the phenomenology of the self* (2nd Ed.). Princeton University Press.

Kaihovirta-Rosvik, H. (2009). *Images of imagination: An aesthetic approach to education*. Åbo Akademi University Press.

Lafer-Sousa, R., & Conway, B. R. (2009). Vision and art: An interdisciplinary approach to neuroscience education. *Journal of Undergraduate Neuroscience Education, 8*(1), A10–A17.

Magsamen, S. (2019). Your brain on art: The case for neuroaesthetics. *Cerebrum: The Dana forum on brain science*. Retrieved March 13, 2023, from https://www.researchgate.net/publication/340163628_Your_Brain_on_Art_The_Case_for_Neuroaesthetics

Markham, T., Mergendoller, J., & Larmer, J. (2006). *Project based learning handbook: A guide to standards-focused project based learning for middle and high school teachers* (2nd Ed.). Buck Institute for Education.

Miller, A. I. (2014). *Colliding worlds: How cutting-edge science is redefining contemporary art* (1st Ed.). W. W. Norton & Company.

Modi, P., Jha, K., Kumar, Y., Kumar, T., Singh, R., & Mishra, A. (2019). The effect of short-term exposure to red and blue light on the autonomic tone of the individuals with newly diagnosed essential hypertension. *Journal of Family Medicine and Primary Care, 8*(1), 14–21. https://doi.org/10.4103/jfmpc.jfmpc_375_18

Moussawi, Y. (2017, December 18). Street photography: Is street photography a violation of privacy or ethics? *Medium.* https://medium.com/@YarahMoussawi/street-photography-is-street-photography-a-violation-of-privacy-or-ethics-b9ed118dbcc8

Muller, L., Froggett, L., & Bennett, J. (2020). Emergent knowledge in the Third Space of Art-Science. *Leonardo, 53*(3), 321–326. https://doi.org/10.1162/leon_a_01690

OECD Education Policy Perspectives no. 1 (2016). *Improving the teaching profession in Romania.* http://www.romaniaeducata.eu/wp-content/uploads/2020/01/1_Improving-the-Teaching-Profession-in-Romania_with_infographic.pdf

Papademas, D. & The International Visual Sociology. (2009). IVSA code of research ethics and guidelines. *Visual Studies, 24*(3), 250–257. https://doi.org/10.1080/14725860903309187

Papuc, O. (2021). The importance of teacher-student emotional rapport in the foreign language classroom. In R. M. Nistor & C. D. Teglaş (Eds.), *LIMBAJELE SPECIALIZATE: Abordări curente şi provocări pentru viitor* (pp. 145–160). Presa Universitară Clujeană.

Prochazkova, E., & Kret, M. E. (2017). Connecting minds and sharing emotions through mimicry: A neurocognitive model of emotional contagion. *Neuroscience & Biobehavioral Reviews, 80*, 99–114. https://doi.org/10.1016/j.neubiorev.2017.05.013

Reynolds, D., & Reason, M. (2012). *Kinesthetic empathy in creative and cultural practices.* Intellect.

Root-Bernstein, R. S. (1996). The sciences and arts share a common creative aesthetic. In A. I. Tauber (Ed.), *The elusive synthesis: Aesthetics and science* (Vol. 182, pp. 49–82). Springer Netherlands. https://doi.org/10.1007/978-94-009-1786-6_3

Schnugg, C. (2019). *Creating art science collaboration: Bringing value to organizations* (1st Ed.). Springer International Publishing: Imprint: Palgrave Macmillan. https://doi.org/10.1007/978-3-030-04549-4

Shaughnessy, N. (2011). Knowing me, knowing you: Autism, kinesthetic empathy and applied performance. In *Kinesthetic empathy in creative and cultural practices* (pp. 33–50).

Shin, S. (Ed.). (2021). *Legal lab report 1: Art + Tech/Science collaborations.* Serpentine R&D Platform Legal Lab. https://www.serpentinegalleries.org/whats-on/legal-lab-report-release/

Social Data Science Lab. (n.d.). *Lab online guide to social media research ethics.* Retrieved April 21, 2023, from http://socialdatalab.net/ethics-resources

Taylor, J., Riden, B., & Markelz, A. (2018). The arts, project-based learning, and students with challenging behaviors: The alignment of standards with student characteristics. *VSA Intersections: Arts and Special Education, 4*, 55–67.

Thill, R., Pic, A., & Malina, R. F. (2012, December 31). Creations of many minds: Contextualizing intellectual property issues arising from collaborations across the disciplines of Science, Engineering, Arts, and Design. *SEAD: White Papers.* https://seadnetwork.wordpress.com/white-paper-abstracts/final-white-papers/creations-of-many-minds-contextualizing-intellectual-property-issues-arising-from-collaborations-across-the-disciplines-of-science-engineering-arts-and-design-2/

Townsend, L., & Wallace, C. (2017). Chapter 8: The ethics of using social media data in research: A new framework. In *The ethics of online research* (pp. 189–207). Emerald Group Publishing. https://doi.org/10.1108/S2398-601820180000002008

Van der Linden, D., Tops, M., & Bakker, A. (2021). The neuroscience of the flow state: Involvement of the locus coeruleus norepinephrine system. *Frontiers in Psychology, 12.* https://doi.org/10.3389/fpsyg.2021.645498

Vienni Baptista, B., Fletcher, I., Maryl, M., Wciślik, P., Buchner, A., Lyall, C., Spaapen, J., & Pohl, C. (2020). *Final report on understandings of interdisciplinary and transdisciplinary research and factors of success and failure.* Zenodo. https://zenodo.org/record/3824839

Vishmidt, M. (2008). Situation wanted: Something about labour. *Afterall: A Journal of Art Context and Enquiry, 19*, 20–34. https://doi.org/10.1086/aft.19.20711710

Vygotsky, L. S. (1978). *Mind in society: The development of higher psychological processes.* Harvard University Press.

Vygotsky, L. S. (1986). *Thought and language* (A. Kozulin, Ed.; Translation newly rev. and edited). MIT Press.

Weiner, B. (1986). *An attributional theory of motivation and emotion* (1st Ed.). Springer-Verlag.

Wiles, R., Prosser, J., Bagnoli, A., Clark, A., Davies, K., Holland, S., & Renold, E. (2008). *Visual ethics: Ethical issues in visual research* [Working Paper]. n/a. https://eprints.ncrm.ac.uk/id/eprint/421/

Woodfield, K. (2017). *The ethics of online research.* Emerald Group Publishing.

Yew, E. H. J., & Goh, K. (2016). Problem-based learning: An overview of its process and impact on learning. *Health Professions Education, 2*, 75–79. https://doi.org/10.1016/j.hpe.2016.01.004

Van Den Beemt, A., MacLeod, M., Van Der Veen, J., Van De Ven, A., Van Baalen, S., Klaassen, R., & Boon, M. (2020). Interdisciplinary engineering education: A review of vision, teaching, and support. *Journal of Engineering Education, 109*(3), 508–555. https://doi.org/10.1002/jee.20347

Unit 6 Lesson: Coordination Techniques of Instructive-Educational Activities in the Field of Neuroaesthetics Using Problem-Based Learning (PBL)

Oana Geman, Emanuela Motrescu, and Johan Magnus Elvemo

Introduction: Learning Theories

Learning is a process of acquisition, depending on experience, thanks to which certain activities/behaviours are formed or modified under the influence of repetitive and variable world conditions. Learning is a human-specific evolutionary process, consisting in acquiring the experience of life. Schools have an important role in promoting learning, introducing us to the secrets of knowledge.

Questions like 'Why does learning take place?' or 'How does learning take place?', led to theories and models of instruction (learning). 'The theory explains the process, and the model describes it', says Biggs and Tang (2007). The first question is answered by explaining the deep mechanisms of the learning process and its causal determinations. As regards the second question, Chye et al. (2008), for example, finds that learning is associated with several knowledge paradigms, one of which, relevant here, advances the idea that school learning is a process of

O. Geman (✉)
Computer Science, Electronics and Automation Department, Faculty of Electrical Engineering and Computer Science, "Stefan cel Mare" University of Suceava, Suceava, Romania
e-mail: oana.geman@usm.ro

Neuroaesthetics Lab, "Stefan cel Mare" University of Suceava, Suceava, Romania

E. Motrescu (✉)
Neuroaesthetics Lab, University of Suceava, Suceava, Romania
e-mail: emanuela.motrescu@ubbcluj.ro
URL: https://neuroaestheticslab.usv.ro/

J. M. Elvemo
Norwegian University of Science and Technology, Trondheim, Norway
e-mail: johan.magnus.elvemo@ntnu.no

T. Balinisteanu and K. Priest (eds.), *Neuroaesthetics*,
https://doi.org/10.1007/978-3-031-42323-9_18

shaping the subjectivity of the learner, thus shaping his/her awareness and conduct, regardless of his/her choices.

The following six questions illustrate the kinds of problems that are the subject of learning theories amenable to the above-mentioned paradigm:

1. ***Which are the limits of learning?***
   This raises the question of intra- and inter-species individual differences in learning ability, whether persistent or changeable because of changes in the capacity of assimilation due to age.
2. ***How does the practice contribute to the process of learning?***
   The old saying that 'practice perfects' has its reason. Obviously, we learn to skate only by practising.
3. ***How are the impulse, incentive, reward or sanction important?***
   Everyone knows that, in general, the efficiency of learning is ensured by means of reward or sanction or that it is easier to learn what is interesting than what bores you.
4. ***What is the place of understanding and intuition (insight)?***
   Some issues are easier to learn if we know what they are about. For example, we feel better as tourists if we can understand a map or a schedule and we are helpless in front of a differential equation if we do not understand its symbols and rules for using them. We can speak vowels easily without knowing how to move our tongue and we can read without being aware of the movements that the eye muscles make. It seems that we assimilate certain issues automatically, while for others we have to fight hard, first to understand them and only then to master them.
5. ***Does learning in a field become a support for learning in another?***
   This is a problem of the formative virtue of a discipline or a problem of transfer in learning.
6. ***What actually happens in the process of memorization and in the process of forgetting?***
   The facts of memory are usually quite unknown, but in connection with remembering and forgetting, strange things can often occur. Some facts we want to remember are easily forgotten, and those we want to forget are troubling our minds. In cases of amnesia, memory lapses on older or newer events often occur.

E. Hilgard and G. H. Bower (2014) believed that the many theories of learning developed in psychology could be divided into three major groups. The first group includes **stimulus-reaction theories** (Pavlov, Thorndike, Guthrie, Skinner, Hull). I. P. Pavlov, a Russian physiologist, discovered that the body can respond not only to innate, unconditional reflexes caused by absolute stimuli, but also to stimuli that occur before or simultaneously with them, known as conditioned reflexes. By repeatedly pairing a signal (such as a bell) with the presentation of food to a dog at certain intervals, Pavlov observed that the dog began to salivate at the sound of the bell, even without the presence of food (known as a conditional response).

According to Pavlov, such conditioning demonstrates that the animal can create an association between the stimulus, initially neutral (the sound of the bell did not produce salivation at first) and a behavioural response (salivation). For the production of the conditioned response it is necessary to have temporal contiguity between the two stimuli (conditioned stimulus and unconditioned stimulus), and, at each association, the conditioned stimulus must precede the unconditioned stimulus. Pavlov warned of the danger of the system being frozen at some unproductive reductionist level, in which there would be no discrimination between human learning and animal learning.

The process of classical conditioning described by Pavlov was used by Watson (2004) to demonstrate how emotional responses develop. A study was conducted involving a 1.5-year-old boy named Albert, who learned to develop a fear of a white rat through repetitive association of the rat's presence with a loud noise. Later, to achieve the unlearning of the conditioned fear, Watson placed the animal at some distance from Albert, while offering chocolate to the child. Gradually the rat was moved closer and closer to the child, until he managed to tolerate the animal's nearness. Learning theorists believe that this classical learning mechanism could be responsible for the occurrence of several phobias (towards snakes, dogs, etc.).

E. Thorndike, an American psychologist who lived from 1874 to 1949, formulated a learning model based on trial and error. Through animal experiments, he posited that a learner is confronted with a problem situation that can be resolved by choosing the correct answer from several possible options. At first, Thorndike used 'problem cages': a hungry cat was locked in such a cage, and a piece of fish would be nearby; the cage could be opened by pressing a lever. The cat moved about the cage attempting to reach the food until, by chance, it pressed the lever that opens the door and thus reached the food. On this basis, the American psychologist established that learning involves a succession of trials and errors; successful attempts are retained, and those followed by negative consequences begin to occur less frequently. For example, a student will better remember those activities in which he was appreciated and praised, experiencing satisfaction.

The second group includes **cognitive theories** (Tolman, Osgood, Koffka, Wertheimer). Based on experimental work, M. Wertheimer, W. Kohler and K. Koffka argued in favour of the pre-eminence of the whole over the parts in psychic activity. Wertheimer developed the theory of productive learning and Kohler the theory of learning based on understanding. The postulates of perceptual theory, formulated by Wertheimer, are as follows (Baeten et al., 2016; Grave et al., 2004; Hung et al., 2008; Jaques, 2003; Walsh, 2010):

- The perception is structured from the beginning;
- The whole is perceived before the parts;
- There are no distinctions between perceptions and sensations;
- The organization of stimuli in all perceptions is not done by chance.

Kohler's research to discover the mechanisms of learning, which later laid the foundations of the theory of 'intuitive learning', was done on anthropoid monkeys, by creating increasingly complicated problem-situations. For example, a monkey's route to food (banana) was not direct, but required finding solutions through complex problem-solving actions. The monkey could find that a primary configuration ('hand – banana') that had been proven to work in the past, was no longer suitable to a new situation. The monkey would wait until it could capture the existing situation in a new perceptual configuration, for example 'hand – arm – banana – mouth'. This new configuration, says Kohler, is not developed through 'trial and error', but through sudden enlightenment that leads to an understanding of the new perceptual situation.

E. C. Tolman (1886–1959) proposed that in learning we must also consider the 'intermediate variables' between stimulus and response and highlighted the importance of a form of cognitive learning which he called 'slow learning'. He argued that something can be learned without an apparent change in behaviour, the learned element remaining in a latent state until its activity is necessary.

The third group consists of **action theories** (Piaget, Bruner, Gagne, Galperin, etc.). The Russian psychologist, P. I. Galperin, developed the operational theory of human activity and the orientation of the types of cognitive–reflective and action activities. Galperin regarded notions as the result of the crystallization of mental actions: 'some idea – as a psychological phenomenon – is nothing more than an objective action transposed in the mental plane and then passed into inner language'. At the higher mental level, what was material action turns into an intellectual operation, that is, into the learning of knowledge and the formation of appropriate operations.

J. Piaget understands learning in a general sense, as information assimilation followed by accommodation or operational restructuring. Mental operations result from the internalization of actions and, in contradistinction to perceptual preservations, are characterized by reversibility. Due to systems of reversible transformations, conceptual invariations are preserved (as stable cognitive structures), abstraction and generalization occur, and the higher level of intelligence reaches capacity for propositional operations.

As regards the learning–development relationship, Piaget supports the idea that learning is subordinated to development. Intellectual development is seen in a staged succession of the evolution of thought, each stage being characterized by a structure in which the higher level encompasses the lower. The child progresses through each of these stages sequentially and at varying rates of speed. The stages include sensory-motor intelligence (0–2 years), preoperative intelligence (2–7 years), concrete operations (7–12 years) and formal operations (11/12–15/16 years). Piaget's theory has the merit of demonstrating how intelligence evolves, that it has its origin in the sensorimotor interactions of children with the environment even before the acquisition of language.

J. Bruner's theory of training argues that the development of the intellect is dependent on the tools used, education being called upon to ensure the development of mental processes and training through specific activities. The American psychologist formulated what has sometimes been regarded as a shocking idea: any child, at any age, can be successfully taught any educational object, provided that it is translated into one of the systems of representation of reality: action, imagistic (iconic) and symbolic. This led to a conception of learning as discovery, as production and creation of knowledge.

The theory of cumulative-hierarchical learning was developed by R. Gagné and stipulates that human development appears as an effect, as a long-term change, produced by both learning and growth. The process of learning is founded on a sequential and cumulative series of skills, evaluated based on the standard of gradually progressing from acquiring basic abilities to more intricate ones. Learning theories fulfil several functions, highlighted in Table 1. As can be seen here, learning theories cover a wide range of aspects of the learning process. However, the learning process is greatly affected by the teaching methods employed. Teachers who have been trained in traditional teaching schools tend to overestimate the impact of spoken instruction on their students—'taught means learned'. This perspective is quite common in secondary education, where teachers often face a curriculum full of a large volume of complex information. Hence, it may be tempting to adopt the quickest and most efficient teaching method of lecturing by the instructor and passive listening by the students. However, can the students learn by just listening to the lectures? Did all students comprehend what the teacher intended to teach them? **So teaching may not be the same as learning.**

Learning is a personalized process where students construct their own systems of knowledge. They link the new information with what they already comprehend and recognize, utilizing concepts, generating ideas, making evaluations based

Table 1 Functions of learning theories

Function type	Characteristics
Informational	• Focused on a distinct area of knowledge, offers a way to analyse, discuss and undertake research on learning
Explicative	• Explains why a learning phenomenon has occurred or not, reaching a basic understanding of the essence of processes
Predictive	• It is closely correlated with explanatory learning theories • Predicts new elements, behaviours and evolutions of educational subjects which cannot be explained by ad-hoc theories
Summary and systematization	• Summarizes, condenses and unifies a large volume of knowledge regarding the laws of learning
Praxiological, normative and prescriptive	• Facilitates the capture of essences, ensures a better knowledge of the training variables by teachers • Contains methodological indications regarding the procedures and techniques for assimilating and controlling information

on their evolving experience, etc. Students seek meaning and logic behind what they learn, and they determine what is significant and memorable. A 'traditional' teacher should be aware that in the minds of his students there exist as many versions of the lecture as the number of students present, versions that are produced and integrated into each student's meaning systems and cognitive structures. Therefore, one student may perceive the lecture's content as new information, while in another student's perception the lecture contains errors or misunderstandings that need to be corrected. In a constructive frame of mind, we must expect the occurrence of mistakes of logic and thinking, as well as the possibility of misunderstanding information, to be the rule, not the exception—not only in the minds of our students, but also in our own minds.

Reconstructing our cognitive structures is a more intricate process than just replacing old information with new information. In actuality, learning is a prolonged process where contradictory sets of thoughts and notions contend with each other, and it is the students who make effort to deconstruct them, not the teacher. Teachers who attempt to rectify the errors of their students will realize that simply informing them about what is accurate is frequently insufficient. These issues are familiar to all teachers. However, constructive learning alone is inadequate to overcome them. Students must engage in activities that involve the application of their newfound knowledge, as simply learning is not enough. For a teacher, this means, for example (Neville, 1999):

1. No lecture without a subsequent workload;
2. Listening to the students' contributions, for example presentations, to evaluate their learning process and achievements;
3. Empowering students to pursue self-development, for example through task-based learning;
4. Listening to students' feedback, for example 'what I found to be especially important was…, I learn best when…', etc.

The responsibility of the teacher is to furnish appropriate learning prospects for their pupils and to assess and converse with them about what is effective and what is not. Constructive learning, which involves deconstruction and subsequent implementation tasks, requires a significant amount of time. Therefore, the teacher, perhaps in collaboration with the students, must decide which topics are worth investing time in, and follow the principle of 'doing less, but doing well'. The Problem-Based Learning (PBL) approach offers an alternative to conventional teaching methods and has been employed across various fields such as medicine, biology, physiology, psychology, engineering, social work education, etc. The four fundamental elements of PBL teaching are circumstances, problems, students and teachers. The teaching process revolves around circumstances and problems as its central components. Students should work to understand or solve problems, and teachers are the students' partners or organizers. In the process of implementing PBL, first, appropriate settings should be carefully created and clearly introduced to the students. Then, the students should be divided into several groups, each consisting of 5–10 students. The students should develop the curriculum and monitor the process stages on their own. In order to solve practical problems, students will naturally draw upon their prior knowledge and actively seek out new knowledge. Once results are obtained, reflection and evaluation will follow (Dahms, 2014; Hattie and Yates, 2014). There are many differences between traditional learning and PBL learning. First, traditional learning aims to provide systematic, comprehensive and in-depth information to students, while PBL pays more attention to the practical part of knowledge acquisition. The traditional approach relies mostly on textbooks, whereas the modern approach emphasizes the use of practical materials. In the traditional method, the presentation of the materials starts with smaller parts then proceeds to integrate them into wholes, while in the modern PBL approach, the presentation of the materials starts with the whole, then focuses on the parts where identification of the problem by the student is required. The traditional methods emphasize fundamental skills, while the PBL method concentrates on significant concepts but in practical applications. In traditional teaching, assessment is seen as a separate activity and takes place through testing, while with the modern PBL teaching method assessment is seen as an activity integrated with teaching and learning, and takes place through portfolios and observations. In addition, PBL offers students the chance to self-assess. When making the transition to PBL teaching, one of the biggest obstacles for many teachers is the need to give up a certain degree of control over the class and to trust their students. This certainly does not mean that teachers do not teach in a PBL class. Many traditional practices remain, but are being reshaped. In PBL teaching, other information delivery techniques are applied. Students should discuss the issues related to what they learn, mobilizing their previous knowledge. Using their prior knowledge, each student or group is encouraged to propose a hypothesis or working statement that may evolve as they gather more information through research. Students will tackle a list of questions that need to be answered in order to solve the problem at hand, namely: What do I know? What do I need to know? How can I find out? (Biggs, 2011).

For example, at the beginning, students are given an unstructured problem. Even if a problem is poorly structured or unstructured, it is still considered a defined problem, except that it has only a few elements. However, these elements are sufficient to stimulate an investigative process. The problem presented to the students should not be easily solvable with their prior knowledge alone. Additionally, the problem should have multiple acceptable solutions, as the answer is likely to evolve as new information is gathered and integrated. Additionally, the problem should be meaningful to the students, and they should be able to connect with the topics and concerns that the problem raises. This way they will be more motivated to solve the problem and will store the information they find. A second difference between traditional learning and PBL relates to the fact that in traditional course-based teaching, teachers play the lead role in the classroom. Teachers pass on knowledge to their students, and they passively receive information. By contrast, in PBL students play an active role. In a problem-based learning setting, the teacher's role undergoes a transformation, which may require some time for adaptation. The teacher is no longer the sole source of knowledge in the class, and the traditional reliance on textbooks is reduced. Instead, the teacher acts as a coach or guide to facilitate learning. In a PBL class, it is unrealistic to expect students to come up with optimal solutions right away. Because learning to solve problems is one of the main goals of PBL, students will need to be guided through the search and solving process. Therefore, it is important for the teacher to allow students to ask different questions about things. The differences between the role of the teacher in traditional education and the PBL system can be summarized as shown in Table 2. (Duch and Groh, 2001). Thus, the traditional method of teaching involves guiding students to learn through memorization and recitation techniques, so that they do not develop critical problem-solving thinking and decision-making skills, while PBL involves teaching based on identifying information required to solve a problem. Here, the students learn as a team, as the main actors of the problem in question, while the teacher is the director-mediator, who directs the whole process. The PBL principles are Constructive learning, Collaborative learning, Contextual learning and Self-directed learning.

Learning Is Constructive

Learning is easier and knowledge is stored for longer when what is new to learn can be linked to the learner's previous knowledge and experiences. Thus, teaching must start from what those we teach already know and propose a way to integrate new knowledge into the already existing mental structures of the learner.

Learning Is Collaborative

Learning is easier when learners are stimulated to interact and learn from each other. Through collaboration, sharing ideas and providing support and feedback, students understand better the subject being studied. Thus, teaching should provide various opportunities to collaborate, to work in a team to solve various tasks, to ask each other questions, to hear how others think about the topics, and to say how one in turn thinks about the topics.

Learning Is Contextual

Learning is easier when what is to be learned is exemplified by locating the topics in a reality-based context relevant to the learner. Thus, teaching must propose from the outset tasks related to the students' choice of their future job/specialization, using relevant examples from the media, professional practice and/or relevant everyday situations.

Table 2 Differences between traditional teaching and PBL

Stages of the didactic process	Traditional education	PBL system
The learning process framework	The role of the teacher in traditional education is to explain notions through presentations (e.g. using a video projector), the students having during this time a passive role	The role of the teacher in the PBL system is to help students become familiar with, and improve, teamwork. In this situation students have an active role
Didactic act planning	Planning in traditional education is rigid	Planning in the PBL system decides how the learning process will be carried out through tutoring and guides the group in the initial analysis phase
Learning needs	In traditional education, learning needs are ignored and taught according to the prescribed curriculum	In PBL education, the emphasis is placed on the differences between the existing knowledge and those necessary to be acquired to solve problems, and the combination of competencies/abilities with new knowledge acquired by students
Setting goals	Within the traditional system, the objectives are set by the teacher/tutor	Within the PBL system, students are encouraged to formulate precise learning objectives
Designing a learning plan	In the traditional learning system, the teacher presents his own learning plan	In the PBL system, the teacher helps the students to design their learning plans and to develop strategies for consulting the sources of documentation
Involvement in learning activities	In the traditional learning system, the teacher is NOT involved in learning activities	In the PBL system, the teacher serves as the catalyst for the learning process
Evaluating learning outcomes	The teacher in the traditional learning system evaluates the results in exams	In the PBL system, the teacher provides feedback to the students so that they can improve their learning process. The evaluation of competencies must be combined with the evaluation of the knowledge acquired by the students

Learning Is Self-Directed

Learning occurs more easily when the learner's mind is active, when the learner plans, monitors and evaluates her/his own learning, and when s/he acknowledges that s/he is primarily responsible for her/his own learning. Thus, teaching must be

Table 3 Advantages of PB

Long-term knowledge development	Engaging in PBL activities can enhance students' ability to remember and retrieve information as they participate in open discussions with their peers, reinforcing their understanding of the subject matter
Using various types of instructions	Grouping students for PBL allows them to address tangible issues and enjoy team-based learning. Content such as videos, news articles and more can also be provided
Continuous involvement	Students work in teams to solve real-world problems, they communicate directly and get strongly involved
Development of transferable skills	The use of PBL can provide tangible contexts and consequences that enable students to develop a deeper and more sustainable understanding, allowing them to apply the skills they learn to other real-world scenarios
Improving teamwork and interpersonal skills	The completion of a PBL challenge involves a great deal of interaction and communication, which implies that students are expected to develop skills related to teamwork and collaboration

based on the learner's knowledge and provide her/him with opportunities to plan, self-evaluate and reflect on her/his own learning.

Tables 3 and 4 summarize the advantages and disadvantages of PBL. Table 5 lists some of the conflict situations that may arise within the PBL tutorial group.

Stimulating the Involvement of Educators in the PBL Approach

Constructive alignment of assessment with learning objectives and learning activities (Biggs & Tang, 2011) starts from the fact that a teaching process is considered effective if we develop the design of the activity by combining in a constructive way the following elements: goals, activities learning and assessment tasks. Constructive alignment is a way of designing a course or way of learning based on what learners should know and should be able to demonstrate at the end of the course. Learning objectives, assessment methods and learning/learning facilitation activities are intentionally 'aligned' so that learning outcomes are as good as possible (Kurt, 2020).

Our education is focused on skills. Their relevance is that, since we aim to develop skills (general, specific) in students, assessment is an organic component of the learning process. Hence, assessment must also be incorporated into, or 'aligned' with, the learning process (Biggs & Tang, 2011). I need to establish,

Table 4 Disadvantages of PBL

Potentially poorer test performance	Traditional tests often measure fact-based learning through multiple-choice and short-answer questions, which may not adequately prepare students who have engaged in PBL activities
Student training	Due to factors such as immaturity, lack of prior knowledge, and a high number of questions, many students may not be ready to engage in a PBL activity
Teacher training	The teacher may need to modify certain habits, such as excessive correction of students and teaching for the purpose of promoting rapid recall of facts. Instead, they should provide hints and pose questions that encourage independent thinking
Time-consuming evaluation	In a problem-based learning exercise, if grades are to be given, the evaluation of a student's performance requires ongoing monitoring and assessment of both acquired competencies and skills. This means that knowledge should be constantly acquired and evaluated throughout the semester, rather than only at the end

Table 5 Possible types of conflict situations that may arise within the PBL tutorial group and with the proposed modalities of action

Description of the conflict situation	The teacher's response
Poor communication between students	Active listening to each student and establishing rules in the PBL group Brainstorming session
Lack of active participation, involvement of all students	Agree with the leader to speak to each member in turn (setting rules) Establish clear rules for the operation of the PBL group, from the beginning of the PBL
Interpersonal conflicts between students	Establishes rules on how the PBL group works It is recommended that the tutor organize a brainstorming session with the entire PBL group Proposing 'dismissals' or 'resignations' in the group Active listening
Defective management in the PBL group	Clarifies the roles and responsibilities within the group from the beginning of the PBL activity

as a trainer, how I will assess learning and include those opportunities to demonstrate the competencies pursued in the design of the learning process. In other words, learning tasks and assessment tasks are basically one and the same thing. Implication: the paradigm of the three distinct moments (design–teaching–evaluation) must be taken seriously. While 'teaching', that is, while facilitating the learning process, I have to evaluate. Moreover, before I think about how I will facilitate learning, I have to decide what and how I will evaluate, because—since assessment tasks are learning tasks—it makes sense that I have to design these tasks first.

So: I establish which are the relevant observable behaviours based on which I can conclude that the student has acquired a (specific) competence, I describe the behaviour in the clearest possible terms to understand how s/he can demonstrate it (what to do, what to say, what to produce, etc.) and then I think about opportunities to manifest the behaviours I have to engender, i.e. the learning-assessment tasks.

The conclusion is that if learners understand what desirable behaviour looks like, they will strive to manifest it. That is why it is important that the assessment indicators are clear and objectively verifiable. When we pursue the development of skills, assessment design precedes learning design and learning tasks are at the same time assessment tasks. My checklist would include the following questions:

What are the objectives of the course? (What will students know at the end of the course and be able to apply in practice?)
What is the form of organizing the course? (lecture, discussions, teamwork)
What is the ultimate goal of the activities? (What are the skills and attitudes developed?)
What are the preconditions and conditions for promoting the course?
What is the purpose of the test? (understanding, capacity for synthesis, application of knowledge in a new context)
What are the assessment methods meant to help the student learn?
What are the recommended bibliographic references for students?

Specific Assessment Methods to Test the Acquisition of Both Knowledge and Skills and Abilities

This will include the list of questions that students will have to answer, the structure of the presentation or project they are going to support or the list of requirements that the practical work must satisfy if necessary. Depending on the specificity of each course, this part can include any type of assessment that the teacher considers appropriate for testing the acquisitions accumulated during the course.

The products of the problem-based learning process are:

1. Report;

2. Presentation;
3. Annexes of each report (minutes, concept maps, summaries, reported projects).

The evaluation should focus on two directions:

1. Product component and,
2. The component of the process.

Therefore, the on-going assessment should not be something 'appended' to the learning process at the end, but should also take place during the learning process. The report evaluation forms and the evaluation scale for the group report can be used in the assessment. At the end of each project, the study group will be required to submit one of the following documents: a poster, report, oral presentation, web page, drawing or a constructed device. The precise format will be determined during the initial phase. Each individual in the group will be evaluated according to how well they succeed on the following levels:

- Analysis of the problem;
- Innovation of possible solutions;
- Critical evaluation of the group's suggestions;
- Demonstration of both previous and newly acquired knowledge by participating in the case study;
- Using practical skills in solving the problem.

Their position as a team member will also be assessed, including how well they have fulfilled their role of:

- Leader of the discussion;
- Writing/content producer;
- Time administrator;
- Member of the group.

One of the weaknesses of the PBL system is the lack of a formal evaluation because it is often missing or not aligned with the objectives of the PBL. Although there is much written work on student assessment, these assessment methods are not often applied in PBL groups (Alessi, 2001; Capon, 2004; Guerra, 2017; Newby, 1996; Savin-Baden, 2004). However, the strength of the PBL evaluation is that the evaluation criteria include assessments of process component as well as product component. Below are included guidelines for assessment scales:

1. **Individual Work**

For **2 points**:

- Increased interest in identifying the advantages and disadvantages of using lab tools (EEG, behavioural questionnaires, etc.).
- Follow the instructions and use the instruments available in the laboratory.
- Is able to face difficulties in finding criteria to increase the effectiveness of available equipment.

For **1 point**:

- Interest in conducting experimental tests.
- Does not always follow instructions and use available equipment.
- Is not always able to face difficulties in finding advantages, and disadvantages specific to particular devices.

For **0 points**:

- Low interest in conducting experimental tests.
- Does not follow instructions and use available equipment.
- Cannot face difficulties encountered along the way.

2. **Team Work (students are divided into teams of 5–6)**

For **2 points**:

- Excellent collaborative work.
- Able to reach consensus and complete tasks on time.

For **1 point**:

- Difficult collaboration relationships.
- Limited consensus and does not always complete tasks on time.

For **0 points**:

- Low interest in working in a team and collaborating with other colleagues.
- Inability to reach consensus and complete tasks on time.

3. **Use of Resources**

For **2 points**:

- Excellent interest in implementing resources and laboratory guidance information.

For **1 point**:

- Good interest in implementing resources and guidelines.

For **0 points**:

- Low interest in implementing resources (including tutorials) and guidance information.

4. **Quality of Information**

For **2 points**:

- Precise information, clearly presented and sufficient details on the correct choice of advantages/disadvantages of using particular equipment, the correct follow-up of a 'red thread' of the experimental steps, correct collection and interpretation of data.

For **1 point**:

- Less accurate information, yet clearly presented in sufficient detail.

For **0 points**:

- Little accurate information, presented in an obscure manner and in insufficient detail.

5. **Fulfilment of Tasks (Score Awarded by Team Mates)**

For **2 points**:

- All tasks received within the team are completed.

For **1 point**:

- Almost all tasks received within the team are completed.

For **0 points**:

- Few or none of the tasks received within the team have been completed.

The Final Grade is calculated by summing the scores obtained on each evaluation scale in one evaluation out of three.

References

Baeten, M., Dochy, F., Struyven, K., Parmentier, E., & Vanderbruggen, A. (2016). Student-centered learning environments: An investigation into student teachers 'instructional preferences and approaches to learning. *Learning Environments Research, 19*(1), 43–62.

Barrows, H. S., & Barrows. (1988). *The tutorial process* (2nd Ed.). Southern Illinois University, School of Medicine.

Biggs, J. B., & Tang, C. (2007). *Teaching for quality learning at university* (3rd ed.). McGraw Hill Education & Open University Press.

Biggs, J., & Tang, C. (2011). *Teaching for quality learning at university*. SRHE.

Chye, S. H., Neo, W. K., & Chyn, K. Y. (2008). *From sage-on-the-stage to guide-by-the-side: Effective tutor skills in problem-based learning*. Temasek Business School available online in English on the page http://www.ntu.edu.vn/Portals/96/Tu%20lieu%20tham%20khao/Phuong%20phap%20giang%20day/role%20of%20tutor%20in%20pbl.pdf and offered to students translated in Romanian.

Dahms, M.-L. (2014). Problem based learning in engineering education. In V. Villas Boas & O. Giovannini (Eds.), *Attracting young people to engineering: ALE 2014* (pp. 10–21). Associação Brasileira de Educação em Engenharia (Abenge). https://vbn.aau.dk/ws/portalfiles/portal/207465598/Proceedings_ALE_2014_final_version.pdf

De Grave, W. S., Dolmans, D. H., & Van Der Vleuten, C. P. (1999). Profiles of effective tutors in problem - based learning: Scaffolding student learning. *Medical Education, 33*(12), 901–906.

Duch, B. J., & Groh, S. E. (2001). *The power of problem-based learning*. Stylus.

Grave, W., Moust, J., & Hommes, J. (2004). *The role of the tutor in a problem based learning curriculum* (chap.3). Maastricht University, Department of Educational Development & Research. Available online at https://www.researchgate.net/publication/200117120_The_role_of_the_tutor_in_a_problem_based_curriculum and offered to students in Romanian translation.

Jaques, D. (2003). Teaching small groups. *BMJ, 326*(7387), 492–494.

Hattie, J., & Yates, G. C. R. (2014). *Visible learning and the science of how we learn*. Routledge. https://www.mnasa.org/cms/lib/MN07001305/Centricity/Domain/184/Visible%20Learning%20and%20the%20Science%20of%20How%20we%20Learn.pdf

Hilgard, E., & Bower, H. G. (2014). Learning theories.

Hung, W., Jonassen, D. H., & Liu, R. (2008). Problem-based learning. *Handbook of Research on Educational Communications and Technology, 3*, 485–506.

Neville, A. J. (1999). The problem-based learning tutor: Teacher? Facilitator? Assessor? *Medical Teacher, 21*(4), 393–401.

Walsh, A. (2010). The tutor in PBL—A novice's guide (chap. 4). McMaster University. Available online in English at https://fhs.mcmaster.ca/facdev/documents/tutorPBL.pdf and offered students in Romanian translation

PBL Web Resources

[1] https://dash.harvard.edu/handle/1/29738968

[2] https://ocw.mit.edu/courses/womens-and-gender-studies/wgs-693-gender-race-and-the-complexities-of-science-and-technology-a-problem-based-learning-experiment-spring-2009/problem-based-learning/

[3] https://www.cumbria.ac.uk/research/enterprise/tean/teachers-and-educators-storehouse/archive/problem-based-learning/

[4] https://citl.illinois.edu/citl-101/teaching-learning/resources/teaching-strategies/problem-based-learning-(pbl)

[5] https://www.maastrichtuniversity.nl/education/why-um/problem-based-learning

[6] https://www2.le.ac.uk/offices/lli/developing-learning-and-teaching/enhance/strategies/copy_of_active-learning

[7] https://www.queensu.ca/ctl/teaching-support/instructional-strategies/problem-based-learning
[8] https://www8.gsb.columbia.edu/researcharchive/articles/376
[9] https://www.en.aau.dk/about-aau/aalborg-model-problem-based-learning/
[10] https://odee.osu.edu/news/2015/10/06/problem-based-learning-online-courses
[11] https://repository.uwl.ac.uk/id/eprint/2625/
[12] https://www.itue.udel.edu/

Unit 6 LAB: PBL in Neuroaesthetics Case Study: Strategizing the Use of Relevant Research Methods

Oana Geman, Emanuela Motrescu, and Johan Magnus Elvemo

In this laboratory, we will apply Problem-Based Learning (PBL) techniques to focus on understanding the relevance and appropriateness of neuroaesthetics research methods. A series of tasks is to be followed as indicated below.

Task 1: Preliminary discussion

Please find relevant information necessary for giving your own reasoned answers to the questions:

- What is Neuroaesthetics?
- What does Neuroaesthetics do?
- Why study Neuroaesthetics?
- How will we put into practice what we have learned/what we will learn in this discipline?

O. Geman (✉)
Computer Science, Electronics and Automation Department, Faculty of Electrical Engineering and Computer Science, "Stefan cel Mare" University of Suceava, Suceava, Romania
e-mail: oana.geman@usm.ro
URL: https://neuroaestheticslab.usv.ro/

Neuroaesthetics Lab, "Stefan cel Mare" University of Suceava, Suceava, Romania

E. Motrescu (✉)
Neuroaesthetics Lab, University of Suceava, Suceava, Romania
URL: https://neuroaestheticslab.usv.ro/

J. M. Elvemo
Norwegian University of Science and Technology, Trondheim, Norway
e-mail: johan.magnus.elvemo@ntnu.no

T. Balinisteanu and K. Priest (eds.), *Neuroaesthetics*,
https://doi.org/10.1007/978-3-031-42323-9_19

The concept of ´Neuroaesthetics‘ was coined in 1999 by the neuroscientist Semir Zeki, who is a professor at the Wellcome Department of Imaging Neuroscience, University College, London. This field is relatively new and combines cognitive psychology, neurobiology, and art to explore how the brain reacts to aesthetic stimuli (Chatterjee, 2011).

V.S. Ramachandran, a professor of neurobiology at the Center for Brain and Cognition at the University of California, San Diego, is also considered one of the pioneers of our field. Professor Ramachandran proposed *Eight Laws of Artistic Experience* which represents a set of principles, that describe how our brains process and respond to art (Ramachandran & Hirstein, 1999). The eight laws are as follows:

I. **Symmetry:** The brain responds more strongly to symmetrical and balanced compositions.
II. **Contrast:** The brain responds more strongly to contrasts, such as light and dark or rough and smooth textures.
III. **Peak shift effect:** The human brain responds more strongly to exaggerated or caricatured features than to realistic ones.
IV. **Grouping:** The components of a composition often get organized by the brain into larger units or patterns.
V. **Isolation:** The distinct aspects of a composition often catch the attention of the brain.
VI. **Perceptual problem solving:** The perceptual obstacles or puzzles given in a piece of art are enjoyable for the brain to solve.
VII. **Abhorrence of coincidences:** The brain tends to interpret coincidences or chance events in a composition as deliberate, and may find them aesthetically displeasing.
VIII. **Orderliness:** The brain responds positively to patterns, symmetry, and orderliness in a composition.

These laws reflect Ramachandran's belief that the human brain has evolved to appreciate and seek out certain features in art, and that artists can intentionally or unintentionally tap into these features to create more engaging and impactful works of art. However, it's important to note that not all artists or works of art adhere to these laws, and that different people may have different aesthetic preferences and responses to art.

Ramachandran suggests that art typically involves an amplification or exaggeration of reality. For example, *Venus of Willendorf (*Present location—*Natural History Museum in Vienna*, Austria.) and Indian female temple sculptures (literally 'celestial beauty'), a Surasundari at a Khajuraho temple. As well as *Caricature* of Aubrey Beardsley by Max Beerbohm (1896), taken from *Caricatures of Twenty-five Gentlemen.* Ramachandran has termed this amplification the 'peak shift effect', and he has observed similar mechanisms at play in the animal kingdom (Ramachandran & Hirstein, 1998). There was an intriguing experiment conducted on seagulls and their feeding habits. The seagull's beak, which is typically yellow, has a red stripe that the chicks peck at when they want to be fed. Ramachandran states that training an individual to respond to a specific stimulus will result in a preference for an amplified or exaggerated version of that same stimulus.

Task 2: Form 4 groups. Within each group, discuss among yourselves how the information studied in Task 1 relates to the information you have learned during the entire course. As a group, answer the following questions (choose a spokesperson):

1. What is the role of Neuroaesthetics?
2. What concepts are involved in neuroaesthetics studies?
3. What are the advantages and disadvantages of using Neuroaesthetics methods?
4. Why should one study Neuroaesthetics?
5. What are the similarities and differences between Aesthetics and Neuroaesthetics?

Task 3: Create a map of concepts employed in Neuroaesthetics and the relations that may exist between them. Remember: you can use this map in your exam! Before signing off, have a look at the final page for information about your course evaluation!

A map of concepts is a visual representation of the relationships between different concepts within a specific field or domain of knowledge. It can also be referred to as a concept map, a knowledge map, or a semantic network. Typically, the map is made up of nodes, which stand in for distinct concepts, and lines or arrows, which show the connections between those concepts.

Concept maps can be used in a range of sectors, such as science, education, and business, to organize and display knowledge. As they can assist students in organizing and connecting their grasp of various concepts within a subject, they are frequently employed as a tool for learning.

In research, concept maps are also used to show the connections between various ideas and to spot regions of overlap or knowledge gaps. They can be used to investigate the relationships between various ideas or concepts or to assess the organization of a certain topic of study.

Overall, a map of concepts is a useful tool for categorizing and presenting knowledge because it makes complicated ideas and relationships easier to understand and comprehend.

Task 4: Focus on the techniques used in neuroaesthetics as you read the text and examine the images below:

See Figs. 1 and 2

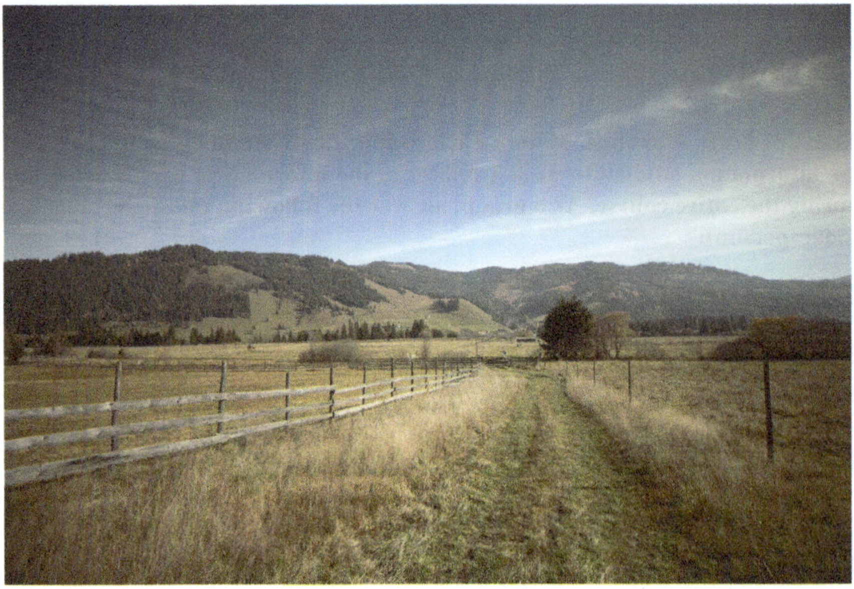

Fig. 1 Landscape 1—© *Ema Motrescu*

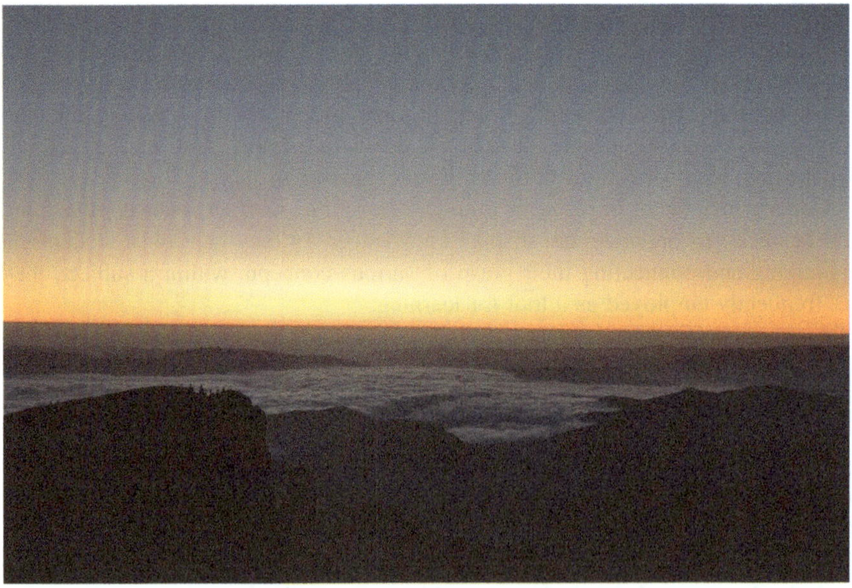

Fig. 2 Landscape 2—© *Ema Motrescu*

Methods in Neuroaesthetics

I. Electroencephalography (EEG) is a technique used to monitor brain waves known as event-related potentials (ERPs). It is possible to explore the temporal dynamics of cerebral processing of aesthetic stimuli by recording these brainwaves.

II. Eye tracking: The measurement of eye movements during aesthetic experiences is conducted using a technique known as eye tracking. By measuring where people look while viewing art or other aesthetic stimuli, researchers can investigate how different aspects of the stimuli capture attention (Fig. 3).

III. Behavioural experiments: Participants in behavioural experiments are rated on how they feel about various aesthetic cues. Researchers can examine how various aspects of the stimuli affect aesthetic preferences by examining these ratings. These are only a few of the numerous techniques employed in neuroaesthetics. Researchers frequently combine methodologies to look into various facets of aesthetic experiences as each method has advantages and disadvantages.

Research question: What effects does the presence or absence of man-made things in a scene have on people's aesthetic preferences for landscapes?

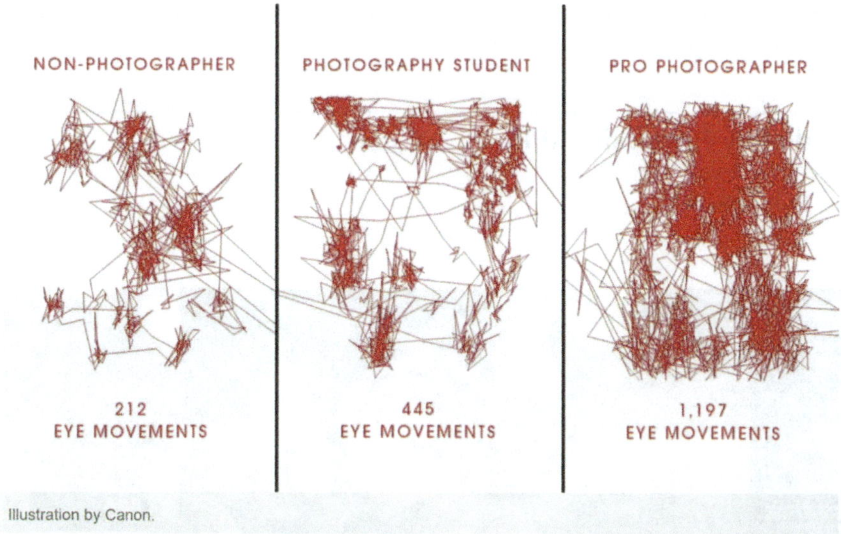

Fig. 3 https://www.slrlounge.com/canons-obsession-experiment-see-average-person-vs-pro-views-image-details/

Method

Participants: A group of participants who have interest in photography, landscapes, or nature scenes.
Stimuli: A series of landscape pictures, some with and some without human-made structures such as a cabin or a fence.
Procedure: A Likert scale from 1 (strongly dislike) to 7 (strongly like) will be used by participants to judge the aesthetic preference of the images after viewing them in a random order. Participants will also score the scenes' apparent naturalness, serenity, and beauty.
Data analysis: The average ratings for each image will be computed and compared for the conditions with and without human-made objects. The relationship between the perceptions of beauty, tranquillity, and naturalness and aesthetic preference ratings will be investigated by a correlation analysis.
Expected results: It is expected that participants will rate photographs with human-made objects as less aesthetically pleasing, less beautiful, less tranquil, and less natural than those without human-made objects. The correlation analysis may reveal that naturalness is the most significant factor influencing aesthetic preferences in winter landscape photography.
Conclusion: This behavioural study can help to understand how the presence of human-made objects in a landscape photograph influences people's aesthetic preferences. The results may have repercussions for landscape photographers hoping to capture visually appealing scenes as well as for those researching the psychology of aesthetic experiences.

Predictive Processing (PP)

See Figs. 4 and 5

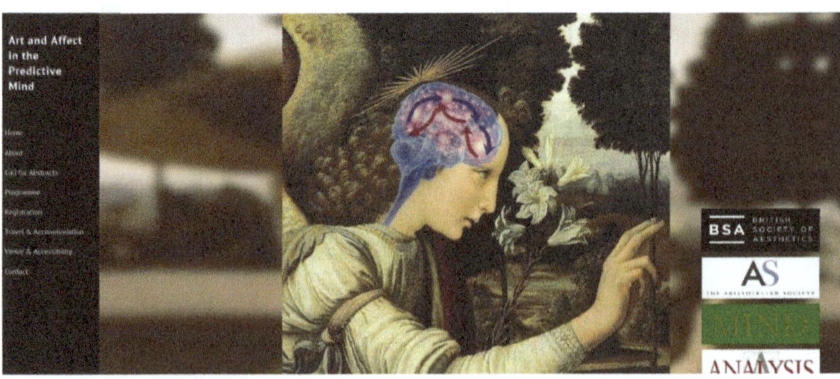

Fig. 4 https://sites.google.com/view/artandaffectinpp/home

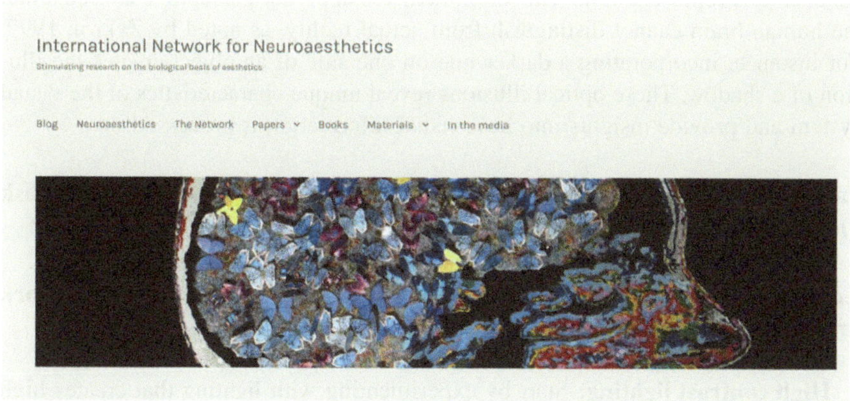

Fig. 5 https://neuroaesthetics.net/neuroaesthetics/

Task 5: According to Ramachandran's *Eight Laws of Artistic Experience* (Task 1) take a series of 4 photographs corresponding to the following techniques:

Symmetry: The brain responds more strongly to symmetrical and balanced compositions.

- **Find symmetrical objects:** Students walk around and find objects that have symmetrical shapes or patterns. Then, they take pictures of those objects from a symmetrical perspective. It is encouraged to play around with the angle of the shot to create different compositions.
- **Reflective surfaces:** Reflective surfaces, like water, mirrors, and glass, can create interesting symmetrical compositions. It is asked to experiment with reflections by capturing a symmetrical image of the reflected object.
- **Portrait symmetry:** Take portraits of subjects using a symmetrical composition. This can involve positioning the subject in the centre of the frame, with the face or body evenly balanced on either side. Alternatively, they could use reflections or shadows to create symmetry in the composition.
- **Symmetrical landscapes:** It is encouraged to look for landscapes that have symmetrical features, such as mountains, trees, or buildings. Then, to achieve a balanced and harmonious composition, a photo must be taken from a symmetrical perspective.
- **Editing symmetry:** After the photographs have been taken, use different editing tools to experiment with the creation of symmetrical compositions. This could involve using mirroring techniques, or cutting and pasting parts of the image to create a symmetrical effect.

Neuroaesthetics finds art to be extremely valuable as it provides a visual representation of reality, which prompts artists to explore innovative methods to enhance this representation. This often involves applying perceptual shortcuts that the human brain cannot distinguish from actual reality, as noted by Zeki in 1999. For instance, incorporating a darker hue on one side of an object creates the illusion of a shadow. These optical illusions reveal unique characteristics of the visual system and provide insights into how visual information is processed.

Task 6: According to Ramachandran's *Eight Laws of Artistic Experience* (Task 1) take a series of 4 photographs corresponding to the following techniques:

Contrast: The brain responds more strongly to contrasts, such as light and dark or rough and smooth textures.

- **High contrast lighting:** Start by experimenting with lighting that creates high contrast in the images. This could involve using a strong directional light source, like the sun or a spotlight, to create stark contrasts between light and dark areas of the image.
- **Contrasting textures:** Look for objects or scenes that have contrasting textures, such as rough and smooth, soft and hard, or matte and glossy. Then, take pictures that emphasize these contrasts, making sure to capture the texture in a way that is visually compelling.
- **Black and white photography:** Black and white photography is an accurate way to learn about contrast, as it eliminates the distraction of colour and allows students to focus on the interplay between light and dark.
- **Colour contrast:** Although contrast is often associated with black and white photography, colour can also be used to create contrast in an image. Find colour contrast by looking for scenes or objects that have complementary or contrasting colours.
- **Editing for contrast:** After the photos have been taken, use editing tools to experiment with to enhancement of the contrast in the images. This could involve adjusting the brightness and contrast settings, or using selective editing tools to emphasize specific areas of the image (Fig. 6).

Left example: intensity of contrast between the two squares.
Centre: example of size contrast between the two squares.
Right: example of position contrast between the two squares (inside versus outside).

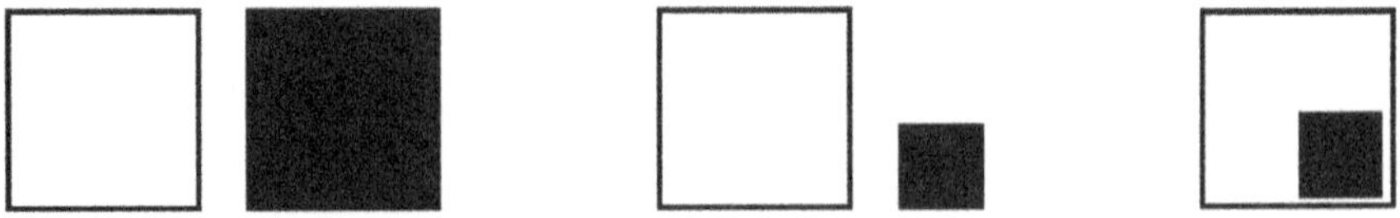

Fig. 6 Examples of contrasts

Task 7: According to Ramachandran's *Eight Laws of Artistic Experience* (Task 1) take a series of 4 pictures using the approaches listed below:

- **Isolation:** The technique of using separating a topic from its surroundings and emphasizing it through composition. This is often accomplished by arranging the subject in a way that provides a striking contrast with its surroundings, or by employing a shallow depth of field to blur the backdrop or foreground.
- **Shallow depth of field:** If you want to separate a subject from its surroundings, use a shallow depth of field. To focus on a small portion of the scene while blurring the backdrop or foreground, use a wide aperture (f/2.8 or f/1.8).
- **Contrast:** Find things that stand out from their surroundings, such as a flower with a bright colour against a dark background or a person wearing a bold colour against a plain background. Then, play around with various compositions to highlight the contrast and focus on the subject.
- **Positioning:** Put the topic in a position that clearly separates it from the background. In order to achieve this, the subject may be set against a plain, uncluttered background or the viewer's attention might be drawn to the subject by employing leading lines or shapes.
- **Still life:** Create a still life composition using a single object as the subject. Choose different lighting and positioning techniques to isolate the object and create a sense of focus.
- **Editing:** After the photos have been taken, use editing tools to experiment to further enhance the isolation effect. This could involve selectively blurring the background or foreground, or using cropping and resizing tools to emphasize the subject (Figs. 7 and 8).

Task 8: According to Ramachandran's Eight Laws of Artistic Experience (Task 1) take a series of 4 photographs corresponding to the following techniques:

Peak shift effect: The human brain responds more strongly to exaggerated or caricatured features than to realistic ones.
Comparing images with similar but different subjects: Compare the two images that have similar subjects, but one image has a more dominant or exaggerated feature. For example, a portrait of two people, where one person's eyes are bigger than the other's. Identify which one they find more striking or memorable. This exercise helps to understand how the peak shift principle works by exaggerating the dominant features to create a more impactful image.
Creating a contrast matrix: Compare this to the square grid, where each square has a different level of contrast. Find the squares on the grid that stand out the most via observation. By boosting contrast to produce a more dynamic image, this exercise demonstrates how the peak shift concept operates.
Adjusting composition: By zooming in or cropping a photo, you can alter the composition by focusing on particular aspects. Determine which photo has more visual impact by contrasting it with the unaltered version. By highlighting specific

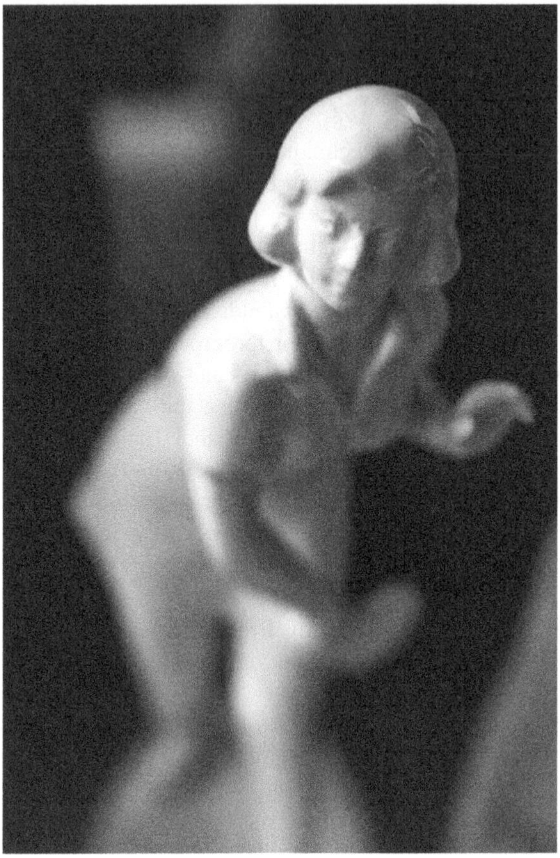

Fig. 7 Example of isolation. © *Ema Motrescu*

parts in the composition to produce a more impactful image, this exercise aids in understanding how the peak shift principle operates.

Experimenting with colour: To emphasize or minimize a particular colour, adjust the colour levels. Compare the original and the modified image to determine which one has the greater visual effect. By boosting or lowering particular hues to create a more colourful or muted image, this activity explains the peak shift principle.

Task 9: According to Ramachandran's Eight Laws of Artistic Experience (Task 1) take a series of 4 photographs corresponding to the following techniques:

Grouping: It represents a concept in photography theory that refers to how elements in an image are viewed in relation to one another. It involves the arrangement of visual components in a way that fosters coherence and unity and enables the spectator to comprehend the composition quickly and simply (Fig. 9).
On the left and centre, the figure is observed to be the letter B.
On the right, the centre figure is viewed as the number 13.

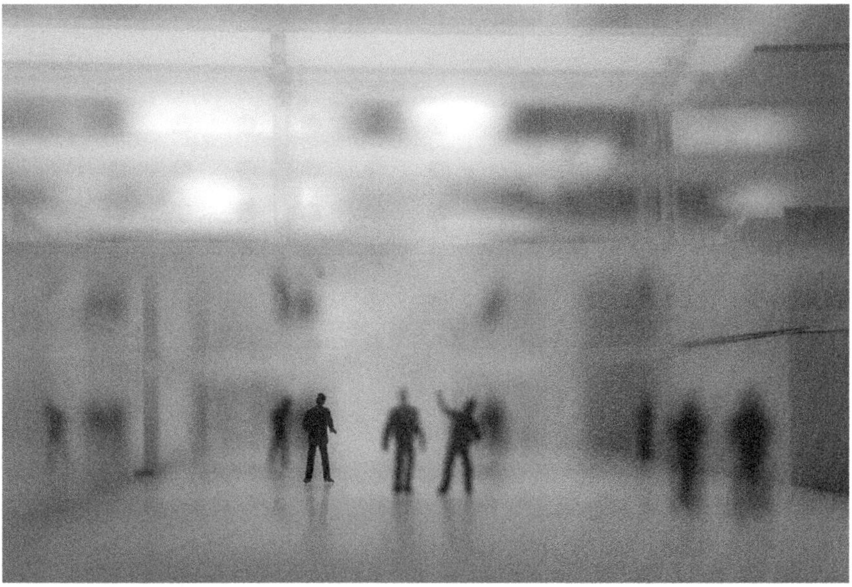

Fig. 8 Example of shallow depth of field. © *Ema Motrescu*

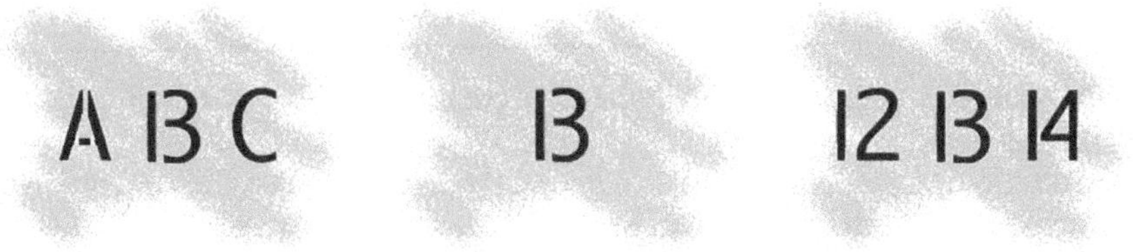

Fig. 9 Example of grouping

In the centre the figure is shown on its own.
The concept of grouping can be broken down into several sub-principles, including:
Proximity: Objects that are located near each other in physical space are interpreted as a collective group (Fig. 10).
In the left figure, the matrix of dots is perceived as being composed of rows while the matrix of dots on the right is perceived as being composed of columns.
Similarity: Similar visual characteristics, such as form, colour, or texture, cause objects to be viewed as one cohesive group (Fig. 11).
Left—grouping by similarity of shape.
Centre—example of grouping by similarity of colour.

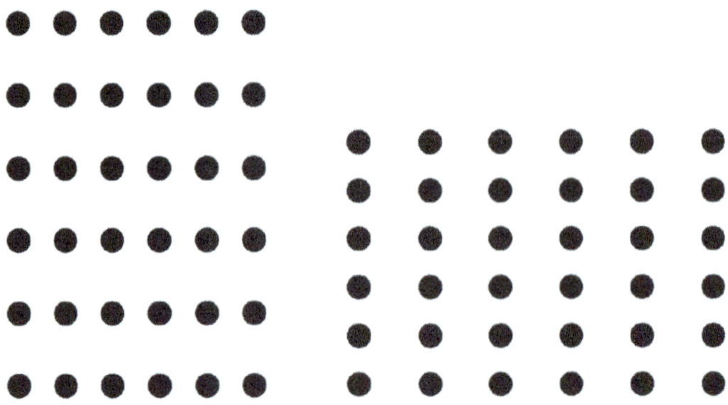

Fig. 10 Example of grouping by proximity

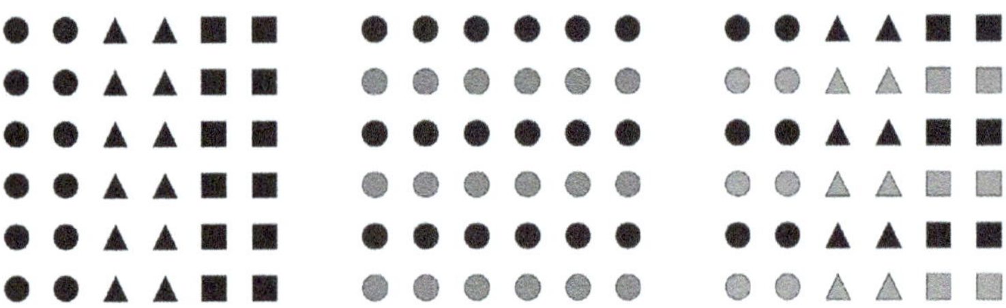

Fig. 11 Example of grouping by similarity

Right—example of grouping by similarity overwhelming the perception of grouping by shape.

Continuation: A set of elements is perceived as a group when they are arranged in a way that suggests continuation or flow, such as lines or patterns (Fig. 12).

Closure: When elements are placed in a way that makes a closed shape, the mind fills in the blanks to produce a complete shape or form, and these elements are regarded as a group (Fig. 13).

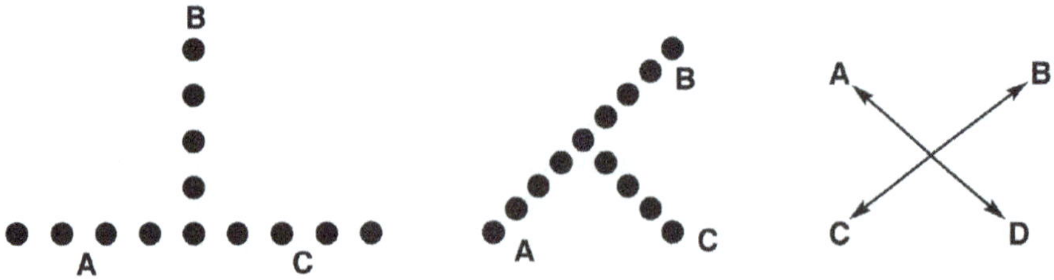

Fig. 12 Example of grouping by continuity

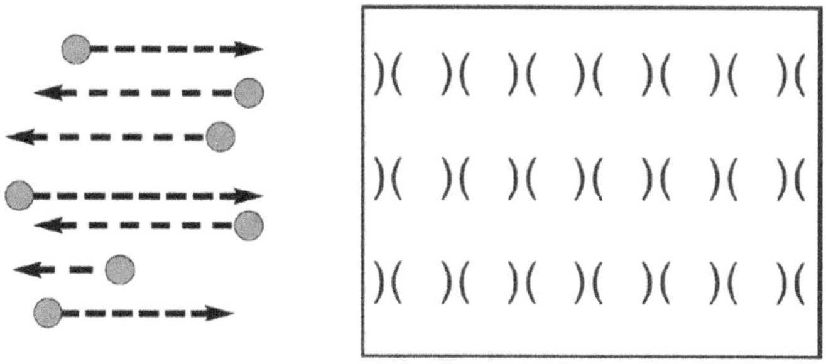

Fig. 13 Example of grouping

Left—an example of grouping by common fate. Items moving on similar paths are grouped into units.
Right—The parentheses could be grouped by proximity to produce hourglass shape figures.
The elements of a picture can be grouped in a way that makes the composition clear to the observer by employing these grouping sub-principles. An effective shot can be produced by using grouping in the right way.
Grouping by proximity: To establish a sense of grouping by closeness, analyse the photographs that contain numerous subjects and experiment with various placements and arrangements.
Grouping by similarity: To generate a sense of grouping by resemblance, examine the photographs that have features in common, such as colour or texture, and experiment with different layouts.
Grouping by continuation: Analysis of photographs with several topics arranged in a way that suggests a continuation or flow, such as a line or a pattern, and experimentation with different arrangements to strengthen the feeling of continuation are steps in the grouping by continuation process.
Grouping by closure: Try different arrangements to strengthen the sense of closure based on images with several subjects grouped in a way that results in a closed shape or form.

Task 10: According to Ramachandran's Eight Laws of Artistic Experience (Task 1) take a series of 3 photographs corresponding to the following techniques:

Perceptual problem solving: To solve issues pertaining to the development and interpretation of photos, it refers to the process of utilizing visual perception and knowledge of photography principles. It involves identifying visual challenges and finding creative solutions to overcome them.
Composition challenges: Re-compose some photographs in different ways, such as using different angles, adjusting the placement of the subject, or altering the

framing. This exercise helps in developing the ability to identify visual challenges and find creative solutions to improve the composition.

Lighting challenges: Using the photographs with different lighting situations, such as low light, backlight, or harsh shadows, experiment with different camera settings to achieve a balanced or unbalanced exposure.

Motion challenges: Using the images with various types of motion, such as sports, cars, or water, take some photographs using different shutter speeds to achieve different motion effects, such as freezing motion or creating motion blur.

Task 11: Using the knowledge about Natural Beauty in the Fibonacci Sequence and the Golden Ratio, the task is to take four photographs while following the given instructions.

- Choose a subject for your photo. It could be a landscape, a person, an object, or anything that catches your eye.
- Use the golden ratio to compose your photo. Imagine dividing the frame into three equal parts both vertically and horizontally, and positioning the subject at the intersection of one of these lines, or in close proximity to the lines themselves.
- Experiment with different angles, distances, and compositions to find the most effective way to incorporate the golden ratio into your photo.
- Take several photos using this technique, and compare the results. Analyse which composition looks the most visually pleasing and well-balanced.
- Repeat the exercise with different subjects and settings to further develop your skills in using the golden ratio as a compositional tool.

The Fibonacci sequence is a mathematical concept that is often used in art and design, including photography. This sequence of numbers follows a specific pattern where each number is the sum of the previous two: 0, 1, 1, 2, 3, 5, 8, 13, 21, 34, and so forth. The Fibonacci sequence and the Golden Ratio, a mathematical ratio that may be found in many natural and man-made objects, are closely related.

By positioning the subject or important parts in the composition at precise points in the frame, photographers can leverage the Fibonacci sequence and the Golden Ratio to produce visually beautiful compositions. The topic can be positioned, for instance, at the intersections of fictitious lines that divide the frame into thirds in accordance with the Fibonacci sequence.

The size and arrangement of various elements in an image, such as the border's width or the distance between other parts, can also be decided using the Fibonacci sequence. Photographers can create compositions that have a balanced and harmonious feel and that direct the viewer's attention to the important parts of the image by using the Fibonacci sequence and the Golden Ratio.

Even while using the Fibonacci sequence and the Golden Ratio in photography is not a rigid law, it is a useful guide that can aid photographers in making compositions that are more practical and aesthetically appealing (Figs. 14 and 15).

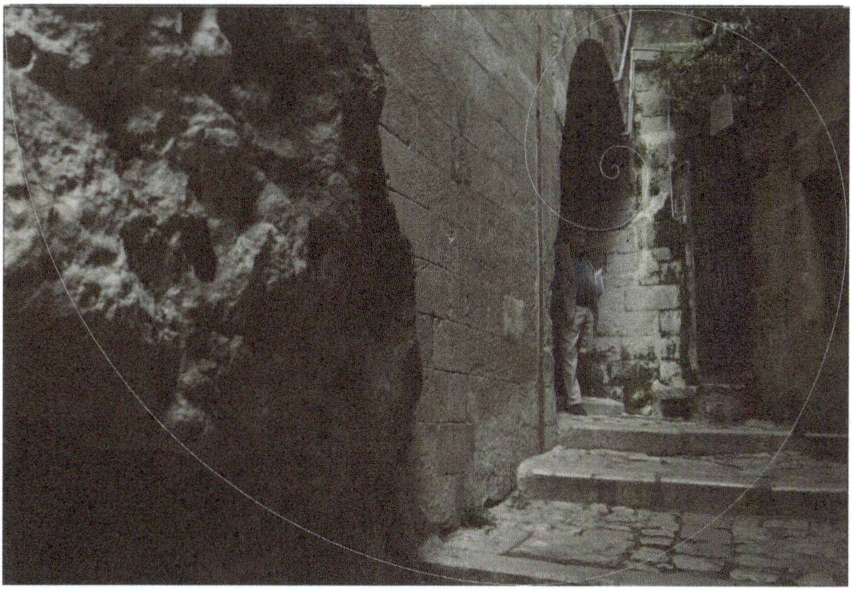

Fig. 14 Golden ratio in photography 1 © *Ema Motrescu*

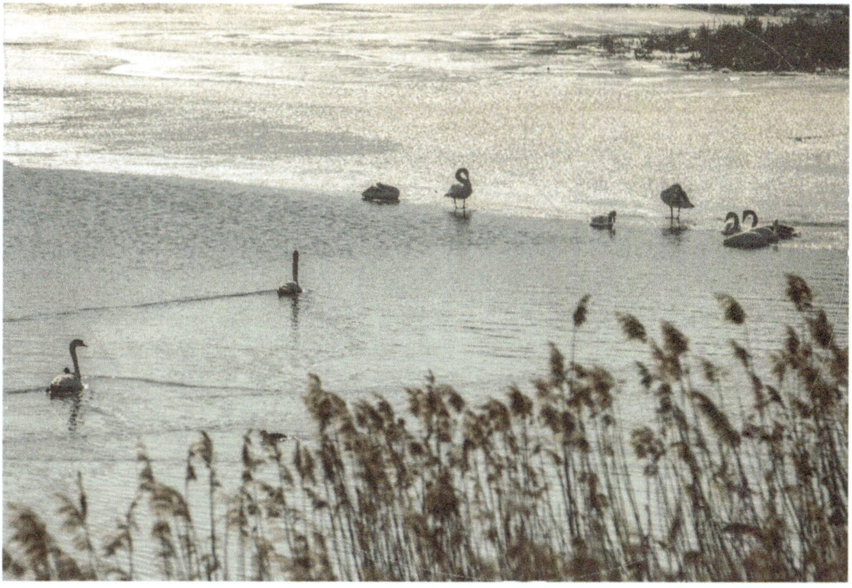

Fig. 15 Example of Golden Ratio in Photography 2 © *Ema Motrescu*

Task 12: Choose a theme or concept to explore. It could be anything from contrasting colours to different textures, patterns, or emotions. Then, take 4 diptychs.

- Take 8 pictures illustrating the theme or idea. A story or message should be presented through the use of aesthetically appealing images.
- Create a diptych with photo editing software. A diptych is only two pictures arranged next to each other, either vertically or horizontally, with a little space or overlap in between. You are free to use whichever program you are accustomed to, such as Canva or Lightroom.
- Try out various arrangements, such as mirroring one image or making one larger than the other.
- Consider how the two pictures function as a pair. Do they contrast one another or do they enhance one another? Compared to seeing the photographs separately, how does the diptych alter your perception of the images?
- Show your classmates your diptych and talk about how you approached the task and what you took away from it.

Diptych—Use of Metaphor

A diptych represents a compositional method in which two distinct images are arranged next to one another. The photos are typically placed in a frame or display that visually unites the two images and can be related thematically, intellectually, or graphically. When examining contrasts, comparisons, or links between two themes or viewpoints, diptychs are frequently employed as a technique. It can be a powerful approach to convey a message, emphasize a point, or provide the spectator with a special and unforgettable visual experience (Suler, 2013).

An illustrative metaphor is 'the atom resembles a solar system' (Clair, 2000). This metaphor draws a comparison between the atom and the solar system by highlighting how they share similar structural components. Specifically, the atom has a nucleus, much like the sun is the centre of the solar system. This metaphor represents a visual analogy between something that we have a mental image of (the solar system) and something that we may not (the atomic structure). Two identical pictures, side by side, with one obvious difference. It represents the perfect visual set up and punch line. For example, you can check Elliott Erwitt‘s diptych (beach chairs), Cannes, France, 1975 (Figs. 16 and 17).

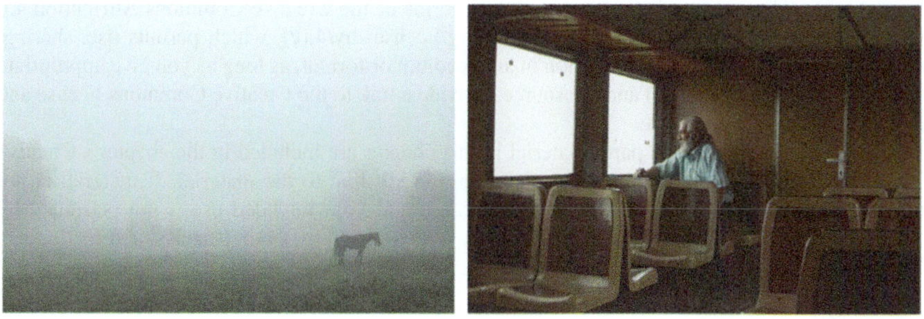

Fig. 16 Diptych 1 © *Ema Motrescu*

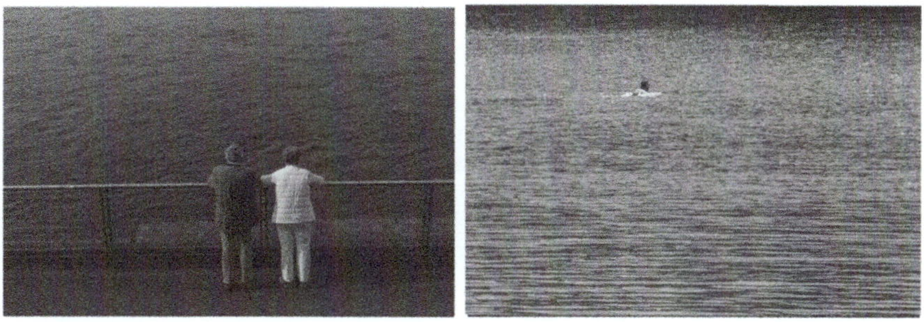

Fig. 17 Diptych 2 © *Ema Motrescu*

References

Chatterjee, A. (2011). Where there be dragons: Finding the edges of neuroaesthetics. *American Society of Neuroaesthetics Newsletter, 31*(2), 4–6.

Clair, R. N. S. (2000). Visual metaphor, cultural knowledge, and the new rhetoric. In *Learn in beauty: Indigenous education for a new century* (pp. 85–101).

Ramachandran, V. S., & Hirstein, W. (1998). The perception of phantom limbs. The D. O. Hebb lecture. *Brain: A Journal of Neurology, 121*(Pt 9), 1603–1630. https://doi.org/10.1093/brain/121.9.1603

Ramachandran, V. S., & Hirstein, W. (1999). The science of art: A neurological theory of aesthetic experience. *Journal of Consciousness Studies, 6*(6–7), 15–51.

Suler, J. (2013). Conceptual photography. In R. Zakia's (Ed.), *Perception and imaging* (4th Ed.). Focal Press (Elsevier). https://www.users.rider.edu/~suler/photopsy/article_index.htm.

Summative Comments: What Is Neuroaesthetics?

Tudor Balinisteanu

Our scientific methods, concepts, and techniques have grown intertwined together with our hermeneutical, phenomenological, or logical-interrogative interpretations of experience. Indeed, scientific research and philosophical enquiry are still gruely (remember Nelson Goodman?) intertwined, even though sometimes this intertwining is not immediately visible, and may require taking some philosophical distance. For example, features of an object that are more easily processed by the brain make that object more likeable with factors like duration of exposure, repetition of exposure, perceptual priming, or artistic expertise modulating the pleasure derived from ease of processing (see, among others, Leder et al., 2019; Reber et al., 2004). The concept of ease of processing, however, may have some of its roots in notions of symmetry. Symmetry has a very long history in both philosophy and science, where it is linked with harmony and invariance, respectively. If symmetry is linked to invariance, asymmetry may be linked to complexity. Perhaps complexity can be linked to creativity? (see Barron, 1963) Adopting the frame of thinking promoted in our lab at the University of Suceava, within the collaborative Romanian-Norwegian project, PoeticA, can we link symmetry, invariance, and ease of processing with more distant concepts such as 'nationalism'? Conversely, can we link asymmetry, variance, and creativity with concepts of 'cosmopolitism'? if so, this could be an example of how science and the humanities can grow together as questions in one realm light up questions in the other. Indeed, it may not even be possible to extricate humanities research from science research when studying aesthetic experience. As Marcos Nadal and Anjan Chatterjee point out, aesthetic experience has both universal and variable features: the universality of

T. Balinisteanu (✉)
Neuroaesthetics Lab, University of Suceava, Suceava, Romania
e-mail: tudor@texmar.ro

T. Balinisteanu and K. Priest (eds.), *Neuroaesthetics*,
https://doi.org/10.1007/978-3-031-42323-9_20

aesthetic experience stems from the fact that the perception and creation of art require neural systems that are common to all humans, and therefore can be studied by harnessing the generalising and extrapolative power of science (requiring an 'aesthetics from below' approach, in Fechner's terms); however, human neural systems are plastic and adaptable to changing contexts, with many neural records or memories of successful past adaptations preserved for possible future use, making aesthetic experience amenable also to the historical, political, or geographical study of those contexts that enabled or augmented its production (Nadal & Chatterjee, 2019).

Arguably, when speaking of cognitive science, statistical analysis, neurobiology, and neuroscience, nowhere is this intertwining more clearly visible than in the 4E cognition debates. The four E's of 4E cognition are embodied, embedded, extended, and enactive cognition. Our summative section cannot do justice to this rich debate that discusses what counts as cognition and the limits of what may be called 'mind'. Is our mental universe bound within our brain, or does it spring from bodily action, embedded in material environments, extended by tools, and always fluidly enacted in interactions with the environment and others? (For an extensive presentation of the debates, see Newen et al., 2018) Without going into too much detail, note that this debate is anchored in both phenomenology, notably in the phenomenology of perception developed by Maurice Merleau-Ponty (1908–1961), and cognitive science. Could this debate provide the elements of an integrative perspective on the dynamic interactions between art objects and perceivers?

Elements of these debates inform the core research direction being implemented at the Neuroaesthetics Lab, University of Suceava. Since the present textbook was initially conceived for this lab's students, it seems fitting to close by outlining a theory about the origins of art that takes in many of the points raised in the lessons, labs, and overviews you have studied, a theory that I am promoting as the core research direction in the lab. Let us then keep within an embodied cognition and phenomenology framework, while highlighting the wealth of existing research on the role of social relationships in cognitive development (Hinde et al., 1985, is a 'must read'). A fundamental, even primordial, as one may put it, role in this respect is played by the relationship between carer, usually the mother, and infant. J. P. Changeux (1994), among others, has highlighted that one may legitimately argue that expressive forms are initially produced and recognised in mother–infant non-verbal communication (also see Hobson, 2004, another 'must read'). On this count, it seems that neural processes cannot be extricated from a phenomenological understanding of human cognition and emotion. Let us take the example of responding to painted portraits. It seems obvious, although arguing it scientifically would take some time, that we react emotionally to portraits because, in previous interactions with other humans, we have learned to understand the emotional expression of real individuals' faces. In our lab, we are interested in developing research that supports the theory that one has learned to mirror another in one's own self as an infant gazing at his/her mother's face, entrained all the while through rhythmic movement, speech, song, regularities in movements of the mother's face, its shifting symmetries and asymmetries, its resolvable and irresolvable ambiguities. If artistic perception and creation are to be traced to the syncretic experiences first lived in the primary mother–infant dyad, then neuroaesthetic approaches to dance, visual arts (ancient Gr. *rhutmos* meant both flow and symmetry), or poetry listening, must account for the psychological range developing within the dyad, such as the experience of empathy, or of surprise born out of improvisation (the root of creative acts). Beauty and taste, inasmuch as they can be theorised in a developmental psychology perspective, are perhaps traceable to the pleasure experienced in the dyad: the 'proper' aesthetic norms of beauty and taste may have emerged from a need to formalise the experiences of pleasure known to the infant, in order to preserve those feelings in adult life, when they drive pro-social behaviour, and, in their formalisation, stabilise society and culture. The formalisation process will by necessity reflect both biological universals (e.g., preference for symmetry, entrainment to regular rhythm) and cultural patterns (e.g., preference for familiar forms or rhythms, along with enthusiasm for rare, and thus auratic, features in objects or bodies, or, indeed, rhythms). In this view, the traditional dichotomy between culture (the humanities) and nature (the sciences) collapses into nature–culture hybridity, the neuroaesthetic study of which requires both scientific exhaustiveness and humanist depth.

What is, then, neuroaesthetics? At the risk of being a little reductive, let us finally, yet still provisionally, propose that:

►**Neuroaesthetics is the study of the neural mechanisms involved in the experience of pleasure of various intensities arising from interactions with art and underpinning a wide range of other psychological experiences, such as empathy and surprise, pleasure caused by universal biological mechanisms specific to humans, but modulated by cultural factors, and commensurate with one's past experiences of the world that can be reported in a language (including artistic languages) validated by consensus.**

At the same time, let us not forget that neuroaesthetics is still a young discipline, in search of identity, on the cusp of adulthood. As Eugen Wassiliwizky and Winfried Menninghaus aptly put it:

> Over the past two decades, research in empirical aesthetics has been propelled strongly by advances in neuroscientific methods, giving rise to the subfield of neuroaesthetics […] The use of artworks provided insights into general brain functioning, including reward, motor control, neuroplasticity, learning, and embodiment […] At the same time, there is overall little agreement regarding the general conceptualization of empirical aesthetics as a distinct research field, the identification and definition of its key concepts, and a methodological framework for its future advancement. What actually is the agenda and what are the main goals of empirical aesthetics? (Wassiliwizky & Menninghaus, 2021, p. 437, brackets added)

We invite all of you, neuroaesthetics students, to attempt to answer this question in your future academic quests!

References

Barron, F. (1963). *Creativity and psychological health.* Van Nostrand.

Changeux, J.-P. (1994). Art and neuroscience. *Leonardo: Art and Science Similarities, Differences and Interactions, Special Issue, 27*(3), 189–201.

Hinde, R., Perret-Clermont, A. N., & Stevenson-Hinde, J. (Eds.). (1985). *Social relationships and cognitive development*. Clarendon.

Hobson, P. (2004). *The cradle of thought: Exploring the origins of thinking*. Oxford University Press.

Leder, H., Tinio, P. P. L., Brieber, D., Kröner, T., Jacobsen, T., & Rosenberg, R. (2019). Symmetry is not a universal law of Beauty. *Empirical Studies of the Arts, 37*(1), 104–114. https://doi.org/10.1177/0276237418777941

Nadal, M., & Chatterjee, A. (2019). Neuroaesthetics and art's diversity and universality. *Wiley Interdisciplinary Reviews: Cognitive Science, 10*(3), e1487. https://doi.org/10.1002/wcs.1487

Newen, A., De Bruin, L, & Gallagher, S. (2018, 2020). *The Oxford handbook of 4E cognition.* Oxford University Press.

Reber, R., Wurtz, P., & Zimmermann, T. D. (2004). Exploring 'fringe' consciousness: The subjective experience of perceptual fluency and its objective bases. *Consciousness and Cognition, 13*(1), 47–60. https://doi.org/10.1016/S1053-8100(03)00049-7

Wassiliwizky, E., & Menninghaus, W. (2021). Why and how should cognitive science care about aesthetics? *Trends in Cognitive Sciences, 25*(6), 437–449. https://doi.org/10.1016/j.tics.2021.03.008

Correction to: Neuroaesthetics

Tudor Balinisteanu and Kerry Priest

Correction to:
Chapters 3 and 9 in: T. Balinisteanu and K. Priest (eds.),
Neuroaesthetics,
https://doi.org/10.1007/978-3-031-42323-9

The original version of the book was inadvertently published with incorrect word "fifteenth century" instead of "seventeenth century" in the chapter "Unit 1 Lesson: Behavioural Experiments—Research Designs, Statistical Power, Sample Size *Case Study: Empathy and Closeness in Partnered Dance*", and missing tilde symbol on page 130, which have now been corrected. The book has been updated with the changes.

The updated versions of this chapters can be found at
https://doi.org/10.1007/978-3-031-42323-9_3
https://doi.org/10.1007/978-3-031-42323-9_9

T. Balinisteanu and K. Priest (eds.), *Neuroaesthetics*,
https://doi.org/10.1007/978-3-031-42323-9_22

Grading Scale

Elaborated by Tudor Balinisteanu

A grading scale is included below for evaluating students who have taken this module. Good luck with your evaluation!

Evaluation Criteria

Level grading starts from 1 point	Introductory level course
3 points	Excellent knowledge and understanding of the principles of, and the concepts involved in, neuroaesthetics research—the student can name and describe 3 concepts and/or principles
2 points	General grasp of the main concepts and principles—can name and describe 2 concepts and/or principles
1 point	Little knowledge of concepts and principles—can name and describe 1 concept and/or principle
0 points	No relevant knowledge
3 points	The student was able to envision ways of applying the knowledge gained during the lectures in the lab practical work. S/he has demonstrated practical skills during the experiment sessions. S/he has contributed original ideas over and above the requested performance level
2 points	The student was able to envision ways of applying the knowledge gained during the lectures in the lab practical work and demonstrated practical skills during the experiments sessions
1 point	The student was able to envision ways of applying the knowledge gained during the lectures in the lab practical work, but was unable to translate these into his/her practical work
0 points	The student was unable to envision applications of theoretical frameworks within the research designs elaborated during the lab sessions

(continued)

T. Balinisteanu and K. Priest (eds.), *Neuroaesthetics*,
https://doi.org/10.1007/978-3-031-42323-9

(continued)

Level grading starts from 1 point	Introductory level course
3 points	The student demonstrated consistency by participating at all labs and lectures. S/he demonstrated team work skills. S/he offered constructive feed-back to colleagues and was able to integrate his/her own ideas within the group's collaborative structure
2 points	The student participated at most labs and lectures and was a good team worker
1 point	The student participated in some labs and lectures and was a good team worker
0 points	The student did not participate in more than one lab and one lecture

Index

T. Balinisteanu and K. Priest (eds.), *Neuroaesthetics*,
https://doi.org/10.1007/978-3-031-42323-9

P

Q

R

S

T

U

V

W

Printed and bound by CPI Group (UK) Ltd, Croydon, CR0 4YY
15/11/2024
01789381-0002